THE EXHAUSTION OF DIFFERENCE

D1611759

THE EXHAUSTION OF DIFFERENCE

The Politics of Latin American Cultural Studies // *Alberto Moreiras*

DUKE UNIVERSITY PRESS // DURHAM & LONDON 2001

© Duke University Press   All rights reserved

Printed in the United States of America on acid-free paper ∞

Designed by Rebecca Giménez   Typeset in Trump Medieval

with Insignia display by Tseng Information Systems, Inc.

Library of Congress Cataloging-in-Publication Data

appear on the last printed page of this book.

CONTENTS

Of such dreams and of the rituals of them there can also be no

end. The thing that is sought is altogether other. However it may

be construed within men's dreams or by their acts it will never make

a fit. These dreams and these acts are driven by a terrible hunger.

They seek to meet a need which they can never satisfy, and for that

we must be grateful. —Cormac McCarthy, *Cities of the Plain* (1998)

ACKNOWLEDGMENTS

This book is particularly indebted to four of my friends whose thought has had a determining impact on my own thinking over the last several years: Brett Levinson, Gareth Williams, John Kraniauskas, and Jon Beasley-Murray. I am also grateful to Abdul Mustapha and Kate Jenckes for their very generous and highly useful commentary of my typescript when I was in dire need of readers. A number of visits to Chile have enabled me to establish and maintain strong intellectual and affective contacts with the group of thinkers around *Revista de crítica cultural:* Nelly Richard, Willy Thayer, Federico Galende, Elizabeth Collingwood-Selby, Carlos Pérez Villalobos, Ivan Trujillo, Pablo Oyarzún, Sergio Villalobos, and others will not, I trust, let people say that my own work is extraneous to their own thinking and thus not Latin American enough. I see my work as a modest form of solidarity with their efforts. Although I would not want my other friends, particularly in the United States, to feel unrecognized by my omission of their names here, I cannot be exhaustive. But I will mention, for reasons instrumental to this book, Teresa Vilarós, George Yúdice, Laurence Shine, Gabriela Nouzeilles, Danny James, Adriana Johnson, and Horacio Legrás. Thank you also to Ana Lucia Gazzola and Wander Melo Miranda, who invited me to present a large amount of material from this book in a seminar at the Universidade Federal de Minas Gerais in Belo Horizonte, Brazil, in the summer of 1997. Much of the analysis that follows is informed by post-Marxian and deconstructive intentions, owing a great deal to my perhaps idiosyncratic relationship with the tradition of subaltern studies. I wish to thank John Beverley and Ileana Rodríguez for their role as mentors in the Latin American Subaltern Studies Group. I also want to thank Duke University for its generous support, and in particular Debby Jakubs, Natalie Hartman, Ariel Dorfman, Fred Jameson, Walter Mignolo, and Cathy Davidson. And I want to thank my editor, Ken Wissoker, for his patience, friendship, and generous judgment.

Earlier version of chapters or parts of chapters have been published in *Revista de crítica cultural,* Jameson and Miyoshi, *The Cultures of Globalization, Siglo XX/20th Century. Critique and Cultural Discourse, Dispositio/n, Journal of Interdisciplinary Literary Research, Revista iberoamericana, Journal of Narrative Technique,* Gugelberger, *The "Real" Thing, Journal of Latin American Cultural Studies,* and *Cultural Studies.* I am thankful to the publishers for permission to reprint the materials involved.

This book is dedicated to my wife, Teresa M. Vilarós, and to our children, Alejandro and Camila.

INTRODUCTION Conditions of Latin Americanist Critique

Latin Americanist reflection today, understood as the sum total of academic discourse on Latin America, whether carried out in Latin America, in the United States, in Europe, or elsewhere, is one of the sites where the separation of intellectual labor from its very means of production is forcefully revealed. This separation shows up as a kind of expropriation—as an expropriating symptom—in the constitutive gap between theoretical discourse and the field of reflection. Granted that Latin Americanism seeks, in every case, something like an appropriation of a Latin American found object, the distance between the object and the appropriative intention remains irreducible. This irreducibility has become thematized as the very name of the Latin Americanist game in an ongoing debate or series of debates involving the relative replacement of the traditional apparatus of literary studies by cultural studies in transnational reflection on Latin American culture. These debates are also influenced by the weight given by Latin Americanists to the intellectual currents that seem to flow all too unilaterally from U.S. university discourse toward the different Latin American academies.[1]

The conditions of possibility for Latin Americanist discourse have shifted over the last decade. What could still be understood in, say, 1985 as a crossing between our-Americanist drives and the centripetal forces of scientific universalism—in other words, the whole apparatus of identity discourse to be paradigmatically applied when-ever it was a question of attuning specific histories to general epis-temologies and vice versa—is in 2000 an even more perplexing en-deavor.[2] The change is not merely because the very concept of a "general epistemology" has consistently come under critical fire. It is also because, inverting Freud's definition of melancholy, when-ever it is now a matter of reflecting on historical specificity, the shadow of the reflecting subject is found to have always already fallen upon the object. Just as the disappearance of any "true" world ends up destroying the very possibility of thinking appearance, the failure of epistemic certainty drives the concreteness of the concrete into its grave. That is to say, Latin Americanism lives, if it is living, in a certain precariousness of experience—that unleashed because the waning of the critical subject involves the dissolution of the critical object itself.

Old philology arose in eighteenth-century Europe as the means the modern university used to separate the social from the cultural legacies of the national community. It was soon hegemonized by the powerful literary apparatus, which came to exclude or subordinate attention to symbolic elements that could have shed some light on processes of cultural constitution. But contemporary Latin Ameri-can cultural studies—lightly and hurriedly accused of being a mere transplant of British and North American provenance—is not under-stood by its critics to be, at least partially, a sort of return to the philo-logical sources at the twilight of the modern Latin American state form.[3] It is rather said to start off from a blind or short-sighted will to negate literature—the latter taken as a promise of aesthetic au-tonomy and spiritual transformation of existence. Cultural studies, it is said, politicizes everything, and thus nothing, and it pays no heed to the preservation of the properly aesthetic values that have grounded the self-reproducing possibility of the humanist intellec-tual since Romanticism. We will have to ask about the status of the aesthetic in contemporary reflection, and whether it can still pro-vide, as it did in previous historical times, a paradoxical opening to some outside of history in relation to which reason could pursue its will to truth against the fetishization of the real. What is at issue in the debate on literature and cultural studies is nothing but the spe-cific valences of the critical function in the humanities. No doubt such a function cannot be claimed exclusively by any of the sides in the debate: but the function of critical reason is the dead center of the discussion.

Those who refuse to indulge in the mere denunciation of emerging reflection should also refuse to validate the nevertheless understandable desire of those who seek to preserve through their critique, at all costs, their unchanged capacity for self-reproduction. Self-reproduction without mutation is no longer politically viable. Of course, in the last instance, as I will attempt to show, the gesture whose possibility opens in cultural studies cannot be reduced to a simple return to the classical—that is, Romantic—roots of philology. If politico-intellectual activity must be understood as the development of a critical relationship with the present, then academic politics in the humanities are fundamentally conditioned by the latter. A critical relationship with the present cannot be sustained by insisting upon modalities of cultural discourse that have passed into the historical archive after having exhausted their analytical productivity. I mean literary studies here, not literature, in the same way that when we say cultural studies we refer not to culture but instead to the apparatus for the study of culture. Literary criticism is today unsatisfactory in its traditional forms and objects, and it can no longer claim the position it once held as the arbiter of national culture. This is not an unannounced phenomenon. The irruption of so-called theory in literature departments—the unprecedented relevance of theoretical reflection for literary studies—after the 1960s was the first clear sign. Thirty years later we witness a new turn in the crisis: theory itself seems threatened and withdraws. Cultural studies is apparently the new tool for hegemonic articulation. Literary criticism is powerless and cannot develop viable counterhegemonic strategies, and theory is in a similar situation. The problem of succession to the old is open, and it involves and interpellates us all.

But we need to move beyond stating the obvious. I find Charles Taylor's differentiation between *cultural* and *acultural* theories of modernity useful because it enables us to establish a distinction between modernity as *modernization,* that is, as a teleological tool or set of tools for the instrumental rationalization of the world, and the more properly historical usage of modernity as what results from the diversified impact of capitalism on social formations across the world (Taylor, "Two Theories" 153–54). For Taylor the ideological notion of modernity as modernization is today obsolete and lacking in philosophical value. He is therefore more concerned with cultural notions of modernity. From his acknowledgment that the world-system, in its imperial expansion, determines modernity, he goes on to suggest that there is not one modernity but many alternative ones and that it is the task of reflection in the humanities to understand them all in their historical specificities. But the notion of alternative modernities is not an exhaustively culturalist notion: it merely registers that the history of capital and the history of social power—understood as the constitutive state of the symbolic sphere in any given social formation—are not the same thing. To investigate what they do not have in common is then to investigate alternative modernities, or what is alternative or multiple within modernity.

Taylor's notion could curiously constitute a basis for the rigorous metacritical defense both of the literary-critical apparatus and of cultural studies, especially in reference to the theoretical analysis of the symbolic production of peripheral and semiperipheral societies in the world-system.[4] The Latin American literary tradition is almost exhaustively definable as the quasi-systematic exploration of the specificity of the Latin American alternative modernity from what today are outdated concepts of identity and difference. Latin Americanist tradition never really subscribed other than marginally to acultural theories of modernity. All the great figures of the tradition, from Francisco Javier Clavijero, Andrés Bello, Domingo Sarmiento, and José Martí to Angel Rama, or Antonio Cornejo Polar through Alfonso Reyes, Pedro Henríquez Ureña, Antonio Candido, Emir Rodríguez Monegal, and Roberto Fernández Retamar, were culturalists in Taylor's sense. But the master concepts of identity and difference keep finding a new if precarious life in the new space of cultural studies. It could be said that a large part of the work of Latin American cultural studies is nothing but an engaged reproduction and transplantation of the old historiographic categories to new texts: the literary referent is often rather mechanically substituted with alternative referents, but the questions remain—a bit farcically—the same.

It is true—it has the truth of tautology—that something is gained when criteria for inclusion are expanded and it becomes possible for a literary scholar to read the cinematographic text, or the text of the new social movements, in a situation where it had not previously been allowed to move beyond the essay, the novel, or the poem. In this cultural studies does return to the philological spring, since philology wanted to explore cultural specificity through an ample repertoire of discursive traces. And it is also tautologically true that something is lost when those who read such texts—the preservers—do it on the limiting basis of a certain weakening of their technical capacity. Their reading capacity is in principle weakened because readers educated in an exhaustive attention to the literary cannot simply transfer their attention to the nonliterary and expect to produce results of a similar strength. But there is no reason to think that the history of reading is ecstatic and that adequate tools for the kind of reading that is pertinent to the widening of textual space will not be developed soon. It is, however, truer, and more interesting, and not tautological, to conclude that if the simple considerations above are more or less accurate, then cultural studies today, from a literary perspective, is still far from having created a new paradigm for Latin Americanist reflection. Cultural studies, from the point of view of its reading practices, its master concepts, and its geopolitical inscription, is, to a certain extent, more of the same. The old and the new thus share a similar anachronism—or a similar novelty.[5]

We then have to wonder about the real motives underlying the dispute between cultural studies and literary studies. If both practices are to a large extent the same, and only the textual object changes, why the mutual antagonism? A perhaps more provoking way of posing the same question is to ask, if the old literary-critical and the new culturalist apparatuses use the same concept of critical reason (and if such a concept is circumscribed to the determination, evaluation, and defense of what is properly Latin American or intra–Latin American in the specific Latin American alternative modernity) and if the concept of critical reason used by all sides of the disputation cannot go beyond the affirmation of an identitarian space-in-resistance, whether from a continental, national, or intranational perspective, then how is any real concept of critique at stake in the debates? And how are the debates handling the potential of a renewal of reason attuned to the needs of thinking for the present? Can critical reason dissolve in identitarian or differential description? Has Latin Americanist reflection ever done anything but engage in the attempt at precisely such descriptions? Can it ever do anything else? Are the debates in question looking for something else? If the present book cannot be said to move toward that something else, then nothing can save it, and it will have failed.

A certain aporetics has become everyday currency. Average non–Latin American Latin Americanists must hear, as a constant background murmuring, that their efforts to think Latin America from their location in the cosmopolitan university have, as a damning condition of possibility, their all-too-comfortable installation in the methodological trends and fashions of world-hegemonic university discourse. The problem is not that those trends and fashions are foreign, but rather that they are excessively familiar as "foreign." Latin American Latin Americanists can invariably confront their boreal counterparts with the disquieting thought that, whatever the intended novelty in their discourse, it is never novel enough: "I already know where you are coming from; before you speak, I already know what you will say—because I know what produces you. What you want to give me is not even yours; it belongs to someone else. I cannot then make it mine."

But look now at stereotypical Latin American Latin Americanists and you will realize that they are by no means off the hook: if the problem of their alien friend was an excessively comfortable installation in the privileges of Northern knowledge, and if such sinister installation in knowledge (sinister because "excessively comfortable," and thus not comfortable at all) was inverted as a mark of unredeemable ignorance, Latin American Latin Americanists may find a dubious legitimation in the positing of location as final redemption. But then location was precisely what always already delegitimized their outsiding others. How can location function simultaneously as a source of legitimation and as its opposite? The apparent answer is: proper location works, improper location does not. The Latin American Latin Americanists must find their truth in a discourse of propriety that is never secure as such: it is simply based on the expropriation of the impropriety of the other. "Take this, since it does not come from elsewhere," they say, without realizing that if it is not to come from elsewhere, then nobody (else) can take it. They are therefore themselves expropriated.

One of the first large institutional forums devoted to the mutual display of less-than-friendly emotion between Latin Americanist literary and cultural studies scholars was the meeting of the Brazilian

Comparative Literature Association (ABRALIC) in Rio de Janeiro in August 1996. The conference theme called for the defense of a space for thinking culture beyond the reinscription of the literary understood as a reactive formation. Or, it could be seen as trying to protect a space of thinking called literary studies from the intrusion of an emergent field called cultural studies. For the audience and panelists alike, a decision had to be made if it had not been previously made. That is, one had to make a decision insofar as what was at stake was not simply to fulfill a program for the acquisition and maintenance of academic or symbolic power for some people or their antagonists. At the Rio meeting literature held the place of truth from the institutional perspective—but it never was literature; it was rather the literary discipline in all its archival wealth and in all of its misery as well. Therefore literature had to guard itself against a graphematic structure that was threatening to divest it of subjective power or even to eliminate its subject position—in other words, against a structure that was threatening to turn it into a lie. But whatever the power negotiations within the Brazilian academy, for an outside observer it soon became obvious that the disputation could not be considered a confrontation between autonomous knowledges or autonomous subjects of knowledge. It was not a confrontation between alternative, but already constituted codifications of institutional value. The discursive battle brought two armies face-to-face who had been born into themselves out of their mutual opposition: two instances or vectors of force whose dissimilarity or heterogeneity was a direct result of the need to cut or divide a territory that had previously been indifferently occupied. In any case a certain violence became visible and it embodied two empirical characterizations: on the one hand, the dividing and founding violence of cultural studies, which I will call *force;* on the other hand, the divided and conserving violence of literary studies, which I will call *power.* It was not, and it is not, a pure division: the division was marked from its inception by mutual contamination. *Power* makes reference to the hegemonic site of the literary in the Brazilian discussion; *force* to the irruptive position of cultural studies. But we will indeed see the precariousness of such distinctions. The irruption of the new soon became conservative, and the preservation of the old revealed itself, through its very spirit of resistance, as the site for potentially new forms of irruption.

The structure that thus came to light was from the beginning

complicated because both power and force were not merely originary instances, endowed with a full capacity for autonomous self-
inscription. They were conditioned, and overdetermined, by their
previous form of presence in a space that was not the same institutional space that was now the site of the battle, even if it was
not totally heterogeneous to it. The mode of preinscription of both
power and force at the Rio meeting was chiasmatic and it depended
on a transnational frame that in itself seemed to have undergone a
hegemonic mutation in which a historically previous relationship
had been inverted. What in the transnational context was emergent
power had become irruptive force in Brazil; and what was residual
force in the transnational sphere was occupying the space of threatened power in Brazil. Thus part of the mutual contamination between dividing and divided violence came because force and power
in Brazil respectively translated power and force in the transnational
space. Or thus ran the story of the Rio discussion.

At the sessions, in the halls, in the bars, during the walks along
the beach it was possible to think that the defense of the literary
apparatus was at the same time a defense of the national or the regional order against an interference that could only be understood
as neocolonial, since it emanated from a transnational space that
was hegemonized by the U.S. metropole; and it was possible to think
that the transnationalizing cosmopolitanism of the irruptors could
be defined, in at least one and not the least significant of its facets,
as imperial serfdom. On the opposite side, that is, on the side of the
irruptors, it could be thought that the defense of the literary space,
granted that it was the defense of a previously constituted national
space, was compromised by the concomitant ideological defense of
established social domination within the nation against new interpellations that would want to dismantle it. And then of course both
positions are simultaneously true and false: they are true because
they describe factual phenomena and they are false because they do
not describe them well enough.

I do not know in any detail how the situation that became schematic at the Rio meeting has evolved in Brazil since 1996.[6] Within
Spanish-language Latin Americanism the controversy, which also
began around the same time, turned quickly and effectively hot, and
it soon drew a peculiar pattern: the open and explicit accusation
made against U.S.-based Latin Americanist cultural studies scholars

of engaging in cultural colonialism on the basis of an undue appropriation and reproduction of the Latin American cultural object. An element that was absent in Rio should now be added to this story, and it may prove to be a decisive element even if at first it appears merely confusing: the attack against U.S.-based cultural studies did not come primarily from literary scholars, that is, it did not come primarily from members of the various Latin American national intelligentsias that could be identified with a defense of more or less residual power positions.[7] It came from prominent academic intellectuals whose credentials as thinkers in the tradition of cultural studies are impeccable. They seemed to have substituted conservation, a certain conservation, for irruption—which is, certainly, not necessarily a bad thing. Everything depends on what it is that is trying to emerge, and on what it is that one wishes to preserve.

Thus the 1996 ABRALIC discussion between power and force, between literary and cultural studies, took a different turn when it reproduced itself as a transnational complaint from some significant Latin American practitioners of cultural studies force against the constituted power of the largely North American academy. But I think this was still a turn within the same controversy and not an alternative or supplementary one. In both cases, we have the two forms of violence, one dividing and founding, the other divided and conservative, and in both cases we have a reaction against a tendential displacement caused by the irruption within the institutional field of a graphematic structure that is both threatening and invasive. The tactical variation that led Spanish-language Latin American critics to launch their attack against their Latin Americanist friends from the north springs from the mutual contamination of the two instituting violences, and it marks simply a second phase of the same dispute.

The growing accumulation of a series of polemical writings within the last few years and, still more significantly, the influence of the controversy on field formation and development—conference discussions, seminar conversations, dissertation topics, and so forth —constitute something like a minor scandal, the effective comprehension of which is still not quite accessible but will have to be pursued. To the extent that we cannot trivialize these accusations by considering them totally justified on the basis of the fact that they attack poorly conceived work, it is necessary to foreground their importance, which encompasses not just cultural and intellectual but also historical, political, and geopolitical fields of reflection and action. A thoroughly fundamental question is at stake, and it is a question about the minimal conditions for an effective critique of knowledge in the contemporary world. Latin American critics of the U.S. academic establishment are quite right that the post-1989 crisis of the area studies apparatus released a specter or two into the world. If area studies was centrally committed to the productive containment of thought within the geopolitical parameters of the Cold War, the current situation of area-based (but not area-bound) university discourse in the U.S. academy—what we could call the dis-orientation and dis-occidentalization of post–area studies—has broken containment and expanded into diffuse borderlands where all cows seem equally colored and no single cat stands out. Under those conditions, there is indeed a risk that the de-Americanization of knowledge that is ostensibly pursued will at times appear undecidably as its opposite; there is also the risk that the calls for diversity and cultural creativity, the abandonment of the national referent, and a newfound theoretical interest in the subaltern may constitute a new avatar of more traditional tools for U.S. cultural domination. It may be that U.S. post–area studies, far from being a new space of experimentation in the freedom of knowledge, is little more than yet another "cunning of imperialist reason," in Pierre Bourdieu's sense (Bourdieu and Wacquant, "On the Cunning" 41)—indeed, imperial reason itself.

And yet that suspicion may itself be implicated in the very same logic it ostensibly fights when it uses blanket indictments that make no differentiations and establish no boundaries. There must be a difference after all between, say, postcolonial studies and neoliberal thought, and the distinction between critical race theory and rational choice conceits is not a mere trifle when it comes to investigating or contesting the North American domination of epistemic fields concerning any and all areas of the world. We all know enough about the correlation between blindness and insight in critical work to understand that no one is free from errors and prejudices that necessarily contaminate that work. But the ongoing controversy, which is now reduced to repeating what everybody already knows for the most part, may be stagnating or may have reached an impasse: a certain disorientation has come to affect all sides and it is apparently impossible to move beyond an endless drawing and redrawing of already staked-out positions and a vague commitment to the necessary reestablishment of redemptive macronarratives. But the fundamental question remains: Is it possible to reaffirm the nonimperial destiny of critical reason, or is such a pretension nothing but the final movement of an exhausted Enlightenment that can barely survive by holding onto the illusion that thought and power are not the same, in spite of all kinds of historical evidence? No call for a more adequate historicization, no pretense about the epistemic privileges of location, and no suspicions about political bad faith can adequately deal with that question: those things are not enough.

We must understand the current discussions as symptomatic of a geocultural change, which is as such necessarily destabilizing for all, but for an understanding of which change the old parameters of cultural imperialism are seriously inadequate. Ways of thinking developed in the north in order to deal critically with ongoing changes are not to be mechanically defined as imperialist simply because they hope to attain some influence in the south. I understand *geoculture* in Immanuel Wallerstein's sense, that is as the "cultural frame" for the current world-system, today undergoing transition according to Wallerstein, and in respect of which 1989, the year that marks the end of the Cold War, remains "a door closed upon the past" (Wallerstein, *Geopolitics* 11, 15). I want to propose three hypotheses about such geocultural change, which I will offer briefly and without drawing from them all pertinent considerations. Something ought to be left for the chapters that follow.

First Hypothesis

The first hypothesis is the most obvious: the presentation of this polemic as a polemic between literary and cultural studies is a decoy whose constitution is ideological and that therefore ought not to deceive anyone—perhaps paradoxically. What is at stake is not literature, nor its study, nor even aesthetics. What is at stake is not the text or any of the ways of reading developed through the many years of hegemony of the literary field, but rather is a matter of dealing with a geocultural displacement that is in the last instance motivated and sustained by a substantive change in the structure of capitalism at the world level. I do not want to suggest that there is a relationship of simple causality between mode of production and cultural superstructure. I am, rather, interested in the mediations that have been taking place over the last decades concerning the expansion and globalization of capital accumulation: in the changes in the financial structures of capital, in the state form, in the sociopolitical regimes of rule; in the end of the division of the world into power blocks; in the development of new antisystemic movements in what some would still call civil society and in their combined effects on the production, distribution, circulation, and consumption of knowledge. All this amounts to a massive geocultural shift in the specific codifications and recodifications of sociohistorical value. We must cipher the origins of the polemic that so markedly affects the until recently leading function of literary studies in a change in the structures of knowledge, a paradigmatic slide whose consequences, although everywhere noticeable, cannot yet be understood with sufficient clarity.

If capitalism in its previous stage produced affective territorializations on the basis of an encoding of social value where literary studies had a key function as preservers of the unified space of the nation, the contemporary mode of production codetermines an alternative kind of affective identification for the rationalization and processing of which literary studies are grossly insufficient.[8] That does not mean one can no longer study literature, even understand literature within the horizon of a thinking of irruption and force—it only means that literary studies have lost their hegemonic function for the ideological production of social value. The game of irruption and conservation must be understood, in all its complexity, within that schematic.

The academic apparatus called cultural studies will thus come to replace literary studies in the ideological articulation of the present. Literary studies will now assume a subaltern function. This process will not occur without problems, since it involves a restructuring of academic power and the subsequent redistribution of cultural capital within university discourse. Interpretative wars are therefore inevitable. But they are also to a certain extent useless if they serve only to vent resentment against ongoing social processes. We can understand and resist the latter—we can proceed, for instance, toward the critique of the emerging apparatus—but we cannot deny that those processes are taking place lest we condemn ourselves to maintaining nonviable critical positions (which lose henceforth all critical power). That is my first hypothesis. As a corollary, I want to say that the new subaltern function of literary studies endows it with a forceful irruptive potential. We are far from having dealt with the literary—but the tools needed for literary reflection must be redesigned in view of the emerging configurations of knowledge. Literary reflection can find a new role in a potential counterhegemonic articulation, an articulation that we could also call *ultrapostmodern* (using Perry Anderson's admittedly clumsy term)—a concept that still needs to be developed (*Origins* 102 and passim). I should refer from this perspective to some questions that I left pending above.

There is an implied possibility in Taylor's distinction that I have not yet commented upon: the possibility that what is fundamentally important for the study of alternative modernities has to do with the lag or lack of overlap between the history of capital and the history of social power. If the notion of critical reason still holds irruptive power and is not simply a citation from some obsolete ideologeme, then critical reason must exert itself, through historical imagination, in an attempt to understand the totality of the social relations that condition us as well as our past. Our immediate past's critical project, at least for those of us who were formed in the Latin Americanist humanities, was very precisely to understand the Latin American alternative modernities in their various specificities. We were trained to do so through the understanding and exploration of an aesthetic mode of production that was determined by a historicist modernism whose first emblematic productions could well be José Martí's "Nuestra América," Rubén Darío's "A Roosevelt," or José Enrique Rodó's *Ariel*. Within that configuration the aesthetic was never an end in itself or it was already fundamentally loaded by historicist weight. Only historicism could allow for an understanding and a strengthening of Latin American social power against the incursions of monopoly capital—the latter blamed as a source of sociohistorical alienation.

The aesthetic was therefore a means toward historicism, although no doubt one could also say that historicism, insofar as it was a culturalist historicism, could simultaneously be understood as a tool for aesthetic satisfaction.[9] The Latin American national-popular state, which defines or sutures symbolic production in the region from the beginning of the twentieth century until the late 1970s, was a form of aesthetization of the political—certainly so for José Vasconcelos, but also, say, for Fernando Ortiz and Angel Rama, not to mention Jorge Luis Borges, Octavio Paz, or the boom literature. Critical reason for that period was an aesthetic-historicist project that looked to preserve and reinforce the specificity of Latin American (and Argentinian, Mexican, etc.) social power against an invasive and threatening outside.

What has changed? How is it now possible to say that the project of critical reason has undergone a fundamental modification, one symptom of which is the contemporary dispute between literary and cultural studies? And in what sense can it be said that cultural studies will only come into its own, that is, will only be able to understand itself as a critical relationship with the present, if it manages to determine its specificity? Can cultural studies develop a style of thinking that will no longer be associated with a mere expansion of the textual corpus within aesthetic-historicist postulates for the sake of the construction and strengthening of the national-popular state and against monopoly capital?

One wishes that the problem would end there: that one could simply proceed toward an answer that would solve the issue. "All right," the Latin American Latin Americanist says, "if those self-appointed cosmopolitans and neocosmopolitans are right, if we can no longer think clearly against capital and for the nation, if the old location of thinking has become a problem and not the solution, let's solve the problem by imagining alternative locations." But there is a further element of destabilization in that the very discourse of location, that is, the substitution of the national or the regional by the local, which only a few years ago seemed to give us a new beginning to think about, from, and of Latin America under the geopolitical conditions of university discourse in the time of post–area studies, has finally revealed itself as a ruinous thinking, or a thinking in the ruins of thinking.

Taylor's culturalist theory of modernity, like all historicisms, depends on a determinate tropology that Martin Heidegger may have defined for our time on the basis of Wilhelm Dilthey's work: the tropology of the hermeneutic circle (Heidegger, *Being* 188–95 passim). The hermeneutic circle marks, for culturalism, the epistemological limit of human existence as such. To understand one's own culture, or even somebody else's culture, means to enter and dwell within that culture's hermeneutic circle. But Taylor's presentation of his culturalist theory of modernity on the basis of a theorization of the lag between the history of capital and the history of social power seems tendentially to dismantle his own constitutive tropology. In other words, if the sphere of social power within any given culture is subjected to historical change, and if historical change is not simply a function of that culture's internal dynamics but is also or above all a function of heterogeneous factors (such as spatial contaminations from the outside in the form of military conquest or political or economic domination), then the hermeneutic circle never closes. That is, the hermeneutic circle, insofar as a cultural world goes, is never a circle, but simply a circle's catachresis. But then the culturalist theory of modernity loses its necessity and becomes a mere tropological approximation to, an ideology of, the truth of the world. What goes for the national goes for any conceivable locality as well, since locational thinking simply alters the expanse of the hermeneutic circle but does not destroy it.

The first tendential contribution of cultural studies to the destruction of the aesthetic-historicist paradigm is no doubt the vague intuition that the understanding of a given social formation's culture as a hermeneutic circle is a mere ideological prejudice. That seems to me the great and quasi-inaugural contribution of Néstor García Canclini's *Culturas híbridas* (*Hybrid Cultures*). To use Deleuzian-Guattarian vocabulary, the hermeneutic circle would stand revealed, in every case, as a striated or segmented space under the pretense of smoothness. The hermeneutic circle is a circle of hegemony. It is in fact a function of the constitution of the public sphere or of the space of social power as a hegemonic relation. Hegemony, as one of the master concepts to represent political modernity, was always itself understood as an imaginary circle, or rather, as a sphere. Power and subordination within the hegemonic sphere were very precisely intraspheric. The constitution of the political sphere around the notion of the nation-state within the political tropology of modernity is no doubt not a circumstantial fact but rather an essential and all-determining one.

But the threat to or the destabilization of the hermeneutic notion of culture on the basis of its insufficiency is a contribution of cultural studies that cultural studies itself does not seem to understand all too well. In the specific case of Latin American historicity, cultural studies must engage in the radicalization of its own postulates and look for the remainder beyond transculturation, the outside of hermeneutic circularity, what has been subalternized as the constitutive outside of the hegemonic relation. This amounts to a proposal for a fundamental revision of the goal of critical reason. Critical reason in cultural studies is no longer (or should not be, according to what this book will try to show) aesthetic-historicist, but it is rather fundamentally committed to the deconstruction of the inside-outside relationship on which any and all historicisms, including the historicisms of intranational or diasporic locality, and therefore all cultural theories of modernity, have always been structurally established. In my opinion such a proposal has not yet come to fruition, whether on the Latin Americanist side or on the side of British or American (or Australian) cultural studies.

The leading question for the project that constitutes this book is: What kind of tropology could today replace the master tropology of the hermeneutic circle, with its corollary, which is the supplemental tropology of the outside as a savage space? What kind of thinking could think the abandonment of the hegemony of hegemony as the master concept to think about culture in our own time, to think modernity alternatively, and to think postmodernity? A fundamental revision of critical reason must abandon its aestheticist or historicist horizon, a legacy of the modernist past, and seek the undoing of the inside-outside polarity on which all aesthetic historicisms and all culturalist theories of modernity rest. We could think then of the irruptive possibilities of the postaesthetic and posthistoricist language that the literary promise still withholds and could provide. But not without a certain effort.

There is nothing, in my opinion, wrong in principle with any kind of ruinous thinking, and thinking in the ruins of thinking may in fact define the conditions of intellectual labor for our age. The problem, here, is also elsewhere. Locational thinking, to the extent that it thought of itself as something other than a thinking of and in the ruins of the local, thought of itself as what we could call translational or translative thinking. For a thinking of location it was always a matter of vindicating the sheer (utopian) possibility of a retrieval of what Walter Benjamin would have called *pure language* by means of the literary labor of translation—understanding translation radically, as the infinite opening to history. If history is, among other things, the story of power and resistance, then locational thinking undertook to retrieve the historicity of resistance as itself a form of power. We could alternately describe this by suggesting that locational thinking was already a thinking of expropriation, of history's expropriation, and of the expropriation of the thinker as well. The labor of translation undertook to liberate what the later Julio Cortázar would have referred to as a sort of intersemiotic ghost: if the ghost is precisely that which can never leave the place of erstwhile dwelling, the rooted trace of history, then the locational thinker is the thinker for whom what remains at stake is precisely what remains. And what remains can only be found, through translative digging, at the very crossing of the intersemiotic systems—for instance, at the crossing of colonial discourse and subaltern negation in Latin America.

If the crossing of colonial discourse and subaltern negation is the very object of this thinking of expropriation, then it is clear that no thinking of propriety is an adequate rendition of it. The fight between the stereotypical Latin Americanists from the south and from the north is a staged fight, a wrestling match between jokers, because what is at stake in that match is anything but what remains. The Latin American Latin Americanists, or those who assume that position, have no real right to assume the representation of subaltern negation, because they also think from colonial discourse, just as, for example, the U.S. Latin Americanists (and all other cosmopolitans and neocosmopolitans, to the extent that they are Latin Americanists) are no impeccable representatives of the system of epistemic domination. Location, here, is always already crossed, and crisscrossed. A critical position is no automatic gift of commodified location. But more on this a bit later.

Second Hypothesis

The second hypothesis is that cultural studies, in an accelerated process of expansion and transnationalization, is already losing its unity as an irruptive and dividing force. As happened to literary studies, cultural studies has been captured by its very iterability and is today in a large measure in a process of consolidation as epistemic power, within each of its alternative possibilities, at the service of the ideological reproduction of late capitalism. This no doubt fuels what was earlier called the second phase of the ongoing debates. If cultural studies' irruptive strategies could at first present or conceive of themselves as endowed with some founding violence—it happened to literature in Latin America some hundred and fifty years ago—such irruptive possibilities are today largely tamed, as I will attempt to show in several of the chapters that follow, in the service of new encodings of social value. The differential and mutual contamination of the two forms of violence, the fact that they grow by division of a given territory, means that the present violence of consolidation will be followed by new forms of founding. It is then a matter of understanding the game so that we can avoid being caught unawares by the reification of social values that accompanies the ideological reproduction of the movement of capital. It is still critical reason that can mobilize thought and make it a producer rather than a reproducer.

The defense of cultural studies, still necessary in the face of archaic or reactionary forms of intellectual labor, is not in any case an unconditional defense. In that sense discussions between intellectuals from the south and the north are as essential as those between north and north or south and south. But they should not be undertaken in the name of the preservation of reactive cultural capital. In other words, effective attacks come from the dividing force that determines critical reason—critiques must come from the grapheme against entrenched truth and not vice versa. Some of the protests come from Latin American cultural studies scholars against a certain excess—against the tendential or potential radicalization of cultural studies into, for instance, subalternism. Historical imagination, which was the condition of possibility of philology, still appears today as the specific strength of reflection in the humanities. Only historical imagination can meditate on the difference between what is coming and what could come, between the present and the past. Holding on to historical imagination is a point of departure for any emergent rearticulation of critical reason. It is essential to fight the tendential reduction of thinking to the condition of a means for the technical reproduction of what there is. In that sense, the division of the intellectual field, or of the humanities, between literature and culture, between literary reflection and cultural critique, between what is radical (or too radical) and what attempts to preserve—the reification of that division into two fields with opposing interests collaborates with the shrinking of thought and can only lead to further disasters of various kinds.

This is perhaps the place to mention two recent books which in a sense belong to my own critical location, Fredric Jameson's *The Cultural Turn* and Perry Anderson's *The Origins of Postmodernity*, because both of them have something to say that affects my argument directly. Anderson's book is substantially a reevaluation of Jameson's theory of postmodernism as the theoretical horizon of our time. Anderson generally limits himself to an exposition and endorsement of Jameson's thought, which he considers the culmination of Western Marxism. I will focus on the last section of his book, entitled "Politics," and concretely on two remarks that will allow me to develop my position.

Elaborating on the notion that Jameson's theory of postmodernity finds its ground in the systematic counterpoint between "a plane of substance (political economy) and a plane of form (the aesthetic)" (*Origins* 125), Anderson detects what he considers a certain reduction of the political into a minor or subsidiary role within the system. He notes the absence of any sustained study of Antonio Gramsci in Jameson's work. Anderson says, "It [Gramsci's work] was eminently political, as a theory of the state and civil society, and a strategy for their qualitative transformation. This body of thought is by-passed in Jameson's . . . resumption of Western Marxism" (131). In the Marxist tradition Gramsci was the great thinker of the hegemonic circle and of its counterpart, subaltern force. The omission of this thematic in postmodernism theory is not just casual neglect; it has to do very precisely with the determination of postmodernity as the moment in capitalist development when "culture becomes in effect coextensive with the economic" (131). In Jameson's own words, postmodernist language "[suggests] a new cultural realm or dimension which is independent of the former real world, not because, as in the modern (or even the romantic) period, culture withdrew from that real world into an autonomous space of art, but rather because the real world has already been suffused with it and colonized by it, so that it has no outside in terms of which it could be found lacking" (*Cultural Turn* 161).

Jameson's postmodernism theory implies the necessary deconstruction of the notion of the hegemonic circle, or even of the hermeneutic circle understood as a definition of culture, because it involves a radical reduction of the notion of an outside, without which a hermeneutic circle cannot constitute itself as such. A maximum reduction of the possibility of an outside pushed the political possibilities of a theoretical reflection on culture in modernist terms toward their limit. If in full-blown postmodernism the history of capital and the history of social power become one and the same, then the very project of critical reason, which was in modernity based on the nonidentity of social form and social content, as Taylor might put it, is undermined in its very formulation. And the same happens to aesthetic thinking, which is always necessarily based on the possibility of an existing if unreachable outside, on the Borgesian "imminence of a revelation that never arrives," which is aesthetically posited as the transaesthetic foundation of the real and therefore as foundation of the aesthetic itself. In one of his more striking formulations Jameson says: "The image is the commodity today, and that is why it is vain to expect a negation of the logic of commodity production from it, that is why, finally, all beauty today is meretricious and the appeal to it by contemporary pseudo-aestheticism is an ideological manoeuvre and not a creative resource" (*Cultural Turn* 135).

What is then the type of historical imagination that could warrant a reformulation of the project of critical reason as a properly politico-epistemological project? In other words, where can we find a force for intrasystemic irruption if the system has expanded in such a way that no productive notion of an outside is permitted? A second remark by Anderson attempts to save the possibility of political articulation in postmodernity as an intrasystemic movement, in reference to Carl Schmitt's theorization of the political field as the field of division between friends and enemies. Anderson says: "the aesthetic and the political are certainly not to be equated or confused. But if they can be mediated, it is because they share one thing in common. Both are inherently committed to critical judgment: discrimination between works of art, forms of state. Abstention from criticism, in either, is subscription. Postmodernism . . . is a field of tensions. Division is an inescapable condition of engagement with it" (*Origins* 134–35).

I will finish this commentary to my second hypothesis by foregrounding that strange possibility of a critical reason that becomes irruptive or disruptive on the basis of the apparent impossibility of any irruption, of any disruption. Friendship and enmity become for Anderson the figures for a perpetual redivisioning of the social field. The critical possibility is thus given in the possibility of friendship, of which Jacques Derrida says that it can constitute, in its radicalization, "an unprecedented thought of rupture and interruption when . . . we come to call the friend by a name that is no longer that of the near one or the neighbour, and undoubtedly no longer the name of man" (*Politics* 293).

Jameson does not negate, but rather postpones, such interruptive possibility, which for him must arrive in some yet unimaginable future after a dialectical modification of the system. Derrida's words, which take here their departure from the Nietzschean thought of the "perhaps," are merely tentative and preparatory: what he imagines as a radical opening to the friend is also based on the absolute subsumption of otherness into sameness, which is an intrinsic part of Jameson's postmodernism. When there is no longer an imaginable outside, by the same token we lose the possibility of an inside that would permit the simple division of the territory of the political between friends and enemies. The collapse of the classical distinction, the end of the friend and the end of the enemy, inaugurates the new aporetic possibility of the friend—as well as the new aporetic possibility of the enemy. A chance must be taken, on the basis of the Nietzschean perhaps, which does not entirely reduce the sinister possibility of the utterly dystopian or monstruous future—a future ruled over by the figure of the new enemy, rather than the figure of the new friend. Something like a Nietzschean "grand politics" comes then to establish a watch and keep vigilant over the possibility of a political reason and a critique of knowledge that Derrida entrusts to the "literary community" (*Politics* 293), but in a sense that is now to be considered postaesthetic and no longer simply modern.

The commodification of location in locational thinking—the conversion of expropriation into propriety and, finally, into property— is an undesirable but structural by-product of the literary labor of translation. That it haunts Latin Americanist reflection today is a given. The irreducibility of a critical distance between conditions of reflection and field of reflection—or, perhaps, the critical irreducibility of such a distance—finds itself put to work at the service of a betrayal of translation. How, then, to undo such structural betrayal? How can we preserve the promise of locational thinking—for instance, Latin Americanism—and at the same time avoid the pitfalls of its recommodification? Is it possible to do both if we insist on translation as the ultimate horizon of Latin Americanist thinking?

But the minute translation comes to its own end, the minute the labor of translation transmutes into a result, fulfilling its structural goal, is also the minute when locational thinking abandons its vocation as a ruinous thinking, a thinking of the ruins of thinking, and becomes ruined thinking: no place left for the intersemiotic ghost, who chokes and must return to the underground. A fulfilled translation cancels the crossing at the cost of the structural conversion of subaltern negation into colonial discourse. A fulfilled translation, a work of appropriation, is always necessarily colonial discourse. There is only one thing that becomes historically more damaging than the separation of intellectual labor from its means of production, and that is their final identification—because it marks the absolute subsumption of intellectual labor into capital.

Third Hypothesis

Just as my first hypothesis involved the first moment of the epochal dispute in the disciplinary fields of the humanities between literary and cultural studies, and as my second hypothesis referred to a second moment when what was attacked was the tendential radicalization of cultural studies toward alternative encodings, the third hypothesis refers to a third moment that we are perhaps entering. The very same catastrophe of the conservative paralysis and reification of what was emerging force only a few years ago, sad as it may be, is also the dawning promise of a real task for thinking. That is my third hypothesis. The task in our present is clearer and more urgent precisely in view of its opacity and obscurity—in view of its aporetic obscurity. The critique of cultural studies must give way to projects for theoretical reformulations that might allow us to advance toward that "literary" dream of unprecedented interruption and rupture. I understand a theoretical practice as the resistance to all processes of commodification or reification of forms, whether aesthetic forms, forms of valuation, or conceptual forms. In that sense only a theoretical practice can preserve the possibility of an irruption of thinking—against conservation there where conservation is a reactionary practice. This book would like to be an exercise in theoretical practice thus understood.

I also believe that Latin Americanist reflection is now in a privileged position to attempt such projects of reformulation. The Latin American civilizational crossings, together with the Latin American threshold or intermediate position vis-à-vis globalization processes, give it a potential role at the crossroads of world history. Wanting to think such crossroads as they require to be thought means assuming a certain risk and a certain danger: the risk and the danger of failure. But not wanting to do that, that is, preferring to continue within intellectual and academic practices that no longer satisfy even ourselves, is gambling even more strongly for a greater danger: the danger of absolute redundancy, of the infinite iterability of the same. Whether all this, and to what an extent, is a matter of personal decision or a matter of carrying out the programmatic calculability of what is already before us, even if in darkness, remains itself undecidable. But there is no critical possibility that does not embrace undecidability—the opposite case is to proceed to the mechanical deployment of a program for the encoding and recoding of value: a service indeed.

The maximum accomplishment of translational thinking is also its total defeat: an adequate integration into the circuits of conformity, when all further translation becomes unnecessary, when language no longer exists as such, when there can be no literary community anymore. If it is necessary to translate so that what is alien does not expropriate us, and if it is necessary to translate so that what is ours does not kill us (and, finally, both of those are the very conditions of possibility of the cultural practice of Latin Americanism), it is also necessary to understand that translation is not the final horizon of thinking. An untranslative excess, then, must mark Latin Americanist reflection as its last and first condition of critical existence: as the possibility of its existence as a theoretical practice and a community of friends. For the same reason, locational thinking must give way to a sort of dirty atopianism, a supplement to location, without which location comes to the end of itself and becomes a ruin of thought. Dirty atopianism is here the name for a nonprogrammable program of thinking that refuses to find satisfaction in expropriation at the same time that it refuses to fall into appropriative drives. It is dirty because no thinking proceeds from disembodiment. And it is atopian because no thinking exhausts itself in its conditions of enunciation. This does not free us from criticism: rather, it makes critique possible.

///

The following chapters attempt to dwell in the neighborhood of the questions I have been raising. They are, certainly, an exercise in situational consciousness from my own position as a Latin Americanist working in the United States—but they also want to be something else. Although I define Latin Americanism as the sum total of engaged representations concerning Latin America as an object of knowledge and make no general distinctions between work produced in the north and work produced in the south (distinctions can be made, but they can never be general), I have not dreamed of presenting a metacritical analysis of it all. Instead, I have opted for engaging a certain segment, or a number of segments, of contemporary Latin Americanist reflection tangentially, metonymically, and selectively. My purpose all along has been to find and then draw something like a possible path for continued reflection under present conditions: I used whatever seemed more useful within the limits of my knowledge.

While attempting to give my own responses to the various Latin Americanist crises associated with the contemporary predicament of region-based reflection within university discourse, I have also critiqued other existing responses. Although I will apologize in advance for the possibly controversial character of many of the chapters that follow, I must confess I have created some of the controversy on purpose. It is perhaps not always necessary to think against others, and that certainly has never been my intention. But, in the process of writing a book that deals with the possible reconstitution of critical reason in a given institutional field, it is unavoidable that the very development of my thinking will come to be perceived by some of my colleagues, no matter how counterintentionally, as inimical to their own projects. That will be, in many cases, a misperception—but I harbor no illusions. On drawing the lines of what I consider historically and theoretically viable options I must talk about what I consider nonviable. For better or for worse, that is my book, and for that I can make no persuasive apologies. It is organized around a small constellation of critical themes that I could also call theoretical proposals. They are interlaced throughout the chapters in ways that make a summary of them too cumbersome. I will forfeit attempting it. But I do wish to point out here that I understand the book to be an organic proposal rather than a disjointed series of essays. Its organicity is, however, somewhat reckless, as it depends, perhaps a bit too much from the perspective of textual economy, on the positing of the impossibility of organicity when it is a matter of the redefinition of the task at hand for Latin Americanist reflection in the humanities. Latin Americanist organicity is in fact presented in chapters 1 through 4 as strictly dependent on geopolitical models of knowledge that have today become impracticable—notwithstanding their constant resurrection as a form of neolibidinal epistemic nostalgia. I think the central theoretical chapters in this book are chapters 3 and 4, respectively the last and the first I wrote, since everything else depends on them. My proposals for modes of destructive critique variously identified as critical regionalism, second-order Latin Americanism, savage atopics, subaltern negation, restitutional excess, or the accomplishing of a reflective space that would open Latin Americanist thought to nonknowledge and that would transform it into a nonholder of the nontruth of the (Latin American) real are continued in chapters 5 through 8 in a sort of archaeological dig through the work of Antonio Candido and Jorge Luis Borges, Angel Rama and José María Arguedas, U.S.-based testimonio criticism, and some important contemporary critics. This archaeology is in a sense also an autographic genealogy of my own itinerary into the rather abyssal but nevertheless fascinating heart of my disciplinary field: let us call it, by now, Latin American cultural studies. Finally, chapter 9 proposes something like a critical machine, which I term subalternist double articulation, as a kind of device to break out of the corner of aporetic reflection and political scandals into which I may have painted myself in the rest of the book. I have therefore tried to finish the book with an affirmative, if not a positive, note.

ONE Global Fragments

The Immigrant Imaginary

James Petras and Morris Morley's 1990 harsh indictment of Latin American institutional intellectuals is unfair only insofar as it limits itself to Latin American intellectuals. In defining them as those who "write for and work within the confines of other institutional intellectuals, their overseas patrons [i. e., funding institutions], their international conferences, and as political ideologues establishing the boundaries for the liberal political class" (*US Hegemony* 152), Petras and Morley are in fact mentioning the general conditions of academic thinking, at least in the West and in Western-dominated areas. Any conceivable counterpractice in that respect is a practice of negation and resistance, and thus it is still determined by what it negates. Can reflection on current political constraints give way to reflection on political possibilities? Some of those possibilities are to be found in the space afforded by the apparent contradiction between tendential globalization and regional theory.

Area studies were never conceived to be a part of antiglobal theory. On the contrary, as Vicente Rafael retells the story, "since the end of World War II, area studies have been integrated into larger institutional networks, ranging from universities to foundations, that have made possible the reproduction of a North American style of knowing, one that is ordered toward the proliferation and containment of Orientalisms and their critiques" ("Cultures"

91). The project followed an integrationist logic whereby "the 'conservative' function of area studies, that of segregating differences, is made to coincide with their 'progressive' function, that of systematizing the relationship among differences within a flexible set of disciplinary practices under the supervision of experts bound by the common pursuit of total knowledge" (96). A secret imperial project comes then to join the more apparently epistemic one: "the disciplined study of others ultimately works to maintain a national order thought to be coterminous with a global one" (97).

For Rafael, the practice of area studies as traditionally understood is today threatened by the arrival of what he calls "an immigrant imaginary" (98), one of the immediate consequences of which is to problematize the spatial relationships between center and periphery, between home and abroad, between the locality of knowledge production and its site of intervention: "Since decolonization, and in the face of global capitalism, mass migrations, flexible labor regimes, and spreading telecommunications technologies, it has not been possible for area studies to be, or merely to be, a colonial undertaking that presumes the metropole's control over its discrete administrative units" (103). U.S. Latin Americanism is certainly conditioned, although perhaps not yet to a sufficient degree, by the drastic demographic changes and the massive Latin American immigration to the country in recent decades. U.S. Latin Americanism can no longer pretend merely to be an epistemic concern with the geographic other south of the border. Instead, the borderlands have moved northward and within. The immigrant imaginary must necessarily affect an epistemic practice that used to be based on a national-imperial need to know the other, insofar as that other is now pretty much ourselves, or an important part of ourselves. As Rafael puts it, "the category of the immigrant—in transit, caught between nation-states, unsettled and potentially uncanny—gives one pause, forcing one to ask about the possibility of a scholarship that is neither colonial nor liberal nor indigenous, yet constantly enmeshed in all these states" (107).

This hybrid scholarship has been theorized by a number of critics under the name of postcolonial studies, even though postcoloniality refers within contemporary university discourse primarily to a history that is not synchronic with the history of Latin America. To speak of a "postcolonial Latin Americanism" is neither to claim an equal history for diverse parts of the world nor to refer to the nineteenth century, which would be the "properly" postcolonial period for most of the region. As an adjective, *postcolonial* refers here more to a scholarly practice than to its object. *Postcolonial Latin Americanism* is a comparatively useful, if not literally exact, term, used in reference to a scholarly practice in times of globalization, to a Latin Americanism informed by the immigrant imaginary—by the Latin American "within" university discourse. By announcing or affirming a split within metropolitan discourse, postcolonial Latin Americanism radically opens itself to encompass university discourse in Latin America as well as in other areas of the world. Postcolonial Latin Americanism, by adopting the immigrant imaginary, becomes a cosmopolitan discursive practice where location needs to be interrogated every time, since it can no longer be taken for granted. It vindicates itself because the conditions for thinking in the present are such that a responsible academic practice must seek necessary articulations between region of study and region of enunciation in a context defined by globalization. Insofar as this academic practice arises out of a politics of location or, rather, out of a counterpolitics of location, since location was already thoroughly inscribed in previous practices; and insofar as this counterpolitics fixates upon differential localities of enunciation in their difference with respect to the smooth space of hegemonic, metropolitan enunciation, postcolonial Latin Americanism conceives of itself as a form of antiglobal epistemic practice geared toward the articulation or the production of difference through the expression of an always irreducible if shifting distance from the global.

The immigrant imaginary thus seems to open the possibility of Latin Americanist counterimaginings to historically constituted Latin Americanism. Through them Latin Americanist reflection becomes an instance of antiglobal theory, insofar as it opposes the imperial formation of knowledge (and its neoimperial variations) that has accompanied the move of capital toward universal subsumption in globalization. But what is to be decided is whether antiglobality can remain strong enough to counter effectively the controlling force of historically constituted Latin Americanism as it moves to reconstitute itself through the immigrant imaginary, by taming it and reducing it to a contingent position or to a set of mobile positions within new social regimes of rule. In other words, there is no guarantee that the immigrant difference will not be ultimately assimilated—indeed, has not already been assimilated—by the global apparatus and its constant recourse to the homogenization of difference in and through its very preservation. Perhaps homogenizing disciplinary developments and the new role of the global university in the reproduction and servicing of the global system are not really in opposition to the academic theorization of heterogenizing, singularizing drives. Perhaps heterogenization is just the other or presentable side of homogenization, or in a sense necessary to it, necessary for the further expansion of global homogenization, a form of self-produced feed. In any case, even if homogenization and heterogenization are not really antinomical but stand in some sort of dialectical relationship, the relationship between them, as actually existing, remains an important site of political engagement. From the point of view of intellectual institutional politics, to the extent to which they relate to global citizenship today, such a relationship might appear to be the proper region for reflection on new kinds of work in what used to be called area studies.

Two Kinds of Latin Americanism

In the middle of the 1995 debate concerning CIA involvement in the Central American counterinsurgency apparatus, the *New York Times* published an article by Catherine S. Manegold that might be taken to stand as an archetypal example of the way the Western imaginary regulates and controls its engagement with alterity in post–Cold War times: "the most improbable of intimacies" ("Rebel" A1). The article embodies a powerful although fundamentally reactive narrative whose subtext sets Latin Americanist solidarity work against the backdrop of obscure jungle desire or some heart-of-darkness fascination: "Jennifer Harbury was 39 when she first saw Efraín Bamaca Velázquez. She was a lawyer working on a book about the women in Guatemala's rebel army, following an idiosyncratic path that led her deeper and deeper inside a well-hidden, war-hardened society of guerrilla fighters. She had traveled from Texas to Mexico City to the jungles of western Guatemala in her research. She was there to tell their story. She made no pretense of objectivity. She did not see gray and did not want to" (A1).[1]

Harbury's guerrilla romance with the younger and beautiful Maya *comandante*, described as "a fawn" in subliminar allusion to Walt Disney's Bambi, becomes a plausible and tendentially exhaustive explanation for an entanglement in social and political struggles that would otherwise seem utterly inappropriate for a graduate of Harvard Law School: "The prospect of death ordered his days. A fear of banality ordered hers" (A1). Death appears as the figure of some exotic authenticity, and simultaneously therefore as the source of a perverse longing—a longing for negation that will not take itself for what it is. Through Harbury's paradigmatic story, an American citizen's engagement with Central American revolutionary social movements is shown to amount to little more than a deluded orientalism of the heart: "Ms. Harbury tells it as a love story, her first, though she was married once before to a Texas lawyer whom she lived with only briefly" (A5). Orientalism of the heart is undoubtedly the mythical underside of the kind of global politics the CIA itself, together with the FBI, the DEA, and other U.S. law-enforcement agencies, would rightfully pursue, according to their criteria, for higher reasons involving global security and transnational terrorism. Within this discourse, orientalism of the heart comes close to being the only possible explanation for an opening to alterity in global times. Through Harbury, in Manegold's account, an entire class of Latin Americanist solidarity workers and left-wing intellectuals, as well as melodramatic citizens in general, are indicted at the level of affect: their desire, it can always be said, is only obscure love and therefore neither epistemologically nor politically viable: "She made no pretense of objectivity. She did not see gray and did not want to."

What Kenneth Frampton has called the "optimizing thrust of universal civilization" is no longer dependent on the imperial projections of this or that national formation, or of a given set of them (*Modern Architecture* 327). Civilization instead follows the flow of capital into a tendential saturation of the planetary field. Totality affects metropolitan self-understanding because it affects peripheral or intermediate localities by constantly reducing their claims to a differential positioning regarding universal standardization. Global difference may indeed be in an accelerated process toward global identity, to be accomplished by means of some monstrous, final dialectical synthesis after which there will be no possibility of negation.[2] And yet negation occurs, if only as a residual instance doomed to self-understanding through death. "The prospect of death ordered his days," says Manegold of the Maya comandante, as if only death could compensate for, or at least present a limit to, the desperate banality of the global standard.

Latin Americanism is the set or the sum total of engaged representations providing a viable knowledge of the Latin American object of enunciation. I take the notion of "engaged representation" from Stephen Greenblatt. Commenting about early European responses to the New World, Greenblatt remarks: "The responses with which I am concerned—indeed the only responses I have been able to identify—are not detached scientific assessments but what I would call engaged representations, representations that are relational, local, and historically contingent. Their overriding interest is not knowledge of the other but practice upon the other; and . . . the principal faculty involved in generating these representations is not reason but imagination" (*Marvelous Possessions* 12–13). Greenblatt's observation also applies to later Latin Americanist representations. In terms of engagement, Latin Americanist desire can claim to have a powerful association with death in at least two ways: in the first, Latin Americanism, as an epistemic machine in charge of representing the Latin American difference, seeks its own death by integrating its particular knowledge into what Robert B. Hall, in one of the founding documents of area studies as we know them today, called "the fundamental totality" and "the essential unity" of all knowledge (*Area Studies* 2; 4). In this first sense, Latin Americanist knowledge aspires to a particular form of disciplinary power that it inherits from the imperialist state apparatus. It works as an instantiation of global agency, insofar as it ultimately wants to deliver its findings into some totality of allegedly neutral, universal knowledge of the world in all its differences and identities. Born out of an ideology of cultural difference, its fundamental thrust is to capture the Latin American difference in order to release it into the global epistemic grid. It therefore works as a machine of homogenization, even there where it understands itself in terms of promoting or preserving difference. Through Latin Americanist representation, Latin American differences are controlled and homogenized and put at the service of global representation. This is so also in the extreme cases where the homogenization of subaltern difference must go through the active production of othering or abjection. Latin Americanist knowledge, understood in this first sense, ultimately seeks its own death as it endeavors to transfigure itself into its own negation and to dissolve into the panopticon.

In a second way, a Latin Americanism that is no longer a purely imperial "practice upon the other," in Greenblatt's sense, but that has a claim at some internal subversion through its new postcolonial imaginary can also conceivably expect to produce itself as an antirepresentational, anticonceptual apparatus whose main function would be that of arresting the tendential progress of epistemic representation toward total articulation. In this sense, Latin Americanism works primarily not as a machine of epistemic homogenization but potentially against it as a disruptive force, or a wrench, in the epistemological apparatus, an antidisciplinary instance or Hegelian "savage beast" whose desire does not go through an articulation of difference or identity but instead goes through their constant disarticulations, through a radical appeal to an epistemic outside, to an exteriority that will not be turned into a mere fold of the imperial self. In this sense, Latin Americanism seeks an articulation with alternative localities of experience in order to form an alliance against historically constituted Latin Americanist representation and its attendant sociopolitical effects.

In the first case, Latin Americanism aims toward its own dissolution in its apotheosic completion: the day when Latin Americanist representation will finally be able to release itself into the final, apocalyptic integration of universal knowledge. In the second case, Latin Americanism engages its own death by operating a thorough critique of its own representational strategies regarding the Latin American epistemic object. But this critical, antirepresentational practice depends on its previous formation and can be taken to be nothing but its negative or its very form of negation. It could even be argued that this critical, second kind of Latin Americanist practice only comes into focus precisely at the moment when the first Latin Americanism starts to offer the early signs of its radical success, which is also its dissolution as such. However, this may not entirely be due to the first Latin Americanism's own merit. Something else has happened, in relation to which the immigrant imaginary is only a symptom: a social change that has radically altered the stakes in the game of knowledge production.

Commenting on Gilles Deleuze's idea that "we have recently ex-

perienced a passage from a disciplinary society to a society of control" (34) in one of the preparatory essays for *Empire*, the book he
later wrote with Antonio Negri, Michael Hardt makes the following
argument:

> The panopticon, and disciplinary diagrammatics in general, func-
> tioned primarily in terms of positions, fixed point, and identities.
> Foucault saw the production of identities (even "oppositional" or
> "deviant" identities, such as the factory worker and the homo-
> sexual) as fundamental to the functions of rule in disciplinary
> societies. The diagram of control, however, is not oriented toward
> position and identity, but rather mobility and anonymity. It func-
> tions on the basis of "the whatever," the flexible and mobile per-
> formance of contingent identities, and thus its assemblages or
> institutions are elaborated primarily through repetition and the
> production of simulacra. (Hardt, "Withering" 36)[3]

If the first Latin Americanism was one of the institutional avatars
of the way disciplinary society understood its relationship to alterity,
a window in the panopticon, as it were, the second Latin Americanism might be conceived as a form of contingent epistemic performativity arising out of the shift to a society of control. No longer itself
caught in the search and capture of "positions, fixed points, identities," the second Latin Americanism finds in this unexpected release
the possibility of a new critical force. This is so only to the extent
that the second Latin Americanism can articulate itself in the rift of
a historical disjunction: that which mediates the change from discipline to control.

If societies of control assume the final collapse of civil society
into political society, and thus the coming into being of the global
state of the real subsumption of labor under capital, what is then the
mode of existence of nonmetropolitan societies in global times? On
one hand, for Hardt and Negri, *empire,* which is the name for the
accomplished global society of control, "posits a regime that effectively encompasses the spatial totality, or really that rules over the
entire 'civilized' world. No territorial boundaries limit its reign. . . .
Empire presents itself not as a historical regime originating in conquest, but rather as an order that effectively suspends history and
thereby fixes the existing state of affairs for eternity" (*Empire* xiv).
But this is only the perspective of *empire* on *empire* itself. On the

other hand, in the perspective that Hardt and Negri elaborate on the basis of the Spinozan concept of the "multitude," "the passage to Empire and its processes of globalization offer new possibilities to the forces of liberation" (xv). I am particularly interested in the notion of passage, that is, in the reluctant temporality of the coming-to-be of empire. If "the society of control might . . . be characterized by an intensification and generalization of the normalizing apparatuses of disciplinarity that internally animate our common and daily practices" (23), and if "in the passage to the society of control, the elements of transcendence of disciplinary society decline while the immanent aspects are accentuated and generalized" (331), I wish to retain the temporal gap or time lag that determines the alternative modality of incorporation into empire of societies for which the history of capital and the history of social power have never been identical. In semiperipheral societies there is a slower temporalization of the passage, that is, a quantitatively larger presence in their midst of elements from previous social configurations, themselves in the process of vanishing, but at a pace that follows alternative determinations and pressures. In other words, if "the whatever" has tendentially taken over metropolitan societies, it is active in peripheral societies still only as a dominant horizon. In any case, it would only be a matter of degree, since one of the characteristics of imperial rule is its tendential release from spatial and geospatial references: "The striated space of modernity constructed *places* that were continually engaged in and founded on a dialectical play with their outsides. The space of imperial sovereignty, in contrast, is smooth. It might appear to be free of the binary divisions or striation of modern boundaries, but really it is crisscrossed by so many fault lines that it only appears as a continuous, uniform space. In this sense, the clearly defined crisis of modernity gives way to an omnicrisis in the imperial world. In this smooth space of Empire, there is no *place* of power— it is both everywhere and nowhere. Empire is an *ou-topia*, or really a *non-place*" (190).

The imperial regime will do away with the old tropology of center and periphery as it will tendentially embrace a "horizon outside measure" (*Empire* 354) where the old "fixed points" of modern or imperialist sovereignty will no longer obtain. Under the regime of control, in Hardt's words, "instead of disciplining the citizen as a fixed social identity, the new social regime seeks to control the citizen as a whatever identity, or rather an infinitely flexible place-holder for identity. It tends to establish an autonomous plane of rule, a simulacrum of the social—separate from the terrain of conflictive social forces. Mobility, speed, and flexibility are the qualities that characterize this separate plane of rule. The infinitely programmable machine, the ideal of cybernetics, gives us at least an approximation of the diagram of the new paradigm of rule. ("Withering" 40–41). Through the radical reduction of space or its conversion into pure virtuality, in the meantime of subjectivity, in the wake of its temporal displacement, in the time lag that separates alternative residual adisciplinarity, disciplinarity, and control—there the second Latin Americanism announces itself as a critical and residually regionalist machine whose function for the time being is twofold: on the one hand, from its disjointed, shifting position from the diagram of discipline to the diagram of control, to engage Latin Americanist representation as obsolete metropolitan disciplinary epistemics; on the other hand, from its disjointed, residual connection with Latin American social formations, to engage Latin Americanist representation as it evolves into the new paradigm of epistemic rule. The second form of Latin Americanism, which grows out of epistemic disjunctures, can then use its problematic status alternatively or simultaneously against paradigms of discipline and against paradigms of control. Thus announced, it remains no more than a logical and political possibility whose conditions and determinations must then be further, and systematically, explored.[4]

Hardt ends his essay with reference to the possibilities of political practice that the shift from societies of discipline to societies of control necessarily opens: "The networks of sociality and forms of cooperation embedded in contemporary social practices constitute the germs of a new movement, with new forms of contestation and new conceptions of liberation. This alternative community of social practices (call it, perhaps, the self-organization of concrete labor) will be the most potent challenge to the control of postcivil society, and will point, perhaps, to the community of our future" ("Withering" 41). The second Latin Americanism, a form of academic social practice, understands itself as fully within the gaze of this alternative community.

If the first Latin Americanism operates under the assumption that alterity can always, and indeed must always, be theoretically reduced, the second Latin Americanism understands itself in epistemic solidarity with the residual voices, or silences, of Latin American alterity. But it does so under certain conditions. To the extent that there should remain some linkage between solidarity practices and Third World, or colonial, localities of enunciation, globalization turns solidarity, epistemic or not, into an orientalist poetics of the residually singular, the tendentially vanishing, the obscurely, if beautifully, archaic, as represented in the *New York Times* piece: "[H]e looked almost like a fawn" (Manegold, "Rebel" A1). Globalization, once accomplished, dispenses with alternative localities of enunciation and reduces politics to the administration of sameness. Within accomplished globalization there is only room for repetition and the production of simulacra: even so-called difference is nothing more than homogenized difference, abjected difference, a difference that responds to always already predefined "lexicons and representations, . . . [and] systems of conflicts and responses" (Mato, "On the Complexities" 32). However, in that globalization is not yet accomplished, and that the time-lag, or the difference between societies of discipline and societies of control, has not closed in upon itself, the possibility of alternative world imaginings will remain dependent on an articulation with the singular, the vanishing, the archaic: this is the other, constitutive side of the displacement of subjectivities toward infinite lability. It is, however, a peculiar form of articulation, as no "organicity" is given to it. If the first Latin Americanism will continue to think its Latin American subject, its Latin American other, the second Latin Americanism is, as such, constitutively barred from thinking its other. It rather thinks what the thinking of the other conceals or destroys. It thinks what the thinking of the other reveals and accomplishes. The first Latin Americanism is an organic part of the regime of social rule, but the second Latin Americanism lives deprived of organicity, in the temporal lag of the passage to empire: hence its freedom, as well as its impossibilities.

Whatever can still speak to us in singularly archaic ways can only be a messianic voice. It is a singularly formal voice, in that it only and endlessly says "Listen to me!" It is a prosopopeic voice, in the sense that it is a voice from the dead, from the dying, a voice of mourning, like all messianic voices. Latin Americanism can only be open to the messianic intimations of its object through an active affirmation of solidarity. Solidarity has epistemic force to the extent that it understands itself to be in critical resistance to old and new paradigms of social-epistemic rule. But there can be no proper epistemics of solidarity, for it is the end of solidarity to break away from disciplinary capture and subjection to control. A Latin Americanist epistemic politics of solidarity is therefore a paradoxical and unstable extension into academic practices of counterdisciplinary or countercontrol movements arising in principle from the Latin American social field.

Solidarity politics needs to be conceived, in at least one of its faces, as a counterhegemonic response to globalization and empire, an opening to the trace of the messianic in an imperial world. Solidarity politics, as it represents a specific articulation of political action with claims for justice originating in a nonhegemonic or subaltern other, is not the negation of globalization: it is, rather, the recognition, within globalization, of an always vanishing and yet persistent memory, an immemoriality sheltering the singular affect, sheltering singularity, even if that singularity must be understood in reference to a given community or to a given possibility of communal affiliation.

There is then another possibility for reading Manegold's story: Harbury does not indulge in orientalism, but, through her politics of solidarity with the subaltern, with the dead and the dying, she opens herself up to the possibility of preservation of what is immemorial, and therefore to a new thinking beyond memory: a postmemorial thinking, aglobal, coming to us from the singularity that remains, residually. If thinking is always a thinking of the singular secret, a thinking of affective singularities, there is no such thing as globalized thinking; and yet globalization reveals that which globalization itself destroys, and by so doing gives it as a matter for thinking: a thinking of mourning singularity, from singularity-in-mourning, a thinking of what is revealed in destruction, and a thinking of what revelation destroys. This is not to say that such a thinking has been given to us as yet, but only that its difficult possibility may be there.

The Singular Dream

Globalization in the cultural-ideological sphere follows in the wake of the subjection of the citizenry to homogenizing drives mostly deriving from what Leslie Sklair has called "the culture-ideology of consumerism." In one of Sklair's formulations, "the culture-ideology of capitalism proclaims, literally, that the meaning of life is to be found in the things that we possess. To consume, therefore, is to be fully alive, and to remain fully alive we must continually consume" (*Sociology* 41). But what is to be consumed is not necessarily only objects: identities are consumable as well. "Global capitalism does not permit cultural neutrality. Those cultural practices that cannot be incorporated into the culture-ideology of consumerism become oppositional counter-hegemonic forces, to be harnessed or marginalized, and if that fails, destroyed physically. Ordinary so-called 'counter-cultures' are regularly incorporated and commercialized and pose no threat, indeed through the process of differentiation (illusory variety and choice) they are a source of great strength to the global capitalist system" (42). Even consumerism itself is effective at the individual level when it calls for an antiglobal, always local and localized appropriation of the product. As George Yúdice has argued, if citizenship is to be defined fundamentally in terms of participation, and if participation is not, today, to be outside the frame of consumerist ideology, which of course also includes, perhaps predominantly, the containment of the emotional effects of the inability to invest in consumption, then citizenship and the consumption of goods, and the deprivation from consumption, whether material or phantasmatic, go hand in hand. Those parameters presuppose that civil society cannot be understood, at this time, as in any sense outside the global economic and technological conditions that contribute to the production of our experience: indeed, those global conditions would be the fundamental producers of experience. As a consequence, as Yúdice puts it, "theories of civil society based on experiences of struggles of social movements against or despite the state, which captured the imagination of social and political theorists in the 1980s, have had to rethink the concept of civil society as a space apart. Increasingly, there is an orientation toward understanding political and cultural struggles as processes that take place in the channels opened up by state and capital" ("Consumption" 8).[5]

Arjun Appadurai makes a similar point about civil society when he describes "the conditions under which current global flows occur" as produced by "certain fundamental disjunctures between economy, culture, and politics" ("Disjuncture" 280, 275). For Appadurai, "global cultural process[es] today are products of the infinitely varied mutual contest of sameness [homogenization] and difference [heterogenization] on a stage characterized by radical disjunctures between different sorts of global flows and the uncertain landscapes created in and through these disjunctures" (287). Appadurai's "radical disjunctures" disarticulate and rearticulate social actors in unpredictable and therefore uncontrollable ways (in "radically context-dependent ways," as Appadurai adds rather euphemistically [292]); they are, today, the purveyors of experience, not the objects of it.

If, as Yúdice says, the culture-ideology of consumerism is ultimately responsible, in the global system, for the very articulation of oppositional social and political claims, in other words, if consumerist globality not only absolutely circumscribes but even produces resistance to itself as yet another possibility of consumption; or if what Appadurai called "the fundamental disjunctures between economy, culture, and politics" are responsible for a global administration of experience that no social agency can control and no public sphere can check, then it would seem that intellectuals are fundamentally conditioned to be little more than purveyors of a smooth incorporation of the global system into itself, along with the whole array of workers in the cultural-ideological sphere. There is no cultural-ideological praxis that is not always already produced by the movements of transnational capital, which is to say, we are all factors of the global system, even if and when our actions misunderstand themselves as desystematizing ones.

Ideology, then, following the movement of capital, is in a certain strong sense no longer produced by a given social class as a way to assert its hegemony; it is not even to be solely understood as the instrument of transclass hegemonic formations; instead it has come to function, unfathomably, through the very gaps and disjunctures of the global system, as the ground on which social reproduction distributes and redistributes a myriad of constantly overdetermined, constantly changing subject positions. Under those conditions even the Gramscian notion of the progressive organic intellectual as someone with a direct link to anti-imperialist and anticapitalist struggles would seem to appear as an ideologically packaged product for subaltern consumption. Petras and Morley's "new generation" of would-be organic intellectuals will indeed have their work cut out for them.[6] If there is tendentially no conceivable exterior or outside of the global system, then all our actions are seemingly condemned to reinforce it. So-called oppositional discourse runs the most unfortunate risk of all: that of remaining blind to its own conditions of production as yet another kind of systemic discourse. But what would insight accomplish? In other words, what good is it to engage in a metacritics of intellectual activity if that very metacritics is ultimately destined to become absorbed in the systemic apparatus whose functioning it was once thought designed to disrupt? Even the willed metacritical singularity of our discourses, whether it is to be thought in conceptual terms or in terms of style, voice, or mood, is to be incessantly reabsorbed into the frame that alone enables it, producing the site for its expression.

A number of contemporary theorists have made similar points, and they all have a Hegelian genealogy, for instance, Louis Althusser talking about the ideological state apparatus, and Fredric Jameson on capital in its third stage. Their discourse is not so drastically different in this respect from the quasi-totalizing parameters Jacques Lacan set in reference to the unconscious, Martin Heidegger and Jacques Derrida regarding Western ontotheology and the age of planetary technology, or Michel Foucault regarding the radically constituting sway of the power-knowledge grids. All these thinkers come to the far side of their thinking by opening up, usually in a most ambiguous manner, the possibility of a thinking of the outside that will then become a redemptive or salvific region. Such a possibility seems to be an imperative for Western thinking, even the essential site for its constitution: an ineffable disjuncture at its origin, or the trace of the messianic in it, which Derrida has thought of, in his book on Marx, as just another name for deconstruction.[7] This messianic trace, which turns up in contemporary thinking as the compulsive need to find the possibility of an outside to the global system, a point of articulation permitting the dream of an oppositional discourse, has been expressing itself, ever since Hegelian dialectics, as the very power of the metacritical or self-reflective instance in the thinking apparatus. If it is true, on the one hand, that metacritics will always be reabsorbed by the system that first opens up its possibility, it seems, on the other hand, as if it were true that at some point, at some place of utmost ineffability or ambiguity, metacritics could disrupt the reabsorption machine, arresting it or paralyzing it even if only temporarily. Such is, perhaps, the utopian dream of Western thinking in the age of mechanical reproduction.

But the age of mechanical reproduction, the age of the global system and the planetary technologization of (disjunctive) experience, is also the age in which the question as to whether there is something other than a thinking that must be called Western retrieves a new legitimacy. The question itself comes from such Western thinking, for only Western thinking is sufficiently naturalized within the global system that constitutes it that it can legitimately, as it were, dream of an alternative singularization of thinking. But it is a special question, in that in it Western thinking wants to find an end of itself as a response to itself. This end would not necessarily have to come from non-Western geopolitical spaces: it would suffice to find the end internally, as perhaps a fold in the question about the end itself.

The end of thinking was paradoxically articulated by Theodor Adorno in terms of the ultimately irrepressible historical victory of instrumental reason. The radical negation of negativity itself, understanding negativity as the force of alienation, was for Adorno the motor of a critical thinking that could then not stop short of negating the very possibility of critical thinking as a thinking of always insufficient negativity, constantly running the risk of a positive reification of its negative impulse. Adorno's melancholy abandonment of hope in the face of what he understood to be the fundamental but also fundamentally inescapable error of totality, which is also total alienation, would still find redemption in an always receding utopian countermove to the extent that the latter could still be at all imagined, although never articulated. Martín Hopenhayn has shown up to what point Adornian pessimism was conditioned by his metropolitan location and by his more or less unconscious assumption of a particular historical standpoint, which was then naturalized as universal. Hopenhayn argues that it is today quite possible, indeed even necessary from the standpoint of Latin American new social movements and other oppositional practices, to understand and use the full force of a critical theory-inspired thinking of negativity insofar as the global system is concerned, *and* at the same time to use such gained knowledge toward the concrete affirmation "of that which negates the whole (interstitial, peripheric)" (*Ni apocalípticos*

155; my trans., here and below). This would be a thinking of historical disjuncture, where a dialectical relationship between negation and affirmation may not quite obtain. Globality may not be overcome or torched by "interstitial sparks," but spaces of coexistence may be implemented, folds within the global system, where an exterior to totality emerges as the site of a possible, concrete freedom: "Negation does not liberate from the negated—the general order—but it acknowledges spaces where that order is resisted. From this perspective, an *absolute* cooptation by dominant reason does not exist, even though micro-spatial, counter-hegemonic logics may not be able to engage in a process of general overcoming of dominant reason. [But this] critical function of social knowledge [preempts] . . . the total closure of the world by the dominant order" (155).

Hopenhayn's interstitial or peripheric spaces are disjunctive sites, of which it is affirmed that they hold the possibility of a singularization of thinking beyond negativity. With negative thinking they share the notion that there will be no historical closure insofar as the historicity of any system can still be understood as historicity, that is, to the extent that something other than it can still be imagined. These interstitial spaces, however, are not postponed, as they might have been for Adorno, to the improbable but still ever more dimly perceivable future of utopian redemption; they are instead found in alternative presents, in the different temporality of alternative spatial locations. Hopenhayn quotes an Adornian sentence, which might in fact define the negativity of the new thinking of the singular: "Only s/he who is not totally caught up in the self-movement of the object is at all able to follow it" (*Ni apocalípticos* 133). Beatriz Sarlo opens her *Escenas de la vida posmoderna* with a similar statement: "Whatever is given is the condition of a future action, not its limit" (10; my trans., here and below). But must a singular thinking then establish its own positivity?

"Negation does not liberate from the negated—the general order —but it acknowledges spaces where that order is resisted" (Hopenhayn, *Ni apocalípticos* 155). If Latin Americanism could find in negativity a possibility of recognition of alternative dwellings, Latin Americanism would still not be a thinking of the singular, but it would have opened itself to the singular event and thus to the possibility of an exteriority to the global. In Latin Americanism, then, an end of thinking comes into operation which is also the stated goal of Latin Americanist thinking: the preserving and effecting of Latin American experiences which would arrest "the total closure of the world by the dominant order."

Neo-Latin Americanism and Its Other

We are not yet outside the region defined by what Jameson has called the "temporal paradox" of postmodernity, which, when thought of in a global scale, takes on spatial overtones as well. In its first formulation the paradox reads: "the equivalence between an unparalleled rate of change on all the levels of social life and an unparalleled standardization of everything—feelings along with consumer goods, language along with built space—that would seem incompatible with just such mutability" (*Seeds* 15). If Latin Americanism could once generally think of itself as the set of interested representations in charge of preserving, no matter in how contradictory or tense a manner, an idea of Latin America as the repository of a cultural difference that would resist assimilation by Eurocentric modernity, for Jameson such an enterprise would today have been voided of social truth, since that specific countermodernity would have, at least tendentially, "everywhere vanished from the reality of the former Third World or colonized societies" (20). The Latin Americanist emphasis on cultural difference must then be understood in the context of neotraditional practices: "a deliberate political and collective choice, in a situation in which little remains of a past that must be completely reinvented" (20).

This particular kind of postmodern epistemic constructivism, which is in itself providing a powerful if perhaps residual possibility of revival to area studies as historically constituted, stands in a paradoxical relationship to the critical function that modernity envisaged as proper to the intellectual. The modern intellectual, again in Jameson's formulation, "is a figure that has seemed to presuppose an omnipresence of Error, variously defined as superstition, mystification, ignorance, class ideology, and philosophical idealism (or 'metaphysics'), in such a way that to remove it by way of the operations of demystification leaves a space in which therapeutic anxiety goes hand in hand with heightened self-consciousness and reflexivity in a variety of senses, if not, indeed, with Truth as such" (*Seeds* 12–13).[8] The risk of Latin Americanism today is to engage in a neotraditional production of difference that could then no longer be interpreted as having a fundamentally demystifying character. The Latin American nonmodern residual, as invoked in journalistic, cinematic, and even academic discourse, is today frequently no more than an already-itself-constructed pretext for an epistemic invention by means of which metropolitan postmodernity narrates itself to itself by way of the detour of some presumed heterogeneity, which is in turn nothing but the counterpart of the thorough universal standardization, the stuff on which standardization feeds in order to produce itself. If Catherine Manegold's rendering of Jennifer Harbury's story has revelatory power, it is because it reveals the deep structure of such epistemic constructionism. If the power of the narrative is fundamentally reactive, it is because it reinforces the story rather than attempting to modify it or to counter it.

The main function of a second, antirepresentational, critical Latin Americanism would be that of arresting the tendential progress of epistemic representation toward total articulation. This second Latin Americanism is to be conceived as a kind of contingent epistemic performativity arising out of and dwelling in the time lag between the shift from a disciplinary society, in the Foucauldian sense, to a society of control, following Hardt's critical use of the Deleuzian notion. This second Latin Americanism would understand itself as an epistemic social practice of nonrepresentational solidarity with singular claims originating within whatever in Latin American societies still remains in a position of vestigial or residual exteriority, that is, whatever actively refuses to interiorize its subalternization with respect to the global system. In fact, this second Latin Americanism emerges as a critical opportunity through the metacritical realization that the first, or historical, Latin Americanism has come to a productive end with the end of the disciplinary paradigm of rule that understood the progress of knowledge as the panoptic search and capture of "positions, fixed points, identities." But it could not maintain its critical force if it were to accept as its historical mission substitution of the old identitarian difference with another kind of difference based upon the repetition of the former—a simulacrum. A solidarity with the singular demands not its reconstruction as a positive difference but rather an opening to processes of epistemic negation and disarticulation vis-à-vis identitarian knowledges that are themselves a product of a disciplinary configuration or of its reconstitution as a regime of control. Solidarity is, precisely, not capture. No positive apparatus of knowledge could result from a practice whose form of action is already a refusal of disciplinary appropriation.

Historically constituted Latin Americanism seeks to reformulate itself at the service of the new paradigm of rule through an epistemic constructivism that homogenizes or abjects difference in the very process of interpellating it, and for which this construction of neo-difference is no more than a post–civil society detour toward the goal of universal subsumption of knowledges into the global standard. It is this new avatar of Latin Americanism, whose direct genealogy is historical Latin Americanism, that should be understood as neo-Latin Americanism properly so-called (thus falling within the purview of Jameson's critique). It appears, today, as the real enemy of critical thinking and of any possibility for counterhegemonic action from the academic institution or through university discourse.

Against neo-Latin Americanism, then, as its negation and secret possibility, there can be another Latin Americanism, whose possibility lurks in the gap between the rupture of disciplinary epistemics (and its constant recourse to "positions, fixed points, identities") and its reformulation as an epistemics of control (and its recourse to "the whatever" as the infinitely contingent placeholder for an identity that can never go beyond its frame and that must therefore continuously produce itself as simulacrum and repetition). Between discipline and control, let us imagine the always contingent performativity of a singular thinking of Latin America that thinks what thinking Latin America destroys: against discipline, against control. Its limit, which is therefore also the condition of its actions for the future, in Sarlo's phrase, might be given in the notion of preempting the total closure of the world by the dominant. It does not seem possible to find a way in which Latin Americanism can offer anything but a construed heterogeneity when attempting to think the Latin American singular. By the same token, however, a radical opening to extradisciplinary heterogeneity through the work of negation remains the mark of this critical and antirepresentational Latin Americanism, which self-reflexivity only prepares.

Opposite Numbers

Catherine Manegold's account of Jennifer Harbury's story has a neo-racist subtext. Etienne Balibar's precise definition of the phenomenon allows it to be understood as the reactive counterpart to Rafael's immigrant imaginary. Balibar explicitly mentions immigration, "as a substitute for the notion of race and a solvent of 'class consciousness,'" as a first clue toward the understanding of contemporary transnational neoracism ("Is There a 'Neo-Racism'?" 20). Neoracism is the sinister counterpart to the cultural politics of difference that the immigrant imaginary and other nonimmigrant but nevertheless subaltern social groups generally invoke as their emancipatory banner. Neoracism works in effect as the mirror image of identity politics, that is, as an identity politics of the dominant, since "it is a racism whose dominant theme is not biological heredity but the insurmountability of cultural differences, a racism which, at first sight, does not postulate the superiority of certain groups or peoples in relation to others but 'only' the harmfulness of abolishing frontiers, the incompatibility of life-styles and traditions; in short, . . . a differentialist racism" (21).

Balibar makes the point that differentialist racism takes the antiracist argumentation of culturalism at its word, promoting a curious and effective "turn-about effect." For the neoracist, "if insurmountable cultural difference is our 'natural milieu,' . . . then the abolition of that difference will necessarily" create problems, such as "defensive reactions, interethnic conflicts and a general rise in aggresiveness," which would be best avoided by preempting, through exclusion in the form of some minor or major ethnic-cleansing procedure, too close a contact between the different human groups ("Is There a 'Neo-Racism'?" 22). Manegold's understated ridicule of Harbury's involvement with the Maya guerrilla as a form of orientalism of the heart or romantic third-worldism is, consciously or unconsciously, meant to promote precisely that need for cultural separation. The result of all this is what Balibar calls a naturalization of racist conduct, in the sense that neoracism ideologically conceives of itself as trying to avoid racist conduct by eliminating the conditions that would lead to its "inevitable" manifestation.

Neoracism is, as it affects, for instance, the Latino population in the United States, the opposite social and political number of the immigrant imaginary. Second Latin Americanism fundamentally orients itself against the culturalist ground of neoracism. If "from the logical point of view, differentialist racism is a meta-racism, or what we might call a 'second-position' racism, which presents itself as having drawn the lessons from the conflict between racism and anti-racism, as a politically operational theory of the causes of social aggression" (Balibar, "Is There A 'Neo-Racism'?" 22), then second-position Latin Americanism is, from the logical and political point of view, also a meta-Latin Americanism that has understood the culturalist dangers of neo-Latin Americanism and its cooptation of difference. But it is above all a meta-Latin Americanism that understands itself as the social, political, and epistemic opposition to a historically reconstituted Latin Americanism in the context of the society of control—whether historically reconstituted Latin Americanism is posited as neo-Latin Americanism, in its liberal variant, or, in its extreme version, as an ideological formation at the service of a globalized technopolitics of selective inclusion and hierarchically organized distribution of planetary resources.

TWO Negative Globality and Critical Regionalism

A Critical-Regionalist Teleology

A sufficient response to the notorious affirmation of the end of the macronarratives of modernity does not exist yet.[1] Instead mirages abound, and a lot of those mirages have been conceptualized, as mirages, in terms of micronarratives of difference and heterogeneity. Difference and heterogeneity permanently run the risk of being understood, and of understanding themselves, as simple negations *within* a false dialectic of consciousness imposed by the supremacy of what we could understand as the neoimperial avatar of imperial reason: the culture-ideology of consumerism. *Narrative fissure, negative globality,* and *critical regionalism* are concepts within the purview of second-order Latin Americanist reflection that attempt to preserve a historical legacy; they are concepts that attempt to deconstruct a historical legacy; and they are concepts that, immodestly enough, also attempt to open up a discursive field where the possibility of new forms of reflection can be prepared.

Michael Geyer and Charles Bright use the expression *narrative fissure* to refer to the contrasts between expectations of modernization and the realities of the course of events. Narrative fissures must be understood in every case as "arising out of world-wide processes of unsettlement (the mobilization of peoples, things, ideas, and images and their diffusion in space and time) and out of the often desperate efforts both locally . . . and globally . . . to bring them under control or, as it were, to settle them" ("World History" 1053). These reversals of expectations, because they are planetwide and affect everybody, produce a sort of *negative globality* that must be culturally figured in the various impossibilities, everywhere observable, of narrative closure and cultural self-understanding.

It is not that modernization has not happened or is yet incomplete. It is rather that modernization has not happened in the sense it was supposed to have happened. A rupture at the level of consciousness has taken place—and it has taken place everywhere. That rupture could perhaps be represented, allegorically, using an old essay by Louis Althusser ("The 'Piccolo Teatro': Bertolazzi and Brecht. Notes on a Materialist Theatre"). Commenting upon melodramatic consciousness, Althusser says of the subaltern characters that share it:

> the motor of their dramatic conduct is their identification with the myths of bourgeois morality: these unfortunates live their misery within the arguments of a religious and moral conscience; in borrowed finery. In it they disguise their problems and even their condition. In this sense, melodrama is a foreign consciousness as a veneer on a real condition. The dialectic of the melodramatic consciousness is only possible at this price: this consciousness must be borrowed from outside (from the world of alibis, sublimations and lies of bourgeois morality), and it must still be lived as *the* consciousness of a condition (that of the poor) even though this condition is radically foreign to the consciousness. (*For Marx* 139–40)

Let me attempt to read these words as if *modernization* were the same thing as *melodramatic consciousness. Melodramatic consciousness* would then be *modernization,* always lived by subaltern subjects as such, in the terms used by Althusser, as a "foreign consciousness . . . on a real condition." The analogy might permit us to understand the underlying connections between imperial reason and modernization; and it permits us to understand modernization as the empty signifier for a certain kind of imperial hegemony at the planetary level.[2] This is a condition for the emergence of what I am calling *critical regionalism.*[3]

We are all now in the position of Nina, the main character in the play Althusser analyses: we have undergone a world-historical experience, which ended with the collapse of so-called actually existing socialism and the ongoing destruction of the welfare state, allowing us potentially to break with a form of melodramatic consciousness whose destruction is, as Althusser puts it, "the precondition for any real dialectic" (*For Marx* 138). Actually existing socialism was no enemy of modernization and imperial reason. The conflict between the so-called First and Second Worlds was an internal episode in a dialectic of consciousness that has now come to reveal itself as the false dialectic of modernization. The rupture with such false dialectic is a historical moment of denarrativization. It has been widely understood as signaling the end of modernity's macronarratives. But it is simultaneously more and less than that. It is not so much an end of particular macronarratives as it is a fissure in modern consciousness itself, a monumental moment of arrest not just for macronarratives but also for any and all supplementary narratives, no matter how "micro-" they claim themselves to be. The rupture with the false dialectic of modernizing consciousness is also ultimately a rupture with all false dialectics, with all melodramas, with all narratives of identity, and with all narratives of difference; and it is so to the extent that these latter narratives depend for their own constitution on a negation of the macronarrative of modernization, which is the great narrative of Western identity itself. Narrative fissure has to be understood, objectively, in the sense of "the fissure in narrative" (that is, not as "the fissure of narrative"). It affects all narratives, and not selectively so, including all (post)modern narratives of difference and all (post)modern narratives of identity and including subaltern narratives wherever they exist. To endorse John Kraniauskas's definition of subaltern studies: subaltern studies, as the proper thinking of the narrative fissures in the discourse of globalization, is "a critique of the total apparatuses of development" whose ground of necessity is its refusal to be complicit with the hegemonic production of narratives of heterogeneity as a product of the movement of capital.[4]

Negative globality is the underside of the great narrative of global modernization; or, even more than its underside, negative globality is the "other than itself" through which the false dialectic of melodramatic, modern consciousness comes to an end *in every case,* that is, not just at the abstract level defined by the hegemony of metropolitan, neoimperial reason but also in its innumerable subsumptions in subaltern consciousness throughout the planet, wherever "a foreign consciousness" developed "as a veneer on a real condition." It has been a long time since there was an outside to Western imperial reason—and it may no longer be possible to think *without* it. If modernization, from the point of view of the subaltern, is nothing but "a foreign consciousness as a veneer on a real condition," could we then invert the proposition and define negative globality in terms of "a real consciousness as a veneer on a foreign condition"? Can negative globality be understood as "genuine" subaltern consciousness? If so, then we would probably want to say that negative globality, like Nina in Althusser's interpretation of Bertolazzi's play, "[which] is for us the rupture and the beginning, and the promise of another world and another consciousness, does not know what [it] is doing. Here we can say that consciousness is delayed—for even if it is still blind, it is a consciousness aiming at last at a real world" (*For Marx* 142).

Because our critical narrative is also fissured, we cannot know if negative globality, which is the formal concept to design the blockage for any reconstruction of melodramatic consciousness at the level of social totality, and which is therefore an absolute condition for the possibility of "a real consciousness" or of "a consciousness of the real," is in itself already seized by a return of melodramatic consciousness at the level of critical argumentation. The possibility that narrative fissure and negative globality are, as critical concepts, nothing but a ruse of reason, another mirage in themselves, is however the very motor of the notion of critical regionalism and the very basis of its effective dialecticity. In other words, critical regionalism already contemplates the possibility that it constantly runs the risk of developing into melodramatic consciousness.

The universal phenomenon of consumerism must be understood, not merely at the anthropological level, as a primary mechanism of socialization, but also at the sociological level, as a secondary or symbolic mechanism of socialization into the culture-ideology of global capitalism. I am thinking of a consumerism that goes beyond the lure of the market: a consumerism that is no longer an effect of the market but is rather its very cause in contemporary terms; of commodity consumption, or its deprivation, as the very basis of a relation to the world, the primary form of "worlding" in the present, including the present of knowledge production, of university discourse: knowledge as commodity, university discourse as a discourse of the market.[5] If such a consumerism exists, could we then establish the theoretical possibility of a nonconsumptive singularity? Non-consumptive singularity would be a code-word for the singularly resistant modality of subjective presence within global capitalism—it would be the name for the theoretical possibility of a residual outside to global consumerism, of an "outsid-ing" trace. Whatever its possibilities, they would have to be thought without and not within the game of identity/difference, for the dialectics of identity and difference has been exhausted and should rather be understood today as the latest avatar of melodramatic consciousness at the global level. Difference, in other words, is no longer an "other than itself," but it has been made into more of the same through the expanding power of cultural commodification that defines our regime of capital accumulation.

A subalternist critical regionalism is the systematic exploration of the fact that no systematic exploration can today be understood as something other than a ruse of universal reason—even if and when such (latter) systematic exploration believes itself to be merely local or subaltern. Critical regionalism is therefore the name for an enterprise of thinking that takes the subaltern perspective, formally defined as the perspective from the constitutive outside of hegemony, as the starting point for a critique of contemporary consciousness. Its goal is twofold: on the one hand, to continue the enterprise of deconstruction of melodramatic consciousness, whether local, regional, national, or global, understood as the false consciousness of a real situation; on the other hand, to move toward alternative, non-hegemonic local and regional histories that will seek to constitute themselves as the real consciousness of multiple and always false situations. I think this is a strong teleology for critical practice, and one that could perhaps sustain a certain historical realignment in the production of knowledge.

The Difficulty of a "Major Realignment"

The Gulbenkian Commission's report on the restructuring of the social sciences associates the development of so-called cultural studies with the ongoing challenge to "the tripartite division of knowledge" between the natural sciences, the social sciences, and the humanities that had been thoroughly institutionalized in the Western academy by 1945 (*Open the Social Sciences* 64).[6] For the Gulbenkian Commission, the rise of cultural studies, which originates in the humanities field, has "undermined the organizational divide between the superdomains of the social sciences and the humanities" to such an extent that it has produced the possibility of "a major realignment" (68, 73) of scientific and disciplinary boundaries. Although the Commission never makes the link explicit, such epistemic shifts are strongly related to changes in the geopolitics of knowledge. So-called area studies has also been undergoing a grave crisis. What is at stake is the substitution of area studies by another global enterprise or epistemic apparatus geared to the production of area-based knowledge.[7] In the words of the former president of the Social Science Research Council, Kenneth Prewitt, "from United Nations agencies to international corporations, from nongovernmental organizations to the State Department, the traditional region-by-region approach is found to be poorly aligned with the tasks and opportunities of the contemporary world" ("SSRC" 10).[8]

The traditional intellectual aim of "understanding the foreign other," which was always defined from a U.S. or Eurocentric perspective that became consubstantial to the area studies enterprise, is to be replaced by a new goal: the code words refer to the integration of problem-oriented scholarship and area-based knowledge in the context generated by the exponential increase in the speed and spread of processes of global integration and fragmentation. Traditional area studies was excessively dependent on reflection on local cultures in view of their particularity and uniqueness. Its reconfiguration as area-based knowledge purportedly promotes the critical and dynamic study of historical localities in terms of the processes of globalization and fragmentation that affect them. The link between cultural studies and area-based knowledge is essential, and it is as such already implied in the very definition of cultural studies the Gulbenkian Commission provides: "The three themes that have come together in cultural studies are: first, the central importance of gender studies and all kinds of 'non-Eurocentric' studies to the study of historical social systems; second, the importance of local, very situated historical analysis, associated by many with a new 'hermeneutic' turn; third, the assessment of the values involved in technological achievements [i.e., modernization] in relation to other values" (65).

Cultural studies is, from this definition, centrally concerned with the activities that have historically occupied area specialists, whose mission was to study the uniqueness or particularity of non-Eurocentric social formations within the previous epistemological paradigm of global modernization. The epochal shift connecting cultural studies to the end of area studies as we know them is genealogically tied to the exploration and theorization of social difference in a globally integrated world from which the allure of modernization as ultimate teleology has vanished. But the study of social difference, when it is deprived of teleology, that is, when done for its own sake, is in itself unproductive—unless the very pleasure of epistemological consumption is considered productive. In the words of Jacob Heilbrunn, in view of current epistemological changes, "to examine area studies itself is to realize that it has become a field without a mission" ("News" 50). The disciplines most seriously affected by the rise of cultural studies today—literary studies, history, anthropology, and communication studies—also find themselves deprived of a clear historical mission for the near future. Even if we accept the epistemological hegemony of cultural studies within area studies, the teleological determination of cultural studies remains fundamentally obscure. But a radicalization of cultural studies in the sense of subaltern studies—of a subalternist critical regionalism— could indeed offer the possibility of a perhaps complex solution to the impasse of the current configuration for critical practice.

According to the definitions given above, which I will use tactically, the basic thrust of cultural studies would be the incorporation of the experiences of dominated groups into the discourse of knowledge. This obviously includes an attention to local and historical specificity. Prewitt insists that "globalization does not render the specifics of place inconsequential. Whatever may be meant by the term 'globalization,' the phenomenon to which it points is clearly constructed from dozens to thousands of separate places, not all marching in some lock-step pattern" ("SSRC" 10). The Gulbenkian Commission finishes its report by referring to the "arduous task of demonstrating how incorporating the experiences of [dominated groups] is fundamental to achieving objective knowledge of social processes." (88). But the crucial question is arguably not "what [does] our understanding of social processes [gain] once we include increasingly larger segments of the world's historical experiences" (88), but rather why should we want to include those experiences into our knowledge; that is, for what purpose?

Geyer and Bright point out a fundamental dilemma that seems to threaten contentions in favor of the possibility of a "major realignment" in knowledge production as something other than a simple continuation of imperial reason: "[the twentieth] century began with the expectation of a modern and thoroughly homogeneous world that would become one as a result of the expansion of the West and the consolidation of its power at the center of an integrated human experience. It ends with people asserting difference and rejecting sameness around the world in a remarkable synchronicity that suggests, in fact, the high degree of global integration that has been achieved" (1036–37). Except, of course, that the achieved global integration does not respond to the admittedly Eurocentric expectations of progress toward modernity—or to any other expectations. As Geyer and Bright say, "the world we live in has come into its own as an integrated globe, yet it lacks narration and has no history" (1037). This lack of historicity, this pointed moment of denarrativization must on the one hand be associated with the disciplinary absence of mission Heilbrunn has mentioned. On the other hand, however, it might guard a critical potentiality having to do with the unfathomable excess of singularity itself: the moment when a narrative, any narrative, breaks into its own abyss is also a moment of flight in which subjectivity registers as noncapturable; indeed, it is a moment of pure production without positivity that will not let itself be exhaustively defined in the name of any heterogeneity.

I would like to raise some questions about the metacritical justification of area-based cultural studies for the specific case of Latin American studies. Latin American cultural studies, accepting the Gulbenkian Commission definition, must emphasize Latin American singularity and heterogeneity even as it attempts to place them in the context of global events going beyond Latin America's geographic borders. The first critical question—the question on which the very constitution of Latin American cultural studies as a kind of critical regionalism in the global context might depend—is then to wonder whether Latin American cultural studies, and its particular fostering of the production of regional difference, is a genuinely productive enterprise and not the mere byproduct of a global phe-

nomenon that is reading us all: the stealthy and radically totalizing "culture-ideology of consumerism," in Leslie Sklair's formulation.[9] The already quoted remark by Fredric Jameson referring to
what he calls the "temporal paradox" of postmodernity might serve
as an epigraph for my argument: "[there is an] equivalence between
an unparalleled rate of change on all the levels of social life and
an unparalleled standardization of everything—feelings along with
consumer goods, language along with built space—that would seem
incompatible with just such mutability" (*Seeds* 15). We do not yet
know whether the intellectual work that may go under the name
of Latin American cultural studies might avoid falling into the trap
of (re)producing local difference for the sake of a merely regionally
diversified consumption of sameness. But the cultural studies enterprise, in its foundational appeal to a dialectics of difference and identity, may in fact not be as protective of subaltern subject positions as
it appears. In that sense, a reframing of cultural studies work under
the twin concepts of hegemony and subalternity emerges as an alternative to the traditional conceptualization in terms of identity and
difference.[10] A certain historical exhaustion of the critical productivity of the dialectics of identity and difference must be put to work
at the service of an alternative understanding of critical reason that
makes of subalternity, as the "constitutive outside" of hegemonic
consciousness, a privileged reference.

Heterogeneity and Fissured Globality

Even as recently as 1990, when Antonio Cornejo Polar published
his essay "Nuevas reflexiones sobre la crítica latinoamericana," he
could not have anticipated how quickly the epistemological ground
was going to shift. It remains his merit to have insisted then that "a
paradigm shift" in literary-historical reflection was at the same time
coming and long overdue (231). What he could not have known was
that his "cambio de paradigma"—in the midst of which we presumably still are—was going to alter the conditions of the possibility of
literary-historical reflection to such an extent that the very viability
of the literary-historical discipline—if its goal is to produce knowledge about a bounded geocultural system—would come under serious questioning (231).

Cornejo's recommendations were radical enough. Drawing on his
work as well as that of scholars such as Rolena Adorno, Martin Lien-

hard, and Walter Mignolo, Cornejo called for a complete redrawing of Latin American literary history on the basis of the heteronomy of its objects: "the great theme of historiographic and critical thought is without a doubt the theme of the heterogeneity and the contrasts in Latin American literature" ("Nuevas reflexiones" 235; my trans., here and below). His notion that Latin American literary historiography had to attempt to reconstruct itself on the basis of the concept of "contradictory totality" went beyond all previous historiographical efforts in the respect it showed in all its implications for the irreducibility of cultural difference and historical heterogeneity in the hemisphere: "A 'totality' . . . because [the modalities of literary production] are inserted into the great stream of our America's social history, which articulates them while keeping their specificity, and 'contradictory' because we are dealing with the faithful if indirect reproduction of the disaggregated, conflictive, and belligerent socioethnical totality of American life" (230).

And yet Cornejo was still calling for a totalizing historiography whose main normative category, Latin America, was arguably a historical construct as much as anything. A fundamental preoccupation with the past and future destiny of Latin America as a historical unit pervades Cornejo's essay even as he argues for the contradictory, irreconcilable character of "Latin American" culture as such.[11] This is a subtle but not unnoticeable contradiction that necessarily contaminates his whole argument. In Cornejo's thesis, Latin America, explicitly named "our America," remains or becomes a privileged object of critical reproduction and consumption. A residually organicist conception of Latin America as a contradictory *totality* is the dominant subtext in "Nuevas reflexiones." Its inaugural gesture is to oppose an operating notion of our America to a supposedly foreign postmodernity that must remain outside the circle of legitimate conceptual categories with which to think of Latin America. However, this undesired postmodernity may at the same time have managed to creep inside, into the supposedly endotopic, bounded horizon of our-American modernity, through what Cornejo seems to consider the stupidity, the frivolity, or the corruption of some. Cornejo asks, self-reflectively: "The encounter with our belligerent multiplicity, is it the organic result of [our] America's self-examination, or does it rather respond to certain ideas—such as the critique of the subject or the heterogeneity of literary discourse—of an undoubtedly post-modern filiation?" (225–26).

I am interested in this latter anxiety, which I will not hesitate to call the moment of truth of the essay. Cornejo's anxiety symptomatically reaffirms the residual resistance of the old paradigm by re-invoking the organicity of a geocultural "us," that is, a tradition of cultural and geographical self-sameness whose main feature would have been to provide for historical articulation and continuity. His project is to foreground, within this self-sameness, the tradition's internally contradictory and heterogeneous nature for the sake of subaltern subjectivities in Latin America. But Cornejo's heterogeneity, at the very moment it is formulated, always already goes too far; it seems to step out of bounds, and Cornejo must then contain it. Thus, the question itself ("is the critical concept of heterogeneity a result of self-examination, or is heterogeneity the result of postmodern, hence foreign, influences?"—where we can already see that the question within the question would be how to embrace the former and reject the latter) reveals a decisive experiential ambiguity according to which such organicity would have always been seemingly fissured, not only by interior constraints but also by an aggressive and destructive outside. For Cornejo what is particularly significant about the present situation is that postmodernism would purportedly speak about heterogeneity and the end or the rupture of organicity, which makes it undecidable whether the fissure in organicity comes from within the historically organic, that is, from Latin American history itself, now understood as a contradictory totality, or whether it is instead the result of a phantasmatic internalization of a presumably postmodern but certainly always already imperial outside.

This undecidability is crucial for Cornejo because it opens up the bothersome possibility that the thinking of heterogeneity may depend on the postmodern situation itself. Heterogeneity, then, as the limit or the goal of thinking, would be nothing but a mask of neocoloniality—that is, the direct opposite of what was intended. Whatever the case, Cornejo lucidly affirms that such an undecidability will only make itself more undecidable, "with all the advantages and the disadvantages that these hybridizations have for the development of a Hispanic-American critique" (227). This paradoxical affirmation of a fissured and heterogeneous globality, from within which it remains necessary to retrieve a lost historical sense of the Latin American multiple singularity, becomes the starting point of the new cultural-historical paradigm Cornejo is proposing. It is also a striking formulation for the possible starting point of a Latin American critical regionalism, where the word *critical* finds centripetal and centrifugal references, that is, a reference to the multiplicity of regional localities within Latin America and a reference to the various global mappings within which the concept of Latin America is to be understood today.

I have pointed out that Cornejo's formulation does not solve but rather opens up a fundamental problem, namely, that all attempts to circumscribe the local are bound to run into their conceptual impossibility—even when the local is understood as a contradictory instance. Cornejo's attempt to limit the ceaseless reproduction of contradiction by the ambiguous appeal to a historically constituted totality that would arrest the spread of the virus and produce a thinkable object is ultimately arbitrary—to the extent that it is not a sanction of the sheer facticity of modernity's hold on our reason. His notion of Latin American cultural heterogeneity has been an important part of Latin Americanist critical discourse since it was first proposed in the early 1980s.[12] In "Nuevas reflexiones," far from recommending that heterogeneity should serve as some kind of wedge to set the new critical paradigm loose, Cornejo insists that, given the great magnitude of the proposed change, it is imperative "to overcome the temptations of Adanism and to rescue the values of the Latin American critical tradition: only then will change happen in history and within it, and not in the self-specular space of pure abstraction" (231). In the name of concrete politics and against pure speculation, Cornejo overemphasizes the importance of the redemptive value of a "Latin American critical tradition." But, if heterogeneity could be taken to express the mark of a Latin American cultural and historical singularity, then those vague "values of the Latin American critical tradition" would be nothing but the precipitate of the numerous historical attempts to come to terms with it, that is, to erase it, more or less successfully: they are themselves the residue, not only of a presumed Latin American resistance to imperial reason but primarily of the cultural regimes of rule that the Latin American(ist) intellectuals have dreamed up to produce historical sense *against* internal heterogeneity. Why does Cornejo need to avoid the thought that those "values" of the Latin American critical tradition are nothing but the ideological counterpart to the various hegemonic articulations in the region as historically constituted? Now, as a new round of historical sense production is called for, the complementary notions of contradictory totality and heterogeneity would seem to be encompassing enough that they could, on the one hand, account for past regimes of rule and, on the other hand, inaugurate a fresh one. But would this new regime of rule be anything different from a reconstitution of the ideological grounds of hegemonic power under a new world configuration?

In other words, can the new regime of sense that Cornejo is proposing be something other than a new version of the old dialectics of singularity and totality? The local and the global do not relate merely dialectically when the local is said to remain resiliently heterogeneous to any notion of globality and when the global is already a fissured, ruptured global of negativity. The anxiety about "postmodern filiations" that Cornejo's essay registers is part and parcel of the old resistance of Latin American left-wing intellectuals to modernization theory, which was the dominant and largely uncontested global paradigm more or less until the 1973 oil crisis. So-called three-worlds theory, as Carl Pletsch showed in his remarkable 1981 essay, "The Three Worlds, or the Division of Social Science Labor," was inextricably connected to modernization.[13] As Geyer and Bright put it, "the paradigm of global modernization . . . predicted, first, that in dominating the world through its mastery of the technical and material means of global integration, the West would actually control the world and be able to shape the course of global development, and second, that in shaping the world, the West held secure knowledge, positive empirical proof in its own development, of the direction and outcome of world history. The world would become more like the West in a protracted period of modernization, and, as the rest of the world moved toward uplift and progress, the division between 'the West' and 'the rest' would diminish" (1051).

But globalization has not followed that course. Global integration has in fact proceeded in spite of the collapse of the various modernizing projects and ideologies throughout a very large part of the planet. Narrative fissures are now a constituent feature of the new regimes of rule—from postmodernism to fundamentalism in

its various guises.[14] The announcement of a Latin American historical heterogeneity or contradictory totality Cornejo offered is thus
only the acknowledgment of such narrative fissures, and, left there,
it is in fact, at a certain critical level, a predictable kind of acknowledgment, "for the progress of global integration and the attending
struggles among would-be hegemons have persistently set loose contests over identity . . . and for autonomy that, time and again, have
renewed difference in the face of integration and thus continued
to fragment the world even as it became one" (Geyer and Bright,
1044). Narrative fissure, in the general sense, following a logic of
negativity, has produced a vindication of difference and a rejection of sameness whose synchronicity with postmodern global integration should make us see how they are in fact but integration's
counterpart at the local level. Cornejo's anxiety was well warranted.
Heterogeneity, whatever it may mean for our America internally
and supplementarily, is also the code word for the cultural paradigm
of global postmodernity. But Pletsch, as he detected the structural
anomalies in three-worlds and modernization theory, which also in
his opinion foretold the necessity of a "scientific revolution" and a
paradigmatic shift, had already warned that "it may be more appropriate to put ourselves on guard against whatever new conceptual
scheme may grow up to replace the three worlds than to congratu-
late ourselves upon having seen through modernization theory and
the three worlds" (589)—which brings me closer to the heart of my
intent.

Counterconsumptive Consumption

In *Escenas de la vida posmoderna* Beatriz Sarlo identifies three
dominant intellectual emphases in the contemporary world, respectively related to the culture industry, to the ruins of popular culture
such as they are, and to high aesthetic reflection. Neoliberal intellectuals would be more or less loosely but always fundamentally connected with the cultural industry in their role as advisory experts.
Neopopulist intellectuals would have some claim to dwell among
the ruins of popular culture from a redemptive perspective. And
critical intellectuals would be individuals committed to nonmediating, nonredemptive reflections on social and aesthetic values, and
would thus be genealogically linked to the figure of the enlightened
intellectuals in the best tradition of negative thinking. What hap-

pens, however, when negative thinking must be understood, as it must be understood today, in the face of global capitalism, within the sphere of a thinking of practices of consumption? One has to wonder whether it is not in fact the case that critical intellectuals must necessarily incorporate into themselves the basic defining features of what Sarlo calls the neopopulist and the neoliberal intellectuals. To conciliate those conflicting or contradictory attitudes—cultural industry advisers, redemptive populists, and nonmediating, nonredemptive negators—is not an easy task, but it might well be the task one is called on to assume. In any case, it represents as good a definition as any of the task that goes under the name of cultural studies. The problem is compounded when cultural studies is pursued from a regional perspective, such as the Latin American one, since regionalist intellectual labor is doubly obligated to confront the paradoxical role of mediation between localities and totality in global times.

Silviano Santiago has insisted on the need "to rethink radically the problem of cultural enjoyment and evaluation in mass society" ("Reading" 248). Santiago calls for an alternative approach to education in Latin America, one that will foster, at the very point of intersection between the state and civil society (the educational apparatus), a different understanding of cultural consumption. Santiago turns the negative thinking of decades against itself by suggesting that the only negativity significantly available today is the one potentially exercised not by intellectuals against mass culture or by intellectuals against the cultural industry, but by consumers at different levels of literacy as they receive, experience, and interpret the cultural object in its very disappearance into, or resistance against, exhaustive consumption. For Santiago it is precisely not a matter of turning consumption against itself. It is rather a matter of admitting that the culture-ideology of consumerism constitutes the inescapable horizon for thinking in our time. Thinking consumption is therefore one of the most urgent tasks for the critical intellectual. Part of that task is of course figuring out ways of teaching it: if that suggested change in the educational field were to be implemented, Santiago implies, then the educational field would turn into the most proper and promising site for a productive, and not merely reproductive, cultural politics.

Santiago's particular proposal is germane to the proposals made by Jorge Castañeda and Néstor García Canclini regarding what they understand as "regional federalism."[15] The proper understanding of this notion, to be thought of as the guided regional response to U.S.-led globalization from an anti-neoliberal perspective, implies a turn away from any rushed idealization of local difference, from all kinds of national-popular statism, and from any celebration of the cosmo-politanism of transnationalization as such. In Castañeda's words, regional federalism is, simply and soberingly enough, "an intermediate solution between a largely unsustainable status quo and a largely harmful progression toward the dissolution of [local] sovereignties" (*Utopia* 313; qtd. in Yúdice, "Civil Society" 18). The purpose of regional federalism is the creation of regulatory policies that would help, in this case, Latin American civil society so that what George Yúdice calls "the affective aspects of cultural interpellation—identity formation—" are not, in his words, "so overwhelmingly determined by US-identified transnational corporations nor by particular nationalist ideologies" (18). Yúdice agrees with Santiago, and with García Canclini's model as proposed in *Consumidores y ciudadanos*, about the need to think of consumption as the inevitable road to the construction of citizenship in global times: "societies may have reached a historical threshold in which it is no longer possible to think such ideas as citizenship and democracy in the absence of consumption" (20).[16]

For all these thinkers, what is at stake nowadays is not primarily the self-conceptualization of critical practice as different from mass-cultural practice but rather the former's insertion within mass-cultural consumption and the particular role it is fated to play there. What is at stake is the possibility of theorizing, and then implementing, what we could call a counterconsumptive, negative instance within cultural consumption itself; that is, the preservation of a sort of residual subject sovereignty or local singularity within the totalizing process of consumption. By *counterconsumption* I do not mean *anticonsumption:* it is not a matter of opposing mass-cultural consumption, precisely because we are always already immersed in it. Rather, counterconsumption refers to a particular mode of relation to consumption from within consumption: an adequate analogy would be, for instance, Homi Bhabha's notion of *contra-modernity* as a form of constitution "otherwise than modernity." For Bhabha, "[the] cultures of a postcolonial *contra-modernity* may be contingent to modernity, discontinuous or in contention with it, resistant to its oppressive or assimilationist technologies; but they also deploy the cultural hybridity of their borderline conditions to 'translate,' and therefore reinscribe, the social imaginary of both metropolis and modernity" (*Location* 6). 'Counterconsumption' is perhaps not an "otherwise than consumption," but is rather an "otherwise in consumption": a trace of discomfort, the fading memory of an experiential otherwise that can also be taken to be the anticipation of an alternative future.

But there are two ultimately divergent ways of thinking about this problem. One of them sets off from the militant, substantive affirmation of counterconsumptive singularity. The second takes a dimmer view, judging that any affirmation of counterconsumption, any supposed resistance to consumption, is nothing but itself a ploy of consumption, a coy niche marketing of the product for a more or less elite segment of the consumer population. The difference is a matter of emphasis, perhaps: it is one emphasis to affirm the moment of counterconsumption within consumption, and it is another emphasis to state its predictable destiny as merely a more exquisite or sophisticated kind of consumer's behavior. The former would be insisting on the need for a categorical (and then practical) distinction between consumption and counterconsumption within the cultural object's paratext and claiming the critical potential of the second in its very materiality as an event. The latter would reduce counterconsumption to ideology and say that counterconsumption is only self-concealing or alienated consumption.

John Beverley's differentiation between two possible intellectual projects within cultural studies follows similar lines. For Beverley, the option is not merely a matter of philosophical deduction, but one that must be articulated along a political cleavage that will determine either the hegemonic or the nonhegemonic destiny of cultural studies itself. He focuses on García Canclini's notion of *cultural hybridity* to note that it has descriptive and normative possible uses, and that the normative use may end up acquiring an unwelcome ideological character whose main function would be to cover up the very possibility of counterhegemonic articulation: "wouldn't [the] central concept of 'cultural hybridity' be a counter-response to the strong binarism implied in the notion of the subaltern?" ("Sobre la situación" 20; my trans.). Similarly, an excessive emphasis upon the totalization or suture of consumption—the notion that there is no anthropological trace of an escape from it, no remainder to the disappearance into it—would indicate a kind of ideological complacency under the pretext or the mask of lucidity.

The regulatory policies Castañeda and García Canclini advocate are in effect elements of statist cultural politics. Santiago's call for a renewed form of education is also part of it. Their suggestions run counter to the neoliberal state and try to set some controls over the terms of global integration. By the same token, however, they can be understood as excessively timid reformist attempts. They can even be understood, counterintentionally, as neoliberal social policy in the sense explained by Carlos Vilas. After establishing that in the neoliberal model "the state has abandoned its role as an agent of social development and integration [in order to merely] help define winners and losers in the marketplace," Vilas calls neoliberal social policy any (semiparadoxical) neoliberal state intervention "intended to compensate for the initial negative effects of structural adjustment among certain sectors of the population." (18). In other words, neoliberal social policy has a minimalist mediating function, which can be described as "putting out fires so that situations of extreme social tension do not become larger political problems" (18).

Once it is understood that neoliberal social policy does not consist, as it is habitually suggested, of the lack or the rejection of any kind of social policy, but that it does exist and that it has an in extremis compensatory character, it will also be understood that there is little in the logic of the statist social policies that we have noted under the name of regional federalism that will keep them from eventually being swallowed by global integration and made radically indistinguishable from neoliberal structural compensation. Even if, at the cultural level, those social policies did manage to control "the affective aspects of . . . identity formation" (Yúdice, "Civil Society" 18), it may well be because a degree of identity diversification, that is, a degree of difference production remains irreducibly essential for the global marketplace and its mechanisms of cultural consumption. Castañeda's "intermediate solution," in other words, would become just another structural part of the neoliberal order: the always surpassable limit upon which it will ceaselessly grow.

It would seem to be essential to look for ways of upholding counterconsumptive singularity in its first emphasis. If education is to form citizenship, it will have to incorporate into itself, as its main theoretical justification, the teaching of counterconsumptive consumption, as it were, or how to consume while resisting the total disappearance of the historical subject into consumption—the total exhaustion of the historical subject into practices of consumption. It will have to find its own ideological resources, not necessarily in local traditions, although it would not exclude them, but more likely in the negative force of historical disjunction, of social difference, of regional solidarity. In this modified sense, federal regionalism could be the social and political articulation of what in educational, intellectual, and cultural terms would better be called *critical regionalism*. Critical regionalism, as a thinking of cultural consumption from regional perspectives, is necessarily then a thinking of the singular resistance to consumption from within consumption through which regional and local identity formation happens in global times. It does not point to the production of any kind of counteridentity; rather, it moves beyond identity as well as difference in order to interrogate the processes of their constitution. It dwells at the border of hegemony, in order to break its circle for the sake of attaining, not a new identification, not even a disidentification, but rather a recalcitrant production of subjectivity as something other than subjection to history: not what obtains at the intersection of historical time-space, but what exceeds it. Critical regionalism is then a regionalism against itself: a savage atopics. At this point the question is whether that notion can be something other than political desire: that is, whether it is intellectually and practically viable in any strong sense. And, if so, which sense?

From Recognition to Compulsion

The critical questions would be how to theorize a tactical engagement of heterogeneity and how to develop it in the intellectual practice of Latin American cultural studies without falling into the regulatory trap of proposing as an alternative to global or dominant ideological interpellations for consumption particular ideological interpellations for counterconsumption that end up producing counterconsumption as yet another consumer's (compulsive) choice. Arjun Appadurai's word on "the fetishism of the consumer" should be kept in mind: "the consumer has been transformed, through commodity flows [which include not just mediascapes, but also ideoscapes], into a sign, both in Baudrillard's sense of a simulacrum which only asymptotically approaches the form of a real social agent; and in the sense of a mask for the real seat of agency, which is not the consumer but the producer and the many forces that constitute production" ("Disjuncture" 286).

Silvia Rivera Cusicanqui's work on *ayllu* democracy in northern Potosí is an example of the difficulties of Latin Americanist work on singularizing practices. Speaking from the collapse of the Bolivian national-popular state, Rivera argues in favor of a new anti-integrational concept of citizenship within Bolivia whereby the ayllus would be left alone to develop their own ways of communal democracy. Her fundamental hypothesis is that the Bolivian ayllus are the potential locus of "a richly democratic communal life," whereas "attempts by liberals, populists, and leftists to impose liberal democratic models on the *ayllus* have actually hindered the emergence and consolidation of democratic practices and institutions" ("Liberal Democracy" 102). Rivera's proposal is for the Bolivian state and hegemonic classes to keep their hands off the ayllus, since "no human right will be fully recognized so long as the indigenous peoples are denied the right to autonomy in their decisions to continue or transform, by themselves, their forms of organization and collective life and their conceptions of the world." Rivera's call for a politics of "recognition of the right to be different as a fundamental human right" has ample resonance in the context of a history of secular oppression of the ayllus by the Bolivian mestizo-creole population (117). And yet things become conceptually and ethically complicated when we find that "tensions have grown between the older and the younger generations: the latter have seen the NGOS as a way to escape collective social controls and to seek individual subsistence alternatives, such as migration, which have a direct, negative impact on the communities' productive potential" (112).

Rivera's notion of multicultural citizenship in Bolivia is akin to what Nancy Fraser has called a "post-bourgeois conception" of the public sphere. According to Fraser, it is necessary to realize, against the "bourgeois conception" ("Rethinking" 26), that "public spheres are not only arenas for the formation of discursive opinion; in addition, they are arenas for the formation and enactment of social identities. . . . [P]articipation means being able to speak 'in one's own voice,' thereby simultaneously constructing and expressing one's cultural identity through idiom and style" (16). But Fraser, who like Rivera is engaged in the theorization of "democratic possibilities beyond actually existing democracies" (26), fails to take account of the fact that, as Judith Butler puts it, "identity categories tend to be instruments of regulatory regimes, whether as the normalizing categories of oppressive structures or as the rallying points for a liberatory contestation of that very oppression" ("Imitation" 13–14).[17] It is easy for any regulatory regime of truth to slip over, perhaps inevitably, from recognition into compulsion. We do not know whether, in the face of a rearticulation of Bolivian citizenship in the multicultural sense proposed by Rivera, the "younger generation" of ayllu inhabitants would no longer wish, through migration or otherwise, to escape collective social controls within the ayllu. Thus the emphasis on the defense of a cultural and social difference secularly reluctant to accept the parameters of the national state can inadvertently move into a contrary emphasis on compulsive identity consumption—even if for the sake of communal redemption.

How, then, to engage, from the perspective of the intellectual producer at odds with the institutional mandate for social reproduction, with a politics of recognition without stepping over into a politics of compulsion? The identitarian claims Rivera and Fraser promote as necessary to the construction of a postbourgeois public sphere involve in the current configuration a "fetishism of the consumer," in Appadurai's sense, which remains blind to the possibility that such claims are not in fact *produced* by the subject, but only *consumed* by him or her. Is this not the case as well for so many other theoreticians of subaltern identity?

Differential Consciousness

Dreamed alternative singularizations of thinking: a different kind of "global dream," to mimic Richard Barnet's expression, but not an alternative to it.[18] Those singularizing dreams today orchestrate the panoply of antiglobal discourses within global discourse. They are more and more thought of as microdiscourses, places where a singularity is enacted and an intensity is affirmed, sites of a resistance that is also a withdrawal, a monadic pulsion, a punctual, discardable identity, or a customized difference: in any case, whatever can be salvaged as the sheer possibility of an alternative articulation of experience outside global homogenization. Even Appadurai seems to concede that much when he mentions the "brighter side" of global culture today. If its central feature is "the politics of the mutual effort of sameness and difference to cannibalize one another and thus to proclaim their successful hijacking of the twin Enlightenment ideas of the triumphantly universal and the resiliently particular" (287), then the brighter side of global culture would reveal the possibility of an enactment, however fleeting, of the singular difference within totality. These singular dreams are not only the dreams of Buenos Aires urban squatters and La Morada feminists, of U.S. queers or Muslim fundamentalists, of neo-Zapatista guerrilla leaders or German cyberpunks, of Catalan greenheads, Galician rockers, or Bangkok S/M practitioners: they are also the dreams of (former) academic area studies intellectuals as they resist their reconversion into corporate intellectuals at the very instant of their absorption by the global university. They are also the metacritical dream as it informs this book that I am writing, here and now—and thus the dream of a critical Latin Americanism.

All dreams of singularization are virtual expressions of a certain distance, a certain inadequacy, a felt disjunction vis-à-vis global incorporation. They can be tenuous dreams, as in the kid who fantasizes herself as one of the players in Mortal Kombat, or strong dreams, such as the ones at the basis of the Zapatista rebellion or the Rio *arrastões*; or nationalist dreams; or Rigoberta Menchú's understanding of the particularity of her people as a people with secrets. But they all express a singular intensity. As Jean Franco puts it, "in the age of global flows and networks, the small scale and the local are the places of the greatest intensity" ("What's Left" 21). Franco is placing intensity at the service of an experience of what I would call "distance-toward-the-global." Such an experience can only be categorized as an instance of self-reflexivity: a particular arrest of the process of consumption or even self-consumption or the emergence of what Chela Sandoval calls "differential consciousness" ("U.S. Third Feminism" 3).

Sandoval's 1991 article on oppositional consciousness in the postmodern world provides a concise theoretical formulation of the possibility of a self-redemptive practice through tactical singularization. But her theory reveals, in spite of itself, a constitutive lack of closure. It is perhaps not so much a theoretical inconsistency or a flaw as it is itself an expression of how tactical singularization is a reactive practice against homogenization: nothing but an alternative consumptive move from within consumption. Sandoval's differential consciousness is based on a formal movement of self-reflexivity, where self-reflexivity is not to be conceived in terms of a synthetic move of the Hegelian spirit but in terms of a self-reflexivity of affect, a self-reflexivity of intensities or affective tonalities. For Sandoval, her theory "focuses on identifying forms of consciousness in opposition, which can be generated and coordinated by those classes *self-consciously* seeking *affective* oppositional stances in relation to the dominant social order" (2, my emphasis). "Differential consciousness" is for Sandoval the self-reflective affect that alone becomes the necessary and sufficient condition for the constitution of a new subject position. She makes a grand claim for it: "Differential consciousness is the expression of the new subject position called for by Althusser—it permits functioning within yet beyond the demands of dominant ideology" (3). The status of that perhaps surprising "beyond" stands in need of questioning—as it is, if the essay's logic is to make sense, the keystone of its articulation.

Within Sandoval's topography of consciousness, the place of that "beyond the demands of dominant ideology" is a function of self-reflexivity: "Any social order which is hierarchically organized into relations of domination and subordination creates particular subject positions within which the subordinated can legitimately function. These subject positions, once self-consciously recognized by their inhabitants, can become transformed into more effective sites of resistance to the current ordering of power relations" (11). The crucial move for Sandoval consists in positing *differential* consciousness as the only effective locus of resistance: that is, the liberatory dimension of difference is the mere form of the subordinated but resistant subject position as such and not its positive content. Yet, without a strong refusal of any positivization, that is, without an active, self-reflective commitment to a radical restraint in the face of any temptation to substantivize subaltern identity, she cautions, "any liberation movement is destined to repeat the oppressive authoritarianism from which it is attempting to free itself and become trapped inside a drive for truth which can only end in producing its own brand of domination" (14). She is interested in arguing not just against homogenization but also against presumed heterogenizations that ultimately resolve themselves into more of the same; in the terms used above, she is opposed to any forms of compulsive recognition.

Sandoval's attempt to escape a politics of compulsion consists of positing a "tactical subjectivity" whose articulation would be purely formal: this tactical subjectivity would open the possibility of a "beyond the demands of dominant ideology" because it would situate itself, by definition, in an oppositional beyond, always in a "variant" site, formally defined as a given differential possibility "emerging out of correlations, intensities, junctures, crises" (14). But, if her "beyond" is always a formal punctuality, always arising out of the negation of the dominant, always an oppositional stance whose very possibility is orchestrated by the dominant, then her "beyond" is just another formulation of the impossibility of an outside to the dominant. From Sandoval's own postulates, in effect, the dominant exhaustively constitutes the nondominant as a merely formal negative relationship to itself—and negation lives only as a function of what it negates.

Sandoval's theory of oppositional discourse can only justify itself on the basis of a previous acceptance of the claim of the global dominant to a complete saturation of the discursive field. It would only be possible to step, from within the saturated field into its formal negation, through an extreme self-reflexivity or differential consciousness, but such a move would come at the cost of a thorough renunciation of any substantive endowment of the content of the differential consciousness as such. If differential consciousness is to be understood as "a [tactical] movement between ideologies along with the concurrent desire for [oppositional] ideological commitment" (15), then oppositional desire is the only positive characteristic of differential consciousness. A radically tactical subjectivity, whose content can only be mimetic negation even as it seems to be affirming something or other, comes close to no subjectivity at all. The negativity of differential consciousness can only preempt the very possibility of its affirmative emergence.

Paul Smith, discussing the "theoretical task . . . of coming to an understanding of how the ideological force of interpellation can fail (and often) to produce a compliant 'subject' for a discourse," understands self-reflexivity as always already produced by ideological interpellation (*Discerning* 39). For him, what is crucial is not only the development of a differential consciousness in Sandoval's

sense, that is, "a conscious and deliberate refusal of particular interpellations and the meanings they proffer for subject positionings,"
but also the theorization of "a radical heterogeneity in the subject-
positions which are constituted in the human agent through interpellations" (39). The fine line here resides, of course, in the difficulty of theorizing a radical heterogeneity while at the same time
avoiding the call for a self-conscious appropriation of it for the sake
of an apparently contestatory practice always already produced by
ideological interpellation. Smith does not solve this metacritical difficulty, and his dream of radical heterogeneity does not therefore
abandon its dream character. There is, to say it once again, a short
step between the recognition of heterogeneity and a compulsive consumption of heterogeneity as a kind of counterconsumption commodity: heterogeneity then becomes a commodified fetish. Sandoval's "U.S. third world feminism," once endowed with self-conscious
recognition as the purveyor of differential consciousness, runs the
risk of turning into yet another cultural fetish, as does, for instance,
Guillermo Gómez-Peña's brand of border performance, the "coming-
out" discourses of closeted sexualities, or even indigenous identities
in times of negative globality.

If subject positions are produced through their actual performance, if there is no essential subject before social practice, but only
subjects whose partial identities must be enacted in order to "be" at
all, and if the field of social practice itself is produced by ideological
interpellations, then what does it mean to dream of theorizing "radical heterogeneity in subject positions"? If heterogeneity can only be
a function or a result of performance, and if performance always already produces a subject position within ideological interpellation,
then heterogeneity must necessarily be self-conscious in order to
be at all. But self-reflexivity immediately reduces heterogeneity into
yet another produced, and therefore not-quite-heterogeneous, subject position. The mechanism becomes a merely formal practice of
contestation insofar as its concrete contents are constantly being
voided or reabsorbed into consumption, no matter how illusorily rebellious or disjunctive.

The Negative Ground of Critical Regionalism

Practices of singularization, or the formation of a differential consciousness, can only be understood as practices *produced* by the very

ideological interpellation that frames them and, by framing them, also performs them. Singularizing practices offer in that sense no beyond to the ideological apparatus of interpellation in response to which they arise, which brings us full circle back to our question. The question concerned the very possibility of Latin American cultural studies as an enterprise of productive and not simply reactive critique.

In the wide definition of the Gulbenkian Commission, cultural studies was to be understood as a systematic effort to incorporate subaltern difference into both nomothetic knowledge (that is, the normative knowledge proposed by sociology, economics, or political science in their best moments) and hermeneutic knowledge (the sort of knowledge that is proper to idiographic disciplines such as literary studies or anthropology). Latin American cultural studies, then, is to be amply understood as the systematic effort to incorporate Latin American–area based knowledge into both nomothetic and hermeneutic science as primarily knowledge of the Latin American subaltern difference in the global context. The systematic effort to account for subaltern difference is hailed by the Gulbenkian Commission as a preliminary to a paradigmatic shift in knowledge production.

Although knowledge of cultural heterogeneity was instrumental in undoing the old dominant paradigm that went under the name of modernization theory, in times of postmodern global integration it is no longer clear that an emphasis on heterogeneity can be made to fulfill the secular requirement for knowledge to be productive, as opposed to having it merely be at the service of social reproduction. Heterogeneity, particularly when used as a critical banner, can only become yet another market option in the marketplace of subjectivities. There is, as we have seen, a certain understanding of local singularity that serves the reproductive interests of the neoliberal order by fostering consumption of (and thus, not coincidentally, annihilating) difference. Heterogeneity, whatever it may have been in previous historical times, is today produced in advance by a social interpellation that at the same time consumes it or prompts its consumption. The consumption of heterogeneity does not guarantee by itself an appropriate teleology for Latin American cultural knowledge.

The concept of critical regionalism offers a potential resolution of this theoretical impasse. Critical regionalism, as a thinking of cultural consumption from regional perspectives, is the thinking of the singular resistance to consumption from within consumption through which regional and local identity formation happens in global times. If critical regionalism refers to the very possibility of simultaneously thinking through the contradictory totality of global integration and fragmentation, then negative globality is to be understood as the structural ground of critical regionalism; within that ground, narrative fissure is the figure of its negativity. Critical regionalism has a necessarily negative ground, for it must proceed through the systematic exploration of its impossibility to constitute itself as something other than a ruse of reason. The theoretical foundation of a radicalized critical regionalism is not constituted by a posited heterogeneity between any world area and hegemonic homogenization. It is constituted by the very impossibility of thinking heterogeneity beyond the processes of globalization that always already determine it as heterogeneity for consumption.

As critical regionalism, therefore, a possibility opens up for Latin Americanist reflection that will no longer reduce it, as the Gulbenkian Commission would perhaps seem willing to do, to the systematic study of Latin American subaltern identities in the global context: it is rather the study of the historical fissures through which the "values of the Latin American critical tradition" disappear into material constraints. It is the study of the aporias of identity formation, and thus also of what could dwell beyond identity formation. And it is the study of the geopolitical fissures through which any kind of cultural universalism will show itself, from a subalternist perspective, as a figure of dominant ideology. These may seem contradictory purposes—but their very tension keeps open the possibility of a productive knowledge of the social totality, even if such a totality is only accessible in negation and from negation. They point toward a materialist thinking that can adjust to present reality without a fear of either postmodern filiations or neoliberal entrapment.

*The university, the totalitarian longing to gather all points
of view into one, cannot tolerate genealogy. Genealogy
weakens the theological-universalist strategy of the state,
throwing it into the quagmire of interests. It reveals that
the universal is an immanent means of facticity and that,
if transcendentally everything comes to the same (nihilism
in act), factically nothing is indifferent. And it reveals that
it is in this factic capacity to discriminate where we must
set up the "true" (erratic) university.* —Willy Thayer, *La
crisis no-moderna de la universidad moderna*

THREE Theoretical Fictions and Fatal Conceits

The Question of Transition in Latin Americanist Discourse

Latin Americanists engaged in what could still be described as the
core of their institutional task, that is, the study of the interrelation-
ships of culture and the state in Latin America, must deal with the
fact that the very concept of culture, the very concept of the state,
and the geopolitical implications of thinking about Latin America
in the context of university discourse have increasingly become precarious and elusive intellectual endeavors. Is it possible to salvage
some kind of antisystemic productivity in our transitional times for
a mode of knowledge that would seem to depend almost exhaustively on epistemological models bequeathed by modernity at the
very moment in which modernity becomes a thing of the past?

A recent debate in *LASA Forum*, the bulletin of the Latin American Studies Association, provides a summary of where the present
discussion lies—and perhaps a warning that the terms of the discussion need to change if the discussion is to move beyond a rather
vicious circle or a series of them. In the lead essay, "Latin America
and Globalization," Jeremy Adelman introduces the problematics of
globalization as little more than a slightly recast version of the old
disputes between *desarrollistas* and *dependentistas*. True, within
globalization "variants of populism" no longer seem a viable political option, since "integrated aspirations and images have been moth-
balled" ("Latin America" 11), whereas the postcolonialist heirs to *de-*

pendentismo are now critical of their ancestors' "economism and reductionism" (10). But in every other sense the "supposed" new world order is presented as a "rhetorical patina" (11), and "globalization-talk" as some "post-modern" superficiality that barely covers over the lack of "debate about the modern experience." The latter "remains open" (12). Of the three respondents, only the one frankly committed to a neoliberal worldview, Albert Fishlow, takes issue with Adelman for his own relative superficiality: "We run the risk of missing the importance of what is happening now by casually designating the subject as 'globalization talk'" (Arias, Fishlow, and Hale, 14). The other two, Arturo Arias and Charles R. Hale, who are "favorably impressed" and see Adelman's piece as "insightful" (12, 13), will not go beyond noting "the apparent contradiction resulting when economic trends toward globalization clash with centrifugal forces moving toward micro-politics and the reconstruction of local subjectivities in Latin America" (12). If Hale takes the dimmer view that Latin American populations will increasingly espouse a "grim realism" concerning the question "where are the havens of minimal human decency and physical security from which to cope with the frightening and depressing daily realities that globalization has wrought?" (15), Arias is actually more upbeat. For him, popular responses to globalization "are the signs of the deployment of a new hybrid community that indeed might signify the death of modern nationhood, but also the hopeful redefinition of a new spatialization/displacement of disenfranchised minorities with at least the illusory perspective of more creative ways (or 'new strategies of resistance,' if one so prefers to name it) to dynamize their peripheral subjectivities within a heterogeneous whole where new ways of making transnational connections already exist" (13).

Of course, all four scholars have strong enough reasons to support their views. I do not claim that they are wrong. I think rather that the discursive parameters of their debate, which are the parameters of mainstream Latin Americanist reflection, as the institutional occasion of their debate might well seem to have advised, limit the scope of whatever they are able to say to an exchange of informed opinions that might fluctuate from expressing skepticism (Adelman, Hale) to different kinds of enthusiasm (oppositional enthusiasm for Arias and a cautious underwriting for Fishlow). Those opinions are, however, by their nature reactive to "what is happening" and can only fail to reset the terms that are critically needed for a stronger reading of the situations that prompt their exchange. In other words, globalization may have accomplished a number of things: it may even have promoted an epochal change in the way people must adapt to everyday and symbolic life. But it doesn't seem to have brought about any radical questioning of the ways in which university discourse shapes or is shaped by its object. That seems to me a serious objection. An epochal change in people's lives cannot be adequately understood through minor adjustments in long-established forms of Latin Americanist representation.

There is a remarkable passage toward the end of Immanuel Wallerstein's *Geopolitics and Geoculture*. After announcing repeatedly throughout the book that our planet finds itself today in the throes of a civilizational change and that its contemporaneity can only be thought, globally, under the figure of a transition ("It is a matter of envisaging the overall framework of a transition, which might be posed as a choice between a controlled reconstruction or a looser, less structured disintegration" [229]), Wallerstein says: "Perhaps we should deconstruct without the erection of structures to deconstruct, which turn out to be structures to continue the old in the guise of the new. Perhaps we should have movements that mobilize and experiment but not movements that seek to operate within the power structures of a world-system they are trying to undo. Perhaps we should tiptoe into an uncertain future, trying merely to remember in which direction we are going" (229).

Although I suspend my opinion on the issue of whether an end to capitalism is already visible in some horizons of thinking or experience, the notion proposed by Wallerstein that our times are transitional times in the sense that we are witnessing through them the possible beginning of the consummation of a capitalist world-system that will eventually come to pass, as all things must, is consistent with the perspective established in previous chapters regarding the ongoing change in the regime of social rule.[1] For Wallerstein the locus of social praxis, understood as the countersystemic form of agency that might guide the transition in relative terms, is not the cultural-ideological sphere but is rather "the arena of the antisystemic [social] movements (broadly defined)" (229). However, his emphasis on the deconstruction of the old cultural-ideological structures as preparation for opening the way to a renewed social praxis is consonant with his notion that the historical social sciences, as they evolved in the nineteenth and twentieth centuries in the wake of the French Revolution, could never break free from their origins as an ideological justification of the capitalist world economy:

> The French Revolution was the moment in the historical development of the capitalist world-economy when the formulations in the ideological arena finally were changed to express a by then long-existing reality of capitalism as a mode of production. The new ideology took account of the fact that, in the capitalist world-economy, the political superstructure was not only a social construct (both the sovereign states and the interstate system) but a social construct that was constantly being amended and reconstructed. The terminology in which this reality was clothed was that of the "sovereignty of the people" which was a way of legitimizing the fluidity as opposed to the solidity of the political structures. To deal with this fluidity, we were bequeathed the antinomy of society/state, and with it the supposed interaction and/or conflict between society and state which was to constitute the largest focus of the scientific activity of the historical social sciences. (116–17)

In just the same way that the most effective antisystemic movements of the nineteenth and twentieth centuries made a strategic decision to invest in the acquisition of state power, the social scientists "who saw their role as contributing to the social transformation of the world had to make a strategic choice as to where they would invest their scientific energies" (117–18). The countermodels that resulted, which allowed for the mobilization and articulation of antisystemic energies, were ambiguous, because "concentrating on the elaboration of a countermodel involved two subordinate decisions: accepting the premises of modern science and accepting the broad outlines of the dominant historiography" (118). Both modern science and the dominant historiography had, after all, originated in modernity as the ideological superstructure or underside of the capitalist world economy. They are "the intellectual premises of . . . the geoculture of the world-economy" (11).

The contemporary crisis in the world-system would mean, for Wallerstein, that the epistemological models of modernity, including their antisystemic countermodels, must be subjected to a thorough questioning. If modernity's geoculture, understood as "the cultural framework within which the [capitalist] world-system operates" (11), is undergoing a fundamental crisis, there is no way out of it unless we manage to understand first the extent to which our discursive tools are themselves compromised by the crisis. Whether our questioning can be radical enough, or whether we are always destined to discover that our presumed deconstructions, far from destabilizing "an inegalitarian system" (229), can only end up reinforcing it, thus perpetuating the crisis—that is indeed the question of transition in epistemological terms. One of its more significant aspects, because it is also one of the sites where the crisis in the sciences meets the crisis in the antisystemic social movements that can lead political praxis, refers to the relationship between universality and particularisms. Wallerstein situates at this point the question of the university: "In a sense, the concept of the university is itself supposed to constitute this rendezvous. After all, the words university and universalism have the same etymological root. And, curiously, in medieval European usage, a *universitas* was also the name given to a form of particular cultural community. Was it then that the university in the sense of the universal was being suggested as the meeting-place of the universities in the sense of particular communities? It is certainly doubtful that this is what they have been historically, but it is regularly suggested that this is what they should become today and in the future" (197).

As university discourse on Latin America, or on any of the particular locations that constitute it, Latin Americanism is a function of modern social epistemology, one of whose main concerns, as Wallerstein puts it, is the thinking-out of the relationships between society and the state. But the concept of *culture* has become today the master trope for the idea of social specificity. If university discourse, that is, a cultural discourse that cannot as such claim to step outside of itself to represent society to itself in terms other than cultural, is in every case a particular modality of cultural mediation between the social and its principle of rule, then Latin Americanism can only speak geoculturally about particular geocultural specifications. The interplay between the universal and the particular is thoroughly intertwined in Latin Americanist discourse. Now, if the crisis in the sciences today is precisely a crisis in the relationship between the universal and the particular, under what conditions can university discourse on Latin America or on any of the locations that constitute it, and particularly when that university discourse expresses itself in English and originates in non–Latin American, metropolitan institutions, constitute, at best, anything other than what Wallerstein calls a "controlled reconstruction"? A subordinate question would be whether that controlled reconstruction can in the end reconstruct anything but itself. We run the risk that our intellectual field, which originated in the need to respond to the structural constraints of the capitalist world economy, will end up in transitional times precariously serving the needs of crisis management, and thus forfeiting even its limited antisystemic capabilities, which were given in the past as a function of modern science's ability to present itself not simply as the geocultural underside of modernity but also as a countermodel for the acquisition of state power.

What kind of discourse is Latin Americanism anyway? I have been using the notion of university discourse to refer to it. I take it from Jacques Lacan, who studies it in the context of his so-called four discourses.[2] According to Lacan, following a certain typology, any discursive formation can be understood through one or several of the following categories: a discourse is a master's discourse, a university discourse, a hysteric's discourse, or an analyst's discourse. Lacan takes from Hegel the notion of the master's discourse. It is the primary discourse, in the sense that it is "the fundamental matrix of the coming to be of the subject through alienation" (Fink, *Lacanian Subject* 130). The master's discourse is the discourse of the nonsensical signifier: the master signifier. It does not have to explain itself, it simply is, and it is "because." Faced with the master's discourse, we are all slaves. As slaves, Lacan says, we may come to learn something, although chances are that what we learn will be appropriated by the master—as all surplus value belongs to him. Latin Americanism is a master's discourse in the sense that our relationship with Latin Americanism, within today's university and within the humanities, can be described as a relationship with the master signifier. There is no escaping "the fundamental matrix of the coming to be of the [academic] subject through alienation." University discourse is the discourse of truth, of knowledge as system, of knowledge as collected into the unity of the university. For university discourse everything has its reason. It is the discourse of the principle of reason. University discourse is little more than a legitimation or rationalization of the master's will as master. Philosophy serves the master. As Bruce Fink puts it, "working in the service of the master signifier, more or less any kind of argument will do, as long as it takes on the guise of reason and rationality" (133). Latin Americanism is a university discourse in the sense that our relationship with it can be defined as a relationship meant to justify our very existence and activity as intellectuals, as academics. Anything will do, provided we stay where we are.

The hysteric's discourse is, for Lacan, the direct opposite of the university discourse. It constantly interrogates the masters by asking them to show their stuff. What is decisive here is that the hysteric constantly interrogates the master and "pushes the master to the point where he or she can find the master's knowledge lacking" (Fink, 134). It is a discourse of the real—the hysteric grabs at the real, which is precisely the failure of rationalization, the other side of the signifier, the point at which systems reveal their truth precisely by coming to the limit of it, by giving it up. Can Latin Americanism be interpellated by a hysteric's discourse? Can we push Latin Americanism so it releases its truth into the real? If we were to succeed in interpellating Latin Americanism from the point of view of a hysteric's discourse, if Latin Americanism were to be put in the dominant discursive position once it has coughed up its position in the real, then Latin Americanism could perhaps start to function as the analyst, in the position of the analyst, and thus something like a scientific status in the Lacanian sense could be given to it. What would it take for us to do that? How can we turn Latin Americanism into a proper interlocutor for the hysteric, that is, an analyst of sorts, the nonholder of the nontruth of the real?

University Discourse and Finance Capitalism

In his book on the contemporary function of the university, *The University in Ruins,* Bill Readings says that "to speak of the University and the state is also to tell a story about the emergence of the notion of culture. . . . The University and the state as we know them are essentially *modern* institutions, and . . . the emergence of the concept of culture should be understood as a particular way of dealing with the tensions between these two institutions of modernity" (6). For Readings the university today "is busily transforming itself from an ideological arm of the state into a bureaucratically organized and relatively autonomous consumer-oriented corporation" (11). This means, first, "that the notion of culture as the legitimating idea of the modern University has reached the end of its usefulness" (5). And second, that "it is no longer the case that we can conceive the University within the historical horizon of its self-realization" (5).

Readings grounds his argumentation in the idea that "the nation-state and the modern notion of culture arose together, and they are . . . ceasing to be essential to an increasingly transnational global economy" (12). Thus, "the University no longer has to safeguard and propagate national culture, because the nation-state is no longer the major site at which capital reproduces itself" (13). Although we could question the notion that the nation-state arose, as Readings seems to say, around the end of the eighteenth century, we could still accept his assertion that the modern university, that is, the university that is theorized first by Kant and then by Humboldt as radically dependent on a notion of national culture as the site where knowledge and power, that is, reason and the state, could be unified, is coming to an end today. And we could accept the corollary notion that this tendential vanishing of national culture leaves in its wake an empty space that can only be precariously filled by either an appeal to de-ideologized "excellence" ("the stakes of the University's functioning are no longer essentially ideological, because they are no longer tied to the self-reproduction of the nation-state" [14]) or by the "de-referentialized" study of culture that goes under the name of cultural studies (17).

The notion of national culture was first centered, by Humboldt, in philology, which we can now perhaps reinterpret as a kind of cultural studies *avant la lettre*, born when the possibility of a full symbolic referentialization of culture onto the state first opened up. For Readings, it was the British and the North Americans that "[gave] a particularly *literary* turn to the German Idealists' notion of culture" (15): there is an "implicit linkage between the way 'literature' gets institutionalized as a University discipline in explicit national terms and an organic vision of the possibility of a unified national culture" (16). When the organic vision vanishes, the principle of mutual accountability between the people and the state is substituted by its fallen or essential form: a principle of accounting. Cultural studies is the apparent alternative to this reduction from accountability to accounting. In Reading's words, "the institutional success of Cultural

Studies in the 1990's is owing to the fact that it preserves the structure of the literary argument, while recognizing that literature can no longer work" (17). Thus cultural studies attempts to become or to represent itself as "the discipline that will save the University by giving it back its lost truth" (18). The solution that Readings presents hangs on a general reconsideration of the university in contemporary times as "a space in which it is possible to think the notion of community otherwise, without recourse to notions of unity, consensus, and communication. At this point, the University becomes no longer a model of the ideal society but rather a place where the impossibility of such models can be thought—practically thought, rather than thought under ideal conditions" (20).

As Mark T. Berger and Fredrick B. Pike, among others, have sufficiently demonstrated, there is no discontinuity between the notion of the University of (National) Culture that Readings presents as an institution of modernity and the fact that such a university developed subsidiary discourses on alternative nations and areas of the world: on the contrary, those subsidiary discourses were part and parcel of the construction of a university discourse on the national. In the case of the United States, the development of Latin American studies, in particular after 1898, served not just the establishment of a hegemonic articulation of national culture but also the self-presentation of such national culture, in geopolitical terms, as the hegemonic culture of late modernity in the planetary context.[3] The interesting question is, then, what is to be the function of Latin American studies, among other area or post-area studies, in the age of culture's dereferentialization vis-à-vis the nation-state? Can they escape the fate of becoming anything but, at best, a "controlled reconstruction" in Wallerstein's sense?

Latin Americanist reflection is not primarily an exterior, or non–Latin American, discourse on Latin America. Although it can certainly also be that, Latin Americanism is first a transnational discursive production, Latin American to a large extent, that forms the total set of engaged representations on Latin America, or on any intra–Latin American location. Beyond the localized, and certainly important, differences that regulate the production of Latin Americanist discourse in its various possibilities of enunciation (since Latin Americanist discourse is not the same in Bolivia, Argentina, Chiapas, North Carolina, California, or Germany), insofar as it is a discourse of reason, that is, account rendering within the context of the institutionalized production of knowledge, Latin Americanism is university discourse: the conflicted discourse of the principle of reason concerning Latin America. Its exteriority vis-à-vis Latin America has less to do with political borders than with the fact that, as university discourse in contemporary times, it constitutes itself in relation to a master signifier, which I will call neoimperial and which remains transcendental, as all master signifiers must.

If Latin American cultural studies is supposed to represent, today, a transformation and a salvaging in reference to the idiographic enterprise that was known as Latin American area studies in the recent past, what is the critical specificity of such a salvaging?[4] Of course suggesting, as I have been doing, that Latin American cultural studies is the proper name for what could also be called Latin American postarea studies, that is, what follows institutionally from the current reorganizations of what was the area studies apparatus in the Cold War years, is at least a residually controversial gesture —although perhaps not so much one for scholars in the humanities. The Gulbenkian Commission Report says, among other things that "the challenge . . . from what we may generically call 'cultural studies' . . . [is such that it is] having a major influence in the institutional arenas of knowledge production for the first time in the two centuries since science, a certain science, displaced philosophy, a certain philosophy, from the position of legitimator of knowledge" (65). But in any case my questions are circumscribed to the reflection on culture. Latin American cultural studies differs from Latin American area studies in one major point, which is that its primary referent is not the nation-state or the Latin American interstate system. Latin American cultural studies is in that sense area based but not area bound.

Latin American cultural studies, understood as the academic apparatus that rises tendentially to occupy the place of Latin American area studies in the transitional time during the rise of finance capital and the decline of national cultures, hasn't been able to establish a working concept of culture because Latin Americanists have given up on the notion of national culture but have little to substitute for it. We have discovered, in practical, empirical terms, that cultural studies does not really have, and perhaps cannot ever produce, a concept of culture that can aspire to a paradigmatic position.

According to Readings, this is not a casual or temporary defect of cultural studies: it is rather its necessity, because cultural studies cannot overcome its very conditions of possibility as a reactive formation that replicates or reproduces the "literary argument, while recognizing that literature can no longer work" (17).

Readings is not saying that literature is no longer legible or that there is no pleasure in it. Rather, his point is that literary discourse, that is, the university discourse around literature as a national institution, has come to fail historically in its operation to produce what Fredric Jameson a few years ago called a "national allegory."[5] This is so because the nation is no longer the site where knowledge and power meet. In other words, literary discourse can no longer sustain or operate the link between culture and the nation-state, can no longer occupy the position of the empty signifier that could suture a hegemonic articulation at the level of the nation-state. In yet other words, literary discourse is no longer the privileged site for the expression of social value, understood as what rules through rule itself —the very principle of the state. If social value, as the master signifier for all meanings, was in modernity articulated with the nation-state through literary mediation, that mediation no longer holds, not because literature can no longer mediate, but rather because the nation-state is no longer the primary referent of social value.

So cultural studies developed in the 1990s as a reactive formation meant to fill the gap in the wake of literature's withdrawal. It presents itself as able to accomplish the missing articulation of the nation, or whatever comes in its place, with itself. Except that nothing quite comes, or has yet come, in place of the nation. Cultural studies is thus dereferentialized, or, even more radically, it is, on at least one of its faces, the very discourse of ongoing dereferentialization. If literary discourse could aspire to the status of a theoretical fiction throughout modernity, following Reading's reasoning, cultural studies would today be no more than a fatal conceit.[6] Let us say that cultural studies is constitutionally barred from becoming the linkage between knowledge and power (or reason and the state) that literature once was, at the same time that it announces itself as the new possibility of linkage between knowledge and power (or reason and the state). The conditions of possibility of cultural studies are, under this understanding, at the same time its conditions of impossibility.

In his reading of Giovanni Arrighi's *The Long Twentieth Century*, Jameson accepts the notion that Arrighi's "finance capitalism" is an appropriate description of the economic underpinnings of our transitional time, the time of postmodernism: "[a] third stage . . .— the withdrawal of profits from the home industries, the increasingly feverish search, not so much for new markets (these are also saturated) as for the new kinds of profits available in financial transactions themselves and as such—is the way in which capitalism now reacts to and compensates for the closing of its productive moment. Capital itself becomes free-floating. It separates from the concrete context of its productive geography. Money becomes in a second sense and to a second degree abstract . . . , as though somehow in the national moment money still had a content" ("Culture" 141–42).

Finance capital, defined as "the highest and last stage of every moment of capital itself" (142), organizes postmodern time as a time where "speculation itself" reigns: "specters of value, as Derrida might put it, vying against each other in a vast, worldwide, disembodied phantasmagoria" (142). As capital shakes loose from its productive moment, it abandons the ground and takes flight: "the results of these lightninglike movements of immense quantities of money around the globe are incalculable, yet already they have clearly produced new kinds of political blockage and also new and unrepresentable symptoms in late-capitalist everyday life." This latter remark prompts Jameson to say, supplementing Arrighi, that "any comprehensive new theory of finance capitalism will need to reach out into the expanded realm of cultural production to map its effects" (143). It must accordingly also map its effects on university discourse.

Jameson traces the cultural effects of the "axiomatic" of capitalism by recourse to Deleuze and Guattari's notion of deterritorialization, which I will claim serves the same function for our purposes as Reading's "de-referentialization of culture." As Jameson explains it,

> The first and most fateful deterritorialization is . . . this one: what Deleuze and Guattari call the axiomatic of capitalism decodes the terms of the older precapitalist coding systems and "liberates" them for new and more functional combinations. . . . [It] implies a new ontological and free-floating state, one in which the content . . . has definitively been suppressed in favor of the form, in

which the inherent nature of the product becomes insignificant, a mere marketing pretext, while the goal of production no longer lies in any specific market, any specific set of consumers or social and individual needs, but rather in its transformation into that element which by definition has no context or territory, and indeed no use value as such, namely, money. (152–53)

There is no need to postulate a total mimesis between the realm of culture and the avatars of capital to imagine that, if Latin American studies, in its old area studies configuration, could be understood as serving the needs of a peculiar kind of deterritorialization consonant with the productive moment of capital and thus ultimately consistent with the apparent preservation of the autonomy of nation-states within the interstate system in the world economy, the further or more radical deterritorialization brought about by finance capitalism marks the time-space of Latin American cultural studies. If either literature or the literary (as ultimate producers of the "national allegory") could in the past be claimed to constitute the principle of closure of the idiographic epistemics of area studies itself, as literature was held to be the moment of self-consciousness for any regional cultural particularism, it is now a de-referentialized culture that marks not any moment of self-consciousness but the absolute abandonment of the ideological, or rather its total identification with the real: just as finance capital operates the deterritorialization of territory ("the becoming abstract of land and earth, the transformation of the very background or context of commodity exchange into a commodity in its own right" ["Culture" 154]), "the real world has [now] been suffused with culture and colonized by it, so that it has no outside in terms of which it could be found lacking" (161).

The Neoliterary, the Neoregional, and Neo-Latin Americanism

Just as finance capital, through its principle of speculation, has torn free from embodiment and become (tendentially) an all-suffusing phantasmagoria, for Readings, in the context of university discourse, cultural studies has also developed a spectral function as what we could call the *neoliterary*. Cultural studies, for Readings, lives in the very tension of its disembodiment: it replicates the literary argument, while recognizing that literature can no longer work. When something is "neo" or can declare itself thus, it means that it resurrected out of the restlessness of having been put to rest. The literary, now in the specific sense of an organic connection between knowledge and power, has become a ghost for us: we have put it to rest, but it still haunts us out of the past, residually. The neoliterary is a fallen reactive formation, a symptomatically unrecognized spectrality. It is the attempt to resuscitate—or "reterritorialize"—the dead body of the literary in the context of the neoimperial game. The literary, in the sense of an organic articulation between knowledge and power, was put to rest by finance capitalism, and now we want to bring it back to life. Let us imagine that the imperial game survives until the 1980s, well after so-called decolonization, until it became obvious that the socialist world was no enemy of the First World. The neoimperial is then another name for globalization or the postideological arm of finance capitalism: the global cultural politics of the dominant. Because it is itself also deterritorialized from finance capital, it is partially also a reactive formation, a symptomatically unrecognized spectrality. But the neoimperial today, under the dominant global power of finance capitalism, has the status of a theoretical fiction, while the neoliterary is no more than a fatal conceit. The neoliterary, if that is all that cultural studies can be, is the attempt to counter the reactive cultural global politics of the dominant: it is a "me-too" game from a position of inadequacy, or even worse, from a position of always already internalized subordination.

The literary, not as literature, but as university discourse on literature, was at some point in history (Readings situates it at the beginning of European Romanticism) powerful enough to occupy the position of the empty signifier, in Ernesto Laclau's terms:[7] it was powerful enough to offer a national allegory, to offer the possibility of sustaining a hegemonic formation. Let us consider that period, which of course lasted well into the twentieth century, the properly libidinal moment of literary discourse, when it could have accomplished something, could have turned itself into an event of appropriation or a seizing of the social. No more. Now we have the neoliterary, that is, a ghost-desire, hence, neolibidinal.

The literary, as literary discourse, was a theoretical fiction once, but it has now turned, under the guise of the neoliterary, into a fatal conceit. Both theoretical fictions and fatal conceits are constructive rationalizations of the world. The former stands a chance, has a potential life. The latter has always already lost it. World rationalizations are a bid for state power. The literary was a bid for state power once. Now, resurrected as the neoliterary, it is a fatal conceit: a neolibidinal machine, the unrecognized spectrality of a minor or subaltern state-desire in a world in which state-desire was put to death and was then reborn as something else. It has been reborn precisely as the neoimperial. The neoliterary exists, perhaps under the guise of cultural studies, and it is a ghostly attempt to retrieve a constructed ideology regarding a national tradition in order to put it at the service of a nonnational, neoimperial resurrection.

Deleuze's announcement that the world is on the verge of going from a regime of rule characterized by discipline to a regime of rule characterized by control can perhaps now be supplemented with the notion that the transitional space marked by "on the verge of" coincides with the time of gradual suffusion of the social by finance capital, in Jameson's terms.[8] When exactly does one society stop being ruled by discipline or by monopoly capital and start being ruled by control or by finance capital? This is like the Aristotelian question about the withdrawing army: suddenly one soldier turns around and flees the scene of battle, then two, then three, then a dozen. At what point can it be said that the army is withdrawing and the battle has been lost? But the question, which is an important one, hides a supplement. It is only at the time of battle that the question can be asked. Only that particular time of confrontation allows for a question about confrontation itself. We live in one such time: for Hardt and Negri it is the time of the "passage to Empire," but Paul Bové has called it a time of interregnum.

Bové's *interregnum* refers to "that place and time [the present] when there is as yet no rule, when there are ordering forces but they have not yet summoned their institutional rule into full view" ("Afterword" 385). From the point of view of intellectual work, this generates a particular form of in-betweenness with important implications: "the fact of being within modernity and the state while trying to be in but not of postmodernity and globalization produces as yet unfulfilled demands for thinking, a process that can only be satisfied in a movement that does not work within the tread-marks of previous intellectual systems themselves principally attendant upon either modern state formations (and their epiphenomena) or romantic embrasures of local 'struggles' against 'global' forces" (377).

The neoliterary, as a reactive formation, amounts to a refusal to respond to the "as yet unfulfilled demands for thinking": the neoliterary is the fallen thinking of the interregnum. Accordingly, the neoliterary can only think within intellectual systems that are attendant on modern state formations or that are following a restricted dialectics of the local against the global. In either of the two versions, our thinking, if it is neoliterary, can only proceed to think the state on the basis of a retrenchment into the cultural, whether under the banner of identity or of difference (or, which comes to the same thing, of the hybrid), understood as the regional, that is, as the localized habitus for a given circulation of meanings. Just as the neoliterary could only reactivate "the literary argument, while recognizing that literature can no longer work" (Reading 17), it can only seize the social under a regime of discipline, while understanding that discipline no longer rules.

I propose to term this modality of thinking the social *neoregional.* What was called in previous chapter neo-Latin Americanism is obviously one of its faces. The neoregional is also a reactive formation in times of interregnum. Faced with globalization as a regime of control based on the tendential disavowal of the unmasterable excess of the social, the neoregional reproduces the same disavowal by disciplining the social, as well as the principle of social rule, through categories of localization that are dependent on modern notions of the state.[9] It is a willful return to a principle of reterritorialization in the face of the very deterritorialization underway in finance capitalism. But it is a dead-end solution, undertaken on the basis of a nostalgic relationship with the residual geoculture of the world-system in the times of monopoly capital. Whether it is still centered on the national or modernizes itself through an appeal to the intra- or transnational, it can only think the world under the spectral form of the state subject (it replicates the state subject argument, while recognizing that it can no longer work). If its bad limit is particularist essentialism or civilizational fundamentalism, its good thinking *aggiornamento* under the guise of hybridity is limited to a compulsive restatement of the advantages of not getting caught up in the dangers of its opposite. In other words, hybridity thinking has accepted

a first deterritorialization but stops short of accepting the wild deterritorialization of territory itself that the reign of finance capital
has made into an absolute, material condition for thinking through
the interregnum as the transitional time-space of the crisis of the
world-system.

If the neoliterary is the attempt, from within university discourse, to resurrect cultural studies as university discourse, the neoregional sustains the attempt, from within university discourse, to
ceaselessly resurrect Latin American cultural studies as university
discourse. They are reactive formations, meant to prop us up as academics at the service of the master. The master's discourse is today
neoimperial. As such, it is also a reactive formation. It means that
a master signifier died and has been resurrected out of its own restlessness. It is also an ideological formation, and it is just as flawed
as the neoliterary and the neoregional. Except that it is dominant,
and therefore it sutures the hegemonic articulation of the world in
times of transnational capitalism, whereas the neoliterary or the
neoregional can only have a subordinate function within it. As sub-
ordinates, they have always already chosen to serve the master.
They remain willing subjects to their own radical heteronomy: slave
ghosts enjoying their own enslavement.

Genealogical Knowledge

What organizes these deaths and ghostly resurrections, these fissures in and of the historical in postmodernity? I have mentioned
three of those fissures: a fissure in the social regime of rule, created by the shift from a society of discipline to a society of control; a fissure in the master's discourse, created by the shift from
imperialism to something else, empire, or the neoimperial; and a fissure in university discourse, which I have exemplified in the shift
from the literary to the neoliterary, from the regional to the neoregional. The neoimperial is a figure of what is today constituting
itself as a new social regime. The neoliterary and the neoregional are
also figures of that transition. They are thus transitional subregimes
of rule—they are subregimes of the postmodern interregnum. And
they are spectral or ghostly, in the sense that they represent resurrections. They'll keep coming back no matter what we do. If historically constituted Latin Americanism once was a theoretical fiction, in the sense that it could articulate a regional discourse in the

context of the imperial production of knowledge that goes under the name of modernity, neo-Latin Americanism replicates or reproduces that geoepistemological argument while recognizing that imperial epistemologies will no longer do. We therefore need reflection on the neo-Latin Americanist incapacity to reassert colonial dominance growing out of Latin Americanism's essential necessity to ceaselessly produce itself as a tool of colonial dominance. Under that determination, the conditions of possibility of neo-Latin Americanism would stand revealed as its conditions of impossibility, in a manner similar to the way the neoliterary or the neoregional proceed out of their own impossibility.

But perhaps the transition from discipline to control—the interregnum—releases a historical possibility for Latin Americanist reflection that is an alternative to its reconstitution as neo-Latin Americanism. Perhaps a second-order Latin Americanism can design the space of a critical difference within the transitional space of the interregnum. Doing it, proceeding to that design, would be our responsibility. Only then could Latin Americanists find an answer to the question that prompts this book: Can Latin Americanist reflection in the present offer itself as effective critical productivity? Our transitional times have drastically undermined the geocultural grounds on which it was possible to claim that the idiographic epistemology of area studies could be put at the transnational service of a counterproject for state power. The current pretensions of much cultural studies work to be considered a discourse of antisystemic resistance through its imagined complicity with what Arias called "peripheral subjectivities within a heterogeneous whole" (Arias, Fishlow, and Hale 13) seem all too often no more than a neoregional attempt at substitute formations. Either Latin Americanist reflection must serve policy interests, which, more often than not, are already themselves as deterritorialized as the finance capital that prompts them; or it must pursue a nostalgic reterritorialization through epiphenomenic embrasures of the local whose epistemic credibility is often dubious and whose political reach is limited to protesting the injustices of the neoliberal utopia. If Latin Americanism could once, in its more reflective manifestations, claim to occupy a theoretical place within the international division of labor, and thus to have the dignity of a noninstrumental knowledge that could allow itself to forget or erase its own conditions of possibility in the instrumental domination of the physical labor of those whom it studied, that possibility is now foreclosed. How can Latin Americanist reflection find new political possibilities within existing political constraints?

In an essay entitled "The End of 'Intellectual Labor' and the Idealist/Capitalist End of History in the 'Age of the Real Subsumption of Capital'" ("Fin del trabajo intelectual y fin idealista/capitalista de la historia en la 'era de la subsunción real del capital'"), Willy Thayer points out that the end of the social division of labor that, according to Marx, would mark the accomplishment of communist society has come to us, rather, by way of the indifferentiation of physical and intellectual labor which is a mark of finance capitalism:

> The creation of a planetary mode of production . . . slowly makes all antagonism with territorial exteriority disappear. All territory is already re/deterritorialized in capital. All exterior is interior, not only as far as precapitalist modes of production go. Also as far as the social division of labor, that is, in reference to intellectual labor as an exteriority to action. Capitalism . . . subsumes intellectual labor into the process of valorization of capital, so that intellectual labor is [now] conjured into existence by the production process that produces it. All antagonisms now develop and find their accomplishment in planetary, multiversal, pluriform, and polysemic capitalism. Capital [in the age of real subsumption], like Hegel's absolute idea, has no exteriority. (188; my trans., here and below)

Thayer's rich analysis is based on the fundamental intuition that the real subsumption of labor into capital, which for Marx defines capitalism properly speaking or its highest moment, implies a "restitution of totality" (175) where the difference between "action" and "meaning" collapses into indifferentiation.[10] The social division of labor, and the very movement of history through the class struggle, implied the possibility of keeping open the difference between action and meaning as a modality of the difference between physical labor and intellectual labor. But the point at which, in the words of Jameson quoted before, "the real world has been suffused with culture [or capital] and colonized by it, so that it has no outside in terms of which it could be found lacking" ("Culture" 161) is also the moment when culture—or meaning—can no longer differentiate itself from "existing practice" (Thayer, "Fin" 174). This is the Arrighian-Jamesonian moment of finance capitalism in postmodernity, the Wallersteinian moment of the crisis of the world-system "from its successes not from its failures" (Wallerstein, *Geopolitics* 15), the Deleuzian moment of the social rule of control, and the Hardtian and Negrian moment of the passage to empire. It is the moment Thayer calls, following a word of Marx, the moment of the real subsumption of labor into capital, where the absence of exteriority, or exteriority as absence, "cancels the possibility of the question about the meaning of action" ("Fin" 187). As Thayer then puts it,

> Sisyphus was not just condemned to repeat eternally the physical labor of pushing a heavy rock up the hill. . . . Simultaneously he had been condemned to the intellectual labor of realizing the senselessness of his action, to the impossibility of finding ideological restitution for it by means of some philosophy, to the impossibility of overcoming it by means of some liberating event, and to the impossibility of bringing it to an end by diluting his intellectual labor into blind manual operation. Compared to the contemporary intellectual, Sisyphus still had the advantage of being unable to sink himself into the end of the history of the social division of labor. But, compared to Sisyphus, the contemporary intellectual has the advantage of disappearing, together with history, into the planetary manual collective worker. ("Fin" 190)

One can imagine Sisyphus's hysteria. Latin Americanism can, inferentially, no longer think of itself as a theoretical discourse of exteriority vis-à-vis the regional that constitutes it. Subsumed within the territory that produces it, but which is itself thoroughly deterritorialized through the rule of finance capital, Latin Americanism, like any other formation of regional knowledge in the era of real subsumption, must accept, not the senselessness of its actions but worse: the indifferentiation of sense and action as its ultimate horizon of representability. Latin Americanism is then, like cultural studies, also a discourse of de-referentialization. As Thayer himself puts it in another work on university discourse, *La crisis no-moderna de la universidad moderna*, "the contemporary crisis should be named a crisis of the modern crisis as we have been having it up to now" (36; my trans., here and below). University discourse "[lacks] categories to analyze the event of the crisis of categories, including the category of crisis" (*Crisis* 45).

An acceptance of the impossibility of thinking past indifferentiation as its own truth potentially distinguishes second-order Latin Americanism from neo-Latin Americanism, which under these terms would be simply the refusal to confront the categorial crisis of its own presuppositions. Under such an acceptance something else also occurs, which marks an epochal difference. At the limit, there where Latin Americanist cultural reflection must confront its own impossibility as university discourse, university discourse opens itself to what Lacan called a hysteric's interpellation. If the hysteric's discourse is nothing but the ceaseless demand that the master release his or her own pretensions to truth, and if it dwells in the empty insistence that the master must be pushed to the point where his or her discourse will be shown lacking, then Latin Americanism, confronted by its own in-different, totalizing interpellation, also confronts itself, Sisyphus-like, "hysterically," dissolves as university discourse, and retrieves its position in the real: it becomes the nonholder of the nontruth of the real. But it only does so through its own disappearance, through its own death, not as integration of its particular knowledge into the "fundamental totality [of knowledge]" (R. Hall, *Area Studies* 2), but rather through a renunciation of representational strategies concerning its own object of epistemic desire given "the impossibility of finding ideological restitution" in them.

University discourse today can move along the lines of a reduction of the world to a principle of accounting, following the neoliberal subjection of the real to representational calculation; or it can proceed along the lines of a reduction of the world to a principle of accountability. Accountability was, in modernity, or at any rate after Kant, the very principle of the university understood as the conflicted space for the tendential articulation of knowledge and power, of reason and the state, within the organic milieu of the nation as the social synthesis of culture and nature. Under current conditions, however, which mark the collapse of the principle of reason as indifferentiation of action and meaning, accountability can no longer properly render itself. The articulation of knowledge and power, or reason and the state, has no national ground to produce itself, so it functions spectrally, as the neoimperial, within globalization understood as the tendential disavowal, or ceaseless capture, of the unmasterable excess of the social.

If university discourse can no longer be understood within the historical horizon of its self-realization, if the idea of the modern university has lost its ground and can no longer assert its principle as the principle of reconciliation of knowledge and power, or reason and the state, then Latin Americanist reflection, as deterritorialized university discourse, shows its stuff. It rips apart and it offers itself as a failure of rationalization: as the nonholder of the nontruth of the real. Wallerstein called for a deconstruction "without the erection of structures to deconstruct," and for "movements that mobilize and experiment" (*Geopolitics* 229). Subjecting the heritage of Latin Americanism to such deconstructive genealogy may be the paradoxical duty of reflection in transitional times: the activity through which historically constituted Latin Americanism coughs up its own violent truth, including the truth of its dissolution as an instrument of power/knowledge. Latin Americanism could not then be salvaged after that labor, that self-labor, of poisoned love. However, with whatever would appear in its place we could perhaps adequately "tiptoe into an uncertain future, trying merely to remember in which direction we are going" (Wallerstein, *Geopolitics* 229) and want to be going.

If university discourse, as the neoliterary, neoregional, or neo-Latin Americanist, can no longer be "a model of the ideal society," it can still be "a place where the impossibility of such models can be thought" (Readings 20). The genealogical or hysterical interpellation of Latin Americanism as university discourse is perhaps then nothing but a counterprogram for the interregnum, a preparatory program against everything that always haunted the existence of historically constituted Latin Americanism as its catastrophic underside. A program against imperial identity, a program against subordinating difference, a program against cultural power, a program against interiority itself: genealogical knowledge, in sum, as the possibility of an opening to the history of the abolition of exteriority, as a contingent epistemic performativity against any imperial closures of the real, including neo-Latin Americanism. Could it then become the form for a new theoretical fiction, for a different kind of epistemological desire? I do not think these questions are rhetorical. To me, they represent conditions for thinking both within and without university discourse: the very stuff of Latin Americanism's task, if we ever get to show it.

Transcoding

The indifferentiation of action and meaning, the tendential end of the social division of labor between physical and intellectual labor, does a bit more than perpetuate the expropriation, the radical separation, between Latin Americanist reflection and its field of reflection: it indifferentiates the two of them. For Thayer, the comparative advantage of the contemporary intellectual resides in the necessary abandonment of the pretension of exteriority: in the real subsumption of the worker into what he terms the "planetary manual collective worker" and we could call, borrowing from Marx, "general intellect" (about which more below).[11] But a comparative advantage for what? At stake is now the question of the possibility of a specific politics: What kind of politics can the genealogical interpellation of Latin Americanism yield? Both historically constituted Latin Americanism and its neoimperial or postmodern avatar are necessarily a submission to the discourse of the master, but the latter is an indifferentiated submission that ignores its own indifferentiation. How, then, can second-order Latin Americanist reflection proceed to its dissolution into general intellect? How does it subsume its residual solidarity with the singular, the vanishing, and the archaic into politico-epistemic action at the time of the indifferentiation of action and meaning? In other words, how can it still be a theoretical practice, in the sense defined in the introduction to this book? The remainder of this chapter will deal with these questions by proposing the possibility of an epistemic machine that would be the result of a double operation of transcoding: in the first place, transcoding postmodernism theory, no doubt another name for what Thayer prefers to call a thinking of "the age of real subsumption of society into capital," into subalternism as the name for a Latin Americanist theoretical practice; and, second, transcoding subalternism into a possibly Latin Americanist form of critical regionalism.

Toward the end of one of the most disturbing sections in *Postmodernism, or, The Cultural Logic of Late Capitalism,* "The Production of Theoretical Discourse," Jameson speaks about the Marxian concept of "separation" as one of the privileged figures for our own time. It is a concept that would explain or help explain the end of ideology in postmodernism. A tendentially accomplished separation, in other words, would be instrumental in determining what he thinks of as the diminishing function of intellectual life in the perpetuation and reproduction of the socioeconomic system. Separation in that sense is close to Thayer's indifferentiation. Jameson relates separation to the other Marxian notion of primitive accumulation by defining it as "the production of the proletariat in terms of their separation from the means of production" (*Postmodernism* 399). An ongoing separation in intellectual labor—the separation between intellectuals and their work, or the production of intellectuals as (intellectual) wage laborers—would be functional in the becoming-optional of any given ideological code. Optionality, market choice, counters the fictional or ideological necessity of a thought's embodiment: "if a code attempts to assert its nonoptionality—that is to say, its privileged authority as an articulation of something like a truth— it will be seen not merely as usurpatory and repressive but . . . as the illicit attempt of one group to lord it over all the others. But if, in the spirit of pluralism, it makes its autocritique and humbly admits its mere 'optionality,' the media excitement falls away, everyone loses interest, and the code in question, tail between its legs, can shortly be observed making for the exit from the public sphere or stage of that particular moment of History or discursive struggle" (397).

The notion of separation is dialectical and not all that easy to grasp in its specificity. In *Grundrisse* Marx says that, even though "the existence of capital and wage labour rests on [the] separation" of labor from its "objective moments of existence—instruments and material," separation itself is "suspended" during "the real production process—for otherwise work could not go on at all" (364). This would be consistent with Jameson's and Thayer's presentations of intellectual labor as subservient to capital's self-reproduction: the separation of intellectual labor from its means of production would also be suspended during the real production process—and such suspension would make possible the production of the ideological code itself in its double reference to individuality and collectivity. It is later, after production is over and other circuits of accumulation emerge, that separation once again shows up as a necessary expropriation—the moment of "optionality" is thus a moment of theft.

The postmodernist notion of the "death of the author" has everything to do with this, of course, and with it the notion of the death of Latin Americanism, and once again, through it, postmodernism would reveal something about global capitalism that was hidden in its previous stages. For separation—as well as the suspension of separation—was always already at work in the process whereby "conscious ideologies and political opinions, particular thought systems along with the official philosophical ones which laid claim to a greater universality—the whole realm of consciousness, argument and the very appearance of persuasion itself (or of reasoned dissent)" were "functional in perpetuating and reproducing the system" (Jameson, *Postmodernism* 398). The new moment, what Jameson would call the properly postmodern moment, appears in the dialectical culmination of the relationship of labor and capital, that is, in the moment of real subsumption. *Grundrisse* puts it this way: "The process of the realization of capital proceeds by means of and within the simple production process, by putting living labour into its natural relation with its moments of material being. But to the extent that labour steps into this relation, this relation exists not for itself, but for capital; labour itself has become already a moment of capital" (364).

Ours—if we can indeed use that pronoun to refer to a process of dispossession or figural death—would be the moment in which intellectual labor, no longer a for-itself, has become a moment of capital. No wonder, then, that the production of theoretical discourse has become at the same time infinitely easy and infinitely difficult, for the moment of separation under real subsumption must be marked as both permanently suspended and permanently overcoming its suspension: the narrowest abyss is thus opened, which, as Nietzsche put it, is also the most unbridgeable one. This is no doubt what leads Jameson to assert that

> what one uses language for becomes an issue of life and death, particularly since the option of silence—a high-modernist one— is also excluded. . . . Language can, in other words, no longer be true; but it can certainly be false; and the mission of theoretical discourse thus becomes a kind of search-and-destroy operation in which linguistic misconceptions are remorselessly identified and stigmatized, in the hopes that a theoretical discourse nega-

tive and critical enough will not itself become the target of such linguistic demystification in its turn. The hope is, of course, vain, insofar as, like it or not, every negative statement, every purely critical operation, can nonetheless generate the ideological illusion or mirage of a position, a system, a set of positive values in its own right. (*Postmodernism* 392–93)

The negativity of critical discourse would be a way into reappropriation, but its positivity is, however, denied to us as such, which leads into a vicious circle. It is within this utterly aporetic or phobic space that Jameson goes on to elaborate something like a phenomenology of theoretical production, which I would like to claim for my attempt to show second-order Latin Americanism as a form of theoretical practice.

Basically we have two options, which will later reproduce themselves into two additional options. The first pair is "transcoding" and "generating new codes." As to the former, "I can *transcode*; that is to say, I can set about measuring what is sayable and thinkable in each of these codes or ideolects and compare that to the conceptual possibilities of its competitors" (*Postmodernism* 394). I would call this the "critical" option, about which Jameson goes on to say that "[it] is . . . the most productive and responsible activity for students and theoretical or philosophical critics to pursue today" (394). The second option, that of "generating new codes," is identified with "the production of theoretical discourse par excellence," and it is not independent from the first but is instead its forceful continuation, by means of which "the setting into active equivalence of two preexisting codes" becomes "a new one" (395). The second pair of options is the consequence of a simple combinatory: within the setting into active equivalence of two preexisting codes, we can proceed by setting them into hierarchical relationship, option one, or we can refuse or negate the hierarchizing, option two. But both of the options ultimately result in reification, which thus serves to characterize "the general fate or destiny of theoretical discourse, as it finds itself thematized into someone's personal philosophy or system" (397). There is, however, a precarious difference between both reifications, since in the first case the hierarchical relation of the codes leads or could lead into what Jameson calls "cognitive mapping" as a kind of conceptualization, whereas the second one is more an operation than a conceptualization, by means of which "a kind of antisubstantial-ist doctrine about sheer process is invoked, and a momentum de-velops . . . that nonetheless yields the old illusion of system and ontology in the pauses between the operations and the reified ap-pearance of discourse served up on the page" (396).

Reification would thus seem to be the inescapable adventure of thinking in the age of accomplished separation. Indeed, Jameson's own recommendation for the practice of thinking, namely, "cogni-tive mapping," as a "more modernist strategy" based on the very failure of totalization but still retaining an appeal to it, is in itself nothing but ideological reification of a peculiar kind, that is, a simply more literal or less metaphoric rendition in symbolic terms of Althusser's notion of ideology as "the Imaginary representation of the subject's relationship to his or her Real conditions of exis-tence" (Jameson, *Postmodernism* 415). Thinking in accomplished separation thus evolves into a form of aesthetics, namely, the "aes-thetic of cognitive mapping" (416), which is, like all aesthetics, also at the same time transaesthetic in its impossible attempt to seize the totality of the social in imaginary terms. Or else, following the option Jameson would rather discard as somehow politically less sat-isfactory, it evolves into an equally aesthetic or transaesthetic form for which I would like to borrow a sentence produced by the sub-alternist historian Dipesh Chakrabarty: this second aesthetic would not be an aesthetics of mapping, but rather an aesthetic of the "stub-born knots that stand out and break up the otherwise evenly woven surface of the fabric" ("Minority Histories" 22): an aesthetic that one should not hesitate to call "of unmapping," were it not that unmap-ping preexisting maps is but another way of drawing charts.

The possibility of a second-order Latin Americanism as critical transcoding has to do with the setting into active equivalence of the ideological code of postmodernism theory itself and the alternative code of subalternism. It would be a matter of showing their phantas-matic compatibility—how they stand in a relationship to each other that ultimately mimics the relation between a photograph and its negative. It is not a simple question of proving that postmodernism theory and a subalternist code for Latin Americanist reflection are ideologically compatible. Rather, their compatibility, if it is going to be productive, has to be shown at their operational level: Can they start to provide the elements for a new practice of critical reason in

late capitalist times? Can they provide them for a new Latin Americanist theoretical practice that could not be considered neoimperial?

Beyond Linguistic Immanence

As we saw in the introduction, Perry Anderson suggests a possible
political articulation in postmodernism as an intrasystemic movement in reference to Carl Schmitt's theorization of the political field
as the field of division between friends and enemies. Anderson says,
"the aesthetic and the political are certainly not to be equated or
confused. But if they can be mediated, it is because they share one
thing in common. Both are inherently committed to critical judgment: discrimination between works of art, forms of state. Abstention from criticism, in either, is subscription. Postmodernism . . . is a
field of tensions. Division is an inescapable condition of engagement
with it" (*Origins* 134–35). For Anderson critical reason in postmodernism becomes irruptive and disruptive on the basis of the apparent impossibility of any irruption, of any disruption. Friendship and
enmity become for Anderson the figures for a perpetual redivisioning of the social field along political lines, which must remind us
of Jameson's repeated references to Nicolas Luhman's differentiation theory. Except that Jameson will also claim that dedifferentia-
tion is ultimately what obtains, at the very limit of differentiation,
as a form of dialectical collapse into its own residue. Of Anderson's
perpetual redivisioning of the field of friendship, which conceptu-
alizes a specifically political form of cognitive mapping, we could
say what Jameson said of operational transcoding—that it "yields the
old illusion of system and ontology in the pauses between the operations" (*Postmodernism* 396), in other words, that it can only proceed
through a reified or instrumental notion of friendship.

   Unless it is the case that Anderson has something entirely different in mind, which would unexpectedly then have to be compared
to Derrida's invocation of the "literary community" (*Politics* 293).
Either an illusion or a utopian desire for nonseparation seems to obtain here, at the limit, as witnessed not simply by Derrida's invocation of community (even if in the Blanchotian and Bataillean sense
of "the community of those who have no community") or by Anderson's reference to the ability of critical judgment to mediate between
the political and the aesthetic. The very notion of a radical interruption of the existent, the "unprecedented thought of rupture" an-

nounced by Derrida and more carefully kept in check by Anderson, who presents it as an ideologeme or placeholder of the portent of an unimaginable dialectical turn coming to us from the future, has to be understood as an interruption of separation, in other words, as a fabulous reappropriation of the very conditions of existence whose model is still what Derrida calls the "event," in clipped reference to the Heideggerian *Ereignis* (which is generally translated into English as "event of appropriation") (Derrida, *Politics* 293).

Jameson refers to deconstruction, in its de Manian version, as an extreme experience of separation as well as a response to it. Paul de Man's endeavor can be characterized as a "nominalism . . . lived to the absolute and theorized with a forbidding and rigorous purity" (Jameson, *Postmodernism* 251). The extreme experience of nominalism, however, since the Borgesian silence of *Funes el memorioso* must be excluded as an option for our age, can only result in a double development that ultimately sets the parameters of deconstruction as a philosophical operation. If no conceptualization can survive a radicalized nominalism, a nominalist operation wills its own exhaustion in linguistic immanence.

Thus, separation is lived in deconstruction: on the one hand, in its conceptualizing side, "as a last-minute rescue operation and a salvaging of the aesthetic . . . at the moment in which it seemed about to disappear without a trace" (*Postmodernism* 251); and, on the other hand, as an operation against any and all reifications, an "ascetic repudiation of pleasure, desire, and the intoxication of the sensory" (254). The difficulty of conceiving an aesthetic of sensory repudiation is no greater than the parallel difficulty of keeping the deconstructor perpetually intent on the experience of accomplished separation, which is also the experience of the perpetual suspension of separation. As Michael Taussig put it, for a different context, somewhere in *Shamanism*, it is a matter of quasi-simultaneously "standing within and standing without in quick oscillation"—no doubt a tiring exercise that is bound to result in a kind of gymnastic reification of the deconstructive body through the final and irretrievable hardening of the required muscles. Thomas Keenan has recently brought the point home by arguing in *Fables of Responsibility* that deconstruction is the attempt "to think about [the] removal [of the subject, agency, or identity as the grounds of our action] as the condition of any political action" (3). Keenan rehearses Derrida's notion of the "literary community" as the thought of an "originary dispersal" which is "the condition or the chance of anything (new) happening at all" (5). The literary community, in other words, emerges "in language, in the terrible way language dispropriates us, precedes and exceeds us, without in its turn offering or constituting itself as a reliable ground" (4) as a phantasmatic negation or counterprojection of radical separation: "when a text . . . exposes us to the difficulties of language, and leaves us to our own responsibilities—but without anything we could call our 'own' anymore" (4). Intellectual primitive accumulation would then seem to produce in late capitalist times the conditions for a cultural revolution—since the intellectual class, now inhumanly expropriated, finds itself with nothing to lose except its own radical experience of loss without reserve. But then, of course, the very appeal to the literary community runs the risk of appearing as an attempt to contain or capitalize the loss, to reconvert it into mere debt, and thus to turn the inhuman operation of late-capitalist language's expropriation into yet another tool for the reproduction of the system. As Marx put it, "to the extent that [intellectual] labour steps into this relation, this relation exists not for itself, but for capital; labour itself has become already a moment of capital" (364).

It is interesting that Althusser, in his conversations on materialism with Fernanda Navarro (1988), should have referred to nominalism as "materialism itself" (*Philosophie* 47; my translation here and below). For the later Althusser, materialism was a nominalism to the extent that it was the thinking of the singularity of the historical event, understood as a struggle against its logocentric or idealist kidnapping by state philosophies. The primacy of practice over theory is the primacy of operation against conceptualization, where the function of operative thinking is to think the constitutive outside of philosophy. Thus, "the 'philosophers of philosophy,' who undertook the task of dominating the world by means of thought, have practiced the violence of the concept, of *Begriff,* of 'grabbing.' They have affirmed their power by subjecting to the law of Truth (of their truth) all the social practices of the people who continue to suffer and to live in the night" (63). A philosophy of practice is precisely, "against the pretensions of philosophy *not to have an outside,* the final affirmation that *philosophy has an outside,* or better, that philosophy does not exist except through this outside and for it. This outside, that philosophy imagines as subjected to Truth, is practice, social practices" (61, see also 152).

Althusser's nominalism goes thus beyond linguistic immanence to the extent that it wills itself as a thinking of the constitutive outside of discourse. A materialist thinking that resists conceptualization as always necessarily a function of philosophical violence will be presented as a practice of resistance against the hermeneutic power of constituted philosophy. But it is still a thinking understood as a sort of internal differentiation, where the practical outside can only be glimpsed as the mediated or determinate form of resistance: *"the true outside of philosophy is in philosophy, it is, in philosophy, this . . . distance from deformation and exploitation. Practice, on the other hand, is the commitment to exist in spite of deformation and exploitation, it is resistance to this philosophical violence"* (155).

The lecture Althusser gave at the University of Granada, in Spain, in 1976, titled "Le transformation de la philosophie" ("The Transformation of Philosophy") and which to a certain extent is the basis of his conversations with Navarro between 1984 and 1987, makes his programmatic intent clearer. The lecture closes with what Althusser considers a "very adventurous hypothesis," namely, "that the philosophy Marxism needs *was not so much a philosophy produced as philosophy but a new practice of philosophy"* (*Philosophie* 174). A philosophy produced as philosophy can only be intent on constituting itself as the production of a determinate order of domination: namely, as hegemonic knowledge at the service of a dominant ideology. It is in that sense that Althusser pronounces philosophy to be nothing but class struggle at the theoretical level. This is not an optional matter but rather a matter of form. Quoting Marx's double definition of dialectics in the postface to the second german edition of *Capital,* where dialectics is presented as a conception "destined to glorify the existing state of things" or, alternatively, as "critical and revolutionary" (174), Althusser maintains that a dialectical philosophy, as philosophical conceptualization, will always fall on the former. Dialectics can only be "critical and revolutionary" when it avoids its own constitution into a philosophy for the sake of becoming "a new practice of philosophy." I will retain a key paragraph from Althusser's elaboration, since a fundamental development takes place in it:

The philosophy that haunts Marx's, Lenin's, and Gramsci's thought must be a nonphilosophical philosophy, that is, a philosophy which is no longer produced in the form of a philosophy, for which the function of accomplishing theoretical hegemony perishes in order to leave its place to new forms of philosophical existence. And in the same way that the free association of workers must, in Marx's point of view, take the place of the State in order to play an entirely different role than the State's, no longer a role in violence and repression, in that same way one can say that the new forms of existence of philosophy that are linked to the future of these free associations will no longer have as their essential function the constitution of dominant ideology, with all the constraints and exploitations linked to that, but rather the function of contributing to the liberation and the free exercise of social practices and of humane ideas. (177)

Althusser's conception of materialist thinking as a practical operation at the outside of philosophy starts to appear as an attempt to think the outside of the hegemonic circle: that is, no longer as the possibility of turning a dominated ideology into the dominant but rather as the possibility of thinking the outside of hegemony: posthegemonic thinking.

Pierre Macherey's notion of philosophy as operation is harder to crack, if only because he seems intent on turning the dialectical screw and putting the very space of postmodernist separation to work in the service of a new notion of philosophical practice: a practice that would also be posthegemonic in the sense we have detected in Althusser, that is, also posthermeneutic, and "determined as a process which is no longer that of the exposition of a subject" (*In a Materialist Way* 33). And yet it is in Macherey's work that we come closest to Jameson's "cognitive mapping"—although at the expense of an extreme ascetic reduction of the nonseparational residue of the subject within the thinking process. The subject is replaced by Macherey with the trace of a situational mediation, or point of view: the "point of view of operation," which expresses "the necessity of submitting to the conditions of an actual and no longer fictitious engagement" (32). If any freedom obtains in Macherey's operation, it is the very freedom of the totality itself, in its aleatory determination: "One can say that such an objective practice is a 'process without a subject,' in the sense that here the process is to itself its own subject: it produces itself rather than being produced, inside the movement that determines it, in relation to the totality of its conditions. It is not a question of a spontaneous production, dependent on some isolated initiative, but of a labour which is collective in the strongest sense of the word, since in its own constitution it requires no less than all of reality, caught up in the differential chain of its moments" (33).

Macherey's collective operation, as it is mediated by the point of view of the operator—itself conceived not as an "autonomous principle" but as "a moment in the development of the order to which it itself belongs" (33–34)—is a grandiose inversion of the principle of postmodernist separation through an appeal to what is an undecidably post/dialectical doctrine: that of the "'knowledge of the union that the thinking mind has with all of nature,' whose possession constitutes, according to Spinoza, the sovereign good." (35). The antagonism of theory and practice, of conceptualization and operation, is in this doctrine not to be reconciled but to be developed unlimitedly—"the end is after all only another beginning" (35): "This is why philosophy's universality genuinely arises not from theory but from practice: philosophy is not the universality of a knowledge which would include everything, and would substitute its determinations for reality once and for all; rather, it is the potential universality of an operation which, without being enclosed within the fiction of a general form, pursues inside itself the movement that leads it beyond its given limits, and thus carries out the encounter of its truth" (37).

But one needs to ask if, in its attempt to think totality as aleatory singularity, which is also a way of refusing any closure of thinking into reconciliation, this "truth" of philosophy's universality can avoid a reconceptualization into reified truth. If ideology is the imaginary resolution of real contradictions, Macherey seems to have gone further than anyone else to prevent the operation of thinking from recoiling into ideological reconciliation. His refusal to turn the philosophical operation into an aesthetic is a function of his reckless striving for unlimited totalization. With this, Macherey turns toward Heraclitean dialectics, as Heidegger himself also did, in order to close the circle of nonclosure in the history of Western thinking: "To philosophize is perhaps, according to a very ancient conception, to identify oneself with the totality. But if this formula can be retained, it is with the qualification that it cannot be a question of a given identity, whose models an actual thought must reject. The identity pursued by philosophy takes shape through the movement that tends to connect philosophy with all of reality: it is the identity of philosophy's operation" (37).

But what happens then is precisely that another simultaneous inversion occurs, and it is no longer philosophy that must be thought of as a practice. Rather, a practice must be thought to be philosophical to the extent that "in every practice, philosophy is that which incites it to think about itself, not in terms of a preestablished knowledge, but by relying on the development of its own operations, in so far as the latter are all, in their way, images of the absolute" (36). Indeed, late capitalism itself, or even postmodernism, comes as close as anything else to be the ideal model of Macherey's philosophical operation. The identification of thinking and totality loses as it wins, to use one of Jameson's favorite formulations, because, at the limit, no space remains to turn totality into a critique of totality. Operation thus becomes conceptualization, and its unlimitedness must now be seen, unexpectedly, as a counteroperational mechanism to liquidate any residue, any critical remainder: after all is said and done, when there is no longer an outside because we have found the absolute, the absolute also vanishes into absolute placelessness or absolute transcendence.

By contrast, Paolo Virno's "political theory of the future" makes no appeal to Hegelian absolutes, and starts by contesting Macherey's very distinction between *praxis* and *poiesis*. Virno's is also a theory of radical separation, where poiesis, or production in the post-Fordist or postmodernist mode, has become indistinguishable from praxis, or from "virtuosic performance." In classic political theory, from Aristotle to Hannah Arendt, praxis was the space for political or ethical action, conducted as an aim in itself and in the presence of others. Praxis defines activities in which, as Marx put it, "the product is not separable from the act of producing," whereas poiesis, as truly "productive labor," produces "commodities which exist separately from the producer" (Virno, "Virtuosity" 190). Macherey accepts the distinction, and takes sides with poiesis as the proper name for philosophy's operation. Virno, however, establishes that "within post-Fordist organization of production, activity-without-a-finished-work moves from being a special and problematic case to becoming

the prototype of waged labor in general" (192). This is rather scandalous for the classics—Marx, for instance, had denied praxis the status
of productive labor, since praxis does not produce surplus value.
But, whereas the classics had celebrated praxis as the space of action
where nonseparation reigned and where intellectual labor could enjoy the fruits of authenticity, Virno finds the current situation such
that the conflation of action and work "represents the true acme of
subjugation. There is none so poor as the one who sees her or his own
ability to relate to the 'presence of others,' or her or his own possession of language, reduced to wage labor" (192): "When 'the product
is not separable from the act of producing,' this act calls into question the self of the producer and, above all, the relationship between
that self and the self of the one who has ordered it or to whom it is
directed. The setting-to-work of what is common, in other words, of
Intellect and Language, although on the one hand renders fictitious
the impersonal technical division of labor, on the other hand, given
that this commonality is not translated into a 'public sphere' (that
is, into a political community), leads to a stubborn personalization
of subjugation" (195). Postmodern servitude goes, therefore, through
the organization of work, or of waged labor, as the expropriation of
intellect and language. Intellect comes then to be absorbed by capital as an attribute of living labor, and the extreme separation between the producer and the means of production becomes visible
in postmodernism as the rendering of "the more general aspects of
the mind: the faculty of language, the ability to learn, the ability to
abstract and correlate, and access to self-reflection" into a public resource for commodification (193).

   If the decline of political action today is because poiesis has taken
over praxis in such a way that "the potentiality of general intellect
comes to be the principal pillar of social production" (206), a political theory of the future must attempt to "elaborate a model of action
that will enable action to draw nourishment precisely from what
is today creating its blockage" (188). This can only be done, according to Virno, by "developing the publicness of Intellect outside of
Work and in opposition to it," that is, by cutting "the linkage that
binds [general intellect] to the production of commodities and wage
labor" (195). The dialectical possibility for what would otherwise appear as a voluntaristic politics starts in the fact that, if production
is today "virtuosic performance," that is, praxis, and if praxis is also

the characteristic trait of political action, then by following the general movement of production it would seem to be possible to rescue the general intellect from its hijacking by the administrative apparatus of capital, that is, by the state, by engaging in what Virno calls exodus as "engaged withdrawal" (196): such would be Virno's new politicality, his "politics of the future."

Two key aspects of Virno's theory interest us here: the first is the production of a new political subject, that is, the multitude, as "a historical *result*, a mature arrival point of the transformations that have taken place within the productive process and the forms of life. . . . Post-Fordist social cooperation, in eliminating the frontier between production time and personal time, not to mention the distinction between professional qualities and political aptitudes, creates a new species, which makes the old dichotomies of 'public/private' and 'collective/individual' sound farcical. Neither 'producers' nor 'citizens,' the modern *virtuosi* attain at last the rank of Multitude" (200). And, insofar as this multitude is not interested in reconstituting itself as a new state subject, that is, as a new subject of the state, but instead contests contemporary sovereignty as the "despotic organization of wage labor" (197), the enmity of the multitude, and its corresponding politics of friendship, no longer aspire "to shift the monopoly of political decision into new hands, but . . . [demand] its very elimination" (204).[12]

Subalternism

A critical transcoding of the relation between cognitive mapping as conceptualization and its operational counterpart should enable us, following Jameson's words on theory production in postmodernism, to draw a comparison by "measuring what is sayable and thinkable in each of these codes" (*Postmodernism* 394). The operation of critical transcoding is therefore in itself an attempt to deal with totalization. But we have broached totalization through the detour of a dialectics of separation—the separation of intellectual labor from its means of production, which is a tendential law or privileged trope for situational consciousness in postmodernism. If a tendentially accomplished separation is historically instrumental in determining the diminishing function of intellectual life in the reproduction and perpetuation of the system, it follows a fortiori that separation would also have to be instrumental in determining political blockage today from the point of view of imagining the possibility of systemic change. Anderson is not alone in detecting a seeming political impasse in postmodernism theory, which he attributes to the theory's inflexible hierarchizing of "a plane of substance (political economy)" and "a plane of form (aesthetic) (*Origins* 125)." Except that this very hierarchizing is itself of course the force of postmodernism theory, and is thus the ground of its epistemic power: no cognitive mapping without this hierarchical relationship of preexisting codes is possible. The objection of antipoliticality is yet another Hegelian ruse of reason whose agent is separation itself. In a situation in which separation reigns supreme, the withdrawal of politicality from, or its suspension in, theoretical production would seem to be a foregone conclusion or a matter of simple honesty. At the same time, this suspension is itself, or can be, a strong form of political action in a world in which the old forms of political action have become exhausted.

The suspension of politicality in Latin Americanist theoretical production can accordingly become a renewed form of politics: Latin Americanist reflection is structurally conditioned to think of itself in terms of an appropriative intentionality. But the minute that Latin Americanist reflection is historically taken to think, within its intentionality of appropriation, the radical expropriation that prompts it, is also the time when a second-order Latin Americanism begins to turn expropriation into its basic strategy of knowledge and critique: an operationalization of knowledge, a theoretical practice of the outside of philosophy.

The classic understanding of political action is related to the Aristotelian notion of praxis, understood as a type of action whose product is not separable from the act of producing. One of the corollaries of separation theory, however, is that, in full-blown postmodernism, separation has infiltrated praxis, turning it over to poiesis. That praxis is today a commodity, that work is today undistinguishable from action, not only defines postmodernist servitude but also serves to unmask most current conceptions of political action as so much historical dribble and dead ideology. The effort to imagine a new operationalization of political action in theoretical production starts with a renewed understanding of the very notion of thinking as operation. That second-order Latin Americanist reflection can become an operation in this sense thus seems to me to depend on the possibility of transcoding conceptualization into operation: from the predicament of the concept in the age of real subsumption, that is, postmodernity, to an operationalization of (Latin American) subalternity as subalternism.

We have developed a certain number of theoretical tools, namely, in summary form: first, the (possible) notion of a critical reason that becomes irruptive and disruptive on the basis of the apparent impossibility of any irruption or disruption; second, the need to take thinking as operation beyond discursive immanence and into social practices understood as the constitutive outside of philosophy's discourse; third, the need to understand the operation of thinking beyond any attempt at reconstituting it as a form of philosophical reconceptualization at the service of hegemonic articulations; fourth, the need to prevent the operation of thinking from recoiling into ideological reconciliation; fifth, the production of a new philosophical subject, even a subjectless subject, whose "general intellect" can sustain the enterprise of operational thinking, as posthegemonic thinking, in times of postmodernism. I believe that all five of those features are constitutive of subalternist thinking.

The project of South Asian subaltern studies ostensibly developed in order to produce not just postcolonial but also postnationalist accounts of Indian histories. It emblematized from its beginnning the notion of historic failure as an operational device. In Ranajit Guha's 1982 quasi manifesto, "On Some Aspects of the Historiography of Colonial India," "the study of the historic failure of the nation to come to its own" is said to constitute "the central problematic" of subalternist historiography (7). But "failure" was used by the Indian subalternists as a notion that would enable them to confront what Chakrabarty called the "two everyday symptoms of the subalternity of non-Western, third-world histories" ("Postcoloniality" 264). These two symptoms correspond of course to one and the same malaise, a "theoretical condition" derived from the expansion and transformation of European capitalism into a world system. From Marx's explanation, quoted by Chakrabarty, of how and why the coming of the capitalist mode of production into European and then world history made history "for the first time *theoretically* knowable" ("Postcoloniality" 266), there develops the need for non-European social formations to understand themselves in relation to the history of capital and its cultural logics. Because the influence of capitalist expansion never made itself felt at the level of the material base alone, but was always embodied through social, political, and cultural agencies of power, its superstructural implications for the production of what Taylor called "alternative modernities" transcend the possibilities of what he refers to as "creative adaptation" ("Two Theries" 163), or Fernando Ortiz, Angel Rama, and others would call *transculturation.* There is no denying these latter phenomena, which refer to non-European social formations's capacity to react productively to capitalist colonization. But such a capacity was not unlimited. The subalternist notion of historic failure points to the identification and study of undigestible blockages in non-European transculturation and purports to find in them a critical possibility for the operational release of modes of cultural-historical interpretation that counter the necessarily teleological bent of "historical transition" or mode of production narratives.

For the fact is that, even accepting that mode of production narratives do not have to be teleological when applied to metropolitan societies (they can be framed, for instance, under Althusser's "aleatory materialism," where history is said to be a process without a subject and without a goal), they turn into structural teleologies when applied to nonmetropolitan histories:

> There is . . . this double bind through which the subject of "Indian" history articulates itself. On the one hand, it is both the subject and the object of modernity because it stands for an assumed unity called the "Indian people" that is always split into two—a modernizing elite and a yet-to-be-modernized peasantry. As such a split subject, however, it speaks from within a metanarrative that celebrates the nation-state; and of this metanarrative the theoretical subject can only be a hyperreal "Europe," a "Europe" constructed by the tales that both imperialism and nationalism have told the colonized. The mode of self-representation that the "Indian" can adopt here is what Homi Bhabha has justly called "mimetic." Indian history, even in the most dedicated socialist or nationalist hands, remains a mimicry of a certain "modern" subject of "European" history and is bound to represent a sad figure of lack and failure. The transition narrative

will alway remain "grievously incomplete." (Chakrabarty, "Post-coloniality" 284)

This predicament is then instrumental in the production of the two symptoms of historiographic subalternity Chakrabarty referred to. They are that "third-world historians feel a need to refer to works in European history; historians of Europe do not feel any need to reciprocate." And that "we find [their] theories, in spite of their inherent ignorance of 'us,' eminently useful in understanding our societies. What enabled the modern European sages to develop such clairvoyance with regard to societies of which they were empirically ignorant?" (264–65). The answer is of course capitalism, which sets the stage for a time lag in economic and social development and simultaneously sets the standard from which development must be judged, whether in terms of similarity or in terms of difference. "As long as one operates within the discourse of 'history' produced at the institutional site of the university [understood by Chakarabarty as an ideological state apparatus within the world system], it is not possible simply to walk out of the deep collusion between 'history' and the modernizing narrative(s) of citizenship, bourgeois public and private, and the nation-state" (285). As a consequence, "a third-world historian is condemned to knowing 'Europe' as the original home of the 'modern,' whereas the 'European' historian does not share a comparable predicament with regard to the pasts of the majority of humankind" (286).

The full operationalization of the concept of historic failure is a byproduct or reaction to these symptoms of cognitive subalternity and has to do with its becoming explicitly what Gayatri Spivak names "cognitive failure" on the part of the historian ("Subaltern Studies" 6). As a counterpart to the necessary failure of the non-metropolitan social formation to come into its own, since an originary expropriation of history has always already taken place within modernity at the hands of imperial capitalism, the historian's attempt to retrieve the outside of expropriation cannot meet with success. Indeed, success is failure and failure is success, in a situation in which both of them cannot be other than what Spivak calls "theoretical fictions" (7). Failure is operational and productive, however, to the extent that "it acknowledges that the arena of the subaltern's persistent emergence into hegemony must always and by definition remain heterogeneous to the efforts of the disciplinary historian. The historian must persist in *his* efforts in this awareness, that the subaltern is necessarily the absolute limit of the place where history is narrativized into logic" (17). For Chakrabarty, subalternity as theoretical production contests the double bind of the nonmetropolitan split subject by simultaneously investigating history and the impossibility of history, thus not simply dismantling Eurocentric narratives but also calling for a dismantling of the historiographic apparatus itself: "the project . . . must realize within itself its own impossibility . . . a history that deliberately makes visible, within the very structure of its narrative forms, its own repressive strategies and practices, the part it plays in collusion with the narratives of citizenships in assimilating to the projects of the modern state all other possibilities of human solidarity . . . a history that will attempt the impossible: to look towards its own death by tracing that which resists and escapes the best human effort at translation across cultural and other semiotic systems, so that the world may once again be imagined as radically heterogeneous" ("Postcoloniality" 290).

This is the radical moment of subaltern studies, which is not necessarily maintained as such by its practitioners. But, even in its full radicality, it is only superficially that such a project could seem sufficiently described by Jameson's notion of postmodernist theoretical production as a "seach-and-destroy operation," whose reification would come from a reckless insistence on negativity. Subalternism is always already an operation of transcoding, starting from the geohistorical experience of extreme separation in intellectual labor and pushing to resist conceptualization, and thus reification, by what amounts to a *negative inversion* of the two preexisting hierarchical codes it subsumes. The two codes that subalternism transcodes are the mode of production narrative and the narrative of cultural heterogeneity. If the former occupies tropologically the position of material base, and the latter a superstructural position, subalternism inverts the order and places historical heterogeneity as material base; simultaneously, it negates the mode of production as an epistemic device of totalization by foregrounding its residual components (which are henceforth no longer residual, but rather central to the epistemic enterprise); and it negates heterogeneity by placing it beyond conceptualization, and only accessible as failure (imagining heterogeneity, in the recent quote, is precisely the impossible).

superstructure	cultural heterogeneity
material base	mode of production
totalization	failure

The tense dialectical equilibrium that results cannot be easily reconciled into a new turn in the thinking of thinking. Rather, subalternism lives in the operational residue of its own conceptualization and thus inverts Jameson's schema for cognitive mapping, becoming its photographic negative, or its other face. Its materialist credentials are safeguarded because it is still a critique of the bourgeois or capitalist mode of production in its different stages. Indeed, it is a critique of the apparatuses of capitalist development as they affect the life of nonmetropolitan social formations—and, when used in the historical context of the former second world, it is also a critique of state socialism as a mode of production. But it poses no resolution other than historical to the contradictions it detects. To that extent, and thus defined, it would not constitute a form of aesthetic ideology.

Aesthetization as reification is in fact the main theoretical concern of Chakrabarty's 1997 essay, "The Time of History and the Times of Gods." Aesthetization as reification takes for Chakrabarty the form of an ethical challenge, the difficulty of translating "the singular times of gods and spirits" into "the secular time of history" (43). The challenge has to do with producing a satisfactory answer to an aporetic dilemma, that the historian's discourse participates "in a general economy of exchange made possible through the emergence of abstract, generalizing ideas" and thereby excludes from view whatever singularities could have held in the past (or the present) that would defy "the generalizing impulse of the sociological imagination" ("Time" 41; 43). But the craft of the historian is, for Chakrabarty, not to be renounced—not any more than the opening toward the heterogeneous singularity which simultaneously justifies and shows the limits of subalternist historiography. It cannot be renounced because the secular time of history is also the abstract time of capital itself, and the contemporary mode of production, and with it any aspiration to change it through human agency, is thoroughly caught up in it. If so, then the impossibility of giving up the secular time of historiography would mean that ideological conceptualization precedes operation even for subalternism—and therefore that reification has always already taken place. The subalternist's work, because it must express itself in the secular language of university discourse, would then be a commodity in its own right in a double sense: a material commodity in the form of a book or journal article and also a commodified thought in virtue of its internalized reproduction of the norms for abstract exchange that rule over disciplinary work. The question for Chakrabarty's relentless self-critique then is: "how this seemingly imperious, all-pervasive code might be deployed or thought so that we have at least a glimpse of its own finitude, a vision of what might constitute an outside to it" ("Time" 56).

A certain change in Chakrabarty's position sets in between "Postcoloniality and the Artifice of History" and "The Time of History and the Times of Gods." In "The Time of History" Chakrabarty no longer elaborates on the need to drive the historiographic endeavor toward its own death or says that it must realize within itself its own impossibility. Instead, here it is a matter of making room, even if in a central way, within the historiographic endeavor, for "the trace of something that cannot be enclosed, an element that challenges from within capital's and commodity's—and, by implication, History's—claims to unity and universality ("Time" 55). Chakrabarty remains sensitive to the need for the operationalization within history of the constitutive outside of its categories—indeed, such is the need that drives him. At the same time, however,

> just as real labor cannot be thought outside of the problematic of abstract labor, subaltern history cannot be thought outside of the global narrative of capital—including the narrative of transition to capitalism—though it is not grounded in this narrative.... This "outside" I think of, after Derrida, is something attached to the category *capital* itself, something that straddles a border zone of temporality, something that conforms to the temporal code within which "capital" comes into being while violating that code at the same time, something we are able to see only because we can think/theorize capital, but something that also always reminds us that other temporalities, other forms of worlding, co-exist and are possible. ("Time" 57).

Although the last sentence of the essay returns to the fiercer mood of "Postcoloniality and the Artifice of History" ("the practice of subaltern history aims to take history, the code, to its limits in order to make its unworking visible" ["Time" 58]), "The Time of History" marks a transitional moment in Chakrabarty's evolution when the radically operational force of subalternism seems to recoil toward a reconceptualization whereby subaltern consciousness would be deemed incapable of, in Virno's words, cutting "the linkage that binds [general intellect] to the production of commodities and wage labor" ("Virtuosity 195). In a sense, the consciousness of the disciplinary historian has taken over and has to the same extent debilitated the irruptive force of subaltern singularity, which now remains as a Derridean trace. Was this an unavoidable realization?

Those tendencies become partially accentuated in Chakrabarty's third essay, "Minority Histories, Subaltern Pasts." It is a matter of keeping alive the radical operational force of the subalternist enterprise against the dangers of conceptualization. Conceptualization creeps in, in "Minority Histories," under the form of a historicism that is precisely not absolute enough. Chakrabarty had criticized historicism in "The Time of History" as a form of reification occurring through "a very particular understanding of the question of contemporaneity: the idea that things from different historical periods can exist in the same time (the so-called simultaneity of the non-simultaneous) but belong to different worlds. . . . One [can], in historicism, look at peasants . . . as survivals from a dead world. This is a fundamental characteristic of historicist thought" ("Time" 49). His concern then was how to keep history open to the claims of gods and spirits, that is, to the living singularity of nonsecular times, whose coincidence with ours is in itself already an ideological prejudice of universal abstract time. In "Minority Histories" Chakrabarty rehearses his preoccupation with heterogeneity and its disciplinary capture:

> To stay with the heterogeneity of the moment when the historian meets with the Santal, the peasant, is then to stay with the difference between these two gestures: one, that of historicising the Santal in the interest of a history of social justice and democracy, and the other, that of refusing to historicise and of seeing the Santal instead as a figure throwing light on a possibility for the present. When seen as the latter, the Santal puts us in touch with the heterogeneities, the plural ways of being, that make up our own present. The archives thus help bring to view the dis-

jointed nature of our own times. That is the function of subaltern pasts. A necessary penumbra of shadow to the area of the past that the method of history successfully illuminates, they make visible at one and the same time what historicising can do and what its limits are. (24)

Subaltern pasts are subversive pasts. They are presented in their singularity as radically destabilizing for state thinking, for university discourse. If subaltern pasts were permitted to substitute for state thinking, they would lead state thinking to catastrophe. The subalternist historian, wavering between the need for historiography as a discipline and the opening toward the radical heterogeneity of subaltern consciousness, would be a state thinker in melancholia who has no choice but to turn the weapons of the state against itself. For the subaltern historian, in all the force of Chakrabarty's presentation, the shadow of the object—that "penumbra"—has always already fallen on the subject. The subalternist historian lives in extreme separation. Within this economy of loss, however, it becomes necessary not to give in. Hence Chakrabarty's double gesture: "The task of producing 'minority' histories has, under the pressure precisely of a deepening demand for democracy, become a double task . . . 'good' minority history is about expanding the scope of social justice and representative democracy, but the talk about the 'limits of history,' on the other hand, is about struggling, or even groping, for non-statist forms of democracy that we cannot yet either completely understand or envisage" ("Minority" 23). This utopian desire links properly subalternist history to a close confrontation with the limits of history for the sake of a democracy to come: the opening to the subalterns' demand for absolute justice as Derrida would put it, or to their negative or ideal universality, as Etienne Balibar would, finds a mediation.[13]

The master mood of the disciplinary historian is Weberian disenchantment: the experience of time as empty and homogeneous. Against disenchantment, the affect of the subalternist historian, who must embrace subversive history as a necessary supplementarity, appeals to the catastrophic work of absolute justice, and thus to the as-yet unconceivable reestablishment of singularity. The subalternist historian fights against extreme separation, against melancholia, by striving to turn it into mourning for what perhaps was and is not yet. But the step into mourning, which always wills its own extinction, although necessary in the path of operationalization, at the same time marks a necessary recoil from operationalization. At the point in which the subalternist historian, won over by the demands of the time of disenchantment, finds a way forward toward the utopian resolution of his constitutive contradiction and can thus affirm the potential conciliation of the supplement (subaltern pasts) with that which it supplements (disciplinary history), the subalternist historian gives up the demand for absolute justice and forfeits his claim to respect for subaltern singularity. The subalternist historian becomes a state thinker on the way to operational reconciliation, and enters the totalizing realm of "good" history.

"Good" history, the object of Chakrabarty's critique, would seem to reestablish itself toward the end of his essay in the movement that goes from "it is because we always already have experience of that which makes the present non-contemporaneous with itself that we can actually historicise" ("Minority Histories" 27) to "a relation of contemporaneity between the non-modern and the modern, a shared 'now' which expresses itself on the historical plane but the character of which is ontological, is what allows historical time to unfold" (28). If contemporaneity proper—that "now" that marks temporal coexistence—sufficiently renders the object of the subalternist historian, then subalternism has veered into historicism in Chakrabarty's own terms. But it is not an absolute historicism, because it is anchored in ontology. The wavering between non-contemporaneity and contemporaneity is the wavering between a thinking of extreme separation or disjunction and a recuperative thinking of presence. The latter does away with supplementarity and constrains the radicalness of subalternist thinking, which now would seem to reproduce ontological difference rather than seem to produce its operational deconstruction. And thinking comes back, through that very wavering, into full separation. It is not the melancholy thinker but rather only the hysterical or genealogical one who can turn the weapons of the state against itself and engage in a full operationalization of critique.

Subaltern Negation

To conclude, I want to present a textual fragment from Latin American revolutionary history as a sort of allegory of Latin Americanist subalternist knowledge. I run a couple of risks, which I assume willingly but not without the following clarification: in the first place, I am aware that the fragment I offer does not come to us directly from revolutionary history, but that it is rather an account of it that is obviously better considered under the conceptual category of "prose of counterinsurgency" in Guha's determination.[14] In the second place, the allegory is not a perfect allegory—no allegory can possibly be perfect. The villistas do not simply represent the average Latin American subject here in the way that the zapatistas would represent the Latin American subalternist, for example. If the villistas are clearly in what follows the subjects of state and disciplinary knowledge, then the zapatistas would allegorically embody the kind of resistance, let us call it subaltern negation, that goes beyond discipline and control in the name of an affirmative refusal of the discourse of the master. But it is not the zapatistas who represent the position of the Latin American subject either (and then the villistas, the position of the Latin Americanist); rather, the whole fragment represents everything chiasmatically, in the dense complexity of its textuality.

But first, on subaltern negation, there is a beautiful and terrible passage in Harriet Beecher Stowe's *Uncle Tom's Cabin* (1852). The passage is:

> "You belong to the church, eh?"
>
> "Yes, Mas'r," said Tom, firmly.
>
> "Well, I'll soon have that out of you. I have none o'yer bawling, praying, singing niggers on my place, so remember. Now, mind yourself," he said, with a stamp and a fierce glance of his gray eye, directed at Tom, "I'm your church now! You understand,—you've got to be as I say."
>
> Something within the silent black man answered No! and, as if repeated by an invisible voice, came the words of an old prophetic scroll, as Eva had often read them to him,—"Fear not! for I have redeemed thee. I have called thee by name. Thou are MINE!" (482).

Subaltern consciousness is here represented through an extreme formalism, although perhaps I should not say "represented." The unconditional "no," the absolute refusal to surrender to hegemonic interpellation, touches on the very limits of representation and is, in fact, also an absolute refusal of representation. "No! I will not be as you say" means that representation will always miss me. Subaltern redemption is simply mentioned in that passage as the absolute capacity to be always elsewhere, always out of reach of hegemonic interpellation even under conditions of domination (such as slavery). It is a kind of consciousness, and even a voice—but it must remain silent as such, hence it is not dialogic. It is in that sense not yet a subjectivity. This silent voice, this silent refusal to submit to consolidated or hegemonic power, is not simply thoroughly political in nature: it defines the conditions of possibility of the political as such. By the same token it also defines the conditions of possibility of subjectivity as such. If subjectivity is always necessarily dialogical, it can only be possible once we establish the possibility of an interruption of dialogism: in other words, if positivity is the other side of negation, there will be no positivity without the negation that grounds it. There is no subjectivity that is not always already based on subaltern negation. And the corollary is: there is no politics that is not always already based on subaltern negation.[15]

The fragment for which the above is a prologue is the chapter entitled "Zapatistas at the Palace" in Martín Luis Guzmán's memoirs of the Mexican Revolution, *El águila y la serpiente*. The zapatistas have momentarily taken the presidential palace. A commission of villista officials visits them. Everybody seems to know that the zapatistas will be presently forced out of the palace by the villistas themselves. And yet, hospitality obtains. Eufemio Zapata, the officer in charge of the palace guard, takes the commission around for a visit. The eye of the narrator, a member of the commission, for whom the present political situation is intolerable and incongruous with his own vision of reality ("Because that palace, which had always seemed to me so identical to itself, appeared to me now, almost empty and in the hands of a gang of semi-naked rebels, as something incomprehensible" [*Aguila* 394; my trans., here and below]), takes great delight in foregrounding the absolute incompatibility of presidential power and zapatista presence: "There was in the way in which his [Eufemio's] shoe stepped on the carpet an incompatibility between carpet and shoe; in the way his hand rested on the banister, an incompatibility between banister and hand. Every time he moved his foot, his foot was surprised not to stumble in the scrub; every time his hand reached out, his hand would vainly look for the tree bark or the stone's raw edge. Just by looking at him one understood that everything that deserved to be around him was missing and that, for him, everything that surrounded him was superfluous" (395).

A "terrible doubt" (395) assails the narrator upon wondering if the commission's own presence within the palace is also incompatible with a historical sense of the real. "[The zapatistas'] tender, awed, and almost religious concentration did represent there a kind of truth. But us? What did we represent? Did we represent something fundamental, something sincere, something deep?" (396). The unreal truth of the zapatista presence will be betrayed with their dislodgment from the palace. The event is prefigured when Eufemio leads the villista group into the president's office and announces "This is the chair!" He then says: "Since I am here, I come to see this chair every day, in order to get used to it. Because just fancy this: before I always used to believe that the presidential chair was a saddle" (396–97). At which Eulalio, one of the villistas, retorts: "It is not for nothing, *compañero*, that one knows how to ride a horse. You, and others like you, should be certain to become presidents the day saddles look like that chair over there" (397). The "terrible doubt" begins to vanish. The villistas are led into the basement, where the zapatista guards have given themselves over to drunken debauchery: "Fifty, eighty, one hundred zapatista chiefs and officers were there when we came in. They were crowded, piled up. Most of them still stood up, body against body or in groups, hugging each other. Others were sitting on top of the tables. Other lay on the ground, toward the walls and near the corners. Many had a bottle or a glass in their hands. They were all breathing a milky and stinking atmosphere, where infinite humors mixed up with the smoke of a thousand cigars. A bit more a bit less, everybody was drunk" (398).

The villistas accept a few drinks, and at some point Eufemio repeats Eulalio's bad joke: "Here the compañero thinks . . . that Emiliano and I, and others like us, will become presidents the day horses are saddled with presidential chairs like the one up there." (399). A sense of the ominous descends on the room—but it does not last. "There was . . . a deep silence, broken only by Eulalio's mocking laughter. Then the murmur of the voices came back, but with a new nuance, vague, disquieting, and restless. Even so, Eufemio poured more tequila, as if nothing had happened." Within an hour some villista troops arrive at the palace and overwhelm the zapatista garrison: "they were so intent on getting drunk," somebody says, "that they did not have any time to fight with us" (399).

Guzmán presents subaltern consciousness at the liminal moment of apparent defeat, in a state of melancholy revelling. The zapatistas have somehow already accepted their vanquishment—before it has in effect taken place. They can still put fear into the villistas, but everything is seemingly abandoned for the sake of drunken stupor. And their drunken stupor is what enables the villistas to take over, to finally eliminate the terrible doubt about their possible compatibility with historicopolitical power. There is a subdued dialectics in the narrative according to which the withdrawal of the zapatistas from the pretense of power coincides with the accession of the villistas to power. The crucial moment of hegemonic interpellation happens when Eulalio makes his joke—"yes, my friends, you guys will have power the day horses are saddled with presidential chairs." But the zapatistas already know it: hence their withdrawal and renunciation. Subaltern negation in this case shares with Stowe's rendering the refusal of representation: "No! I will not be as you say." Subaltern freedom is in the episode exercised as a mere abandonment of the political.

I am not interested in the abandonment of the political but rather in its suspension, through which the text grants counterintentional freedom to the possibility of subaltern action. When the zapatista voices make themselves heard with a "new nuance, vague, disquieting, and restless," something seems about to occur. That is precisely the undecidable moment through which the villistas are forever prevented from answering back with something like "not being as I say is precisely what I expect from you, hence you are still being as I say." Something had seemed about to occur, and yet it did not. This failure to occur, the nonevent that orchestrates the whole narrative, becomes a fundamental political event for someone else, the villistas: it opens their accession to power, and thus the consolidation of a new hegemony within the Mexican Revolution.

The zapatistas' apparent abandonment or suspension of the political is in any case a contingent historical fact—but one that subaltern negation makes possible. If the zapatistas had chosen to imprison the villista officers and had taken positions for an adequate defense of the palace, the course of history could have been different—and that would also have been made possible by subaltern negation. The zapatistas' failure to act in a sense that would have potentially enabled them to preserve some kind of military control over the Mexican state is still a condition of the political even though it presents itself contingently as a suspension or momentary abandonment of the political. What if, for the zapatistas at the palace, the apparent abandonment of the political had been nothing but an alternative understanding of the political, a radicalization of subaltern negation in a final "non serviam"—"I will not be as you say"—conducive to a secret triumphant redemption? Zapatista atopics: I will not be where you place me, in a context in which hegemonic thinking can only at most place everything, place obsessively, and find itself exhausted in a thinking of the place. But who determines the place if not always already the villistas, that is, those who take it on themselves to define interpellation in the vanquishing of the terrible doubt about their ability to hold power, to administer knowledge? If subaltern negation is a simple refusal to submit to hegemonic interpellation, an exodus from hegemony, is that not a new assumption of political freedom that remains barred to any and all thinking of hegemony, to any and all thinkings of location? What do the zapatistas retreat from if not sovereignty? Can a thinking of the retreat of sovereignty then appear as an excess of thinking itself? A thinking that will not be bound to respond affirmatively, or to respond at all, when the master insists upon masterly recognition.

*One cannot say "here are our monsters" without
immediately turning the monsters into pets.*
—Jacques Derrida, "Some Statements and Truisms"

FOUR Restitution and Appropriation

The Dissymmetrical Gaze

Latin Americanist reflection, perhaps particularly in its avatar as
Latin American cultural studies, suffers from the start from the
double and contradictory injunction that constitutes it, namely, that
it must at the same time actively preserve a Latin American (or
any kind of intra–Latin American) singularity and reduce it to its
own (nonsingular) parameters. Doubly caught between appropriation and restitution, to the extent that it is a border discourse that
expresses and regulates relationships between groups with conflicting claims over it, Latin Americanist representation embodies a
structural dissociation. Whether this dissociation must submit to the
negative markings of epistemic and political defect will depend on
our notions regarding the beneficial effects of nondissociation, of
historical self-presence, of seamless communal integration, even of
monolingualism. But, as Geoffrey Bennington says, it may be the
case that "dissociation . . . is an absolute condition of the political
rather than the unfortunate failure of community it is often taken
to be" (*Legislations* 193). This chapter examines some aspects of
the structural dissociation of Latin Americanism, of its constitutive
double injunction.

My first aim is to introduce the way in which such structural dissociation offers itself to us as present predicament and regulates the
need for a metacritical engagement of Latin Americanism and of the

manner in which it may and may not think alterity. I will then elaborate on the interplay of appropriation and restitution in Latin Americanist work, at the same time that I will endeavor to present the possibility of a metacritical outside to appropriational-restitutional drives. An engagement with Geoffrey Hartman's notion of restitution in relation with the deconstructive process will be related to Enrico Mario Santí's concept of restitutional excess, by way of a detour through restitutional thinking in Martin Heidegger and its critique by Fredric Jameson and Jacques Derrida. The fourth and final section of this chapter will attempt to sum up and develop some of the implications of my position by looking at work by Diamela Eltit and Doris Sommer.

Representation is never the simple reflection or product of a subject's reaction to an object in the real. Instead, the object itself has already come into light as object through representation; that is, the object is not given except as an always already socially articulated phenomenon. Stephen Greenblatt, referring to the European encounter with the New World, makes the related point that "any given representation is . . . itself a social relation, linked to the group understandings, status, hierarchies, resistances, and conflicts that exist in other spheres of the culture in which it circulates. This means that representations are not only products but producers, capable of decisively altering the very forces that brought them into being" (*Marvelous* 6). Greenblatt is not suggesting that the New World had no form of existence before the Spanish arrival; only that the Spanish could not understand what they thought of as the "New" World except in terms of their own social and political designs on it, and that their specific understanding was itself already a form of political action. One of the implications of this conceptualization is that there is no such thing as exotopic knowledge of the other: by that definition knowledge is always endotopic, since it can only proceed on an object that was first experienced as such in the process of representational appropriation. Another implication is that representational appropriation is never socially innocent but proceeds on the basis of a multitude of social interpellations that are already active on the representing subject and will find symbolic translation in the representing act itself.

Edward Said established the basic and radical contention in *Orientalism* and *Culture and Imperialism* that Western attempts at knowledge of the oriental other *cannot* be divorced from designs for social (imperial) domination. Transcultural knowledge is already a problematic conceit from that perspective, and one could argue that it cannot in effect exist in any kind of pure form. And yet it exists, as endotopic projection on the other culture, in variously impure forms, all of them marked by their conditions of production in social relations. Latin Americanism shares with orientalism the fact that it too must be understood as an apparatus of mediation for transcultural social relations. As such, it suffers from the start from a dissymmetry that in fact constitutes it. Mediation does not operate as merely communicative action, that is, as a neutral apparatus of dialogical exchange. As a social relation itself, the Latin Americanist structure of mediation embodies a power differential. Latin Americanism is a dominantly Western producer of engaged representations regarding a largely subalternized set of cultural formations, instead of the other way around, even if "Western representation" in the case of Latin Americanism (as opposed to orientalism) is to a large extent intra-Latin American and reflects the much longer and more exhaustive colonial history of the area. The language itself in which the transcultural exchange takes place—the exchange between knowledge about culture and culture itself—is always already dominated by Latin Americanist representation. The dissymmetry of the Latin Americanist gaze is thus not to be reduced, because it is consubstantial to Latin Americanism itself.

It is in that sense that Latin Americanism cannot opt for a relativist framework—the question of relativism would seem to come too late for a dissymmetrical gaze always previously in place. S. P. Mohanty remarks in his investigation of the relevance of cultural relativism for contemporary critical practice that conceiving the other "outside of our inherited concepts and beliefs so as not to replicate the patterns of repression and subjugation we notice in the traditional conceptual frameworks" does not posit the need "to conceive the Other as a radically separable and separate entity" ("Us" 4, 5). In fact, insofar as the other is always caught up in the representation that delivers it as such, its separate positing would seem not so much relativism as untenable idealist voluntarism. The dissymmetrical gaze, however, does not entirely preempt the possibility of transcultural exchange. Endotopic knowledge of the other still must, at the limit, retain the possibility of a genuine opening to alterity if only because without the latter alterity would be radically unable to constitute itself. Even if epistemic representations of the other become, on being produced, themselves the producers or coproducers of the social field on which contact between human groups occurs, this social production must mediate forces of various kinds and thus remain, by definition, a site of political negotiation. Mohanty's call for the recognition of a common "minimal rationality," understood as the capacity of every human group to possess an alternate "meaningful history" (22), is acknowledgment that the hermeneutical moment requires interpretation and not explanation of a discursive object: in other words, that the discursive subject can never exhaust its object. "Two systems of understanding encounter each other to the very extent that both are contextualized as forms of life; this encounter leaves open the possibility of a fundamental change in both" (16). The political and critical negotiation of alterity necessarily incorporates an element of unpredictability: alterity is never in advance exhaustively dominated or even contained.

Latin Americanist appropriation is complex. The Latin Americanist gaze, whose historical origins are in colonial discourse, can in effect no longer be reduced, if it ever simply could, to the dissymmetry obtaining between an imperial site of knowledge production (and its attendant regional subsites of mimetic replication) and the colonial field on which it would exert itself. Even that seemingly relatively uncomplicated relation was limited by structural conditions regulating contact in general between human groups—conditions brought about because groups do not exhaustively know themselves and therefore, alterity is always present within every given group and contact only happens at the unrepresentable border or outer edge of the groups themselves. The Latin Americanist gaze was always more subject to the inconsistencies imposed by structural dissociation than its more faithfully imperial or proimperial practitioners would have desired. Under today's conditions that structural dissociation is no longer simply to be understood as colonial.

Dissymmetry still powerfully obtains in the form of historically conditioned epistemic constraints, but Latin Americanism can no longer be said to represent the discursive property of empire. As Walter Mignolo puts it in a programmatic essay on the matter, "Colonial and Postcolonial Discourse," globalization, new social movements, and immigrant demographic flows have had as a side effect the presence of an increasingly large number of what we could call points of inscription of heretofore subjugated voices and localities of enunciation within Latin Americanist discourse. Latin Americanist discourse must increasingly reconsider the received idea of itself as primarily metropolitan (or even metropolitanist) discourse on Latin American alterity. The irruption and multiplication of alternative sites of enunciation within the field means that the old and more or less stable and always in any case relative discursive monology no longer consistently holds. The metropolitan(ist) position of enunciation—and let me insist that such a position has historically not been the exclusive property of metropolitan intellectuals or institutions but has found ample productivity in Latin America as well, where it has codetermined all particular constructions of hegemonic formation and thus also the production of the Latin American subaltern in all of its complexity—cannot be taken for granted or accepted as an unquestioned or natural a priori of knowledge production. Thus, the structural dissociation within Latin Americanism itself, as a complex stage for the negotiation of social-epistemic alterity, has moved to the center of disciplinary preoccupations.

This state of affairs may be understood to represent either an unwelcome crisis in cultural epistemology or a more or less fateful opportunity for epistemology to address its historical conditions of production and redress some of its social and political determinations. In any case, Mohanty's comment on it, although by now rather a commonplace of liberal theoretical reflection, bears repetition: "For in our 'postmodern' world, History is no longer feasible; what we need to talk about, to pay attention to, are histories—in the plural. This position builds on the pervasive feeling in the human sciences these days that the grand narrative of history seems a little embarrassing; what we need to reclaim instead . . . is the plurality of our heterogeneous lives, the darker and unspoken densities of past and present that are lived, fought and imagined as various communities and peoples seek to retrace and reweave the historical text" (13).

Paradoxically enough, the existing plurality of heterogeneous enunciations within Latin Americanist discourse and the attendant shaking of dominant monology it implies have had as a direct consequence the reopening of the question of radical alterity. As that radical alterity no longer pertains in principle to those who for one reason or another have found a way to legitimize their voices, as women, as indigenous peoples, as members of new social movements, through testimonio, through oral history initiatives, or through documentary enterprises coordinated by NGOs and international foundations, if not through the direct passage into transnational circuits of cultural commodity production and distribution, undoubtedly something like what we might call an anxiety of the hybrid is at stake in these developments.[1] But there are other presumably stronger reasons why the questioning of historical monology should incorporate an investigation of alterity at the very same time that alterity is seemingly reduced by the irruption of heterogeneous voices within Latin Americanism: some are reasons having to do with historical restitution, and there are also reasons connected to present and future political articulations of claims for the preservation and promotion of whatever cultural heterogeneity might still be left to care for.

The breakup of historical monology produces attendant effects at all levels of Latin Americanist discourse. Michael Taussig symptomatically expresses the incorporation of the singular or individual voice of the Latin Americanist researcher within epistemic discourse in political terms. Reflecting on the explicit use of self-reflexive instances in anthropological work, he says: "This is not autobiography. This is not narcissistic self-indulgence. It is neither of these things because it first opens up to a science of mediations —neither Self nor Other but their mutual co-implicatedness—and second because it opens up the colonial nature of the intellectual relationship to which the contextualized other has for so long been subjected" (*Nervous System* 45). Taussig attributes to this practice alone the possibility of what he calls, following Walter Benjamin, a "redemption" of the Latin American object within Latin Americanism. It is a self-reflexivity that would shake Latin Americanist appropriation, thus leaving open the possibility of an irruption of alterity in the strong sense, that is, not alterity as the occasion for its reduction to familiarity, but alterity as the possibility of an event, of a legislation or a legitimation coming from the subjugated other. As he describes his own intellectual itinerary in *The Nervous System*, Taussig says: "The focus of worry shifted from the object of scrutiny to the mode of its presentation, for it is there, in the medium of presentation, that social theory and cultural practice rub one against and inform the other such that there is the chance, small as it might well be, of what I will call 'redeeming' the object—giving it another lease of life breaking through the shell of its conceptualizations so as to change life itself" (6).

The redemption of the object is then understood as a chance event, happening—perhaps—in or through the self-reflexive questioning of Latin Americanist presentation. It is interesting to note that Taussig will not claim that self-reflexivity is in itself a new kind of knowledge, or the possibility of a new epistemic paradigm, but only that it discloses the possibility of a heterotopic irruption or event of meaning that was blocked as such by an unrevised, oppressive conceptualization of the Latin Americanist object in Latin Americanist presentation. It is as if the implicit violence of Latin Americanist representation were now to be turned in on itself—as if, somehow, Latin Americanist representation could be taken as the alterity on which a new form of epistemic appropriation needs to occur, whereby the possibility would be released of an alternative politico-epistemic dispensation—"another lease of life . . . so as to change life itself."

Taussig's self-reflexivity, by questioning the Latin Americanist medium of presentation as precisely that which blocks communication with its object of reflexion, inaugurates a radical uncertainty as to whether communication with the object—or its effective recognition as a *subject* properly called—is at all possible. But it is then in this uncertainty itself that Latin Americanism would find the aleatory condition of its possibility as redemptive, including self-redemptive, knowledge. As Bennington says, only a self-motivated opening to the intrinsic violence of communication with the other can warrant the possibility of communication, since "communication takes place, if at all, in a fundamental and irreducible uncertainty as to the very fact and possibility of communication" (2).

What is at stake in alterity is certainly not alterity itself, but precisely this uncertain possibility of communication whereby the other can break through preconstituted representation and assert something like a new word: "The other, in so far as he, she or it *is* an other, always might be bringing me a new law. There is no real alterity unless the law I know is being cast into doubt. The problem, which looks in principle as though it ought to precede all questions that might be asked about meaning, or about determinate ethical and political issues, is that of knowing whether I am faced with an other, therefore a legislator, or not" (Bennington 2).

Any kind of opening to an endotopic knowledge of the other, such as Latin Americanist knowledge, is necessarily if uneasily open as well to the possibility of alterity as a radical excess in respect of itself. In this dangerous openness something like a Latin Americanist responsibility is at stake—in its acceptance, Latin Americanist knowledge runs the incessant risk of undergoing epistemic collapse. If knowledge of the other is always endotopic, then the possibility of irruption of alterity as legislation introduces—has always already introduced—something different from knowledge or domination of the other at the very heart of Latin Americanism: it introduces the founding possibility of nonknowledge, which is also the possibility of exotopic or heterotopic legislation, as the necessarily excessive ground of Latin Americanism.

But, once the possibility is granted as an "internal" possibility of Latin Americanist constitution, investigating its implications becomes a need of theoretical reflection. Latin Americanism must study its own excessive ground even if it is not yet willing to take the additional step of studying heterotopic legislation itself (through, for instance, subalternism). In other words, Latin Americanism must attempt to understand, and then incorporate into its discourse, the way in which its structural opening to alterity modifies or regulates its presence as social-epistemic production. There is a new urgency to this essential metacritical or theoretical preoccupation. As the old and relatively consistent historical monology of Latin Americanism breaks open, and as it starts to dawn on most Latin Americanist practitioners that, in Mignolo's words, "the Third World is not only an area to be studied but a place (or places) from which to speak" ("Colonial and Postcolonial Discourse" 123), a new and sustained reflection on the very bases and conditions of possibility of heterological production becomes determinant.

This gesture should be understood, politically, in the overall academic context of knowledge globalization as well. Post-area studies, in the United States and elsewhere, have become the new site for a politics of knowledge production whose main impetus generally emanates from the "clash of civilizations" paradigm articulated by Samuel Huntington on behalf of the U.S. political establishment, from the feeble multiculturalism of consumption that is the corporate response to the conflict model, or from both.² In any case, it would seem, a new epistemological neocolonizing machine is on its way, the epistemic counterpoint of the passage to empire, the parts of which are under frantic construction *also* in and through area studies' transdisciplinarity. It is important to begin engaging in a counterdiscourse to the regime of control whose primary aim should be not to oppose globalization but to question its epistemological thrust insofar as it may wish to remain blind to its own historical determinations and conditions of production. A Latin Americanist critical-regionalist counterdiscourse to globalization can only occur if Latin Americanism first understands itself as a historical subjugator of Latin American knowledge localities. Any appropriate revision of Latin Americanist discourse must be consistent with the metacritical realization that, even if the representation of radical otherness is not available to Latin Americanism except as idealist voluntarism, a precarious, contradictory, and perhaps unmanageable experience of alterity is at the material basis of its constitution.

If, through Latin Americanism's double injunction to reduce and preserve alterity, the conditions of possibility of Latin Americanism are shown to be at the same time the conditions of its impossibility, then such a momentous critical realization—not a new one but perhaps usable in new ways today—must be given appropriate leeway. It is incumbent on us to examine the conditions for the development of an alternative or second-order Latin Americanism in the understanding that it will not be possible to abandon the reduction and subordination of radical alterity. Latin Americanism is constituted in a double and contradictory injunction. Short of altogether renouncing it or of willingly suppressing the unsettling fact of its abyssal grounding, the double injunction must be brought to bear on Latin Americanist work. But the abyssal grounding of Latin Americanism is not necessarily to be understood as a merely negative determination: in good hermeneutics, its abyssal grounding, once recognized, is as much the source of its critical power as it is its defining limit.

The very conditions of possibility of Latin Americanist knowledge are given in an unequal transcultural exchange by means of which the dominant culture perpetuates its epistemic dominance as an extension of its social and political dominance. But the Latin

Americanist dissymmetrical gaze also secretly looks at its constitutive alterity, and by so doing it holds the possibility of its articulation as an alternative politico-epistemic dispensation. Through its opening to the alterity that founds it and gives it a field of vision a way seems to exist, perhaps precariously, in which Latin Americanism may step out of itself in order to arrest itself in its always necessarily unequal determinations.

The conditions that regulate Latin Americanist knowledge also and simultaneously regulate the conditions of its nonknowledge, of its essential blindness to the alterity it has always wanted to master; and the conditions that regulate Latin Americanism's foreclosure of alterity are also the conditions that force alterity into the foreground of Latin Americanism's self-understanding as epistemic endeavor. Two alterities, then, confront Latin Americanism: on the one hand, there is the alterity that comes to it from the Latin American singularities it has always *impossibly* at the same time attempted to tame into familiarity and to preserve or even restitute as singularities; on the other hand, there is the alterity that comes to it from its own distance with respect to Latin Americanist representation itself, from its own internal disengagement from itself, since Latin Americanism has always already known that its responsibility to the other—be it an internal other—made it impossible to fulfill the conditions that its responsibility to itself seemed to impose; it has always known it at the very least to the extent that it has already silenced or repressed it.

Like Abraham, Latin Americanism is caught in a double injunction: sacrificing Isaac can only be done at the cost of privileging obedience over love; but privileging obedience over love makes the sacrifice itself trivial—so that love must be privileged in order for some impossible sense to be restored to the sacrificial injunction. A difficult mediation obtains here—the field of vision that the dissymmetrical gaze articulates is always already disarticulated by it.[3] To begin thinking this difficult mediation is the overall goal of this chapter—and a fortiori of this book.

Standing Within and Standing Without

There is a rather enigmatic moment in Jorge Luis Borges's "Tlön, Uqbar, Orbis Tertius" in which the narrator, Borges, after telling us about the reduplication of lost objects, which is a feature of a universe already colonized by Tlön, mentions another kind of object: "Stranger and purer than any hrön is sometimes the ur: the thing produced by suggestion, the object educed by hope" (420; my trans., here and below). Since a *hrön* is a "secondary object" (419), an *ur* would be something like a primary object: as the object of desire, an ur is the thing itself, that is, not so much the real as its imaginary elaboration and concretization. It is then a properly ontological object, in the sense that it can give rise to an ontology. Latin America, as the site on which Latin Americanist representations develop, is precisely that sort of ontological efficient object for Latin Americanism: for Latin Americanism Latin America is also a "thing produced by suggestion, . . . educed by hope," where both "suggestion" and "hope" are understood as social producers, in consonance with the metaliterary articulation of "Tlön, Uqbar, Orbis Tertius." If the story narrates the history of the appropriation and substitution of "our world" by the Tlönian universe, the ur object would be the constitutive symptom of appropriation itself, or the site of its primary possibility. As primary object, over against the secondariness of the hrön, which is the properly Tlönian object and which we could therefore translate as the "proper" object of Latin Americanism, the ur object embodies the infrastructural possibility of Tlön itself as primary articulation, ontotheological ground, or being of beings: the "originary" positing, which is always postoriginary, in the sense that it occurs on what is previously indeterminately given.

"Tlön, Uqbar, Orbis Tertius" can be understood to allegorize a process of colonization of the real by the imaginary, in what amounts to one of the most extraordinary anti-utopias of modern literature. Within it, Borges's ur object metafictionally represents the Tlönian universe itself. But the metafictional function of the ur object conceals its ontological preeminence as ground, as the very condition of possibility of each and every colonization of the real by the imaginary. It is therefore, among other things, the founding object of Latin Americanism.

Latin Americanist representation can be said to be the libidinal projection, or the sum of libidinal projections, whose work historically constitutes Latin America as epistemic object. Within this understanding nothing of a representational nature can precede representation, because as Kant put it in his first critique, "the conditions of the *possibility of experience* in general are at the same time conditions of the *possibility of the objects of experience*" (*Critique of Pure Reason* A 138; B 197). Latin America is an ur object of Latin Americanist representation. But Borges has another way of talking about the ur object: the object that he calls a *joya* in "La perpetua carrera de Aquiles y la tortuga": a "limpidity that does not exclude the unpenetrable" ("Perpetua" 187; my trans., here and below). Of this joya he says at the end of "Avatares de la tortuga": "We (the undivided divinity that operates in us) have dreamed the world. We have dreamed it resistant, mysterious, visible, ubiquitous in space and firm in time; but in its architecture we have allowed tenuous and eternal interstices of unreason in order to know that it is false" (204). *Joya:* a tenuous object, a break in the real, or perhaps a break of the real. For Borges it is the Greek paradox of Achilles and the tortoise that constitutes such a jewel, because the paradox would offer an absolutely resisting instance of epistemic disarticulation. The disarticulation of the truth of the world is therefore reconceptualized, in turn paradoxically, as epistemic truth: not the consistency of the given but its fundamental inconsistency is the given. The ur object under this determination does not give rise to an ontology but will still remain as the necessary precondition for any ontology. As the object around which, or in the presence of which, presence itself flounders, this "tenuous" jewel points to the unpresentable site of siting or the abyssal ground for any ontotheology: still an originary positing, revealing this time the indeterminateness of the ground on which it occurs. This alternative conceptualization of the ur object unconceals the imaginary quality of its production and of any epistemic production in general. It signals, therefore, the very possibility of a radical critique of representation. Under this determination, Latin America is still always the ur object of epistemic representation, except that now it appears as the site of resistance to it or as its abyssal moment. From the perspective of the ur object, we could say, any Latin Americanism of the hrön is nothing but "prose of counterinsurgency."

Let me then appropriate the Borgesian ur object as the allegorical cipher of my own critical determination to go beyond Latin Americanist representation. I would claim that Latin Americanist representation is necessarily a failed thinking of the ur object, in the double sense specified above: on one hand, it projects Latin America, and with it any given Latin American object of representation, as an object "produced by suggestion" and "educed by hope," an epistemic object of desire that nevertheless includes as its own ontological specification that it be not only an object of appropriation, but, also even more significantly, an object of restitution. Without this internal self-determination of the object to be returned to the real, as it were, or to escape the network of desire that in the first place produces it, the Latin American ur object could not (have) become the foundational ground that it constitutes for the vast epistemic enterprise of Latin Americanism. In other words, even if nothing representational preexists representation, representation feeds on the radical alterity in whose denial and through whose denial as such it constitutes itself.

On the other hand, then, Latin Americanist representation is necessarily a thinking of the ur object in the second Borgesian sense — which I will not hesitate to present as a sense whose acceptance is of essential importance for a subalternist articulation of Latin Americanist reflection — because it incorporates this nagging resistance to itself as an apparatus for appropriation and restitution, on awareness that there is an essential falsity to any given representation as such and that it is this falsity of representation that, once revealed, is alone able paradoxically to preserve the possibility of epistemic truth through the radical opening to alterity it first grants. If Latin Americanist representation in the first Borgesian sense is the necessary locus for epistemic mediation, then Latin Americanist representation in the second sense leads into a suspension or arrest of the mediational enterprise. I argue in several ways in what follows that, even if both senses of Latin Americanist representation are equiprimordial (one cannot exist without the other, in the same way that a second-order Latin Americanism cannot exist without its historically constituted counterpart, dirty atopics means nothing without locational thinking, and there is no passage to real subsumption without apparent subsumption), only the second has the potential to flourish into an effective metacritical articulation, against the appropriation and beyond the restitution that the first one institutes. It is not in any case a matter of positing two different kinds of Latin Americanist representation:, but instead, of positing two senses of it, thoroughly co-implicated, the second of which makes a destabilizing or ruining move regarding the first. The destabilizing move, *insofar as it be made explicit,* can ruin the focus of the dissymmetrical gaze and thus shake its hold on its object. I will first offer two examples of this move toward metacritical articulation; these are also examples of a move to go from within Latin Americanism toward the outside of Latin Americanism, to its limit.

The double and contradictory as well as strangely complementary possibility of the Borgesian ur object, as possibility of representation *and* as impossibility of representation, is replicated by another Latin American commentary on the paradox of Achilles and the tortoise: Roger Bartra's "Axolotiada" (*Jaula* 81–83). For Bartra the race is imagined as a race between a porpoise and an axolotl, the latter understood as a mythical or traditional symbol of an alleged Mexican difference. In Bartra's rendering, the porpoise can never catch up with the axolotl, which produces a double effect, or at any rate the possibility of a double effect, derived from the "moral" of Bartra's fable: "the civilized porpoise should never concede any kind of advantage to the primitive axolotl, since it is known that its presence causes strange distortions in the normal course of time's reel" (82; my trans., here and below). According to this first possibility, a disarticulation ensues: the porpoise "must accept that there are things that are alien to the universe he knows; that there are separate and incoherent worlds, between which there are no congruous connections. . . . to the extent that, thanks to modern reason, the world becomes more consistent, more evidence appears that there are truths that escape the dominant system. The only way some have found of grasping the Other, the other truths, consists of dismantling the consistency of their world; but then one falls into the vertigo of total disorder, the delirium of the absence of limits and borders, the realm of entropy" (82–83). The latter part of this passage insinuates the second possibility.

For Bartra, the perplexity of the porpoise is a function of the fact that his speed is in inverse proportion to his capacity to overtake the axolotl: the more speed he develops the more perturbing his inability to reach his goal. The porpoise must therefore accept that the axolotl swims in an alternate space, or that the time lag between his course and that of the axolotl is irreducible. What must the porpoise do? But Bartra now engages in pronominal ambiguity: in one reading of the text, the porpoise confronts his own presumption of living in a coherent, closured universe and opens himself to the Borgesian thought of the ur object; under a different reading, the porpoise pro-

ceeds to destroy the consistency of the axolotl's universe by disavowing it: "the only way some have found of grasping the Other . . .
consists of dismantling the consistency of their world" (82). "Their"
undecidably refers to "some porpoise" or else to "Other," that is, to
the axolotl.

According to the latter reading, the porpoise, in the position of
epistemological subject, relates to alterity following a paradigm of
violent, interested, and reductive conceptualization, where alterity
is put at the service of epistemological self-reassurance: "when some
ideas—escaped from the Other—are transposed into this world in
a mythified and domesticated way, they create a sensation of tran-
quility, legitimacy, and power" (83). The price to be paid is always
charged to the other: "vertigo of total disorder . . . delirium of the
absence of limits and borders," where the axolotl must accept the
melancholy fact that her world has withdrawn, has fallen into loss,
and is no longer there.

According to the first reading, however, the porpoise accepts the
destruction of his own world's consistency in view of the irreducible
heterogeneity of the axolotl's space. What the porpoise gains in the
order of knowledge he loses in the order of affect: it is now the porpoise's speed that vanishes as such, since he must confront its illusory quality, and his world comes to loss. As epistemological subject the porpoise can no longer believe that "the entire universe [is]
mediated by infinite connections, in such a way that we can reach
any point from where we are, jumping from one connection to the
other, in a chain of transcendences that leaves us with the illusion of
escaping contradictions, always progressing toward synthesis" (82).
The porpoise has suffered epistemic arrest in the collapse of his
grand recit, and it would be up to him to turn his predicament into a
merely nostalgic or an affirmative opportunity. Except that affirmation, in this reading, can no longer seemingly mediate itself through
the appropriation and substitution of the axolotl's universe. The porpoise must apparently then renounce Latin Americanism, in the recognition that difference is not simply a contradiction to be negated,
mediated, and subsumed in a final synthesis but that, precisely, the
very presence of the axolotl signals the positive presence of a disaster in dialectics, an interruption of the incessant possibility of Latin
Americanist closure. And yet perhaps things are not so simple.

In the 1987 book that includes "Axolotiada," *La jaula de la melan-*

colía, Bartra is not directly speaking about Latin Americanism as such but about its avatar or substantiation in the context of the Mexican post-revolutionary state. Bartra's project is to link Mexican discourse on national identity to the Mexican state's need for political self-legitimation. In that sense, Bartra shows how "the definition of 'the Mexican' is rather a description of how the Mexican comes to be dominated and, above all, of the way in which exploitation comes to be legitimated" (22). In other words, Mexican thinking on Mexican national identity is understood by Bartra as an important part of what he calls "the imaginary networks of political power,"⁴ a structure of mediation whose effectivity resides in the fact that it manages the resolution, at the level of the epistemic imaginary, of "the deepest structures of social conflict" (35). Bartra understands this process, in the context of Mexican history, as the continuation of colonial power—not its mere product or a secondary manifestation, but an essential aspect of the implementation of postcolonial state power as such; that is, in itself a producer of social domination: "in the process of construction and invention of the nation—and therefore of national character—we always stumble on a paradoxical confrontation with otherness. In this confrontation the space of one's consciousness becomes populated with stereotypes and master tropes that, in turn, effect a relative influence in the behavior of the people" (50–51).⁵ We begin to see that the axolotl, once understood by the porpoise as an irreducible alterity, may be something other than irreducible alterity: that it might in fact only be—or, at any rate, *also* be—the precipitate of alterity into stereotype: a hrön, and not an ur object.

Mexican national identity would be an elaborate *transposition* (Bartra's word) of social conflict into the cultural sphere, and therefore a symbolic cipher of a peculiar kind of state domination as well as a tool of domination in itself. Mexican intellectuals are said to be generally complicitous with it, insofar as their role in the production of a national-popular culture helps the consolidation of state power: "there is nothing particularly Mexican in the structure of this metadiscourse [on Mexican national-popular identity]: it amounts to an adaptation of patterns that are narrowly linked to capitalist development and the consolidation of national states. That is, to what we call the modern West" (*Jaula* 230). The cultural domestication of class struggle through the recourse to national-popular identity myths guarantees the continued stability of the state apparatus. But what Bartra calls "the axolotl canon," that is, the cultural basis for an affirmation of Mexican difference or alterity, in counterdistinction to the Mexican national identity promoted by the ideological state apparatus Bartra describes, is in turn reappropriated for identity thinking in its conversion into "symbol, sign, and mask" (203). The porpoise can ultimately conclude that the axolotl resists him because . . . , well, because she is an axolotl. At that point the axolotl can no longer keep claiming irreducible alterity, because her alterity has been domesticated and reduced through the simple devise of identification. The possibility must then be considered that the axolotl was never anything but a figment of the porpoise's imagination, its imaginary other, the very slack he cut himself in order to have some space for his enterprise of self-legitimation. Of this realization, Bartra says, "it was necessary to flee from unendurable *patrioterismo*, and search for reality. There it was possible to pay homage to radical alterity, to critique, to dissidence, and to freedom. But this alterity soon turned into metaphor and mask, and it was necessary to start anew" (203).

We discover in this last citation its metacritical component, in the sense that Bartra thinks of his own critical project as a new departure, beyond all national populism, in search of the radical alterity of which the axolotl could once seem to have held the secret. Bartra's Latin American(ist) paradigm of self-conceptualization proceeds through a constant critique of state identitarianism. Historically, if national-popular identity was the privileged product of Mexican intellectual articulation between, roughly, 1915 and 1955, although it had precedents in Porfirist positivism and sequels all the way down to the present, then the constitution of the axolotl canon can be linked to the Latin American boom novel and its promotion of magical realism: "how to transform an opaque, oppressive, and prosaic subjectivity into a amorous, poetic, and spiritual reality? The answer was precise: magical realism is the means to conjure up a wonderful history full of promises. The axolotl, in her stubborn and childish refusal of change, reveals to us a real-marvelous world where immobility can be a discovery and solitude a way of calling for the mutiny of the new species" (202–03). The destruction of the axolotl canon that Bartra accomplishes in his book would seem to warn us that no tenuous break in the real can stop the pull of the efficient toward ontotheological identity formation unless we can find a way to dwell in the disjuncture that would enable us to turn Latin Americanist reflection into a contrary apparatus of representation: an apparatus of counterrepresentation whose possibility would be granted in the blinding side of the Borgesian postoriginary primary, the side that looks at the unpresentable site of Latin Americanist reflection.

Bartra goes a good way toward this, but his own model must also in turn become appropriated by the dissymmetrical gaze. His critique of state appropriation, insofar as it is a critique, would seem to presuppose a secure ground from which to stage it: the ur object in its first possibility as infrastructural determination secretly haunts Bartra's text, until it overtakes it. Bartra also speaks from a position of Latin Americanist distance: his Latin Americanism is still a form of representational appropriation in which the alterity that remains is ambiguously put to work for the critical enterprise as the formal alterity of Latin Americanism itself. Once all identity and all difference have been showed to be state mediations furthering the political self-legitimation of the postcolonial state apparatus, then Bartra's appropriation can do nothing but claim for itself the sort of singular exteriority that is, precisely, only accorded to the state as ground for the universal mediation of social conflict. With this, Bartra acknowledges that the conditions of possibility of his state critique are also at the same time the limiting conditions of its impossibility: the substitution of the counterlucidity of the thinker for the lucidity of the state is no solution to the constitutive alterity of representational thinking, since it merely reestablishes it. What happened to the axolotl, thought of as ur object? Should we simply abandon it?

The axolotl canon is for Bartra intrinsically linked to magical realism as embodiment of a particular kind of Latin Americanist response to the problems of cultural difference. In *Shamanism, Colonialism, and the Wild Man*, however, Taussig talks about two sides of magical realism. Firstly, Taussig says, magical realism, insofar as it responds to "the persistence of earlier forms of production in the development of capitalism," insists on images "that intermingle the old and the new as ideals transfiguring the promise offered yet blocked by the present" (167). Magical realism points to the past in a radical way, so as to elicit those Benjaminian "dialectical images" by means of which "the dreaming collective of the past" could be reawakened in order "to break out of history's mythic spell" (166).

Magical realism, thus, would offer the possibility of "rescuing the 'voice' of the Indian from the obscurity of pain and time. From the represented shall come that which overturns the representation" (135). In this characterization, magical realism is a practice of the efficient object as well as a redemptive practice. As such, it looks for the presentation of the unpresentable: it wants to bring to life the "fiesta innombrable que nunca se llegó a realizar" (the immorable feast that never took place) (Sarduy, "Imágenes" 5), although it can only do so in a surrogate way, that is, through representation. This understanding of magical realism is doubtlessly congenial to the one Bartra identifies and critiques in the Latin American boom novelists. The basis of Bartra's critique was that magical realism was merely a form of compensation for a fallen reality emanating from elite writers who understood themselves as educators of the people following the model of the state. Taussig, however, in this first characterization, chooses to emphasize its anti-state, messianic, or even revolutionary potential. As a restitution of voice, magical realism lets us hear the promise of a transfigured present. Magical realism would thus constitute a differential, counterrepresentational instance of Latin Americanism: something like an axolotl canon.

But secondly, Taussig offers an alternative characterization, one that overturns magical realism, puts it on its head, and makes it appear as, in his words, "not just primitivism, but third-world modernism, a neocolonial reworking of primitivism" (*Shamanism* 172). These are strong words indeed, based as they are on a painstaking analysis throughout the book in which Taussig shows how "the colonizer reifies his myths about the savage, becomes subject to their power, and in so doing seeks salvation from the civilization that torments him as much as the savage on whom he has projected his anti-self" (211). From this perspective, magical realism shows its hidden face as an always necessarily demonizing representation of the subaltern by the hegemonic. The othering at stake here is engaged with the reification of alterity, not with its mere presentation. Under this characterization magical realism is still a redemptive practice, but its character has fundamentally changed, in virtue of being understood differently. Under this new hermeneutic light, magical realism appears as an aberrant redemption, one that has gone astray in its representational strategy in the thorough reification of its subject. In this version, magical-realist representation has thoroughly overturned the represented. Its second sense has overtaken the first: by being made explicit, it has operated a destabilization of its object. Taussig's critique of magical realism is configurative of a theoretical practice, slightly different from Bartra's, in which thinking is put at the service of an arrest of thinking. Taussig's critique of magical realism looks at the unpresentability of the presented, and unveils representation as a purely hallucinatory practice with concrete political consequences. And through it we see that magical realism is not the simply redemptive affair of differential representation that Latin American boom novelists had attempted to persuade us it was. Once again, the possibility of magical realism shows itself to be also its impossibility.

Borges's, Bartra's, and Taussig's reflections are faithful to the contradictory and double injunction of Latin Americanism. They follow a particular kind of Latin Americanist appropriation, with personal variations, and they respond to the dissymmetrical gaze according to a certain call of responsibility. This responsibility of and to the double injunction attends, on the one hand, to the Latin Americanist call for the representation of the singular (Borges on the real resisting colonization by the imaginary, Bartra on the axolotl canon and the abandonment of the axolotl canon, and Taussig on magical realism as voice restitution); but, on the other hand, it also attends to that which in Latin Americanism organizes the political dominance of endotopic representation (Borges on the ur object as libidinal appropriation, Bartra on the Mexican state apparatus, and Taussig on magical realism as a neocolonial reworking of primitivism). By following this double injunction, these authors respond to Latin Americanism's double alterity: to the alterity of unrepresentable singularity, of which Taussig had said that it might irrupt as if by chance, as an event that could only be aleatorily announced but never concretely organized; and to the alterity of Latin Americanism itself as the epistemic apparatus of the dissymmetrical gaze. Something other than epistemic appropriation seems to be at stake in these gestures, even something contrary to it: in spite of Bartra's ultimate subsumption of the object into epistemic desire, which is suspended in Borges and in Taussig, there is in all three of these endeavors a renunciation of knowledge or an opening to nonknowledge that is, however, far from a fall into blindness; an attempt to give back to alterity what alterity claims, in order to let alterity collect its dues, to cover the debt. Let me call it restitution.

Restitution as Excess

At the end of "The Philomela Project," his essay on restitutive criticism, Geoffrey Hartman makes the seemingly obvious point that restitution can only restitute a lost object. Hartman's critique of restitution—a project that he generally identifies with New Historicism and its attempts at "righting wrongs" "giving voice to the voiceless" (170, 175)—is, as I understand it, twofold: in the first sense he says, "if there is a symbiosis between a discipline and what it seeks to recover, [then] criticism today is engaged in a project of *self-restitution.*" (168). Restitution as self-restitution would be a compromised endeavor, Hartman implies, because, through it, "criticism would exercise its power to revalue an alienated practice and enlarge itself at the same time" (168). There is but a short step, often taken, between "[revaluing] an alienated practice and [enlarging] itself at the same time" and revaluing said practice *in order to* enlarge itself.

Self-restitution in restitution would certainly seem to come close to a mercenary criticism of the worst kind. Self-restitution, understood in this sense, would be the dangerous limit of any kind of positing of the axolotl canon as well as of any deconstruction of the axolotl canon: that in restitution that makes of the restitutional enterprise a self-deluded attempt at aberrant self-redemption. In terms of the above discussion, self-restitution would sum up Taussig's words about the colonizer's reification of the savage as a sort of general allegory of criticism's engagement with the other for the sake of self. But it could also sum up Bartra's gesture regarding the establishment of the exceptional singularity of the critic who can see through it all. In other words, self-restitution would be the cipher for a disavowed and thus an all the more insidious form of critical appropriation: a restoration of Latin Americanism to its position as a discourse of the dominant under the guise of its opposite number as counterrepresentation.

I will come back to self-restitution. Hartman's second critique is engaged with contemporary identity politics or what Cornel West has called, in what is by now a fairly old essay, "the new cultural politics of difference."[6] It directly affects, in however mediated a way,

the assumption that in one of its two faces Latin Americanist restitution is to do with the representation, as well as the impossibility
thereof, of the Latin American singular. Let me then tackle it first.
Although Hartman affirms that "it is not restitution that is attacked
by deconstruction but the use of restitutive pathos," (172), he sets
up the kind of restitution articulated in and through identity politics as somehow deconstruction's betrayal. The restitutive pathos of
identity politics seems to imply for Hartman "a reactive desire for
charismatic closure, and so the movement of a metaphysics of presence into the political process" (172). This is the "bad" ingredient of
restitution, from which we should take our distance, as it amounts
to an "instrumentalism in disguise" (173), concealing in its pathos a
"politics of desire once associated with messianic religion and now
responsible for political theologies" (172). In this sense, of course,
Hartman's second critique appears as a mere development of the
first, because restitutive pathos would be but an extension of self-
restitution as aberrant redemption: "There is no end to the demand
for 'identity,' as something available to groups or individuals, yet denied them by the social order. The new emphasis on identity is like a
rash left by movements that have rigorously questioned it in philosophy, fiction, and social thought. We seem to be passing from exquisite scruples about the 'question of the subject' to a credal insistence
on the 'subject position.' To confess 'where one is coming from' is
no longer a modesty topos but a required affirmation" (169).

Self-reflexivity would then be the blind extension of self-restitution into the critical engagement with the other. But critiquing
the "bad" restitutive pathos of identity politics, important as it may
be, hardly does justice to the more fundamental importance of restitution as a critical opening to alterity—to the alterity of the general, as in, for instance, Latin Americanist representation, and to the
alterity of the singular, as that on which the general exerts its dominance. In fact, Hartman's text takes a rather bizarre critical turn
at this point: his use of deconstruction, or of the legacy of deconstruction, as stabilizing jetty against the barbarous waters of pathetic
identities effectively blinds him to the force of restitution in the deconstructive process. Hartman's final endorsement of restitution as
achieved recognition ("Recognition is the key rather than restitution, though restitution is often the acknowledgment of an achieved
recognition" [174]) puts an end to his critical consideration of resti-

tution by offering it as a static, reified, limiting notion of something that should be accomplished or achieved, as opposed to offering it as a dynamic counterconcept to critical appropriation and its ruses against alterity.[7]

If restitution can only restitute, as Hartman says, a lost object, then it will behoove us to interrogate the possibility and dimensions of lost-object restitution—which Hartman doesn't do, because it appears that for him restitution is not really of a lost object but rather of an object allegedly refound. His abandonment of that which will be always and already lost may well betray or reveal a kind of politics of desire more essentially concerned with presence and with the appropriation of presence than it itself would ever be willing to admit. A political limit seems to be in place here that forces Hartman to withdraw the positive critical force of restitution from its use in identity politics. Hartman himself says that "the problem facing us is that this age of restitution is also an age of resentment" (169). But Jameson had already shown that this ideologeme of resentment is hardly a purely theoretical tool of analysis, because, it would seem, every time it appears, it appears as "little more than an expression of annoyance at seemingly gratuitous lower-class agitation, at the apparently quite unnecessary rocking of the social boat. It may therefore be concluded that the theory of ressentiment, wherever it appears, will always itself be the expression and the production of ressentiment" (*Political Unconscious* 202).[8]

Through the entanglement of his essay in social resentment Hartman is carried away into setting up an aberrant figure of deconstruction as institutional resistance to restitutional pathos. The institutional articulation of Hartman's reflection is clear in his peculiar arrest of critical history: "Perhaps only one thing is certain after such movements as deconstruction. . . . Essentialism is instrumentalism in disguise; and instrumentalized reading has been the norm [in identity politics]" ("Philomela" 173). But resistance to restitution under the form of resistance to the restitutional pathos of identity might be covering up a resistance to deconstruction as what Derrida has called the *destabilizing* jetty ("Some Statements" 84). And yet there is the critical possibility of a destabilizing force of restitution as restitution of a lost object even within the context of identity politics, which is also the cultural politics of an impossible difference. Restitution would then be that in identity that exceeds identity and that is beyond identity: "the force of the movement which throws something or throws itself forward and backwards at the same time, prior to any subject, object, or project, prior to any rejection or abjection" ("Some Statements" 84), for it is not restitution that is the pathos of identity but rather identity that is the pathos of restitution, its lost object or mourning affect, and in this different genitive restitution throws itself out as the excess of all articulations of difference and identity, which is why restitution is the contrary element of appropriation. There is no end to restitution, for restitution exceeds the end and the beginning, remaining as the call of thinking wherever thinking must think following its necessity.

Restitution, thus defined, appears to be the very ground of thought, a kind of longing for the ur object which mimics both the ur object's stability as ontotheological ground *and* its destability as ontotheological abyss. This is itself an old thought, indeed one of the oldest philosophical themes in the Western tradition, going back as far as Anaximander. Anaximander's fragment talks about *tísis*, variously translated in the tradition as *retribution, penalty, recompense*, and which Heidegger (rather, his English translators) translate as *reck*, so that *didónai tísin* would be letting reck belong, and the operation would take place "in the surmounting of disorder" ("Anaximander Fragment" 57). As letting reck belong in the surmounting of disorder, being restitutes, following necessity and *katá ten tou khrónou taksin*, that is, according to the ordering of time. "Following necessity" is *katá tó khreón*. For Heidegger, "*tó khreón* is the oldest name in which thinking brings the Being of beings to language" (49). As this khreón is also the way logos dwells, khreón is the need of thought and the usage of thought. Thought dwells in restitution, as thought, and in particularly concrete ways disciplinary thought means to give back to things what belongs to things according to a certain necessity. That necessity of thinking is its restitutional dimension. Without it no ur objects would ever become a problem for the solipsistic subject, who could no longer be considered a subject of knowledge.

In his essay on Derrida's *Specters of Marx*, Jameson has identified the Heideggerian reflection on Anaximander as "virtually the dead center of all of Derrida's meditations on Heidegger" ("Marx's Purloined Letter" 88). Heidegger's "The Anaximander Fragment" not only originally thematizes restitution of Being as the lost object of

Western thinking, but at the same time it explicitly focuses on restituting Anaximander's fragment into its rightful place as "the incipient saying of being" *and* constitutes, in Jameson's words, "one of the rare places in which Heidegger is willing directly to evoke [and thus restitute] a spatio-temporal system radically different from our own, and even willing to make a stab at describing it for his (necessarily) modern readership, [and where Heidegger] attempts to underscore the radical distinction of a pre-Socratic experience of the world from the one familiar to us from Aristotle to Hegel (and no doubt beyond)" (88).[9]

I think Jameson is right in relating the importance Derrida accords to this engagement of Heidegger with the singular other to spatio-temporal enjoinment/disjoinment (*Fug/ Unfug*), since the latter play of enjoinment and disjoinment would be one of the classical themes of deconstruction (going back to Derrida's early readings of Husserl). But Jameson is perhaps even more correct in arguing that "The Anaximander Fragment" is also a symptomatic place where Heidegger falls prey to the voluntarism of "positing a phenomenon whose fundamental formal trait lies in its radical difference from everything we know, its resistance to all the categories by which we currently think our own world" ("Marx's Purloined Letter" 89). Jameson's objection is of interest to us because it links up with the question of whether Latin Americanism, or any epistemics of the other (including, of course, philology in its full sense) can ever think, and if so under what terms, of representing singular difference following restitutional parameters. Something like the relative consistency of Latin Americanism, and any epistemics of regional knowledge, with Western metaphysics is at stake. It is necessary in this sense to reflect on the fact that Latin Americanism, in its epistemic and political possibilities, may (or may not) stand and fall with Western philosophy, with Western philosophy's thinking of alterity, and even with Western philosophy's capacity to open itself to that that does not come from within itself but that remains stubbornly exotopic and heterogeneous to it.

For Jameson, Heidegger engages in idealist voluntarism in positing radical difference, "an idealism which conceives of the mind as being free enough to range among the possibilities and sovereignly to choose to think a form radically excluded by the dominant system" ("Marx's Purloined Letter" 88). This sort of idealism is certainly not Heidegger's property, although it would have played a part in his interest in the Nazi "revolution," but "[it] is equally at work in other (extreme leftist) versions of radical social change, and even, in a different form, in liberal fantasies of the ways in which rational argument and public persuasion might be capable of bringing about systemic modifications in the logic of our social life" (89). The tension between restitution and what we could think of as its accomplishment (or, to use a term that will be discussed in chapter 8, its "arbitrary closure") in the positing (in Jameson's use of the term meaning the explicitation or substantiation) of radical difference is certainly strong, and it frames a serious danger or sets a trap for Latin Americanism and other similar epistemic endeavors. Achieved restitution was the basis of Hartman's caveat regarding the reactive work of identity politics, which was certainly linked in our own analysis with Bartra's and Taussig's critique of aberrant-redemptive appropriation of Latin American alterity. Jameson's argumentation, however, seems at the limit to preempt the very possibility of legitimation of philological and ethnographic work: insofar as philology, for instance, seeks to understand the truth of an older symbolic system, which would also by definition seem to be excluded by the present dominant. Between restitution, then, as the necessity of thought, and its accomplishment as achieved restitution, a way must be found to restitute the very possibility of thinking alterity (which is not the same thing as restituting alterity's positivity as found object).

It could be argued that there is no real scarcity of Heideggerian lapses into the representation of radical difference, insofar as, from a certain formal perspective at least (that is, in reference to philological method), there is no substantial difference between what Heidegger does with the fragment in question and what he does elsewhere in his numerous engagements with pre-Socratic philosophy, and also with Hölderlin, with Rilke, and with Trakl, given that all these poets are taken to embody an uncanny singularity (albeit Rilke to a lesser extent). Thus, although for Jameson "it must be this side of Heidegger's thought which is necessarily unacceptable to Derrida, [for whom] the positing of a realm of difference, the positive description of such a realm, is inadmissible" ("Marx's Purloined Letter" 89), I do not quite think that Heidegger's philology of otherness would merely warrant Derrida's antipathy. Heidegger's attempt at the concrete articulation of "a realm of difference" in Anaximander is after all perhaps no more than an extreme case of his frequent investigations concerning the poetic saying or articulation of what consistently remains the vortex of his own thinking: the beckoning Unsaid of onto-historical being. It is in that sense also a site for the possible arrival or "invention" of the other, which Derrida theorizes with intense sympathy in "Envois" (*Postcard* 11–273) and "Psyché" among other texts and which constitutes the basis of his affirmative politics of justice in later texts such as *Specters of Marx* and *Politics of Friendship*. Justice is nothing but restitution. The opening to an "invening" or other arrival, always in that sense "messianic," is the necessary and sufficient restitutional demand within any epistemics of the other.

So, even if it is true that, carried away by the restitutional need (the restitution of the Being of beings) that oriented his thought at least since the preparatory seminars for the writing of *Being and Time*,[10] Heidegger simply falls into what could be considered the idealist trap of explicitly representing pre-Socratic singularity, we nevertheless need to see that representing or "positing" the singularity of the other is not the forceful outcome of the restitutional process. It is true that restitution first enables or makes it possible. However, the singularity of the other remains in restitutional excess because it is the necessary excess of restitution, the beyond that beckons restitution and sets the ground for its necessity: its ur object, always beyond the phenomenological events of "losing" and "finding." And if this is so in terms of general historical-philological time in its conjunctions and disjunctions, it is so a fortiori for transdisciplinary discourses concerned with alterity, such as Latin Americanism. From the perspective of those who must listen to beckoning singularities, the formal differences between a pre-Socratic experience of the world and the Aymara experience (or even the Salvadoran experience during the recent civil war) are not as significant as their structural condition of alterity and its ceaseless restitutory claim on us. This is true even if we are also structurally conditioned by actually existing epistemic paradigms into being unable ever to accomplish restitution, so that restitution therefore remains essentially related to the loss or permanent withdrawal of the object of restitution.[11]

It is time to approach two essays by Enrico Mario Santí, who first explicitly thematized and then developed the fundamental relationship between restitution and Latin Americanism. The first published essay, "Latinamericanism and Restitution" (1992), is the first essay I know of to make use of the term *Latin Americanism* in explicit connection with Said's notion of orientalism. It is however in Santí's second essay, "Sor Juana, Octavio Paz, and the Poetics of Restitution" (1993), which incorporates much of the first, where we find a foundational, full-fledged, and densely textured reading of restitution in the sense in which I am using the term (which, therefore, I am pleased to genealogically restitute to him). I conclude this section with an analysis and elaboration of some aspects of Santí's text because it will serve as a point of encounter for several of the major themes I have so far presented in this chapter, and it will also appropriately frame the next and final section.

Santí understands restitution as a form of compensatory hermeneutics of the lost object in Hartman's sense: "As a means of symbolic exchange, . . . restitution exacts more than what was originally taken away. Yet a corollary of the same symbolic logic would be that, if so, then we can never exact what was originally lost. For better or for worse, restitution returns more of the same or something else" ("Sor Juana" 105). Restitution embodies then a "surplus economy," one of whose enactments would be philology: "philology is directed at disengaging the *meaning* of a text, deemed to be a function of its linguistic structure and historical context, from the *truth* of a text, which is a function of its interpretation and therefore subject to the changing ideological needs of its readers." The interplay between meaning and truth in the philological enterprise is a necessary feature: in interpretation meaning is never uncontaminated by truth or vice versa. However, insofar as it remains the case that interpretation is always undertaken from within a historically given hermeneutics properly speaking, then "in interpretation truth exceeds meaning" (106) and not the other way around. And with this the ground is set for Santí's definition of restitution (which is however given earlier in the text): "restitution is supplementary in character—in compensating for a previous lack, it exceeds rather than simply restores the original" (104).

Santí associates restitutional excess, through a brief excursion into nineteenth-century philology, with Hartman's notion of self-restitution: "Rather than represent the past in its irreducible otherness, its purported goal, philology translates and reinvents it in the name of mastery of the present Self" ("Sor Juana" 107). For Santí, however, in this ideological mission of philology it was not the critic's self that was in need of self-mastery; instead, what was involved was philology's own self-mastery at the service of national restoration: "to overcome alienation and restore wholeness and harmony, viewing the past not merely as an antiquarian object but as broken pieces of a past whose reintegration into present life would restore a continuity between past and present" (107). Santí's understanding of self-restitution in disciplinary-political terms gives us an important clue that will enable us to pull away from the restrictive notion that ciphers it in the individual critic's recuperation of a stable locus of enunciation.

What is primary in self-restitution is not necessarily one's own self, that is, the self of the individual critic or scholar, but the epistemic self such as the power-knowledge grid permits it or constitutes it. Self-restitution in this sense attends to a certain kind of professional responsibility as much as it manifests itself in tension with it because there is also restitutional excess in self-restitution. The excess in self-restitution refers to the alterity of Latin Americanism itself, and it organizes the very possibility of epistemic change on one of its sides. Without self-restitution, in effect, there would be no need for epistemic development, as epistemic discourse would simply come to be a static location of blissful self-concordance. Self-restitution is the place of disciplinary or epistemic politics, precisely the site where the multiple negotiations among subjective localities of enunciation, the singular alterity of the object, and the general alterity of disciplinary discourse take place. Self-restitution is therefore not a limiting condition of knowledge but an enabling and hermeneutically positive one; it is also essentially necessary. Self-restitution is, in terms discussed before, university discourse. But it is also something else.

Self-restitution, understood in individual terms, was at the basis of Hartman's accusations against critical sympathy with a certain understanding of identity politics. Santí also effectively condemns it: "Be they called academic exoticism, colonial tolerance, or plain tokenism, benign forms of restitution usually have one thing in common: when unchecked, they subordinate the Other to the Self's salvational perspective. Rather than recognize the Other's stubborn difference—which would lead to a further humbling recognition of the Other's equality, or perhaps, superiority—our restitutions often pigeonhole the Other within prescribed institutional roles that are designed to fit the Self's mystified self-righteousness. They claim to work on behalf of the Other but they actually work to ease the Self's historical conscience" ("Sor Juana"128).

I have no quarrel with these remarks in themselves, as I also did not have with Hartman's similar protests.[12] My objection is rather to the implication that self-restitution must always necessarily lead into the traps Santí describes. By claiming it, Santí's critical operation, like Hartman's, becomes an operation of arbitrary closure through the drawing of a political limit and thus is no longer deconstruction. If, according to Santí, the epistemological or philological grid that first makes the disciplinary object possible at the same time conceals the object and constitutes it in partial loss, thereby assuring that the demand for restitution will continue to make itself heard (and therefore guaranteeing the survival of the discipline), there would not seem to be a good reason to claim that the same mechanism does not apply to self-restitution: the epistemic subject is always also constituted in partial loss. Self-restitutional excess is a destabilizing mechanism at the very heart of disciplinary constitution: it is as such the site where disciplinary politics are essentially played out, as much for Bartra as for Hartman and Santí, and not just for the critics or the institutions targeted by them.

Self-restitutional excess can be used in at least two radically opposed senses, which parallel the senses in which the restitutional need of thought must and must not exert itself in terms of the positing of radical difference: on one hand, self-restitutional excess can organize the site for theoretical or metadisciplinary reflection, that is, it can be the region where disciplinary restitution seeks to interrogate itself (as in Hartman's essay, Santí's essay, and this chapter); but on the other hand, restitutional excess can also choose to negate itself as such; it can look for its own point of closure in an attempt to come to the end of itself. In reference to the magical realism example given above, the metacritical reflection that Taussig interpolates within his interpretation of magical realism belongs to self-restitutional excess; however, if systemic closure were to be claimed for magical realism in the notion that it can effectively open up to the voice of the Indian, that it can therefore redeem the Indian from its historically destitute position, and if that were to be stated in what would always amount to a foreclosure of further interrogation concerning literary restitution, then magical realism would be an example of accomplished restitution. What I am here saying of magical realism holds true for any redemptive or critical practice that comes to rest on representation—even if, or precisely if, such redemptive representation claims to be a resistant or overturned representation.

Accomplished restitution is the cipher of the dangers for self-delusion that the restitutionary paradigm entails. There would then be a particular form of restitutional practice whose overt or hidden premise places the theoretical end of the discipline it enacts in the horizon of accomplished restitution. We could call it a form of aesthetic utopianism, in so far as, in Neil Larsen's words, it constitutes a "promise of emancipation through the spontaneous cultural subversions of the dominant order." Through it culture "in reality becomes a surrogate for a politics of social emancipation" ("Latin America" 60). This is consonant with Jameson's critique of the Heideggerian positing of radical difference as "idealist voluntarism," which he compared to "liberal fantasies of the ways in which rational argument . . . might be capable of bringing about systemic modifications in the logic of our social life" ("Marx's Purloined Letter" 89).

The full political and epistemological impact of the disciplinary reconfiguration of Latin Americanism can only come from the recognition of restitutional excess as an impassable site. Restitutional excess, as the theoretical site of Latin Americanism, seeks to undo Latin Americanist representation. To Taussig's sentence, "From the represented shall come that which overturns the representation" (*Shamanism* 153), we must add: but only if the overturning does not result in a new representation." To engage engaged representations on the side of the represented can only be to undo representation. Representation rests in accomplished restitution. Latin Americanism's accomplished restitutions form the disciplinary alterity of Latin Americanism, and therefore also what Latin Americanism must resist, at the same time that it engages in it, if Latin Americanism is to remain open to the call of its discursive object. Santí ends his article saying of Sor Juana: "By resisting restitution, she preserves her difference and otherness; and by thus resisting, she urges the question about 'Sor Juana,' like all important questions, to remain" (129).

Reckless Gazing

If restitutional excess is the theoretical site of Latin Americanism—that is, the place where Latin Americanism opens into a second-order Latin Americanism; the place where university discourse confronts the hysteric's interpellation; the place where the Latin Americanist apparatus of capture comes to deconstruction—then restitutional excess is also the ground of its metacritical articulation. Excess in restitution figures as the destabilizing possibility of Latin Americanist representation. It indicates that which belongs to representation as such, to its "truth" in Santí's sense, which would also by the same token constitute its essential falsity. But it also indicates that "meaning," understood in the philological sense as the intrinsic singularity of the object, remains irretrievably lost to anything but aesthetic utopianism. Restitutional excess is in that sense the excess of philology itself, and it marks the condition of philology's impossibility to operate a closure of representation, to achieve a restitution of its object in ultimate self-appropriation, which would amount to achieving self-restitution in the thorough appropriation of its object.

Restitutional excess is then the very site of Latin Americanist alterity with respect to itself: the cipher of its impossibility to ever rest in epistemic self-assurance. But it is also the site of an other alterity, the ceaseless singular alterity to which the Latin Americanist object excessively refers as its ur object of constitution. Restitutional excess thus remarks the occasion for Latin Americanism's double injunction: to be always in excess of its double responsibility to restitute itself as well as its object and thereby to meet its responsibility. In conclusion, perhaps only the insistence on restitutional excess can shake off the hold of discursive power and thus redress the dissymmetry of the Latin Americanist gaze itself. Restitutional excess cannot operate a redemption of the Latin Americanist object but, insofar as it dwells on the illusory constitution of representation, it can limit or contest its pretensions to articulate social relations, to serve as the mimetic-discursive assistant to social power. It is in that sense alone that an insistence on the continued explicitation of the second dimension of the Borgesian ur object within Latin

Americanism can have a chance at "a new lease on life" without falling over into idealist voluntarism.

I will briefly mention two apparently contradictory recent instances of Latin Americanist work on alterity: Doris Sommer's "Resisting the Heat: Menchú, Morrison, and Incompetent Readers" and Diamela Eltit and Paz Errázuriz's *El infarto del alma*. I want to look at the other side of their seeming contradiction: their common opening to heterotopic legislation in representational self-arrest. Sommer and Eltit and Errázuriz choose to open their texts to the experience of epistemic disarticulation, thus following the call to make explicit the second sense of their Latin Americanist object of representation: its potential to cause nonknowledge, to interrupt the flow of meaning as well as of truth, risking something else. That something else that appears in their texts is difficult to verbalize, as it attests to a certain scandalous unpresentability, a certain monstrosity. My own mention will have to remain on this side of restitutional excess, pointing at its other side, where restitutional excess turns into a reckless form of *docta ignorantia* beyond appropriation.

El infarto del alma is the result of a visit or a number of visits by the photographer Errázuriz and the writer Eltit to an asylum for the terminally insane operated by the state in Chile. Errázuriz's photographs are perturbing: from most of them, two faces look at us from their confinement in the Putaendo insane asylum. Or more accurately, they look at the camera, an eye defined in the unpaged text as "a gift for the confined," as it gives them "the certainty of their images" (my trans., here and below). Their gaze: those photographs of couples in amorous engagement disclose the dissymmetrical gaze at the same time that they show its impropriety. Something escapes it that comes to us, and confinement, whether in the asylum, in the photograph, or in the text, cannot capture the irretrievable loss of sense that Eltit announces without celebrating. Who then is the other for the other? Symbolic disorder: "the subject, ex-propriated from self, yields her will and becomes a hieroglyph." The sanatorium: an "intermediate space," where there is no community and no memory, but only love as "pure affective expenditure" ["gasto y desgaste afectivo y . . . despilfarro puro"]. Are the text and the photographs also love? Are they also pure affective expenditure? *El infarto del alma* collapses representation by pointing at its impossible center: in the extreme staging of appropriation/restitution, appropriation/restitution simply misses its mark and is shown as it does so.

Sommer's essay, which I discuss more extensively in chapter 7, locates in Rigoberta Menchú's testimonio an exemplary Latin American instance of a text that, by insisting on the secret that gives it origin, puts off any attempt at critical textual mastery and leaves no room for critical self-recuperation. Sommer's resistant texts effectively signal "an epistemological dead end" ("Resisting" 410). If a text claims indeed that the reader is incompetent to penetrate its deepest layers, that is, if the text claims that it gives itself off as its own secret, then the impasse is in place, and that impasse traces an impassable discursive limit. Resistant texts radically resist appropriation as well as they resist restitution. "The purpose of intransigence and refusal is to cast doubts on our capacity to know, without allowing incapacity to float into the comforting, unmanageable mists of ambiguity" (413). What is a reader to do in order to "read appropriately and responsibly texts which ceaselessly call attention to their difference from the reader and to the danger of overstepping cultural limits" (419)?

But then Sommer, in a self-doubling gesture, before requiring once again "a break, a destabilizing irruption outside the self," comments: "the ethical dissymmetry of a meek self . . . may turn out to be the mirror image that reinscribes the older violent dissymmetry of the voracious subject before its objects of knowledge" (425). A new refusal, then, whereby resistant texts will also resist the self-resisting reader, will not spare the well-intentioned Latin Americanist, even the metacritical one. Instead, beyond resistance from self or resistance from other there is the complex responsibility of reckless gazing, without remainder, without restraint.

Eltit and Sommer explicitly thematize what I have called the structural dissociation of Latin Americanism and make it the center of their texts. Their reflections force us to confront our representational inability to come to terms with the singularity of our epistemic object. Through this work the Latin American other, or singular instances of it, appears as the troubling occasion to dismantle Latin Americanist representation as embodiment of social power. It is not power that comes to us from these limiting counter-representations, merely its resilient and always excessive other side. That self-restitution is nevertheless always at stake in these exercises, that is, that these limiting counterrepresentations are then put to use for an enhancement or a renewal of Latin Americanist work seems clear. The point is not that Latin Americanism should wish itself powerless. It is rather that its force should be made to serve against the obliteration of its object, not merely for the sake of respect of otherness or because epistemic objects are subjects in their own right but ultimately because without otherness there is no Latin Americanism, even if under the form of a deconstruction of Latin Americanism—there is only the certainty of a sameness in the face of which rather different forms of epistemic and political collapse will prevail.

FIVE The National-Popular in
Antonio Candido & Jorge Luis Borges

Discussing Brazilian slave society Roberto Schwarz says that the displacement of ideas caused by the social consequences of slavery produced "[a debasement of] ideological life and diminished the chances for genuine thought."[1] Schwarz's formulation is particularly challenging for scholars working on or from peripheral or semiperipheral societies: accepting that a debasement of ideological life diminishes the chances for genuine thought seems to imply that a nondebased ideology would foster them. If such were the case, then, paradoxically enough, "genuine thought," by which I understand Schwarz to mean true situational consciousness, a consciousness that is attentive to social contradictions and is reflexive regarding its own implication in them, is more likely to occur at the center of dominance, where ideological saturation is most intense and, so to say, purer and freer from doubly deceiving mirages. No doubt some dialectical contradiction is at work here—a contradiction that is also present in Fredric Jameson's essay "Third World Literature in the Era of Multinational Capitalism" and that in fact forms its very ground: the "truth" of first-world texts is revealed in third-world texts but only because third-world texts are unable to abandon the "objective relationship of politics to libidinal dynamics" and are therefore "deficient" in that sense, even if it is a form of deficiency that keeps us closer to the truth of things ("Third-World Literature" 80). For

Schwarz, in a similar manner, the lack of opportunities for genuine thought became the breeding ground for Machado de Assis's phenomenal texts.[2]

That kind of dialectical reversal is oriented toward establishing that certain "deficiencies" in capitalism's periphery, to the extent that they are symptomatic at the cultural level of real contradictions in the notorious "universal-expansionist tendency of capital," are at bottom a kind of epistemological privilege. A first theoretical formulation of that thesis in the modern, post-Hegelian, and post-Marxian sense may well have been given by Gyorgy Lukács in *History and Class Consciousness* where Lukács sustains that the subaltern are in a better position than the dominant to understand social totality. Lukács's argument is closely related to Hegel's master-slave dialectic. In Jameson's words: "in the end, only the slave knows what reality and the resistance of matter really are; only the slave can attain some true materialistic consciousness of his situation, since it is precisely to that that he is condemned. The Master, however, is condemned to idealism—to the luxury of a placeless freedom in which any consciousness of his own concrete situation flees like a dream" ("Third-World Literature" 85; ref. Lukács 87–88)

The impossibility of abandoning knowledge of the "objective relationship of politics to libidinal dynamics," defined as the most proper situation for subaltern communities of experience, far from constituting a limitation in every sense is in fact the foundation of a certain epistemological privilege. But study of this privilege does not come to subalternists without some rather extraordinary complications. Cultural singularity is the utopian field of subalternists. Subalternists by definition let themselves remain caught in the founding predicament of simultaneously asserting and abandoning cultural singularity. Subalternists need to assert and subsequently find and represent—that is, precisely not "construct"—the cultural singularity of the subaltern, understood as a positive difference vis-à-vis the dominant cultural formation. At the same time, however, subalternists must give up the notion of cultural singularity, through the very effort of its representation, as an ideological delusion, that is, as a simple variant in the objective relationship between politics and libidinal dynamics. It is a complicated predicament but it is an inescapable one. Without the assertion, which implies a claim to radical if relational difference, subaltern studies would be deprived of everything in its archaeological apparatus that is not inherited from the discipline it is trying to redraw or break away from (i.e., literary studies, history, or anthropology in its traditional configurations). But without abandoning its claim to cultural singularity (at the very moment in which cultural singularity is recognized as a simple variable in the connection of politics to libidinal dynamics), subaltern studies could not establish its peculiar claim to materialist knowledge and would remain prey to accusations of upholding a necessarily idealist culturalism.[3]

We can find an example of this paradox in the founding statement of the Latin American Subaltern Studies Group, in its double and contradictory appeal to a necessarily spectral subject without positivity, that can only appear in "structural dichotomies, . . . fissures" and can only speak in "blank spaces," but which subject is also, rather mysteriously, knowable in or through "'lived experience'" ("Founding Statement" 136, 144, 140). "Lived experience" is meant to refer to unrepresentable immediacy and singularity, that is, to a necessarily unrepresentable positivity, which must nevertheless be posited, whereas the subaltern subject's negativity must be affirmed precisely on the basis of the subalternist's inability to represent without contradiction (or even on the basis of the impossibility of self-representation on the part of the subaltern subjects themselves).

I do not see this founding paradox as a limitation—at least it does not have to be a limitation. On the contrary, I believe that the contribution of subalternism in both its political and its epistemological dimensions entirely depends on that constitutive problematic. And it is precisely for that reason that a critical examination and probing of the paradox is in order. Subaltern studies must not only engage in the archaeological analysis and reconstruction of silenced knowledges but must also, simultaneously, engage in what we could call an auto-archaeology, without which it would remain blind to its own conditions of enunciation, that is, blind to its own cultural singularity. One cannot simply "disagree with" subalternism in that respect; disagreeing with it is productive only when disagreement is based on a deeper agreement. The reasons for this are historical in nature rather than theoretical, to the very extent that not theory but contemporary history has made previous paradigms for cultural interpretation obsolete or insufficient. As is well known, the work of the South Asian Subaltern Studies Group is geared toward finding the repressed voice of the subaltern through and beyond the mystifications of neocolonial and national-popular historiography.[4] Clearly the conditions for the study of culture in India are far from being the same as those determining Latin Americanist work. And yet what we shall understand as the collapse of the national-popular state in Latin America after the debt crisis of 1982 marks as well the historical collapse of a number of critical paradigms associated with developmentalist, antidevelopmentalist, and modernizing ideologies: transculturations, universalisms, and cultural interdependencies of various kinds are thereby revealed to a certain extent as complicitous with neocolonial genealogies, often channeled through nationalist positions, and they must therefore give way to alternative ways of conceptualizing the difficult predicament of Latin American cultural knowledges in the face of neoliberal globalization—of the passage to empire. Understanding Latin American culture in its critical and relational subalternity, where subalternity is not meant to constitute a fixed or essentializing category but rather a differential relationship with the transcendental subject of transnational postmodernity, seems to be the only way in which that very same differentiality can be put to productive epistemological and critical use in contemporary times.

Two well-known collections of essays, *The Postmodernism Debate in Latin America* and *Posmodernidad en la periferia*, edited respectively by John Beverley, José Oviedo, and Michael Aronna and by Hermann Herlinghaus and Monika Walter, opened up a second stage in the debate on Latin American postmodernity by exhausting the possibilities of the first. What seems important now is to investigate the practical consequences of previous definitions for intellectual and political work. The canonical texts of Latin American postmodernity must be reread, perhaps reinterpreted, in the search for the way in which their own understanding of historical self-positioning can illuminate, rather than obscure, our own. If subalternism then comes to appear as the inescapable horizon of critical Latin Americanism in times of late-capitalist globalization, the previous traditions of Latin American thinking and writing survive as the genealogical cipher of a history that cannot be merely refuted; on the contrary, it must be actively affirmed at the very moment in which one takes critical distance from it.

A historical archaeology for Latin Americanist subalternism is therefore in order. This chapter can only pursue it in partial ways. Its organizing question is how to understand both the continuities and the discontinuities between the enterprise of cultural criticism as defined by the Latin American "master thinkers" of the recent past and the redefinition or rearticulation of that enterprise in Latin Americanist subalternism. Is subalternism to be understood as a radical break from the tradition in whatever disciplinary configuration of knowledge it manifests itself? Although I think that subalternism is a new model for the interpretation of Latin American culture that will develop in ways that are not strictly predictable, I am not sure that the subalternist mood, or move, in its present or incipient stage, can yet be understood as a radical break from a previous disciplinary mood. It is perhaps, rather, still no more than an opening up and expansion of disciplinary borders, whether we live in it from a posthistorical, postliterary, or postanthropological perspective.[5]

I want to look at the work of two improbable precursors of Latin Americanist subalternism, Antonio Candido and Jorge Luis Borges, with autoarchaelogical interests and intentions. I think that in Candido's "Literature and Underdevelopment" and in Borges's "The Lottery in Babylon" we may find two anticipatory ways of thinking the crisis of the Latin American national-popular state, which marks a crisis of aesthetic historicism at the superstructural level. My intention is not to think of Candido or Borges as protosubalternists; it is rather to find nontrivial links between past thinking and the present. If subalternism is to be considered the most consistent cultural contestation to the neoliberal state formation (the historical successor to the Fordist-Keynesian state whose Latin American passing became increasingly obvious after the public debt crisis of 1982), then subalternism must find its own critical-historical depth in the selective confrontation with alternative models of thinking—provided, that is, that such models do indeed refer to genuine thinking in the Schwarzian sense.

///

"Cultural dependency," said Antonio Candido, "is a natural fact" ("Literature" 127). He was writing in 1970 and trying to come to terms with what he then considered "the present phase" of cultural experience in Latin America, which he called "the consciousness of underdevelopment" (132). For Candido, the consciousness of underdevelopment is the third of the three basic categories that could summarize the evolution of literary culture in modern Latin America: the first is called "new country nativism" and corresponds to a period characterized by a euphoric faith in the developmental potentialities of the region; the second is called "preconsciousness of underdevelopment" and starts to make itself clearly visible in the thirties, when "[literature] abandoned pleasantness and *curiosity*, anticipating or perceiving what had been disguised in the picturesque enchantment or ornamental chivalry with which rustic man had previously been approached. It is not false to say that, from this point of view, the novel acquired a demystifying force that preceded the coming-to-awareness of economists and politicians" (121).

After World War II a "catastrophic consciousness of backwardness" set in, one that was "pessimistic with respect to the present and problematic with respect to the future," and where "the only remnant of the previous phase's millenarianism perhaps might be the confidence with which it is acknowledged that the removal of imperialism could bring, in itself, an explosion of progress" (121, 120). But the removal of imperialism is not, for Candido, such a simple thing, and it is not simple because "cultural dependency . . . is . . . a natural fact, given our situation as peoples who are colonized, or descendants of colonizers, or who have suffered the imposition of their civilization" (127). This means, above all, that a certain unsettling paradox would have to be absorbed: imperialism in the political and economic orders must be rejected, while, on the contrary, imperialism in the cultural order must be radically embraced, so that through the thorough appropriation of Eurocentric cultural forms dependency evolves into something other than dependency. It is a paradox that Candido only glimpses in order to refuse to accept it as such. Indeed, he ends up neutralizing the paradox itself, disavowing its paradoxical content: "the more the free man who thinks is imbued with the tragic reality of underdevelopment, the more he is imbued with revolutionary aspirations—that is, with the desire to reject the political and economic yoke of imperialism and to promote in every country the modification of the internal structures that nourish the situation of underdevelopment. Nevertheless, he confronts the problem of influences more objectively, considering them as normal linkages on the level of culture" (132).

Thus, for instance, the Latin American appropriation of the forms of the European novel must not be understood as "imitation" or "mechanical reproduction" but rather as "participation in resources that have become common through the state of dependency, contributing to turn it into an interdependency" (134). Candido is of course thinking of the great formal accomplishments of the Latin American boom novel, which by 1970 had started to naturalize, at least to all appearances, a countermovement to cultural dependency, seen in the fact that those novels had become part of the international circuits of cultural consumption. And yet those novels were not Latin American novels for nothing. In fact, in Candido's explanation, we begin to see how his understanding of the history of the Latin American novel embodies a clear teleology whose end result proleptically anticipates the founding predicament of subalternism: that is, the constitutive hesitation between the affirmation of cultural singularity and its abandonment as ideological delusion. This structural similarity is in no way free from political complications.

Candido distinguishes three phases of the Latin American novel, roughly coincidental with his three phases of cultural consciousness. In the first, he recognizes a "picturesque regionalism" corresponding to the euphoric phase of new country nativism (gauchoism, sertanejism, Rivera, Gallegos). In the second, he identifies a "problematic regionalism" (the social novel, indigenism, novels of the Brazilian northeast, etc.). And then there is a third phase, "which could be called . . . *superregionalist.* It corresponds to a consciousness distressed by underdevelopment and explodes the type of naturalism based on reference to an empirical vision of the world, a naturalism that was the aesthetic tendency peculiar to an epoch in which the bourgeois mentality triumphed and that was in harmony with the consolidation of our literatures" (139). This superregionalism constitutes for Candido "a new [universalist] species of literature, which still is connected in a transfiguring way to the very material of what was once nativism" (140). Superregionalism is therefore at the same time new and anchored in the staunchest traditions of creole Latin American culture, the latter rather generously understood in its most integrationist and inclusive sense.

The regionalist emphasis, present in all three phases, is nothing but an emphasis on cultural singularity, and it is the properly Latin American defense against absolute absorption into Eurocentric cultural paradigms; in other words, it is the element without which dependency would never reach its own metamorphosis into (so-called) interdependency. Conversely, however, at the same time that this history of the novel emphasizes regionalist singularity, a countermove to regionalism develops along the phases to find its apotheosis only in the third one: through it, Latin American singularity, to quote the title of a novel by Carlos Fuentes that is radically connected to this adventure, "sheds its skin" as a regional particularity in order to accomplish what Candido calls "the universality of the region" (139–40). It can also be said of this second element that it is through it, although in a different, complementary way to the first, that the very site of Latin American dependency is culturally transfigured into (so-called) universal interdependency.

In Candido's history (and we shouldn't forget its massive influence on several generations of critical writing), regional singularity is at the same time upheld as subversive or resistant within the very same apparatus of literature that represents it; and it is, yet once again, subalternized by the literary apparatus itself, which *cannot not proceed* to its appropriation and tendential erasure while claiming to do it from the perspective of a supposedly theoretical universality. Perhaps subalternism proceeds in a similar manner regarding the subaltern subject. But if it partially proceeds in a similar manner, it also proceeds, as we will see, in a dissimilar manner on which the novelty of subalternism is established.

Superregionalism shares some important structural elements with subaltern studies. Just as the superregionalist novel "explodes the type of naturalism based on reference to an empirical vision of the world" (Candido, "Literature" 139), subalternism in the same way abjures empiricism and becomes, in its own terms, a practice of the spectral. If empiricism had everything to do, in Candido, with the consolidation of bourgeois hegemony, subaltern studies is nothing if not, at least, a counterhegemonic practice. As the founding statement of the Latin American Subaltern Studies Group puts it, the subaltern is "by definition not registered or registrable as a historical subject capable of hegemonic action," which immediately means that the subaltern is never just an object of empirical interpreta-

tion but must rather be found, spectrally, "in the seams of the previously articulated sociocultural and administrative practices and
epistemologies, in the cloning of cultural mentalities, and in the
contingent social pacts that occur at every transitional juncture"
("Founding Statement" 136, 144). In other words, the subaltern is
precisely the counterempirical subject, "the unavoidable, indestruc-
tible, and effective subject who has proven us wrong" (146). And this
seems to be its only possible definition. There is, no doubt, something slightly disconcerting and perhaps not entirely welcome in
these structural similarities between the superregionalist and the
subalternist projects. After all, superregionalism is another name for
the obviously hegemonic boom novel, which organizes, or at least responds to, the master paradigm for the interpretation of Latin American culture throughout the 1960s, the 1970s, and even the 1980s.
Subalternism is born in willed opposition to it, as a form of questioning "the master paradigms used in representing colonial and
postcolonial societies both in the cultural practices of hegemony
developed by elite groups and in the disciplinary discourses of the
humanities and social sciences that seek to represent the workings
of these societies" (136).

Where then is the difference, the discontinuity? In order to find
it we should turn to what we earlier detected as an unresolved, even
unrecognized paradox in Candido's formulation. For Candido, the
struggle against imperialism in the political and economic spheres
was a natural consequence of the consciousness of underdevelopment. However, imperialism in the cultural sphere created a radically different set of demands for counterhegemonic action. Candido
even says that nativism, taken to an extreme, to the extent that it
would question "the use of imported *forms*" such as "the sonnet, the
realistic story, and free associative verse," is "always ridiculous" because it would be "like opposing the use of the European languages
we speak." "At the deepest levels of creative elaboration," Candido
says, cultural dependency "is no longer dependency, but a way of par-
ticipating in a cultural universe to which we belong, which crosses
the boundaries of nations and continents, allowing the exchange of
experiences and the circulation of values" (130). That is why, for him,
the problem of cultural influences should be confronted "more objectively, considering them as normal linkages on the level of culture" (132).

This "normalcy" or "naturalness" of cultural dependency becomes the decisive issue upon which Latin American subalternism can and should build its claim to oppose or redraw previously articulated critical paradigms. In other words, the naturalness of cultural dependency and of its corollary interdependency *is* the master paradigm against which subaltern studies reacts. Furthermore, the historical force of such subalternist reaction depends on the failure of the previous paradigm and not on subalternist voluntarism. That is to say, it is only because superregionalism succeeds in its efforts at cultural integration that superregionalism's integration can be perceived as merely hegemonic self-integration. It then becomes obvious that such self-integration excludes—indeed, that it is based on the exclusion of—so many subaltern cultural formations in Latin America and even on the exclusion of what Veena Das has called the "subaltern as perspective" itself.[6]

With superregionalism, only the superregionalist segment of Latin American culture achieves interdependency. This might seem like a tautology, but it is a tautology with a bite. Superregionalist success simultaneously reveals its deeper failure or inability to operate the cultural redemption of those vast segments of the Latin American population for whom interdependency becomes an even more extreme form of historical dependency. The "transfiguring" element of superregionalism, at the moment of superregionalism's integration into the global circuits of cultural circulation, radically fails to transfigure what prompted its existence in the first place: call it Latin American underdevelopment, backwardness, or social and economic difference, or call it the Latin American subaltern, which rests unredeemed. Now, this failure is not a failure of will, and it is not ultimately a cultural failure. It is rather, as these things always are, a failure whose referent must be found in the political and economic spheres.

Euphoric nativism must be related to the reaction by the emergent Latin American national bourgeoisies against the so-called neocolonial order of economic and economic-political dominance, which suffered a systemic crisis in 1929. The two phases in Candido's consciousness of underdevelopment correspond to the two defining moments (before and after World War II) of the Latin American national-popular state formation, whose construction was undertaken concomitantly with the so-called Import-Substitution Industrialization model of economic development. This was a historical period in which the Latin American state was forced to pursue a state-orchestrated developmentalist strategy, which lasted roughly five decades and ended in the 1982 debt crisis. As Gary Gereffi and Lynn Hempel put it, "in the 1970s, the main source of external financing for ISI [Import-Substitution Industrialization] shifted from foreign direct investment to increasingly heavy amounts of foreign borrowing, which culminated in the debt crisis of 1982. The 1980s was labeled the 'lost decade' for many Latin American nations, as they suffered through economic recession, spiraling inflation, severe budget cuts in social expenditures, high levels of unemployment, and pervasive poverty" ("Latin America" 20)

The 1982 crisis resulted in the dismantling of the national-popular planning state and the institutionalization of neoliberal policies at a very high social cost. The 1980s transition from import substitution to export-oriented development strategies marks the period in which the Latin American economies underwent a drastically accelerated pull toward "globalization," understood as their partial "functional integration between internationally dispersed activities," where "transnational corporations are key actors" (Gereffi and Hempel 19, 27). Latin American dependency on transnational corporations has increased exponentially over the last two decades, and at the same time the severely damaged Latin American state has proven unable to extract adequate social and economic concessions from the corporations. As a result, an always more uneven development has become endemic to the region. As Gereffi and Hempel understate it, "for the majority in the region—workers in low-paying and low-skill jobs, peasants in subsistence of traditional export sections, consumers hurt by devaluations and eroding standards of living, and firms unable to compete in increasingly open markets—the cost of globalization appears to exceed its benefits" (27).

The dream of interdependency through an internationalization of linkages based on sustained development and paralleling the cultural integration of Latin American symbolic production and its metropolitan counterparts is over. The fall of the national-popular state has given rise to centrifugal new social movements that are no longer as interested in transfiguring themselves into the national and then the international spheres as they once might have been. Superregionalism ends when the conditions sponsoring its ascent (that is, the possibility of a successful, reasonably egalitarian, middle-class–led national integration to the global economy) are no longer there. Latin Americanist subaltern studies is ultimately a consequence of the collapsed dream of Latin American nationally integrated modernizations. And it is a response to the exhaustion of superregionalism, whose aesthetic procedures seem today singularly unable to come to terms with the fragmented state of Latin American societies—in the absence of nationally redemptive master narratives.

What then is the positive characterization of subalternism itself, beyond its status as a counterhegemonic, counterempirical, anti-superregionalist critical practice? If subalternism is going to be able to offer itself as a viable redrawing and expansion of epistemological borders; in other words, if it has the possibility of becoming an alternative critical paradigm, beyond nativism and its transfigurations, then it must incorporate to itself a properly theoretical rearticulation of its relation to the previous paradigm. Such theoretical rearticulation must include an account of how subalternism is to reread the historical sequence that it has come to substitute or supplement. Regionalism, since the nineteenth century, has constituted a master paradigm endowed with epistemological privilege for the interpretation of Latin American history. As the dominant ideology for Latin American self-interpretation, regionalism, in its last avatar as superregionalism, suffers a hard crisis at the hands of the neoliberal order from which it may not recover. The question is, who or what can today claim epistemological privilege? From what geocultural position is it possible to develop a re-formed critical position? From the perspective of globalization itself? Or from the contrary perspective of the globalized locality? Subalternism aspires to respond to such questions. By developing the perspective of the subaltern, or the subaltern as perspective, subalternism understands itself in a strong sense as an anti-integrationist and anticreole movement. What is however its specific positivity?

The Latin American Subaltern Studies' founding statement says: "High culture forms such as literature are bracketed by the critiques developed by deconstruction, feminism, black and Chicano studies in the United States, and in their place, an anthropological sense of culture as 'lived experience' comes to the fore" (140). Would rather magically introduced "lived experience" (which I have already mentioned) embody some radical transparency to which subalternism would have ready and immediate access? Or is it only, precisely, a deferral of theory that might also infinitely defer subalternism's possibilities to revamp Latin American regionalism into a new and truly effective form of cultural critique for the New World Order? Perhaps "lived experience" is the counterintentional mark and the mirror image of what in superregionalism ended up showing itself unable to account for its exclusions.

The second part of this chapter, which is a reading of Borges's "The Lottery in Babylon," attempts to trace in the Argentinian writer's textual thinking certain elements for the theoretical rearticulation of a critical enterprise in the neoliberal age. It is not a question of forging a reading of Borges as an *avant la lettre* subalternist. Subalternism can benefit, however, from the response given by "The Lottery in Babylon" to the essential problem of the critical foundation of oppositional action within a social and economic regime in which superregionalism has been transfigured into global control. Perhaps subaltern difference is the last hope of what in more hopeful times used to be called freedom.

///

Borges's central position in the postmodern canon is accepted, but in trying to understand him from or for our own time one never knows whether the most proper reading is to be historical or ontological. With Borges, or at the very least with the Borges of *Ficciones* and *El Aleph*, any merely ontological reading becomes immediately reductive, as does any historical reading. An oscillation between history and ontology is a condition of possibility for a reading of Borges, who should be considered as a thinker of situational consciousness for whom a passage into theory is always already determinant or as a theoretical thinker for whom historical knowledge is the ultimate goal.[7] To use the old Lukácsian formulation, in Borges *science* becomes *consciousness* and "consciousness" becomes "science"—understanding "science" ontologically and "consciousness" historically. The interpreters should not reify Borgesian thought into any one of those poles, and they should not understand any of the poles in a reified manner.

I want to read "The Lottery in Babylon" (1941) both as a reaction

to the state form that had been developing in the West, and consequently in Argentina, during the 1930s and as an anticipation of the
evolution of the state form into its present configuration. In other
words, I think "The Lottery in Babylon" offers a symptomatic reading of the constitution of the Keynesian state, the planning state, or
the interventionist state, and at the same time an ominous anticipation or prognosis of what would historically result from the interventionist state, namely, what Deleuze called the society of control, for
which the alternative expression "neoliberal state" is a misnomer.[8]
Borges then appears as a precursor thinker of what Thayer, Jameson,
Negri and Hardt, and others (as we saw in chapter 3), making use
of Marx's political economy, call "the real subsumption of society
under capital" (Negri and Hardt 14). A similar reading could be made,
for instance, of "Tlön, Uqbar, Orbis Tertius," and even of "La biblio-
teca de Babel." But if it is true that Borges anticipates in his textual
work the evolution of social forms, then critical analysis should not
stop at the point of discovery of his prophetic powers but should
go beyond it to question the particular way in which his work is
not only descriptive but also critical, that is, historical in the proper
sense. By offering an anticipated account of empire, in Hardt and
Negri's expression, Borges also gave us the possibility of a critical
relation to it.

From a perspective that I would then have to call, I imagine, im-
properly historical, I will propose that in "The Lottery in Babylon"
Borges interprets the Keynesian state, which in Latin America as
elsewhere is a direct result of Black Thursday of 1929. As Tulio Halperín Donghi puts it, "[after 1929] national states were . . . the only
economic entities rugged enough to navigate in such high seas . . .
and Latin American states began to exercise functions and adopt
techniques unimaginable only a few years before. . . . The multiplication of state functions signaled a total abandonment of the laissez-
faire principles that had guided neocolonial economic policy. Awareness of the emergency was so widespread that . . . none disputed the
expansion of state power per se" (*Contemporary History* 209–10) The
state that started its new life after 1929 is the planning state, whose
most acute phase was in Argentina the Peronist national-popular
state and which would only find its final collapse during the debt
crisis of 1982.

And then, from an ontological or theoretical point of view, I will suggest that Borges, in his short story, radicalizes historical phenomena into a proleptic understanding of what was, for him, the postcontemporary: the passage from the interventionist state into the state of control as the teleological truth of the modern state. Its Latin American contemporary manifestation, euphemistically called "neoliberal," has meant, among other things, a drastically accelerated pull toward globalization, whereby the Latin American dependency on transnational corporations increases exponentially. In late-capitalist times, the Latin American states become subsidiaries of a perhaps inexistent but nevertheless effective transnational state apparatus whose function is merely to ensure the ceaseless reproduction of labor power through and for "functional integration between internationally dispersed activities" (Gereffi and Hempel 19). The spectral transnational state of flexible accumulation replaces the national-popular state and its old legitimacies. What obtains is a new social regime "of perpetual metastability" based on the market as final mechanism of control (Deleuze, "Postscript" 4). I take my departure from the primary hypothesis that the Borgesian notion of the lottery in its last stage, there where it comes up against the limit of its own nonexistence (when the lottery no longer really matters, for its effects are all-pervasive already), is an allegory of perpetual social metastasis (what neoliberal theoreticians call simply "the market") as a regime of total social control.[9] But my real question goes beyond description into attempting to read, through description, the Borgesian modality of historical critique.

"The Lottery in Babylon" is the account given by an obscure narrator (who happens to find himself temporarily outside Babylon) of a very peculiar state institution and its history: the lottery, in its Babylonian form. The narrator tells us early on that in Babylon "the Lottery is a major element of reality" (101). How it has come to be such a principal part of reality is his topic—a topic, by the way, that the logic of the story leads us to believe has been given to him by the lottery system itself, a result of its hazardous but rigorous prize distribution. The lottery develops historically from a game sponsored by a private corporation—the narrator calls it "the Company" (102)—into the total administration of experience by the "shadowy corporation" (106). If at its historical beginning the lottery is an institution of civil society depending on market mechanisms, by the end, the very notion of civil society has become impossible and unsustainable since the lottery has merged with life to the point where they are experientially undistinguishable: the results of the lottery affect or determine every facet of human and even cosmic events. The lottery, at the end of its evolution, has become such a "major element of reality" that it is in fact the primary mechanism of the real. At the end of the story the narrator hints that it is undecidable whether the lottery should be considered the primary mechanism of the real or, on the contrary, the real as primary mechanism: "it makes no difference whether one affirms or denies the reality of the shadowy corporation, because Babylon is nothing but an infinite game of chance" (106).

Since the very writing of the story could (or could not) be a result of the lottery itself, the truth of the statement is infinitely suspended. The very statement already suspends historical truth, but that suspension is itself suspended, in double undecidability. The readers are called forth to make a preliminary ideological judgment, faced with at least three options: first, the lottery exists, and the narrator is its unwitting servant; second, the lottery no longer exists, but the narrator is unable to decide on its nonexistence; and third, the lottery exists, and the narrator is willingly mystifying us. The real choice for readers is not to decide in favor of one of them, or in favor of their negations. The readers must instead enter an alternative order of decision that the first (and false) choice at the same time announces and introduces: if the truth of the narrator's statement is infinitely postponed and can never be ascertained, then it is up to the readers to let themselves remain caught in perpetual entanglement or else to break free and refuse the very terms of the question. The latter requires, as it is usually the case in Borges, a complicated act of metacritical analysis where the text's general theoretical perspective finds itself at stake.

Right at the point in Babylonian history where the pressure of the people clamoring for equality succeeds in imposing "a *novus ordo seclorum*, a necessary stage of history," "the Company" is asked to assume "all public power" and becomes the state or its substitute (103): "The fair and reasonable desire that all men and women, rich and poor, be able to take part equally in the Lottery inspired indignant demonstrations—the memory of which, time has failed to dim. Some stubborn souls could not (or pretended they could not) understand that this was a *novus ordo seclorum*, a necessary stage of history. . . . There were disturbances, there were regrettable instances of bloodshed, but the masses of Babylon at last, over the opposition of the well-to-do, imposed their will; they saw their generous objectives fully achieved. First, the Company was forced to assume all public power" (103).

"A new order," that popular triumph, an accomplished national-popular integration operated by the Company at the apparent prompting of the multitude, is then the remote beginning of the society of control. The state, which is in principle nothing but the corporation running the lottery, keeps its extraordinary expansion (which is necessary to keep the lottery running more smoothly and consistently) until a moment is reached where every human act happens as a function of state power. It is then that the narrator affirms that the total and real subsumption of life into the state form has been accomplished, perhaps in order to further the claim that such an accomplishment also marks the point where the state form becomes subsumed into the total reality of life. A dialectical inversion has taken place: the planning state has metamorphosed into its own specter in order to better saturate the field of the real, which is now equivalent to the spectral. Proleptic anticipation is thus accomplished in Borges's text: the society of control, our present, is announced in the 1941 text as a teleological consequence of the development of the state apparatus from its national-popular configuration.

A critical objection becomes necessary, but it should be understood that it is a critical objection made possible by the short story itself. Borges's ironic disengagement, or the narrator's stated "indifference," does not hide but in fact reveals the all-determinant difference: the passage from an interventionist lottery to a total lottery is also a passage into the total domination of the human; and it is, epistemologically, a passage from history into its reification as ontology. "To affirm or deny the reality of the shadowy corporation" is precisely not indifferent, because it makes all the difference. "To affirm" means to opt for history and to keep open the difference between knowledge and experiential consciousness; "to deny" means to opt for the reification of history and to collapse knowledge into experience.

Granted that "Babylon is nothing but an infinite game of chance," everything depends on deciding whether such a game is fated to occur through ultimately human determination, because it is orchestrated by the state form as site of power, or whether such human determination is or becomes nature itself, and as such cannot be alternatively imagined. The very notion of historical freedom is at stake in the metacritical decision that the narrator paradoxically offers to us by claiming that there is no decision to be made, or that the decision is indifferent. What is at stake, in other words, is the theoretical possibility of an outside to ideology or, as Louis Althusser would put it in his autobiography, "how to escape the circle while remaining within it" (*Future* 319); in the story's terms it is a question of "how to escape the lottery while remaining within it," or, if you want, how to escape the state of control while remaining within it. The text's historical-critical consciousness thus depends on the possible form or forms of responding to the question it embodies.

It is naturally only the theoretical possibility of an escape that will leave open the possibility of a historical change, and a final destruction of what we are understanding, through this reading, to be the late-capitalist mode of production under the allegory of a total state lottery (only a future possibility for Borges in 1941). If the lottery exists, then to understand it as a contingent and not a necessary historical fact is fundamental. But even if the lottery no longer exists, only realizing that such is the case matters. For Althusser, in his classic formulation, "it is this knowledge that we have to reach, if you will, while speaking in ideology, and from within ideology we have to outline a discourse which tries to break with ideology, in order to dare to be the beginning of a scientific (i.e. subjectless) discourse on ideology" ("Ideology" 173).

One has to wonder, by the way, how Althusser would have modified his notion of ideology and the ideological state apparatus if he had read and seriously meditated on "The Lottery in Babylon." Or perhaps he did, and perhaps he did it to an unfathomable extent. We shall never know, but that should not prevent us from recognizing that "The Lottery in Babylon" is one of the theoretical sources for the Althusserian notion of ideology. Uncannily enough, Borges's text includes a reference to Althusser that Borges could not know would be a reference to Althusser. Perhaps, then, it was Althusser who retrospectively made it a reference to himself. Toward the end of the story

Borges's narrator asks: "the dreamer who suddenly awakes to choke the woman who lies at his side to death, [does he not] carry out a secret decision by the Company?" (71).

As is well-known, on Sunday morning, November 16, 1980, Althusser found himself in the position of that Borgesian dreamer. In Althusser's words, "I surfaced after an unfathomable night which I have never been able to fathom, and found myself standing at the foot of my bed, in a dressing-gown, with Hélene stretched out before me, and with me continuing to massage her neck and feeling intense pain in my forearms, obviously due to the massage. Then I realised, without knowing why, other than from her motionless eyes and the pitiful tip of her tongue showing between her teeth and lips, that she was dead" (*Future,* 253–54). There is no telling how Althusser's own theorization of the discourse of the unconscious as the discourse of "the Order of the human signifier" relates to his own inscription in a Borgesian text that is also a text about the other as absolute signifier (Althusser, "Freud and Lacan" 213). The Borgesian narrator compares the workings of "the Company" to the workings of God ("that silent functioning, like God's" ["Lottery" 106]), just as Althusser theorizes that "the interpellation of individuals as subjects presupposes the 'existence' of a Unique and central Other Subject" ("Ideology" 178).

The position of the narrator in "The Lottery in Babylon" is objectively constitutive of ideology in Althusserian terms. Ideology is for Althusser a necessary condition of what he terms "reproduction of labour-power." In effect, whether the lottery exists actually or spectrally, the narrator's mission is ideological through and through. He could either be an unwitting servant, therefore positioning himself as a worker, or a willing collaborator, and therefore an agent of exploitation. Either way, he serves the same interests: "the reproduction of labour-power requires . . . a reproduction of its submission to the rules of the established order, i.e., a reproduction of submission to the ruling ideology for the workers, and a reproduction of the ability to manipulate the ruling ideology correctly for the agents of exploitation and repression, so that they, too, will provide for the domination of the ruling class 'in words'" ("Ideology" 132–33). The final sentences of the story would at first reading simply seem to ensure the reproduction of labor power, in other words, the perpetuation of state power through the preservation of the lottery system's social hegemony: "it makes no difference whether one affirms or denies the reality of the shadowy corporation." The dreamer will forever strangle his wife, after all. But something else is also being said.

Is "The Lottery in Babylon," as a total textual act, meant to contribute to the reproduction of labor power in the Althusserian sense, that is, by ideologically sustaining it through either submission to it or through its naturalization as equivalent to life itself? Or is it, on the contrary, a way of opening into the subjectless process of history, into the outside of interpellation by the lottery apparatus, into a rupture of the order of the signifier? The narrator of "The Lottery in Babylon" tells us a monstruous story, because it encompasses all stories to the same extent that it kills them all, by voiding them of autonomy. If the lottery orders and determines every human event, every story is simply *that* story and no alternative perspective can ever be developed. The total administration of life through an infinite and unceasing lottery means that life is thoroughly denarrativized, as it responds in every one of its moments to an order issuing from above, from state power in its guise as the absolute administrator of thoroughly universalized capital.[10] From the perspective of the total lottery, life is always already heteronomous, "nothing but an infinite game of chance" and, therefore, a realm of absolute compulsion. But there is an alternative perspective.

Paradoxically, but inevitably, the thorough denarrativization of life as the ideological apotheosis of global lottery returns us to an alternative possibility of understanding. The final closure of the story, that is, the successful allegorization of social totality as always already alienated, always already disappropriated, "redirects," in words that Jameson applies to a different context, "our attention toward history itself and the variety of alternative situations it offers" ("Postmodernism" 288). There is certainly, in Borges's text, no affirmation of human autonomy—there is only, through the metacritical dimension of the text, a loosening up of radical heteronomy, which is, to a given extent, also a (nonhumanist) affirmation of the human potential for freedom.

"The ignorant assume that infinite drawings require infinite time; actually, all that is required is that time be infinitely subdivisible, as in the famous parable of the Race with the Tortoise" ("Lottery" 105). In another text on the Greek paradox already cited in chapter 4, Borges says: "We (the undivided divinity that operates in us) have dreamed the world. We have dreamed it resistant, mysterious, visible, ubiquitous in space and firm in time; but in its architecture we have allowed tenuous and eternal interstices of unreason in order to know that it is false" ("Avatares" 204; my trans.). Such falsities destroy ontology. Through the destruction of ontology history returns, and with it historical consciousness. Would that fundamentally denarrativized historical consciousness—that we can also understand as the radicalization of Schwarz's "genuine thought" into Jameson's situational consciousness, that is, "a demystifying eyeball-to-eyeball encounter with daily life, with no distance and no embellishments" ("Postmodernism" 286)—be translatable in subalternist terms as "lived experience"? "Lived experience," the "lived experience" of the concretely historicized and localized subaltern, interpreted, in Gyan Prakash's words, "postnationally" and "postfoundationally," that is, as nonsubsumable or as particularly resistant to any form of heteronomous narrativization of experience, brings us back to the identity between politics and libidinal dynamics, which is a condition of subalternism as epistemological privilege.[11] Subalternism cannot be made simply to depend on the voluntarist affirmation of an ethico-political ground for solidarity with nondominant subjects. If the subalternist perspective arises out of a critical confrontation with neocolonial and national-popular forms of thought, it is because the subaltern radically marks the site of contradiction in the expansionist tendencies of global capital to saturate the field of the real. The subaltern remains, in its singularly resilient position, beyond the collapse of the national popular, beyond the total allegorization of life into a thoroughly state-structured game of chance, as the perpetual promise and the perpetual necessity of another life and of another organization of life.

Das, having determined subalternism to be "a perspective in the Nietzschean sense," goes on to say that "the development of [the subaltern perspective] will also mean a new relationship with the chroniclers of the cultures under study" ("Subaltern" 324). Antonio Candido and Jorge Luis Borges cannot without mystification be understood as precursors of the subaltern perspective. I have, however, attempted to show that there are advantages to including them in the "new relationship" Latin Americanist subalternism must develop with its own past. If it can be understood that Candido belongs, however problematically, in the Latin American genealogy of a thinking of the positivity of the subaltern, given his insistence on the necessary hypostasis of cultural locality or singularity, then it should also be understood that Borges, for whom the denarrativization of ontology is the precise goal of most of his stories, contributes to another equally necessary genealogy. By showing that everything depends on either affirming or negating the subsumption of life under the domination of capital allegorized as state power, Borges opens up the possibility of an alternative history: a history of the radical negation of ideological universality, or of its revelation as false consciousness. This is certainly not enough for the constitution or even for the recognition of a subaltern perspective. But constitution or recognition cannot fully happen without it. Candido and Borges do not develop the subaltern perspective. At the limit of their thinking, however, its possibility obtains.

What would happiness be that is not measured
by an immeasurable grief at what is?
—Theodor Adorno, *Minima Moralia*

SIX The End of Magical Realism:
José María Arguedas's Passionate Signifier

Transculturation: The Implosion of Meaning

Magical realism developed in the first half of the twentieth century as a result of the cultural fights within the Latin American intellectual public sphere—Angel Rama's "ciudad letrada"—between the centripetal forces of regionalism/nationalism and the centrifugal forces of the artistic avant-garde.[1] What James Clifford has called "ethnographic surrealism," a project largely associated with a certain French avant-garde that came programmatically together in the College de Sociologie (Michel Leiris, Georges Bataille, Roger Caillois, and Pierre Klossowski were some of the people involved), joins a Latin American cultural-political will to difference to produce in the first works of Aimé Cesaire, Miguel Angel Asturias, and Alejo Carpentier the inception of that Latin American semiotic practice.[2]

But perhaps ethnographic surrealism and political will to cultural difference are not sufficient to define such a complicated phenomenon. At its base, in the social body that originates magical-real objects, a disparity among two or more modes of economic production is always present. As Michael Taussig puts it, referring to a felicitous expression by Ernst Bloch, "the nonsynchronous contradiction comes to life where qualitative changes in a society's mode of production animate images of the past in the hope of a better future" (*Shamanism* 166).[3] Irlemar Chiampi argues that magical realism is

a writing of nondisjunction, in the sense that in it the nonsynchronous contradiction wants to find mediation, and therefore to disappear as contradiction (*O realismo* 134). As a writing of nondisjunction, following on the Cuban José Lezama Lima's vision of Latin
America as "incorporative protoplasm," magical realism endorses
the ideologeme that names Latin America as a site of transculturation: not just a melting pot of races and cultures but also a region of
radical assimilation where difference does not operate according to
conventional, Aristotelian logic. The principle of the contradiction
of opposites (be they opposite rationalities) or its corollary the *tertio
excluso* is not operative for Latin American culture. Magical realism allows, as it were, for the simultaneous textualization of both
A and non-A without scandal. The conciliation of the disjointed, according to Chiampi, is the textual effect in which magical realism
comes to constitute itself as such. I will take a different position,
perhaps opposite, to claim that magical realism is radically or primarily a writing of disjunction—regardless of what it itself purports
to be.

Magical realism is a technical device within a larger and more encompassing apparatus of transculturating representation. There are
two main uses of the word *transculturation:* in a loosely anthropological sense, it is used to describe any kind of cultural mixing
(some acquisition, some loss, and some creation are always ingredi-
ents in it). And then it is used to refer to a critical concept, that is,
an active, self-conscious cultural combination that is a tool for aesthetic or critical production. In the sense developed by Angel Rama
from Fernando Ortiz' first use of the term, literary transculturation
is a "revitalized examination of local traditions, which had become
sclerotic, in order to find formulations that would allow for the absorption of external influences. External influences would thus be
diluted into larger artistic structures that can still translate the problematics and the peculiar flavors they had continued to preserve"
(Rama, "Procesos" 207; my trans., here and below).[4] Transculturation
is thus a form of "cultural plasticity," an active receptivity that regulates "the incorporation of new elements . . . through the total rearticulation of the regional cultural structure" (208). In Rama's use,
literary transculturation is a form for the promotion of cultural survival undertaken as a reactive response to modernization. As Rama
puts it, it comes to strengthen and coconstitute the contemporary

"Latin American literary system, understood as a field of integration and mediation, and with enough leeway for self-regulation" (217).

In Rama's definition, transculturation has come to fulfill a foundational role for contemporary Latin American cultural critique. As a foundational notion, transculturation is and is not a return to Latin American cultural origins. It is not a return because, as Silvia Spitta argues, post-Ortiz transculturators—the kind of people Rama wrote about in his own book on transculturation—"open the door to a radical rewriting of the tradition" (Spitta, *Between Two Waters* 10). But it is a return because, once that rewriting is done, it would finally be established that transculturation is indeed at the traumatic source of everything that is literary and not-so-literary in Latin America: in other words, at the teleological end of the transculturating process, the technical, critical, or literary use of transculturation would revert to its anthropological use, now understood as infinitely accomplished.

If the critical insistence on transculturation is meant to counter the colonialist "whitening" of Latin American culture against which Ortiz warned, the task at hand for transculturation analysts is to further Ortiz' enterprise by "reinterpreting" and "reconstructing" the tradition so that the transculturated Latin American subject can survive within a full, and fully known, representational genealogy. In Rama's work, the political epistemics of transculturation go beyond the description or the incorporation of a given state of affairs into a willed critical interference with its very conditions of possibility: in other words, literary transculturation (and, for that matter, transculturation in the extended anthropological sense) is not simply a response to modernization, understood as an "external influence"; but it is necessarily also a critical relationship to modernization. Literary transculturation is oriented transculturation.

Such critical relationship, however, has some limitations, which Rama may not have fully seen. Transculturation analysts must realize, following the very logic of their practice, that transculturation, as oriented transculturation, is in itself always already transculturated, that is, that transculturation, in their sense, does not name a "natural" or primary fact, but that it is itself an *engaged* representation, that it does not simply refer to a social relation but rather is "itself a social relation, linked to the group understandings, status, hierarchies, resistances and conflicts that exist in other spheres of the culture in which it circulates" (Greenblatt, *Marvelous Posses-sions* 6). As a hermeneutic concept, transculturation is as histori-cally produced as the phenomena it would seek to interpret. To that extent there is no such thing as a stable or accomplished "reinterpre-tation" or "reconstruction" or a proper genealogy of the transcultur-ated subject. The possibility that a full Latin American subject in its complex historicity can emerge or be constituted, even at the level of literary representation, through more or less exhaustive analysis or critique is simply not given—and it wouldn't be given even if we replace, as indeed we should, the notion of *a* Latin American his-torical subject by a sufficient plurality of them: subjects. There is no transparency in transculturation, which means that literary trans-culturation, as oriented, is simultaneously always beyond control, always outside its function as a technical device for the integration of external influences into an enterprise of cultural preservation and renewal. This latter sense is, however, the sense in which Rama for the most part theorizes it.

Transculturation, as a genealogical critical apparatus for a certain cultural and historical expression, will have extreme difficulty pro-tecting itself from the history it attempts to critique or vanquish for the sake of the history it attempts to preserve in mediated form, because both histories, and not just the latter, are simultaneously part of its own constitution: transculturation cannot step outside of itself to establish clear-cut "objective" or disengaged distinctions. As a radical concept, insofar as it is oriented toward a possible resti-tution, preservation, or renewal of cultural origins, and not toward a mere phenomenology of culture, transculturation runs into the theoretical wall that marks its conditions of possibility as hetero-geneous with respect to itself: the critical concept of transcultura-tion, paradoxically enough, seems to originate not in the anthropo-logical concept but rather in a different, nontransculturated realm of (unexamined) truth: the realm of ideology. There is no critical trans-culturation without an end or a limit of transculturation, through which end the critical concept of transculturation appears as some-thing other than or beyond what it is purported to be—and it is precisely that "end" or excess in the self-conscious use of transcul-turation that interests me here. Without its explicit critique, trans-culturation loses its edge and is good, at best, as a concept for factical analysis.[5]

Although Rama is quite aware of the difference between literary and anthropological transculturation, transculturation for him is still something "to be accomplished" rather than something that simply happens. In that sense he thought of Arguedas's work as "a reduced model for transculturation, where one could show and prove the eventuality of its actualization, so that if it was possible in literature it was also possible in the rest of the culture" (Rama, "Arguedas" 15; my trans. here and below). All of this of course depends on Rama's notion of transculturation as necessarily "successful" transculturation, that is, a transculturation where the dominated culture is able to register or inscribe itself into the dominant. That an inscription into the dominant culture as such may be considered to constitute a success (and the noninscription therefore a failure) implies a strong ideological positioning concerning transculturation as an everyday anthropological phenomenon: in fact, it ultimately implies the acceptance of modernization as ideological truth and world destiny. For Rama (and not only for Rama), transculturation is therefore always excessive with respect to itself, and it always already incorporates a certain goal. It is obvious that such a goal may or may not be shared by other subjects of transculturation, who may have different goals or may be blind to their goals or may not have a goal. But if they do not have a goal, they are not transculturators in the critical sense but only in the anthropological sense.

I will explore the excess of transculturation in two complementary ways: on the one hand, the end of critical transculturation will be understood as a historical self-subjecting to Eurocentric modernity; on the other hand, that same end of transculturation will also be understood as an opening toward an aporetics of meaning. Once the second sense is realized, however, transculturation comes to the end of itself and must mutate into alternative forms of confronting the materiality of history and its cultural precipitate. As oriented, in other words, transculturation necessarily reaches a final de-orientation. My contention is that only the de-orientated use of transculturation has the potential for critiquing empire—whereas its oriented use falls right into its ideological articulations.

In his foreword to the English translation of Néstor García Canclini's *Culturas híbridas,* Renato Rosaldo remarks that there is always a conceptual polarity involved in the critical concept of cultural hybridity: "hybridity can imply a space betwixt and between two zones of purity in a manner that follows biological usage that distinguishes two discrete species and the hybrid pseudospecies that results from their combination. . . . hybridity can [also] be understood as the ongoing condition of all human cultures, which contain no zones of purity because they undergo continuous processes of transculturation" (xv). The concept of transculturation is naturally entangled in the same unresolved and ultimately unresolvable polarity. The militant or critical version of literary transculturation on one hand must posit both a (utopian) zero degree and a full degree of transculturation, a point of origin and a goal, which are always and equally unreachable but without which transculturation would find itself deprived of a teleological reason for its own practice. The phenomenological usage of transculturation, on the other hand, can survive safely within the second term of the polarity, which ultimately makes it redundant or merely tautological, in the sense that if everything is transculturation then the concept itself has no particular critical validity. The conditions of possibility of critical transculturation, to the very extent that they refer back to or ground themselves in the anthropological notion as their natural ground, are therefore aporetic, because the critical concept is only made possible by the invocation of a reason for transculturation that is itself beyond the reach of transculturation: transculturation is always already transculturated. The way out of the aporetic conflict is of course always pragmatic: the end, or the limit, of every transculturating practice or analysis determines in every case its specific relevance as a hermeneutic tool. But that is no excuse to stop reflecting on the theoretical difficulty.

In Spitta's definition, "the transculturated subject is someone who, like [José María] Arguedas, is consciously or unconsciously situated between at least two worlds, two cultures, two languages, and two definitions of subjectivity, and who constantly mediates between them all." Transculturation would then organize that "ambivalent and indeterminate space" (24) where the transculturating artist or critic would be free to give herself over to the task of, in Rama's words, "recomposing from [previous cultural] material a superior discourse that could match or confront the most hierarchic products of a universal literature" ("Procesos" 228). Perhaps our historical times, different from Rama's, no longer advise or enable us to be so relentlessly enthusiastic in the evaluation of the cultural power of the world's semiperiphery—at least not in the sense invoked by Rama. The celebratory or heroic telos of oriented transculturation cannot respond to a rather simple question: What if that indeterminate space of in-betweenness should prove to be not the purveyor of a new historical coherence but rather a mestizo space of incoherence, in the definition of Claudio Lomnitz-Adler? "Mestizaje is the process wherein communities are extracted from their cultures of origin without being assimilated into the dominant culture. This is a process that entails fracturing the coherence of a subordinate . . . culture. It also entails undermining the conditions for the creation of a new, independent, coherent culture" (*Exits* 39). Hasn't transculturation theory assumed for too long that meaning is always already available, always already to be either found or produced? Such an insistence comes at the price of a certain foreclosure. What if transculturation were shown to be not a path to meaning but rather a path into the implosion of meaning? In other words, what if a given transculturating practice turned toward the site of its aporetic impossibility and not toward its possibility? It is merely a matter of emphasis, perhaps, but with rather portentous implications. Rama preferred to dwell on an optimistic or celebratory possibility, understanding the end of transculturation as the "ample overcoming of modernization" from a Latin American or regional perspective ("Procesos" 215), and perhaps that is what he had to do. It may now be time to examine the opposite or sinister side of transculturation. The thesis I propose is that critical transculturation, once it goes to the end of itself and explores, as it is wont to do through its own logic, its own excess with respect to itself, can no longer go on and so suffers collapse. Arguedas has given us perhaps the paradigmatic example in the Latin American tradition of this final transculturation of transculturation—its overturning, which comes to be, in the final analysis, its ownmost theoretical possibility.

Arguedas's dramatic staging of the implosion of meaning in transculturation takes place in his last, posthumously published novel, *El zorro de arriba y el zorro de abajo* (1971). Roland Forgues has succinctly expressed the major theoretical conflict with which Arguedas was forced to deal in the writing of *El zorro*: "On observing the deep mutation suffered by Chimbote's society, a mutation that radically questioned the ideas he had previously formed about mestizaje and the social and cultural integration of the Indians and other marginalized sectors, the writer had to confront the destabilization of what had until then constituted the very foundations of his work" ("Por qué bailan?" 314; my trans.). I plan to draw some of the theoretical and political conclusions for Latin American literary and cultural historiography that the novel not so secretly offers in the working out of that conflict.[6] The strong optimistic version that Rama offered us of Arguedas's writing obscured the already dark truth Arguedas explores in his last work: a truth that destabilizes not only the alleged foundation of Arguedas's previous writing but, more concretely, the reading that Rama gave us, and with it the dominant version of critical transculturation in Latin American thought.

A Writing of Disappropriation

Jean Franco has argued that several Latin American novels written before *El zorro* but also dealing with "the motif of the dying community or the wake around the body" must be understood as a textualization of the impossibility of construction of the modern Latin American state ("Nation" 206, 205). The writings of Gabriel García Márquez, post-*Zorro* work such as Augusto Roa Bastos's *Yo el Supremo*, and two texts by Edgardo Rodríguez Juliá are also presented by Franco as a representation of the impossibility of a nationalist ideology. Franco's readings are for her a sufficient demonstration that contemporary Latin American literature is not necessarily national-allegorical. In Franco's opinion, however, the fact that those texts do not seem to fall for nationalist state representation should not automatically make them fit the alternative mold of so-called Latin American postmodernism. Resistant to both nationalist narrativization and Latin American postmodernism, Franco prefers to speak of contemporary Latin American symbolic production as "an irrepressible process of appropriation and defiance" where we must detect "a Utopia glimpsed beyond the nightmare of an as yet unfinished modernity" (212).

Franco is engaging in a polemic with Fredric Jameson on the necessarily allegorical import of contemporary third-world literature, and to that extent she chooses her examples carefully.[7] But *El zorro*, which falls entirely within the purview of Jameson's model while at the same time, in a sense that will be explained later, turning it against itself, is not mentioned in Franco's essay. Would she

also think of it as part of the "irrepressible process of appropriation and defiance" of modernity that she finds in her exemplary
Latin American texts? There are solid grounds to do precisely that—
grounds offered, for instance, by Martin Lienhard's and Antonio Cornejo Polar's splendid research on the Arguedas novel.[8] However, if it
were true, as I will contend, that *El zorro* is a narrative of the end of
narrative, it would be reductive to call that writing of writing's collapse an "appropriation and defiance" of modernity. What else can it
then be?

Arguedas's writing in *El zorro*, which is a work between autobiography and fiction, between the personal and the social, is the expression of an event that does not easily yield to available critical-
ideological determinations. If *El zorro*'s fiction, that is, the attempt
at realistic representation of the postsymbolic world of Chimbote,
can perhaps still be understood as an appropriation and a defiance,
as the sort of successful transculturation Rama repeatedly described,
the autobiography that simultaneously writes Arguedas's way toward suicide is *also* a radical disappropriation and *also* a radical defeat, whatever else it may be. Of the two opposing tendencies, appropriation and disappropriation, which one leads and what remains?
Which one constitutes the ultimate horizon, or the end, of the novel?

Following Franco Moretti's argument in *Modern Epic: The World
System from Goethe to García Márquez, El zorro*, like García Márquez' *Cien años de soledad*, as a "novel of uneven and combined
development" (243), is one specific response to the situation that
arises when "the pressure of the world-system forces your country
into a more complete . . . integration. A thousand and one possibilities then really do become a thousand and one dead ends; the
multiplicity of possible developments, a set route. It is the hour of
black magic: an 'incredible' that is no longer bound to a whirlpool
of bizarre combinations, but to the enormity of the crimes committed" (245). Moretti's reading of *Cien años de soledad* has it that
García Márquez' novel arises in a complicity between "magic and
empire," whereby modern literature's "rhetoric of innocence" takes
its strategy of denial and disavowal one step further, into the heart
of the victim. If "the rhetoric of innocence" had been Goethe's discovery in *Faust*, the means by which the West, while being "most
lucid in recognizing the necessity of violence for [its own] civilized
life," simultaneously establishes "the necessity of its disavowal [i.e.,

disavowal of violence] for the West's civilized consciousness" (26),
then García Márquez' brand of magical realism subserviently incorporates such a rhetoric into the literary resources of the world-
system's semiperiphery. In *Cien años de soledad* "forced modernization [becomes] a story of extraordinary delight" (*Modern Epic*
249). A certain appropriation occurs, a certain transculturation has
taken place. But both appropriation and transculturation are pur-
chased at the price of service to historical hegemony: not so much
an overcoming of modernization as a submission to it. Submission
is the price of transculturation's appropriation. In Moretti's words:
"A really strange place, Macondo. A city of madmen, where nobody
has anything in common with anybody else. But where *language is
the same for everybody*. While you are reading you pay no attention
to it—it is all so lovely. But if you reopen the novel with a little de-
tachment, you find that the narrator's impersonal voice covers more
or less *ninety five per cent* of the textual space . . . a real triumph of
monologism" (245–46).

Moretti's unsettling point is simply that magical realism has historically functioned as an apparatus for the capture of nonsynchro-
nicity, of heterogeneous contemporaneity, through the incorporation of the periphery's "reserves of magic" into a global enterprise of
world "re-enchantment" (249), which serves as an ideological justification of the world-system. Its primary technical innovation would
be the conflation of the rhetoric of innocence (which uses the periphery's "magic" for an enterprise of disavowal) and the ideology of
progress and modernization: "For in magical realism the heterogeneity of historical time is also, for the first time, *narratively interesting:* it produces plot, suspense. It is not just the sign of a complex,
stratified history: it is also the symptom of a *history in progress*"
(243).

There is therefore a surface agreement between Rama and Franco,
on the one hand, and Moretti, on the other, which is only the ob-
verse of a deeper disagreement: if Franco and Rama read the Latin
American text as a symptom of "an as yet unfinished modernity,"
Moretti sees the path to modernization as a relentless dissolution
of heterogeneity "according to an ascending genealogy—which will
then end by legitimizing the dominion of the 'advanced' West over
the 'backward' periphery" (*Modern Epic* 51). Everything may then
have to do with our own critical position concerning moderniza-

tion. But is it possible to turn magical realism against itself, or to use it otherwise? What if a Latin American text, such as *El zorro*, had given us the means for understanding a diametrically opposite possibility within magical realism whereby the magical-real apparatus could reveal itself to be not simply a machine of appropriation but its opposite? The critical game would then be to expand our notion of magical realism and make it open itself to a deeper articulation. If the conditions of possibility of magical realism, or of literary transculturation in Rama's sense, are determined by "appropriation and defiance," in Franco's expression, out of a certain temporal heterogeneity or noncontemporaneity of the material, perhaps what we could call the "defiance of disappropriation" *within* magical realism would reveal an altogether different ground for its theoretical definition. In Arguedas's text, as we will see, the double sound of gunpowder and lead, the fatal scar showing up at the end of its writing as sign and signature of the identity between the writer and the text, tragically brings to effect and completion the theoretical moment of the magical real as textual event. But the event is here nonconjunctive: it is rather a fissure in sense, designated by Arguedas with the Quechua word *huayco*, which is an abyss, a precipice. With it, we begin to see *appropriation* as an inadequate concept for understanding what is truly decisive about magical realism as the dominant manifestation of literary transculturation in contemporary Latin American times.

Los zorros, as it is said that Arguedas always referred to what is now known as *El zorro de arriba y el zorro de abajo*, published in 1971 and long considered a failed, insufficient novel, certainly not one of Arguedas's best and certainly not part of the so-called boom of the Latin American novel, is an epochal text for Latin American culture in which the possibility of a new commemoration, that is, a new reading of both the past and the future traditions of Latin American writing, is given.[9] I propose to read *from* Arguedas's epochal text (and *in* it) an event of heterogeneity that might alter our understanding of magical realism as a central ideologeme for Latin American cultural self-understanding. I will contend that *Los zorros*, written between 1966 and 1969, closes Latin American magical realism, or, better, reveals that its conditions of possibility are also at the same time its conditions of impossibility. Magical realism after Arguedas, at least where it is not a neocolonialist commercial mystification, can only begin to repeat Arguedas' gesture, but cannot, structurally speaking, take it any further than Arguedas did, precisely because what Arguedas ultimately did was to undo magical realism and its system of representation. If the very tendency of magical realism is to seek its own undoing (by familiarizing the unfamiliar), the destruction of the possibility of magical realism will be shown to be the moment of its maximum effectiveness. Could the same be said about transculturation?

Incalculable Loss

Cornejo Polar's theory of literary heterogeneity in Latin America, in which I read disjunction as the inescapable dimension of cultural encounter within the Latin American literary artifact, has been largely disattended.[10] The Latin American critical establishment, in the wake of the boom years and still totally possessed by the mirage of cultural presence in the global market, preferred to follow a simplified version of Rama's ideas on transculturation, which form more or less the hegemonic if often unstated paradigm for critical reflection on Latin American literature.[11] Transculturation—that is, the macroprocess of translation by which elements of one culture are naturalized in another culture, although not without undergoing some changes during the process—of course insists on conciliation, conjunction, and dialectical unification of the global cultural field. It is a productive model, but it is also a model that must work and even feed on the systematic erasure of what does not fit into it. And this Rama knew well.

In Rama's historical analysis, the group of narrators he calls "transculturators" (fundamentally, Juan Rulfo, João Guimaraes Rosa, José María Arguedas, and Gabriel García Márquez) constitutes a particular form of response to the crisis of accelerated modernization and integration into the world-system that Moretti also referred to. In this specific historical sense, transculturation retains, from the previously dominant paradigm of regionalist or *criollista* writing, the need for "the conservation of those elements from the past which had contributed to cultural singularization" and tries to "transmit them to the future as a way of preserving acquired formations" ("Procesos" 205). But this kind of conditioned preservation comes at a price.

Transculturation is a war machine, feeding on cultural difference, whose principal function is the reduction of the possibility of radical cultural heterogeneity. Transculturation is a part of the ideology of cultural productionism, indeed a systemic part of a Western metaphysics of production, which still retains a strong colonizing grip on the cultural field. Arguedas's destruction of magical realism as a conjunctive or mediating possibility is a gesture against transculturation. By returning heterogeneity to where it belongs, Arguedas unmasks the reconciling tactics of transculturation as cure or "appropriation and defiance." In a brief but important speech delivered in October 1968 at the Inca Garcilaso de la Vega Award ceremony, Arguedas said: "I am not acculturated, I am a Peruvian who proudly, like a happy demon, speaks Christian and Indian, Spanish and Quechua" (my trans., here and below).[12] For Arguedas, transculturation could not be more than a remedial step taken after acculturation has sadly happened. And he has strong words for acculturation: "a vanquished nation giving up her soul . . . and taking up the soul of the victors" (Zorro 257). Arguedas's demon is the uncanny will to speak two languages, to live in two cultures, to feel with two souls: a doubled demon, a demon of doubling, perhaps happy but also mischievous, as we shall see. In his affirmation of doubledness, Arguedas makes manifest his forceful rejection of the ideology of cultural conciliation, indeed stating his final conviction that, at the cultural level, there can be no conciliation without forced subordination. Arguedas was writing his last novel at the time of the Garcilaso Award ceremony. He knew then that everything was at stake in his bitter attempt to confront the experiential problematics that had always been at the core of his writing. He also knew that his previous attempts were no longer of any use: he was approaching a dangerous edge where theory, and life, started to taste uncannily like lead.

Los zorros is apparently only the presentation of life in a new industrial center of the Peruvian Pacific Coast. In Chimbote a huge industrial conglomerate developed during the 1960s, whose main purpose was to process the bountiful fish of the South American Pacific into fishmeal for agricultural and other purposes. Before this happened, Chimbote was only an isolated Peruvian beach. During the fishmeal boom years it grew, through massive immigration, into a city many tens of thousands of people strong, most of whom were relatively recently proletarianized peasants. The sociocultural conflicts that immediately originated fascinated and horrified Arguedas, who came to see Chimbote as the apotheosis of the Andean future. For Arguedas, at this point, a drastically urgent if perhaps already desperate task lay at hand: to reappropriate, to resymbolize, life in Chimbote into a possible utopia, the only hope for the future. The magical-real machine was then emblematically in place—or apparently so. But in that limit-situation transculturation could only happen as a failure of transculturation—through the failure itself.

Arguedas's presentation of the Chimbote universe is thoroughly demonized in two specific and thoroughly diverse ways. The first is in the forceful interpolation within the text of diary fragments in which Arguedas repeatedly manifests his intention to kill himself unless the novel somehow saves him. The second is by means of the conventional repertoire of the magical real represented by the enigmatic and defamiliarizing presence of the two foxes: the fox from down below and the fox from up above, obviously two *huacas*, as is said in Quechua, two demons or minor deities who make a brief but significant appearance in the sixteenth-century Andean Huarochirí chronicle, from where Arguedas takes them. Descriptions of actual life situations that Arguedas witnessed in his research trips to Chimbote alternate in the novel with magical-real moments in which the conflict of cultures is violently thematized, and these both are interspersed with self-reflective moments in which characters talk with calm or despair about their predicament.

Both Arguedas's text and the very location of the text, Chimbote, the beach where Peru finally meets transnational capitalism, are presented as holes of the real, dark pools or dark wounds of the world, where a world catastrophe is happening.[13] The wealthy capitalist Braschi and the other fishmeal entrepreneurs (who are not merely, the text says, mealmakers but also madmakers, because they produce madness) have taken things "hasta donde no hay sol ni luna" ("to where there is neither sun nor moon"; *Zorro* 116; my trans., here and below). They have, that is, impossibly taken things even beyond the realm of the black sun, there where, as Freud puts it, the shadow of the object has fallen on the subject.[14] In Chimbote, in Arguedas's textual hell, where even the notion of shadow has vanished because everything is a shadow, melancholy is an optimistic delusion, a welcome relief from the overwhelming, always pending, psychotic collapse. *Los zorros* is a text written in the fold of a death wish whose most intimate sense, explicit in the diaries, may have been to ward off a psychotic collapse that would have had more than personal implications. It is here where the two dimensions of the novel, the fictional-ethnographic and the autobiographical or auto-thanatographical, come together seamlessly.[15] Arguedas's narcissistic psychosis finds its world-catastrophic symbol in Chimbote. That is why Chimbote, in Arguedas's representation, is a postsymbolic world where conciliation has yielded to renunciation: a limit world where Arguedas wants to fight the losing battle of resignification.

Arguedas's last word on the possibility of resignification, as we will see, comes to us not through magical-real demonization but through its other side: through suicide as transculturation's end. It is suicide that reads the magical real. The fact that it does not happen the other way around is of course crucial not just for the history of Latin American literature but also for the theoretical understanding of the limits of transculturation. Arguedas's suicide must be read not as the end of the novel, but necessarily as the novel's own end.[16] In a letter the definitive redaction of which takes place on the November 5, 1969, after Arguedas has already made a final decision concerning his death, he says: "I will not survive the book. Since I am sure that my abilities and weapons as a creator . . . have weakened to near-nullity and I only have left those who would reduce me to the condition of an impotent and passive spectator of the formidable struggle that Humanity is carrying on in Peru and everywhere, it would not be possible for me to tolerate such a fate" (*Zorro* 250).

This "formidable struggle," which is not just a struggle of the Quechua people and not only a Peruvian struggle but humanity's own struggle, is the struggle for the new beginning in which Arguedas had attempted to believe, which he had attempted to bring into existence, his whole life. Another epistolary text, which, like the one just cited, is also incorporated in the novel as such, is even clearer: "Perhaps with me a cycle is beginning to close and another one is opening up in Peru and what Peru represents: the cycle of the comforting lark is closing, of the whipping, the muleteering, the impotent hate, of the funereal uprisings, of the fear of God and the dominance of that God and his protegés, his makers; the cycle of light and of the invincible liberating force of the Vietnam man is opening up, of the fire lark, of the liberating God" (*Zorro* 245–46).[17] Arguedas's new beginning (in which the old Tawantinsuyo notion of the *pachacutiy* or cosmic cycle is quite active), his belief in the new beginning, which forces him to remove himself once he is no longer strong enough to share in the "bloody struggle of the centuries" (246), dominates the totality of the textual construction of *Los zorros.* At the opening of the novel the foxes are conversing; they tell each other that this is only the second time they have met in twenty-five hundred years, an ominous event (49). Arguedas's madness and suicide are a result of his lifelong struggle to remove himself from a system of reason that constituted itself in and through the exclusion of Quechua peasants from the very possibility of sanity. If Lienhard is right when he says that "in contemporary Quechua poetry" there is an "almost obsessive presence" of Andean messianism, prophecy, and utopianism, if that messianism is always understood to be the announcement of a historical break, and if that break is consistently related to the *pachacutiy* (Lienhard, *Voz* 221), then a work written on the horizon of the break and leading, as *Los zorros* led, to vital exhaustion, cannot just be read as a symptom of personal despair. Rather, Arguedas's personal is political, and his libidinal economy must indeed be read in the context of the difficult, perhaps impossible (re)formation of a national allegory whose necessity, in today's Peru, does not need to be emphasized.[18]

Arguedas was born in 1911 in a small village of the Peruvian Andes (Andahuaylas) and his mother died when he was three years old. His father, a traveling judge, was forced to leave his child for long periods of time in the company of Quechua servants. Quechua was therefore his first language, but with it he also necessarily learned his social difference from it, a painful split that would haunt him throughout his professionalization (first as a teacher of Spanish, then as an ethnologist of Quechua culture, and finally as a writer) and his socialist politics, possibly to his death. Roberto González Echevarría, among others, has not hesitated to point out that Arguedas "felt within himself the contradictions and the tragedy inherent in the relationship between anthropology and literature with an intensity that in 1969 led him to choose suicide" (*Myth* 15). For Arguedas, of course, the conflict between anthropology and literature was always something more and something less than a disciplinary conflict; it was also the violently felt conflict between two parts of his soul and the source of a serious narcissistic wound, which he ultimately came to love too passionately, more than life itself.

Can Arguedas's suicide be read as an act of "unwriting" such as the one González Echevarría claims is implied in every modification of the Latin American archive? If, as González Echevarría has argued, anthropology, or an anthropological desire, marked the hegemonic literary paradigm in Latin America in 1969, is *Los zorros* just another instance of that dominance, or, on the contrary, does it announce the end of the anthropological paradigm and in so doing prefigure a reconfiguration of the archive whose break with the previous one goes further than anything yet seen since 1492? Arguedas's unwriting of himself, his self-erasure, which is also, as we shall see, a portentous form of self-inscription, is not too far from matching, all too literally, González Echevarría's notion of archival gaps.[19]

Magical realism finds its final theoretical moment, or its abysmal moment, in November 28, 1969. That day José María Arguedas committed suicide in his office at the Agrarian University of La Molina, in Lima. A previous, failed attempt, which had taken place in April 1966 (there had been an earlier one in 1944), is mentioned in the very first line of *Los zorros:* "I attempted to commit suicide . . . in April 1966" (7). *Los zorros* ends with the following words: "Nov. 28, 1969. I choose this day because it won't interfere so much with the functioning of the University. I think the registration period will be over. I might make my friends and the authorities waste Saturday and Sunday, but it [*sic*] belongs to them and not to the u. (J. M. A.)" (255). After writing those words, Arguedas put two bullets through his head, two final affirmations of his will to death. Perhaps unsettlingly, the end of the novel figures them or allegorizes them in those repetitions of the last sentence: a bullet for my friends and a bullet for the authorities; a bullet for Saturday and a bullet for Sunday; a bullet for them; and a bullet for the university. Arguedas is addressing the voices that would still yell at him from the depths of his neurosis, but he is also perhaps calling attention to the fact that two bullets were coming, had come, and not just one: two powerful diacritical marks symbolizing the final identity of the novel and the writer's dead body.

Does this book, which Arguedas's widow, Sybila Arredondo, would publish two years later, end with the prefiguration of those two shots, or does it end with the shots themselves? They are not a final period through his brain but a colon, signing (off) an equivalency between the text that Arguedas left on his office desk and his doubly perforated corpse. *El zorro de arriba y el zorro de abajo* will always have to be read as fantasmatized by the writer's cadaver, given Arguedas's signature effect, given that Arguedas signed the end of the book with two bullets. *El zorro de arriba y el zorro de abajo* is really a crypt where the dead body of the writer still lives, an undead writer, an undead author, as every reader who has read in utter perplexity how death silently and inexorably comes Arguedas's way knows very well. The death of the author is here truly inseparable from the novel's very status as an artwork, that is, it can't be read away from it.

Forguco has warned against the possible superficiality of thinking that the apparent inconclusiveness of the narrative "can be a [willed] mode of articulation of the text with History, and that [Arguedas's] suicide would amount to a kind of justification of the open-narrative technique taken to its last consequences" ("Por qué bailan?" 313). I agree that it is not a matter of being reductive or of oversimplifying. At the same time, however, *Los zorros* comes to be absolutely cannibalized by that which constitutes it as a posthumous object: Arguedas's suicide, after all, cannot in any way be understood or even thought of independently of the problems that the text exposes, for the very fact that suicide *is* thematized and presented by Arguedas himself as something that will happen unless the text saves him, while all the time saying that it probably will not. We know, from a letter written on October 31, 1969 to his department chair at the university, that the writing of *Los zorros* is, as Arguedas puts it, "a part of the therapeutic treatment I was told to undergo" after his second attempt at suicide in April 1966 (*Zorro* 295). The novel itself says it over and over again: "It is not disgraceful to fight death by writing. I think the doctors may be right" (19). And, "I have fought against death or I believe to have fought against death by writing this faltering, whining narrative. I had few and weak allies, hesitant; her allies have won. They are strong and they were well sheltered in my own flesh. This unequal narrative is an image of the unequal fight" (243). Writing his text was a fight against death that ended up being a yielding to, and an embrace of, death, as if death were indeed a restful presence.

Understanding how the author's death can also be here the figure of an utopian space of regeneration is of course a task of extraordinary difficulty, but it is one in which the very possibility of a writing of mourning comes to be decided. Edmundo Gómez Mango, in a brilliant and unfortunately brief paper, has acknowledged this with good critical economy, "Arguedas' novelistic language is never more inebriating and powerful than when he comes to the edge of the *huayco* of his own destruction; it is as if he could only find or invent the plenitude of his writing in the imminence of his own, final, and silent disaster" ("Todas" 367; my trans., here and below). For Gómez Mango *Los zorros* is a writing of the lost object, and it is all the more successful as such, the more the writing is implied in its own catastrophe. "Mourning for the lost object has not been accomplished. The magical rite of writing in order not to die fails in its own victory" (368)—since, I would add, dying is postponed for as long as writing lasts, but no longer. Because the writing in *Los zorros* is a commemoration of an incalculable loss, it can only satisfy itself within a horizon of loss. In this sense Arguedas's death, within the textual context in which we learn of it, is essentially a writing event, an event of writing. But Arguedas's death is also an opting out of writing altogether. In suicide, Arguedas comes to the end of writing. By coming to the end of writing, Arguedas takes writing to its very end, there where it reveals itself as an instrument of signification, precisely because it loses the power to signify. I want to read this fact in the light of the magical-real machine that Arguedas is all the while trying to set into unfaltering motion in Chimbote.

A Negative Accomplishment

Los zorros opens up a new cycle of Latin American writing because it closes the possibility of an anthropological writing in González Echevarría's sense, or even in the sense in which Lienhard, one of the leading Arguedas scholars, has theorized what he calls "ethnofiction." It is not that after *Los zorros* ethnofiction or anthropological narrative is no longer possible, but that *Los zorros* offers itself as a decisive text in which the conditions of impossibility of anthropological fiction are shown as such—conditions of impossibility, that is, insofar as we make them depend on epistemological paralysis rather than on ethical or even political grounds. *Los zorros* marks the theoretical end of anthropological ethnofiction because *Los zorros* takes anthropological ethnofiction to a breaking point. At that breaking point, magical realism, as the organizing principle of ethnofiction, is epistemologically shattered because it is revealed to be inexorably dependent upon the subordination of indigenous cultures to an always already Western-hegemonic machine of transculturation: to modernization itself.

Referring to Lienhard's extensive investigation on Quechua elements within the text, Cornejo Polar risks the following statement: "In *El zorro de arriba y el zorro de abajo* the Andean components are of such a magnitude and they exert such decisive functions, that it is legitimate to think that in that novel, for the first time, indigenous rationality comes to account for modernity [da razón de la modernidad]" ("Ensayo" 303). That it may indeed be legitimate to think so gives us an idea of the very high, epochal stakes that *Los zorros* had set for itself. We do not need to accept the literal truth of Cornejo Polar's statement in order to accept that such an intentionality had partially orchestrated the writing of the book. The other side of the novel's therapeutic failure is then the gift of a cultural instrument in which, for the first time, as Lienhard and Cornejo Polar underline, the oppressing rationality comes, at least tendentially, to be contained by a form of understanding that cannot be accounted for within its parameters.

What I would consider the epochal fact that *Los zorros* embodies is that such (tendential) upturning of perspectives is necessarily and irrevocably framed in the catastrophic aura of a suicide that absolutely suspends all feelings of victory or of liberation, and thus any possibility of "accomplishment," unless we speak of an accomplishment of "negation" in the same way in which we could speak of a negative theology (which is, by the way, the object of a rather secret but extensive treatment in the book). Let me make it clear: if those two shots at the end of the book, the sinister colon, signal the symbolic identity between *Los zorros* and Arguedas's dead body, then it is undeniable that Arguedas is dead because he paid the price, or at any rate he thought he paid the price, writing imposed on him, and it is undeniable that such a price is literally the impossibility of paying the price. The upturning of the cultural perspective within the book, the substitution of what Forgues calls tragic for dialectical thinking, of Quechua for Spanish rationality: all that drained him and made him suspect that his own personal sacrifice, redundant at that point as it may have been for anybody but Arguedas himself, was essential for the novel to accomplish what it had to accomplish—negatively.

Arguedas's epochal accomplishment was against any and all

transculturation, namely, a text where a nonhegemonic rationality could be thought to account or to give the very principle of reason for modernity itself. I do not think such an accomplishment, on which we will never have reflected enough, can be read over, beyond, or apart from Arguedas's textual, literal, suicide. At the moment when Arguedas's inner tension made it possible for him to bring the magical-real machine into its most proper position, at that moment the nonsynchronous contradiction reversed itself and arrest ensued. The result was, of course, not a punctual moment of noncontradiction but rather an aporetic gap of meaning, and disjunction offered incalculable loss, a final arrest of productivity.

But with it the Latin American transculturating machine came to its end, in the double sense of epochal culmination and of equally epochal exhaustion. It is in that sense, in the sense of the double sense, that the novel triumphs through its very failure. Cornejo Polar possibly points in the same direction when he says: "Paradoxically, the highest interest and value in Arguedas' last novel is to be, tragically but enlighteningly, testimony . . . of unresolved contradictions, on which . . . it configures itself as a work of art" ("Ensayo" 301). I, however, do not think the contradictions are unresolved: the most extreme moment of transculturation, the transculturation of transculturation, results and resolves itself in aporetic, unreconstructible loss. Through it Arguedas's suicide marks the beginning of an alternative system of writing: a "defiance of disappropriation," a writing of dis-affect, an antimodern writing whereby his text comes to present itself as a passionate signifier of the end of signification. But the end of signification is not yet the last word.

Arguedas will remove himself, the last man of the old cycle, so that a new cycle may begin. That is why in a letter written on November 27, that is, the day before his suicide, and included as such within the novel, Arguedas mentions, almost casually, that his novel is "casi inconclusa" ["almost unfinished"] (*Zorro* 252). It is "almost unfinished" because he had not yet killed himself, but he had already made the irrevocable decision to do so. After Arguedas's suicide the novel will and will not be finished, simultaneously and undecidably: no other interpretation of "casi inconclusa" is, to my mind, possible, although I realize that this interpretation is based on the very unreadability of Arguedas's phrase. Arguedas's suicide is, properly speaking, the end of the book. Arguedas's radical disincorporation is

also the investiture of his book, through an unheard-of act of identification, with the phantasmatic aura of his own split, melancholic
identity, thus testifying to the final impossibility of transculturation.
With and through Arguedas's suicide, the conditions of literary possibility of *Los zorros* open themselves onto their conditions of impossibility. We are far from "an ample overcoming of modernization"
in Rama's sense.

But what about magical realism? Beyond any and all magical-real
episodes in the text, every intervention of the foxes, every piercing
sound of the bug called Onquray Onquray, the ominous messenger,
every *yunsa* and every *yawar mayu*, and every song of the mountain
ducks that gives the foxes the ability to understand the soul of the
world, Arguedas's death is the truest magical-real event of the novel,
as it gives itself as testimony to a violent conflict of cultures that
will not be mediated away. Arguedas's death is a fissure in the textual sense that paradoxically organizes the text's plenitude of sense:
meaning, in this novel, results from meaning's absolute implosion.
As an event of writing placed between the novel's failure and failure's other side, a rift, a gap, a bullet hole of total disjunction opens
itself: as soon as meaning emerges, it needs to be erased anew. Or
better, meaning is here the necessity of its erasure. Guido Podestá
has pointed out that *Los zorros* represents "the irresolution of an
aporia," (101), implying that in what we could call the andeanization of modernity there is nothing like emancipation. For Podestá,
Los zorros witnesses "the emergency, understanding it as the unexpected appearance, of the postmodern condition in Peru" ("*Zorro*"
101; my trans.). This emergence/emergency, at the same time event
and danger, is aporetically resolved in the text: doubt, the extreme
perplexity between the andeanization of modernity and therapeutic
failure, will not remain stable. Every aporia induces a moment of
loss, in which the fight for sense is negatively solved, solved in negativity: that is ultimately the "unequal-ness" of Arguedas's struggle,
and his legacy. Arguedas's renunciation of the "rhetoric of innocence" destabilizes to an extreme the conciliation of "magic" and
"empire," in Moretti's terms, which is the price of the incorporation
of Latin American writing into the world-system.

The loss at the end of magical realism makes it difficult to read
the magical-realist tradition as a tradition in which national allegory is the ultimate account. Arguedas shows that the magical-real

moment is tendentially a moment in which the national allegory, on the other side of its utopian directives, opens onto its colonizing substratum. Magical realism comes with Arguedas to its theoretical impossibility because Arguedas shows how magical realism is an impossible scene of emancipatory representation staged from a colonizing perspective. Arguedas destroys the good faith of a deluded enterprise. And he offers no alternative, other than insight. Arguedas's posthumous novel follows a path that is diametrically opposed to the one denounced by Moretti and counterintentionally supported by Rama's theory of transculturation and by so many other critics. Arguedas offers a new possibility for Latin American writing by radicalizing his own theoretical investigation—which, as often happens, was also an affective investigation his psychic texture could not bear. Arguedas's novel, at its limit, opens transculturation theory to the presence of a silent and unreadable event. Arguedas's suicide occurs, for us, as a language event. It is an illegible one, in the sense that it opens a fissure between language and signification. Maybe all language events do that: they produce themselves by showing illegibility, disparity between meaning and the materiality of the sign. Perhaps then an event is more of an event, the more illegible it is. As one opens one's self to the event, the event becomes more and more difficult to inscribe in a process of signification. An event, a language event, is an excess whose sense is only given in its recess, its withdrawal. As Jean-Luc Nancy puts it, an event is that which exposes the excess of meaning over any accomplishment of signification.[20] The language event offers a possibility for thinking in which thought fleetingly becomes a total resistance to sense. Thinking, an excess of sense, will depend then on the possibility of loss of sense.

This loss of sense within narrative organizes the language event as an instance of denarrativization. Arguedas's suicide, the end of the narrative, is a moment of denarrativization. It has an epistemological import that affects the Latin American literary tradition at the archival level and brings it closer to the indifferentiation of action and meaning that we saw in chapter 3, following Willy Thayer, as the condition of intellectual work in the age of real subsumption. Arguedas's suicide, the denarrativization of narrative within the narrative, is the most intense, and therefore the most illegible accomplishment of magical realism. Because it brings magical realism to its fulfillment, it breaks magical realism; it brings it to the end of its narrative and it opens it, in all the strength of the paradox, onto the possibility of an actual critique of empire.

With Arguedas's literary act, Latin American foundational utopianism comes to its end. Arguedas loses for us all traces of the possibility of a magical-real mediation of cultures, just as much as he loses the possibility of a final conciliation between land and the human, between cultures and what we, against all evidence, have insisted on calling culture. He therefore also signals the end of the anthropological paradigm for literary practice and, with it, for all critical practice: so the cycle of the fire lark may, perhaps, begin.

Testimonio and the Question of Literature

The 1999 publication of David Stoll's *Rigoberta Menchú and the Story of All Poor Guatemalans* gave some readers the impression that the apparently radical incompatibility between the two opposing armies of the late 1980s cultural wars was going to be adjudicated somewhat scientifically. If Rigoberta Menchú's testimonio could be shown or had been shown to be largely a fiction, well then, those critics who had put all their chips on the abandonment of the high literary canon for the sake of the new referentiality of the subaltern experience would be taking one on the head. Either they were going to have to accept that Rigoberta Menchú and Elizabeth Burgos-Debray's account was simply literature and that it had to be measured in its value as a literary text, or they were going to have to backtrack and denounce Menchú as a liar and Burgos-Debray as a credulous dupe and denounce themselves as willing dupes as well. Either way, Stoll won, and his victory seemed to go beyond Menchú's particular case: Menchú was taken as a symptom of the general politicization of culture in a situation in which the difference between politicization and a highly Machiavellian use of referential truth was not easily discernible. For these readers, Stoll set the record straight and brought it all to the surface; his indignant berating of the gullible critics was simply the sort of corrective on which a better, more finely attuned interpretation of the text would be finally established. Supposing that Stoll had not, after all, gotten all his facts right, surely some facts at least were right, and that already meant that the testimonio was not a real testimonio. Once that conclusion was reached, the literary merits, but no longer the truth claims, of the Menchú–Burgos Debray text would determine whether the text would continue to be read. The centuries-old values of the literary tradition would be reestablished.

The situation appeared schematically simple: testimonio critics had based their claims on the Menchú–Burgos-Debray text on its textual truth, not on its literary value. Stoll had established that the textual truth was faulty. The testimonio critics, tail between their legs, were then going to have to recycle themselves as literary critics if they still wanted to read the text that had meant so much for them, since it is the privilege of literary criticism not to set so much store on the historical truth of the text it reads: the truth of a literary text is its tropology or its fictionality. But what if this conflict of interpretations were not to be understood through a supposedly neutral reading, whose mission would be to evaluate their respective merits on the basis of the weight of their different claims to reason? What if the different positions could not be adjudicated from something like a positionless point, or what Peggy Kamuf calls an ultimate "ground of consensus upon which division and dissent are merely staged as in a theater" (*Division* 18)? Perhaps the conflict of interpretations on which the critical profession is said to flourish is too "stable and stabilizing [a] model," and "something else, something more fundamentally destabilizing and detotalizing has shown itself to be at work on the very borders of the institution" (20). Could that "something else" be related to John Guillory's notion of cultural capital? For Guillory "literary works must be seen . . . as the vectors of ideological notions which do not inhere in the works themselves but in the context of their institutional presentation, or more simply, in the way in which they are taught" (*Cultural Capital* 9).

In recent years high literature has suffered a drastic loss of cultural capital. Traditional literary preoccupations seem at times almost residual even in what one would have assumed to be among their most powerful strongholds, namely, literature departments in U.S. universities. In retrospect, it is easy to say that the rise of theory in the 1970s contributed to the loss of prestige of literary-critical endeavors; it is equally easy, however, and possibly more accurate, to believe that poststructuralist theory was in fact for a few years high literature's last hope for revival in the present sociocultural configuration. The situation may seem paradoxical in that this downturn of literary cultural capital is coincidental with the continued influence, dating from the 1970s, on other disciplines of methodological and theoretical tools first developed in literature departments. But the contestation of traditional cultural canons and the ongoing theorization of emerging transnational, translinguistic, and transmedial loci of enunciation do not exhaustively explain the seemingly radical reduction of the literary field.

In the case of Latin Americanist reflection, the exhaustion of the boom-postboom literary models has occurred not only because metropolitan postmodernity has erased the possibility of a convincing allegorization of the national (boom), and therefore also of its deconstruction (post-boom). Instead, current changes are a function of the decline of a way of conceiving sociopolitical and cultural praxis that had a lot to do with the Cold War and its attendant phenomena. Under Cold War conditions the Latin American national security state made politics center on the issue of revolution understood as a national revolution.[1] Cultural workers of all shades in the political spectrum were forced to confront the revolutionary question, because that was what ultimately regulated their relationship to the state. The perception of culture was therefore heavily determined by national politics, although national politics was seen, according to individual political positions, through the prism of class and interclass alliances around the primary revolutionary possibility. Literary production came heavily and predominantly to figure as national-individual allegory in relation to the revolutionary configuration—a revolution that, for the cultural elite, was most significantly thought of in cultural-national rather than in socialist, anticapitalist terms. Whether an individual was for or against revolution was of course simply a supplementary matter that did not change the structural fact of the need to take a position.

But under current post–Cold War conditions identity politics has replaced class and even nationalist politics as the best way to fight for the albeit limited democratization that financial capitalism can accommodate. Identity politics seems to have become the primary means for contesting the homogenizing apparatus that an increasing socioeconomic globalization is imposing in the cultural sphere.[2]

And of course identity politics drastically questions the self-awarded credentials that the cultural elite had appropriated in terms of vertical representation of its mostly national, but sometimes continental, constituencies. From the point of view of identity politics, literary artifacts such as the boom and even the postboom novel have little to offer, if and when they are not perceived in the first place as in themselves part of the cultural structure to be dismantled. The cultural dimension of identity politics is mostly committed to identitarian representations that no longer pass through revolution or through national-individual allegorizations and that are best, but not exhaustively, understood as resistance against the homogenizing pull of global postmodernity, even though necessarily mediated by power configurations at the national or intranational level.

As preservers of cultural capital, literary critics could comfortably justify their endeavors sheltered in the unquestioned assumption of literature's hegemony and its organic link with the self-understanding of the given national or multinational tradition and its projections for change or continuity or both. Those national traditions reached a historical breaking point all over Latin America in the ominous decades preceding the final collapse of the socialist block, especially in Southern Cone national security states and in Central American counterinsurgency regimes. When global conditions during and after the years of gestation of that collapse preempted the possibility of reconstitution of national traditions according to the old parameters, then Latin American literary writing lost cultural hegemony and literary critics started acknowledging the possibility that a belated death of (high) literature follows the dissolution of national grammars and the withdrawal of the communal gods. High literature is no longer effective, it would seem, in the fight against late-capitalist globalization; instead, other cultural possibilities must be investigated.

When looked at from the perspective of identity politics, literature may indeed appear as colonial discourse, because the literary demand can apparently no longer be recognized, cannot even be heard in its compensatory, potentially preparatory tones.[3] For identity politics the literature of the boom/postboom becomes no more than an obsolete melodrama where the forces in confrontation are relevant for the sake of historical appreciation but not for the history of the future. If it is true, as the critical commonplace has it, that the

Latin American boom novel occurs around the historical event of the Cuban revolution and the continental hopes it elicited, then let us suggest that the (assumed) end of revolutionary hopes at the very least closes a vast literary cycle in Latin America that did not really start with the Cuban Revolution but with Enlightenment hopes for social emancipation and the rise of the European novel. Is this the cycle that Arguedas had in mind when he resorted to removing his literary practice from it?

It is often heard that testimonio is the most significant cultural production to have come out of Latin America in the 1980s—although the beginnings of testimonio as a consciously cultivated discursive option or genre go back to Cuba of the late 1960s and early 1970s.[4] The literary status of testimonio is a hotly debated issue. Elzbieta Sklodowska has repeatedly called into question the more or less naïve, more or less ideological attempts at turning testimonio into a purely referential discursive act. Her discussion of testimonio's paratextual apparatus is a useful and necessary reminder that the literary, even in its merely aesthetic dimension, is in any case a constant and irreducible presence in the testimonial text (*Testimonio* 7–53; see also 68–76, 93–101). Nevertheless, the cultural significance of testimonio includes an extraliterary dimension that is just as irreducible. That extraliterary dimension is certainly tenuous, and perhaps it would be best defined in the negative, as a mere insistence on the referential limits of the literary and, thus, as an insistence against the globalizing elements of the modernist literary apparatus, which is now perceived as not too distant from, if not in itself a part of, the ideological state apparatus. I am not suggesting that testimonio can exist outside the literary; only that the specificity of testimonio, and its particular position in the current cultural configuration, depends on an extraliterary stance or moment, which we could also understand as a moment of arrest of all symbolization in a direct appeal to the nonexemplary but still singular pain beyond any possibility of representation.[5] Once again Arguedas's final act appears prophetic. Testimonio is testimonio because it suspends the literary at the very same time that it constitutes itself as a literary act: as literature, it is a liminal event opening onto a nonrepresentational, drastically indexical order of experience.

The attraction of testimonio is not primarily its literary dimension—even though it is true that the most successful testimonios are also those that have a better claim to literary eminence. But what can make the reading of testimonio an addictive experience, from the literary as well as from the political perspective, is that testimonio always already incorporates an abandonment of the literary. Testimonio provides its reader with the possibility of entering what we could call a subdued sublime: the twilight region where the literary breaks off into something else that is not so much the real as it is its unguarded possibility. This unguarded possibility of the real, which is arguably the very core of the testimonial experience, is also its preeminent political claim.

The significance of testimonio, even when used as a weapon against the traditionally literary, is more political than it is literary. In fact, as George Yúdice has observed, the rise of testimonio criticism, which is an obvious gauge of the consecration of testimonio as one of the primary objects of critical reflection for the Latin Americanist cultural left, cannot be understood without reference to the solidarity movement of the early 1980s.[6] At that time, a proliferation of civil wars in Central America and the quasi-genocidal practices of the Central American military made the dissemination of testimonial accounts one of the most important ways for those in a position to do so (which generally meant outside Central America) to express solidarity. A similar point could also be made for the urgency of dissemination of a different kind of testimonial accounts: those concerning torture and political murder in the Southern Cone. John Beverley and Marc Zimmerman, among others, have also emphasized the importance of the solidarity element not just in testimonio's dissemination, but even in its production: "Testimonio is not . . . a reenactment of the function of the colonial or neocolonial 'native informant,' nor a form of liberal guilt. It suggests as an appropriate ethical and political response the possibility more of solidarity than of charity. . . . Testimonio in this sense has been extremely important in linking rural and urban contexts of struggle within a given country, and in maintaining and developing the practice of international human rights and solidarity movements in relation to particular struggles" (*Literature* 177).

The solidarity movement has today almost waned, but testimonio criticism has come to be an important academic activity in the context of Latin American literature and cultural studies departments. For many of us, testimonio became one of the main bridges between traditional literary concerns and a different, not necessarily more critical but apparently more relevant, way of articulating our reflection on Latin American cultural production under current conditions. If "testimonial literature is emerging as part of a global reordering of the social and economic contexts of power/difference within which 'literature' is produced and consumed" (Gugelberger and Kearney, "Voices" 6), then testimonio criticism must also react to that aspect of the cultural game. From this perspective, solidarity, although not in any case to be excluded, can no longer be our sole motivation for engaging testimonio as its readers and disseminators. But the contemporary attraction of testimonio for literary or postliterary reflection does not depend solely on the fact that testimonio introduces suppressed and subaltern voices into disciplinary discourse; it does not depend solely on the welcome possibility of articulating, through disciplinary discourse, a political praxis of solidarity and coalition; and it does not depend solely on the intriguing promise of expansion of disciplinary discourse to cultural practices that seem to threaten as much as they revitalize discussions about what exactly constitutes literature.[7] There are two other determinant factors to account for the contemporary emblematic importance of testimonio criticism among the Latin Americanist left: the first is that testimonio allows for a conceptualization that is not only useful but also necessary to Latin American identity politics, insofar as testimonio signals the discursive irruption of alternative, that is, nontraditional subjects of enunciation; and the second is the fact that testimonio allows the literary critical enterprise to break out of the high-literature impasse described above—indeed, perhaps even to recognize it as an impasse in the first place. In this second sense, epistemic constraints seem to take precedence over political articulation.[8]

Testimonio criticism differs from testimonio in a very special way that is not parallel to the way in which traditional literary criticism differs from literary practice. If testimonio, in one form or another, can conceivably be affirmed to represent the cultural entry of Latin American identity politics into the transnational public sphere (ignoring that its first practitioners would not have thought of it in this way), it is because the testimonial subjects are themselves immediately recognized as the voices around which new social movements must be articulated.[9] The voice that speaks in testimonio—I am referring to the testimonial voice and not to the paratextual voice of the author or mediator—is metonymically representative of the group it speaks for. But this is not true for the critic of testimonio, who is at best—in this sense not unlike the paratextual voice of testimonio—in a metaphoric relation with the testimonial subject through an assumed and voluntaristically affirmed solidarity with it. There is thus a radical break between testimonio's subject and the enunciating subject of testimonio criticism that does not bear comparison with the merely positional distance between the literary author and literature's paraphrastic or exegetic critic.

Such a radical break or discontinuity has equally drastic epistemic implications. In virtue of the experiential distance between enunciators and receptors around which testimonio is essentially constructed, the enunciators of testimonio can only become "one of us" insofar as they signal themselves to be primarily an other. Solidarity is precisely the emotional apparatus that enables our metaphoric identification with the other, and a double conversion of the other into us, and of us into the other. This conversion has a strong emotional-political character, an ethical character if you will, but its epistemological status remains severely limited, and structurally so. Solidarity allows for political articulation, but it cannot by or in itself provide for an epistemological leap into an other knowledge, understood as a genuine knowledge of the other. The basic consequence of this structural limitation is that the testimonial subject, in the hands of the Latin Americanist cultural critic, has a tendency to become epistemologically fetishized precisely through its (re)absorption into the literary system of representation. In other words, solidarity, which remains the essential summons of the testimonial text and what radically distinguishes it from the literary text, is in perpetual risk of being turned into a rhetorical tropology. But there can be no poetics of solidarity when it is the function of solidarity to produce a break away from poetics. Solidarity, although it can indeed be represented, is an affective phenomenon of a nonrepresentational order—as such, unless it manifests itself as praxis or operationalization, it is by definition nothing but the epigonal false consciousness of a Hegelian beautiful soul. The intellectual in solidarity is no longer an organic intellectual—and this is not a condemnation, of course, but simply a statement of fact.

The disciplinary importance of testimonio for Latin Americanist

criticism turns the risk of fetishizing testimonio, in a farcically ideological gesture of willed compensation for what may be perceived to
be a domestic political stasis as well as a global disciplinary catastrophe, into a particularly urgent problem. Since Latin Americanist cultural criticism, given high literature's loss of cultural capital,
has come to need testimonio for its own partial rearticulation as
an epistemologically viable enterprise, testimonio has paradoxically
and dangerously come to be the main source, or one of the main
sources, for a Latin Americanist "aesthetic fix," to borrow a sentence
that Yúdice uses in a different if related context, a sort of metha-
done in the absence of an effective literary critical practice. As an
aesthetic fix, of course, testimonio produces not solidarity but only
a poetics of solidarity of a fallen and derivative kind.

This literary question that I am attempting to develop in connection with testimonio has strong implications. Given power-knowledge constraints and the difficulties for any disciplinary knowledge
to assert total lucidity over its object of study and the conditions
that determine its constitution as such, what is ultimately at stake
here is nothing less than whether the attraction of testimonio for the
Latin Americanist critic is a function of Latin Americanism as an
instrument of colonial domination or a function of Latin Americanism as an obstacle to colonial domination. This question goes well
beyond the intentionality of the critic on whom it falls, since colonial discourse, which is radically constitutive of Latin Americanism, although not its only ingredient, talks through and by means of
power-knowledge constraints that are by definition beyond purely
subjective control. If "the imperial power cannot represent itself to
itself, cannot come to any authentic form of representational self-
knowledge, unless it is able to include within that representation
the represented realities of its own colonies" (Jameson, "Americans"
59), it needs to be asked whether testimonio criticism might end up
becoming, or is in constant danger of becoming, a tool for imperial
representational self-knowledge in the place where it was supposed
to be its very opposite. Of course only testimonio itself has handed
over this question, in virtue of its tenuous abandonment of the literary, which has paradoxically enabled us to see, under a better light,
the deep implications of literary discourse with power-knowledge
effects.

The controversy surrounding the publication of Stoll's book had everything to do with these questions. It was a bit too easy for Stoll to turn his painstaking labors to demonstrate the inaccuracies in Menchú's account into an indictment of the transnational Latin Americanist left. Of the three reasons he offers for his interest in questioning the "reliability of *I, Rigoberta Menchú*" the third one is epistemic in nature and aims at a critique of contemporary knowledge that falls, however, short of its object. In his words, the third reason

> is to raise questions about a new standard of truth gaining ground in the humanities and social sciences.
>
> The premise of the new orthodoxy is that Western forms of knowledge, such as the empirical approach adopted here, are fatally compromised by racism and other forms of domination. Responsible scholars must therefore identify with the oppressed, relegating much of what we think we know about them to the dustbin of colonialism. The new basis of authority consists of letting the subalterns speak for themselves, agonizing over any hint of complicity with the system that oppresses them, and situating oneself in relation to fashionable theorists. Certainly there is much to be said for listening, but which voices are we supposed to listen to? What I will show in the case of *I, Rigoberta Menchú* is that critical theory can end up revolving around romantic conceptions of indigenous people, mythologies that can be used to sacrifice them for larger causes. (*Rigoberta* xv)

Although the concern against the appropriation of the ostensible object of solidarity is commendable, the fact that Stoll's critique of critical theory turns on the issue of Western intellectuals' identification with the oppressed falsifies most metacritical discussions in Latin Americanist testimonio criticism. Leaving aside the fact that politico-epistemic appropriation and simultaneous identification with its object are strictly incompatible endeavors, to the extent that testimonio criticism embodies the (impossible) project of a poetics of solidarity, testimonio criticism is foundationally conditioned by the impossibility of identification, as we will see. The conditions of possibility of testimonio criticism are precisely the conditions of impossibility of an organic link with the testimonial subject, which leads us into a much more interesting problem, namely, the problem of abjection. In Nelly Richard's words, abjection today emerges as a possibly structural condition of knowledge production in metropolitan regionalist knowledge, not in accordance with metropolitan critical theory, but rather in resistance to it: "Perhaps the political consciousness of Latin Americanism requires, in order to continue to be mobilized by utopias of change, a mechanism for the production of an other that must take the form of a radical exteriority regarding the all-too-familiar metropolitan bibliography" ("Intersectando" 351; my trans., here and below).

The danger is to fetishize testimonio as a merely new disciplinary, that is, aesthetic, literary, or cultural object—a redemptive one, insofar as it comes to save the literary critic from the doldrums of forced and repetitious disciplinary pieties. If testimonio signals the irruption of a new kind of Latin American politics into the transnational public sphere and if it founds the possibility of a dismantling and rearticulation of the disciplinary literary-critical apparatus in what we may have to call, following Beverley, a postliterary sense, then it is incumbent on testimonio criticism to follow the call of its object and attempt an alternative politics of knowledge. Richard's warning, contrary to Stoll's, is directed against the formalization of such a politics along the lines of an excessive disidentification. Thus, the positing of the Latin American subaltern as other "confines the force of *lo latinoamericano* into a mute and savage exteriority regarding discursive norms and their cultural mediations: an exteriority that contains the Latin American force in a prediscursive or extradiscursive zone . . . [and] that condemns it to remain . . . marginalized from the . . . battles around metropolitan knowledge codes that . . . determine the meaning of Latin America" ("Intersectando" 352).

Take another polemic that developed quite independently of Stoll and from a different political context: one between Gordon Brotherston and Brett Levinson. Brotherston accused Levinson of attempting to deprive (symbolically) Menchú and the Maya-Quiché people of their territory, their history, their culture, and their beliefs in the wake of depriving them of their very capacity to testify to a long history of oppression. In truth, in my own reading, Levinson did nothing of the kind. On the contrary, his essay managed to operate a concrete historical restitution that may have no precedent or continuation in testimonio criticism: he undid the structure Richard defines, not through its simple denunciation but through performing a reading of the text where that structure was nowhere to be found. To understand the Maya-Quiché community, on the basis of textual evidence offered in Menchú's text, as invested in a form of patriarchy is not to slander the community or to deprive it of its purity. It is rather to respect its history, by rejecting the double standard according to which third-world or resistant texts should only be treated abjectly, with "affect, empathy, or commiseration" (Levinson, "Neopatriarchy" 38) and never "intellectualized." But Levinson's "intellectualization" of Menchú's text, that is, his submitting it to a certain kind of "critical knowledge," in Richard's expression, does not preempt a thoroughly political commitment to restitution and justice. Indeed, Levinson's essay shows that *Me llamo Rigoberta Menchú* "does something that other indigenous testimonies were never able to do: it renders both the destruction and appeal to justice . . . of the indigenous peoples legible to the West, although that legibility betrays [and, thus, preserves] the illegibility, the 'secret' marks inscribed into the Quiché-Mayan experience itself" ("Neopatriarchy" 48).

What, then, prompted Brotherston's annoyance? The consequence of Levinson's writing act, according to Brotherston, is nothing less than a stifling of all differences "between the spaces respectively inhabited by Menchú's people and most postmodernist critics" ("Regarding the Evidence" 98). This practice, that is, to read Menchú's text as one would read any other text from the point of view of Stoll's critical theory, is assimilated by Brotherston to the neoliberal or right-wing onslaught against any kind of resistance to the thorough colonization of the world by capitalist globalization. Levinson's essay would be a willing participant in a cosmic struggle between the "local versions of postcolonialism" and "the matching universals of postmodernism" (Brotherston 101)—a cosmic struggle that marks in fact a division within testimonio criticism between those who "make political commitment a priority" and those who "stray so far into the supposed sophistication of postmodernism as to render quite null the very concept of testimonio" (93). Levinson would of course be on the latter side.

But there is another, perhaps more telling characterization by Brotherston of this professional divide, which would be a divide between "the politically committed who require 'empathy' and those who intellectualize" (93). The latter, following the equivalential logic which is the substance of Brotherston's contribution, are also the ones who would "apply western theories to non-western cultures," and also the ones who would deny the very existence of the Third World as such, for the sake of a thorough homogenization of the planet into an equal, seamless, flat space where no difference would be possible. Brotherston's neat divisions of the critical world between the empathetic and the intellectualizing ones, which can only prepare a textbook example of the production of abjection Richard refers to, should give us pause. Imagine the different relation both groups would have to establish with their impossible interlocutors if the division were to hold. On the one hand, the empathetic ones, barred from intellectualizing, would have to dwell on the contemplation of their own unbridgeable distance, implicit in their defining emotions of solidarity and commiseration. On the other hand, the intellectualizers would simply impose the infinite iterability of their Western techniques on their human objects, thus erasing them as others. In both cases, no interlocution would be possible. In order to guarantee proper interlocution to only one of the positions in conflict, Brotherston must add to the former and withhold from the latter the supplement of "political commitment." But then of course political commitment, as a supplement, is by definition not essential to the first side and cannot be arbitrarily refused to the second. Brotherston's divide can only remain stable at the price of condemning in advance the potential political claims of the second group. It is a condemnation that can never come to rest; it must endlessly be repeated so that the first position can retain, through its very reassertion, whatever legitimacy its proponents insist on according it.

Brotherston's overt strategy of disidentification for the sake of preserving the exteriority of the other, and thus the possibility of a poetics of solidarity, is a paradoxical investment in what was presented as restitutional excess in chapter 4. For Enrico Santí, "restitution is supplementary in character—in compensating for a previous lack, it exceeds rather than simply restores the original" ("Latinamericanism" 89). The excess in restitution, as Santí says, is not avoidable and belongs in the very structure of disciplinary restitution. Restitutional excess is the other side of the fact that a discipline constitutes itself by means of a foundational restitution in which the disciplinary object is first brought to light. That the object should be brought to light by means of a restitution already implies the previous existence of a system of symbolic exchange. Within this system, the act of restitution restores anew the disciplinary object but in so doing makes it a disciplinary object, that is, an object loaded from the start with an epistemological burden that exceeds it. For example, a text that summons us to solidarity with previously unheard voices appears, and the text is then made to function as exemplary for a new cultural-political critical practice. We see here at the same time a critical act of object restitution and its reverse, that is, a disciplinary act whereby an excess with respect to restitution announces itself and burdens the object of restitution.

Thus, the epistemological grid that first makes the disciplinary object possible as such, that is, as disciplinary object, at the same time conceals the object and constitutes it in partial loss. It constitutes it as a partially lost object, thereby assuring itself that the demand for restitution will continue to make itself heard. Restitution carries within itself its own need for excess, its own need to exceed itself, so that it can, in a sense, survive itself, and therefore guarantee the survival of the discipline. Without restitutional excess no metacritics of testimonio would be possible, but then, also, testimonio criticism would not have been able to constitute itself over against traditional literary criticism. Restitutional excess is a destabilizing mechanism at the very heart of disciplinary constitution: it is as such the site where disciplinary politics are essentially played out. Restitutional excess can be used in at least two radically opposed senses: on the one hand, restitutional excess can organize the site for theoretical reflection, that is, it can be the region where disciplinary restitution seeks to interrogate itself (as, for instance, in metacritical practice, or in the sort of relentless interrogation that Levinson practices); but, on the other hand, restitutional excess can also choose to negate itself as such; it can look for its own point of closure in an attempt to come to the end of itself, as in Brotherston's response to Levinson. I define spectacular redemption as a particular form of disciplinary practice whose overt or hidden premise places the theoretical end of the discipline it enacts in the horizon of accomplished restitution. "It is only if we leave them alone, offering no more than our empathy, or perhaps working silently for them, that they will come back to being fully themselves," the spectacular redemptors want to say. Spectacular redemption is a paradoxical form of disciplinary practice in that its completion would tendentially mean the end of the discipline. In other words, if the ultimate goal of the discipline is the redemption of the object so that the object can go back to being fully itself with no remainder, or if the discipline plays itself out in the wager for the self-identity of its object of study, then that self-identity, once accomplished, would void the need for reflection, would abolish the discipline as such. But, of course, the discipline cannot be abolished by its object, insofar as it is the discipline that first creates the demand for the self-identity of the disciplinary object.

An Auratic Practice of the Postauratic

If Richard is right, the ongoing reconfiguration of the Latin Americanist cultural field would seem to have fallen prey to a powerful trope similar to the discursive practice set forth in Pablo Neruda's "Alturas de Macchu Picchu."[10] The end of "Alturas" enacts a prosopopeia of the dead which is prefigured in section 6, when the poetic voice, after having climbed through "lost jungles" (131) reaches Machu Picchu. The famous verse says, "Esta fue la morada, este es el sitio" [This was the dwelling, this is the site] (132; my trans., here and below). The ruined, fallen dwelling is reconstituted and refigured as the new site of utterance, the primary if postoriginary region of attunement. As an empty dwelling, as a literal cenotaph, the sacred city can only set a voiceless ground which therefore requires the prosopopeic positing of the dead as living, talking dead. Later, in the mention of "la rosa permanente, la morada" ["the permanent rose, the dwelling"] (133), we find the beginning of the foundational trope that will bring posthumous, metonymic life to those who have already died: "una vida de piedra después de tantas vidas" ["a life of stone after so many lives"] (134). The life of stone becomes the living stone, the site of interpellation that can only be constituted as such in the affirmation "el reino muerto vive todavía" ["the dead realm still lives"] (136). Those living dead are the ones who must then accept the injunction of the poet: "Hablad por mis palabras y mi sangre" ["Speak through my words and my blood"] (141). Such problematic resurrection of the dead, a tenuous tropology, is the historical foundation of the Latin American poetic site understood as what we could call an auratic practice of the postauratic. It is also the historical foundation of the contemporary Latin Americanist critical site along the same lines. Auratic practice here means the constitution of a self-legitimizing locus of enunciation through the simultaneous positing of two radically heterogeneous fields of experience—the experience of the dead and the experience of the living, their experience and mine or ours—and the possibility of a relational mediation between them through prosopopeia. It is a practice of the postauratic because the relational mediation between the heterogeneous realms is no longer based on mimesis but is rather based precisely on the impossibility of mimesis: a simulation, then, a repetition, whose moment of truth is the loss of truth itself, "Esta fue la morada, este es el sitio."[11] The poetic voice can only now perform in an intransitive sense, since the object to be performed is a lost, ruined object.

This auratic experience of the postauratic is based on the production of abjection. The abject in Neruda's poem is an unlivable zone, a zone of ruinous death without whose textual reproduction as such the possibility of the poem itself and of the discursive practice that founds the poem would not exist. Abjection would be, in the sense in which I am using the notion here, a certain originary and founding outcasting whose most concrete task is to produce empowerment but whose most precise discursive result is the constitution, or the repetition, of a realm of social unlivability. Judith Butler opens her book on the discursive limits of "sex" with the following definition: "The abject designates . . . those 'unlivable' or 'uninhabitable' zones of social life which are nevertheless densely populated by those who do not enjoy the status of the subject, but whose living under the sign of the 'unlivable' is required to circumscribe the domain of the subject" (*Bodies* 3). But whose subject? In Neruda's case we could confidently respond that it is the poetic subject who is seeking self-empowerment through prosopopeic activity. The mass of the dead, and in particular of the dead insofar as they were oppressed while alive, the slaves and peasants of Machu Picchu whose memory survives in double abjection, constitutes in Neruda's poem the very foundation of the self-enabling voice of the redemptive poet: a voice that is therefore constituted, even attuned, in the production or the reproduction of abjection.

Auratic practice is that which consists of producing a self-legitimizing locus of enunciation through the simultaneous positing of two radically heterogeneous fields of experience. In "Alturas de Macchu Picchu" the dead and the living were the poles of heterogeneity. The aura is produced at the expense of what in translation becomes represented as the silent pole, which the expressive pole vampirizes, as it were, in ventriloquy. "Yo vengo a hablar por vuestra boca muerta" ["I come to speak through your dead mouth"] (141) is thus not coincidentally coupled with the injunction to "speak through my words and my mouth." The second expression only becomes sayable after the living have been endowed with the voice of the dead through prosopopeia. Prosopopeia refers to a mask through which one's own voice is projected onto another, where that other is always suffering from a certain inability to speak. The relational mediation is then always unequal and hierarchical, even at its most redemptive. It is a practice of the postauratic because it turns away from mimesis, or in other words, it pronounces the impossibility of mimesis. I understand mimesis in the Aristotelian and Benjaminian sense, as a repetition of truth where the repeating term follows the lead of that which is to be repeated. Neruda's representational strategy understands itself as emanating from the ruins and ashes themselves, and it finds authorization in the loss of the object of representation, to which it brings purely symbolic restitution, always of a supplementary character.

Beverley thinks that testimonio in general and *Me llamo Rigoberta Menchú* in particular are textual configurations where a radically other model of self-legitimation is enacted. Beverley calls it a "horizontal" representation, since "the narrator . . . speaks for or in the name of a community or group, approximating in this way the symbolic function of the epic hero without at the same time assuming his hierarchical and patriarchal status" (*Against Literature* 74). For Beverley, testimonio breaks the vertical form of representation to be found in Neruda in favor of "a fundamentally democratic and egalitarian form of narrative in the sense that it implies that *any* life so narrated can have a kind of representativity" (75; see also Beverley and Zimmerman 175). At stake is what Beverley identifies as the erasure of the authorial function in testimonio, with the implied consequence that the reading experience calls for a different form of hermeneutics, a hermeneutics of solidarity. Beverley recognizes that the positional distance between the literary text and the literary critic is different from the radical break separating the testimonial subject and its reader. The testimonial subject, by virtue of its testimonio, makes a claim to the real in reference to which only solidarity or its withholding are possible. The notion of the total representativity of the testimonial life, which in fact points to a kind of literary degree zero in the testimonial text, paradoxically organizes the extraliterary dimension of the testimonial experience: solidarity is not a literary response but that which suspends the literary in the reader's response.[12]

But, beyond that, what happens when the unlivable zones produced in testimonio meet a critical reception that rearticulates them as privileged sites of until-then subjugated knowledges? What happens when those abjected knowledges are reaffirmed as such in order to be posited as the foundation of a critical-political practice that is then assumed to be new, or performed as new? Those abjected knowledges are then made to speak prosopopeically, through the voice of its critical representation. Even though I agree with Beverley that testimonio itself as a discursive practice is substantially different from what I am calling the auratic practice of the postauratic occurring in Neruda's foundational poem, I do believe that the appropriation of testimonio in critical discourse may not in fact go beyond that auratic practice.[13] When Latin Americanist criticism reads testimonio it seems to regress to the prosopopeic position emblematized in section 12 of "Alturas de Macchu Picchu." But this critical return to Neruda's redemptive site is generally blind to itself, because the return to the site is produced in the very affirmation that claims to have overpassed it. As testimonio criticism grounds itself in the affirmation of the extraliterary dimension of the testimonial text, it unavoidably puts that extraliterary dimension at the service of a literary-critical performance that reabsorbs the extraliterary into the literary-representational system. One cannot have a hermeneutics of solidarity without a poetics of solidarity to go with it. The price of testimonio criticism's appropriation of testimonio may be that such an appropriation necessarily reabsorbs the testimonial subject into a system of prosopopeic (that is, literary, or tropological) representation. But there can be no poetics of solidarity when it is the function of solidarity to produce a break away from poetics.

If the attraction of testimonio, as a postliterary genre, depends upon the fact that in testimonio the literary breaks off into the unguarded possibility of the real, then testimonio's attraction is radically undermined when its postliterary character is elided into prosopopeic representation (since testimonio is now, and can only be after the critical intervention that so defines it, that which guarantees a reading following a critical poetics of solidarity with the subaltern). In prosopopeic representation solidarity turns into a production of abjection where the producing agency, testimonio criticism, retains an aura that has been sucked off the testimonial subject, now abjected. It is as if testimonio criticism were forced to operate under the injunction of the literary: in principle and origin oriented by the extraliterary dimension of its object, testimonio criticism can be only a literary supplement, and a dangerous one, whose effect is to tenuously repress and substitute for the extraliterary dimension of the testimonial text.[14] As a consequence of this turning of solidarity into a critical poetics, or a hermeneutics, of solidarity, testimonio criticism reauthorizes itself within the epistemological power-knowledge grid at the expense of that which it originally sought to authorize. Testimonio will then be institutionalized within a strict codification: the canonization of testimonio in the name of a poetics of solidarity is equivalent to its reliteraturization following preassigned tropological and rhetorical registers. Thus, in the hands of testimonio criticism, testimonio loses its extraliterary force, which now becomes merely the empowering mechanism for a recanonized reading strategy.

Restitution and the Secret

Rigoberta Menchú's word is founded on the continuous insistence on a secret that will not be revealed. The secret is foundational in Menchú's text to the extent that, as secret, and therefore as impassable limit, it produces "a constitutive outside to the subject, an abjected outside, which is, after all, 'inside' the subject as its own founding repudiation" (Butler, *Bodies* 2). For Doris Sommer, this secret in Menchú's text is emblematic not so much of testimonial production as of the strong identity claim that testimonio makes. It is interesting to note that the testimonial claim in Sommer's interpretation is also a claim to identity and that this identity should to a large extent determine the reader's counteridentity as reader, in the sense of establishing for her or him an ethical non plus ultra: Menchú's secret becomes the key for the development of the notion of a "proper and responsible reading," a reading respectful of a cultural difference that is presumed to be radically heterogeneous (see Sommer, "Resisting," 419).[15]

Sommer's position should perhaps be compared to what Jorge

Luis Borges tried to outline in a short story called "El etnógrafo." The story tells us about Fred Murdock, a student at some large university in the North American Southwest who doesn't really know what to do with his life. He is a quiet man, unassuming. Having suggested to him that he study indigenous languages, his professor, a rather old man, eventually asks him to go and do fieldwork on an Indian reservation, try to find out what the shamans tell the initiate during a certain ceremony, try to get that secret, then come back and write his dissertation. Murdock goes into the reservation and lives with the Indians, goes native, takes his experience seriously, does what the Indians do. One of the wisemen asks him to remember his dreams, and he dreams of buffalo. Finally, one day, he is told the secret. Eventually he leaves the reservation and goes back to his university. He tells his old professor that he has the secret but has decided not to write his dissertation after all. Borges's story talks about a difference of a kind such that, precisely, it cannot be bridged or resolved. It would be something like absolute difference—a difference whose very recognition as such already implies a coverup, since it disciplines it as difference and attempts to tame it. The story suggests that Western ethnoscience is but an attempt to erase that difference. Perhaps the proliferation of differences in which ethnoscience seems to relish is nothing but a coverup of that absolute difference that cannot be expressed, cannot even be erased, and can only be contained. Borges's story raises a set of questions to which Sommer gives a particular answer: What should we do with the secret, once we know it is there? Should we keep away from it? Should we be ethical, or proper, and let whoever has it keep the secret?

Insofar as Rigoberta Menchú is talking to us as a testimonial subject, she seems to have no choice but to foreclose that which enables her to talk to us, that which had kept her from talking to us before her performative act became possible. She does not foreclose her people, but she forecloses the content of the secret, thereby creating a fold that becomes not only the site of identity but precisely the site of abjected identity, as well as the site of a certain resistance to abjection. Menchú's secret is in my opinion at the same time the metonymic displacement of the necessary (re)production of abjection in Menchú's text and its most proper cipher. On one hand, Menchú's text must produce or reproduce unlivability, in order to be persuasive as testimonio; on the other hand, however, Menchú's word is lucid enough to make of that necessary (re)production of abjection, which gives her a place to speak, the region for a counterclaim where abjection is reversed and passed on to the reader. As far as *we* are concerned, Menchú seems to say, our place will remain uninhabited by you, the truly abject ones. Going so far as to speak, in speaking to us, the very unsayability of what must remain unspoken is what makes Menchú's word an epistemologically privileged text in the tradition of Latin American testimonio. I would claim that the secret, in Menchú's text, stands for whatever cannot and should not be reabsorbed into the literary-representational system: the secret is the (secret) key to the real as unguarded possibility.

Once we as readers, however, accept the injunction to become abjected from Menchú's textual site, our relationship to the text is in one specific but crucial sense undistinguishable from the relationship enacted by Neruda with the Machu Picchu dead: a fissure opens, across which only prosopopeia can take us. The border, that without which there would be no outcasting, and therefore no abjection, then once again must be understood as a limit to the expansion of knowledge as a war machine: a limit to be overcome by a further expansion or else a limit to be defended and protected from conquest, which is Sommer's position. Sommer's essay goes a long way toward recognizing and absorbing the radical break that separates the testimonial subject and the enunciating subject of testimonio criticism. By recognizing the break as such, and by positing the necessity of respecting it, Sommer moves away from a poetics of solidarity insofar as her solidarity is precisely enunciated in an alliance against any possibility of a prosopopeic representation. And yet the danger of fetishization (and therefore of tropological reabsorption) has not been conjured away by Sommer's effort.

Sommer's essay is framed as a disciplinary attack on the discipline and on disciplinary reading in particular. According to her, disciplinary reading has traditionally understood itself as appropriative, with a kind of appropriation that would reproduce stereotypical male sexuality: "Difficulty is a challenge, an opportunity to struggle and to win, to overcome resistance, uncover the codes, to get on top of it, to put one's finger on the mechanisms that produce pleasure and pain, and then to call it ours. We take up an unyielding book to conquer it and then to feel grand, enriched by the appropriation and confident that our cunning is equal to the textual tease that had, after all, planned its own submission as the ultimate climax of reading. Books want to be understood, don't they, even when they are coy and evasive?" ("Resisting" 407). Sommer contends that a resistance in the text could under some circumstances signal what she calls "a genuine epistemological impasse" (409) . If a text claims indeed that the reader is incompetent to penetrate its deepest layers, that is, if the text claims that it gives itself off as its own secret, then the impasse is in place, Sommer would argue, and this impasse traces an impassable disciplinary limit.[16] Sommer is willing to concede that a disciplinary limit, that is, a resistance to reading, should be recognized and accepted as such under some circumstances. Recognition and acceptance here, far from expressing a disciplinary failure, are on the contrary enabling gestures, gestures that enable us to transcend "our still deaf ears" (408). In those gestures, Sommer implies, we can address a demand for restitution that had up to now gone unheard. But it is not that restitution makes itself felt as a new demand; instead, we are finally able to radicalize restitution, insofar as we have already seemingly rejected the paradigm of object-appropriation, which was and has always been a false paradigm, just as stereotypical male sexuality has always already misunderstood the real. Restitution, over against appropriation of the object, is the moment of truth in disciplinary practice. In Borges's story, Fred Murdock opts for silence, and it is an active silence that impugns the very possibility of disciplinary appropriation. Murdock opts for restitution.

Radicalizing restitution may be another name for the entry into the unguarded possibility of the real. For Sommer, Rigoberta Menchú's testimonio has an irreducible extraliterary dimension that is constituted in the enunciation of the textual secret as impassable literary limit. It would then seem that Sommer has accomplished a reading that, by renouncing a poetics of solidarity as the only way to keep solidarity as such and by refusing to engage in prosopopeic representation, succeeds in making an antidisciplinary gesture that would take testimonio criticism beyond the auratic and into the postauratic; that is, into the possibility of a postliterary disciplinary politics. The properly political task is to find, in the tenuous borders of subjective self-grounding, "a critical resource in the struggle to rearticulate the very terms of symbolic legitimacy and intelligibility" (Butler, *Bodies* 3). In Menchú's use of the secret we understand precisely that struggle for the legitimation of her ability to speak, for its very intelligibility as a thoroughly political, thoroughly historicized locus of enunciation in the context of colonial and anticolonial practices. I think that both Beverley and Sommer have broken ground for that understanding. Within the realm of questioning they themselves have opened, however, there is room for further questioning. In their critical practice, the critical practice that they have enacted in their analyses of the Menchú text, are they are still residually engaging in what I earlier called an auratic practice of the postauratic? Are they therefore residually caught up in a certain representational strategy that they themselves claim to have overcome? In other words, does their concern for restitution pass over into spectacular redemption? For both Beverley and Sommer, and they are here themselves emblematic of a seeming inevitability within the epistemological field (although it is quite undetectable in Levinson), the legitimation of their critical practice takes place in the (re)production of abjected objects. Beverley must assume an epistemological privilege, which is not in a mimetic but in a supplementary relationship with its object, even as he chooses to model his own critical practice on the discursive production of the Latin American poor and disenfranchised. He does have the choice, which shakes the possibility of mimesis and makes it become a simulatory tactic, no matter how deeply felt, called solidarity. But in order for us to articulate solidarity from an alternative region of experience we must engage in a prosopopeic mediation: we must incorporate the abject, for only the abject, which lives in the unlivable, requires solidarity.

Sommer is more explicitly forceful in her rejection of mimesis, which she understands as an appropriative apparatus. Her model of resistant texts and incompetent readers opens onto a fissure that is not to be crossed if we are to follow the injunction of the texts themselves for us to develop, to use a phrase by Emmanuel Levinas that Sommer herself quotes, "a non-allergic relation to alterity" ("Resisting" 423).[17] Sommer would protect the border that resistant texts trace, for that border is itself the mark of a resistance to the mimetic apparatus, in which an unassailable and nonmimetizable textual truth lies: "Perhaps they withhold secrets because we are so different and would understand them only imperfectly. Or should we not know them for ethical reasons, because our knowledge would lead to a preempting power. Like Nietzsche's meditation on the nature of rhetoric in general, the difference between cannot and should not is undecidable. Because even if Rigoberta's own explicit rationale is the nonempirical, ethical reason about keeping powerful information from outsiders, she suggests another constraint. It is the degree of our foreignness, our cultural difference that would make her secrets incomprehensible to the outsider" (417)

Mimesis is not possible and also not ethical. But to discover the truth of the text in the text's refusal to give up its truth is to bring the (re)production of abjection to a culminating, extreme point, which may indeed indicate the need for what Sommer calls "a paradigm shift" ("Resisting" 426). The true epistemological impasse that Sommer's text presents is set forth in the question, "If our training assumes that learning is a progression, that it is always learning something, how does interpretive reticence make sense?" (427). Well, perhaps it does not, if interpretive reticence comes to represent the site of a new interpretive paradigm, for reticence speaks too, and not unlike prosopopeia. A tenuous fetishization thus insinuates itself into Sommer's reading. Testimonio becomes the privileged site for the critical affirmation of an interpretive reticence in which radicalized restitution finds its own excess and passes over into criticism's self-redemption. Criticism is thus able to refigure its own aura at the expense of textual reticence and precisely in virtue of its relationship with it. Brotherston critized Levinson for not being reticent enough, for speaking too much. In Sommer's essay there is no prosopopeic chatter, but silence, identical to itself, and therefore in itself its own end, has here been made to speak, and thus also tropologized as that which is beyond the "impassable" limit. Spectacular redemption reaches thus its own specularity.

The Aesthetic Fix

In yet another text centrally and in fact foundationally concerned with the analysis of the chiasmic relationship between "Alturas de Macchu Picchu" and *Me llamo Rigoberta Menchú*, Yúdice makes resistance to abjection the paradigmatic site for an understanding of the cultural politics of testimonio and, by extension, of Latin American postmodernity. For Yúdice, abjection is "hegemonic postmodernism's privileged aesthetic principle" ("Testimonio and Postmodernism" 23), whereas nonhegemonic postmodernity, that is, the Latin American one, announces an alternative aesthetics of solidarity that becomes the foundation of a new political practice for the Latin Americanist intellectual. Yúdice seems to be in agreement with both Beverley and Sommer. Perhaps Sommer has expressed more concisely than the others the fundamental thrust of this variety of postmodern politics: "The strategically demure posture allows us to imagine, I want to speculate, a politics of coalition among differently constituted positionalities, rather than the identity or interchangeability of subjects as the basis for equality. And a political vision adventurous enough to imagine differences, yet modest enough to respect them, may be the most significant challenge posed by learning to read resistance" ("Resisting" 421).

Yúdice understands abjection as the fetishization of otherness, the latter being what resistant texts would allegedly make it impossible for their readers to develop. The call to complicity, solidarity, and coalition in these readings would tendentially or logically preempt the possibility of the abjection experience, which comes to be seen as the "aesthetic fix" (Yúdice, "Testimonio and Postmodernism" 25) of hegemonic postmodernity's dealings with alterity. Yúdice is thinking of a critical resistance to abjection as the only way to avoid the impossible reconstitution of solidarity into a poetics of solidarity. A resistance to abjection is for him precisely a recognition of the extraliterary dimension of the testimonial text, which is what properly summons us to solidarity. Yúdice is in that sense not so much disagreeing with Julia Kristeva's elaboration on the abject as "the violence of mourning for an object that has always already been lost" (qtd. in "Testimonio and Postmodernism" 23; see also "Testimonio y concientización" 217), where that lost object is constitutive of the subject's own subjectivity, as he is asking for the displacement of the production of abjection toward nontestimonial texts. If for Kristeva the contemporary subject comes to terms with its own need for abjection in art and literature, that is, in the aesthetic experience as hegemonically understood, then Yúdice is saying that testimonio, in view of its extra-aesthetic, extraliterary moment, should be considered a discursive space totally beyond the purview of abjection. In other words, for Yúdice it is the extraliterary dimension of testimonio that preeminently makes testimonio a site in resistance to abjection. Abjection should come to serve as an aesthetic fix only there where the fetishization of otherness is structurally entitled to take place, that is, in the literary, in the aesthetic, and, thus, not in testimonio if it is true that, as we have been saying, testimonio's truth is essentially extraliterary.

However, Latin Americanist discourse needs abjection to constitute itself, for only the (re)production of abjection can draw the perpetually receding border along which the negotiations between the subjects and the objects of Latin Americanism either align themselves or are aligned. For Latin Americanism there seems to be no way of avoiding putting itself in the position of the dangerous "literary" supplement vis-à-vis the claim of the object. Within Latin Americanism, it seems, restitutional excess is always tropologized at the service of the self-legitimation that Kristeva posits as the function of literature and art in secularized times. With Yúdice the self-legitimating event can also be read against the grain of his own writing, as in Beverley and Sommer, at the moment when he claims that testimonio provides for a resistance to abjection, which is in itself constitutive of an aesthetics of solidarity in which an alternative, nonhegemonic postmodernity is born. But an aesthetics of solidarity is a break away from solidarity, insofar as it takes the radical summons of solidarity into an alien realm, the realm of the aesthetic. I am not suggesting that this unwanted diversion is easy to avoid, or even that it can ever be avoided, just that it happens.

If abjection is indeed a fetishization of otherness, then the abjection of abjection becomes a counterfetish that partakes of the essence of the fetish just as fully as non-A is always implied in A. One does not have to embrace abjection, but rejecting it, reducing abjection itself to an abject position, is an insufficiently critical gesture whose most direct consequence is that it returns us to an auratic practice of the postauratic that does not dare look itself in the face. In the abjection of abjection, we miss the opportunity to understand the nature of the relational mediation between readers and texts as always already conditioned by a rupture, a fissure, a border alongside which the force of disciplinary epistemology creates radically unequal determinations. The issue is then whether it is structurally possible for testimonio criticism, indeed for Latin Americanism, to avoid falling into Yúdice's notion of the aesthetic fix. The aesthetic fix is here understood to be the reabsorption of the extraliterary dimension of testimonio into the disciplinary system of representation: a system that, as we have seen, cannot dispense with the production of abjection insofar as it needs to abject the other in order to speak about it. The best testimonio criticism has always understood itself to be an antidisciplinary gesture, where a newly conceptualized practice of solidarity was trusted to preempt the very possibility of vertical representation on which the production of abjection rests. But the game of attempting to avoid vertical representation has proved to be exceedingly complex, insofar as it must be played out from a disciplinary perspective.

The question I am posing does not limit itself to testimonio criticism. If testimonio as we understand it today is a primary form of cultural manifestation for a wide variety of social movements whose politics are politics of identity, then the question ultimately affects all the disciplinary possibilities of dealing with the identitarian claims of social movements. To formulate it again: it remains to be decided whether it is possible for Latin Americanism to avoid reifying extraliterary experience into mere tropes for a systemic representational poetics. Is it possible for academic criticism to deal with the cultural-discursive production of nonliterary subjects from a perspective other than the one subsumed under the term "auratic practice of the postauratic"? If so, how?

It would seem that an auratic practice under Latin Americanist power-knowledge conditions (and all Latin Americanist practices are necessarily auratic) is still and always on the side of the epistemological subordination of the represented and can then only with extreme difficulty avoid the charge of exerting itself in the interests of colonial or neocolonial domination. This is so particularly when the auratic practice seeks accomplished restitution in a practice of spectacular redemption. Spectacular redemption, that is, the auratic call for the absolute self-identity of the object of study, which will presumably put an end to disciplinary necessity by making it redundant, is always made from within disciplinary constraints. Spectacular redemption is only the shamefaced, embarrassed other side of disciplinary power/knowledge, working in spite of itself to give the discipline further legitimacy, providing it with an alibi, blind to the fact that the discipline speaks through us, always and everywhere, no matter what we say and what we do not say. Admitting that is in a sense Levinson's breakthrough: in his text Menchú is treated not as a radical other, which, as such, can only properly be the object of solidarity and commiseration, but as a fellow human whose actions need to be interrogated and understood, like those of the rest of us, following a certain technical iterability of procedure, which is given to us in advance by our institutional position as cultural critics and which we cannot renounce without ethical violence. That Levinson chose not to hide his technical competence in cultural analysis—is that an undigestible scandal for Latin Americanism? In Brotherston's stunning association of "the malignant practice" of capitalism with Levinson's critical work ("Regarding" 101), spectacular redemption shows its teeth, no doubt counterintentionally, as a disciplining apparatus that will not allow its own disarticulation.

I will finish with two partial references: the first, to Neil Larsen's introduction to *Reading North by South*.[18] As it happens, Larsen also concentrates on the essays by Beverley, Sommer, and Yúdice that have been the main focus of my commentary. Larsen's perspective on those essays, although different from mine, will nevertheless enable me to come back to the question of literature with which I began. Larsen duly notes that a "significant revision" in the way the (Latin Americanist) north has sought to authorize itself for reading Latin American texts has been underway for a number of years (3). After proposing the term *canonical decolonization* to refer to the previous moment, the moment in which Latin Americanism was avidly reading boom novels and seeking to incorporate Latin American culture into the supposedly universal modernist paradigm (7), Larsen suggests that the recent "counter-canonical development, notwithstanding what appears to be its status as a 'paradigm shift,' indicates not the *supersession* of the older, boom-fixated mode of readerly self-authorization but rather its *crisis*" (8). In fact, Larsen says, "the elevation, or *counter-canonization* of the testimonial as post-literary, post-representational, and the like, effectively exempts the reader-as-theorist from questioning his own dogmatically modernist preconceptions regarding the nature of the 'literary' itself" (10).

What Larsen intends, as he will tell us later in the text, is to open the way for a vindication of an antimodernist, realist literature. He therefore needs to do away with testimonio criticism's insistence on the death of (high) literature, as well as with the notion that the extraliterary dimension of testimonio is somehow connected with a better possibility than the one obtaining in realism for a full restitution of the object of representation. This is Larsen's significant conclusion:

It is not only the general crisis of radical political consciousness in the North that foregrounds the peculiar idolatry of testimonial theory, but the fact that this consciousness could only
project itself as universal, that is, as historically integral with the
South, in an aesthetic and cultural plane. The act of "discover-
ing" in the testimonial both an "end of literature" [Beverley] and
a cultural frontier of pure, unrepresentable, and unreadable "difference" [Sommer] discloses, by the very *conjuncture* of these
two antipodes, modernism as the still dominant framework of assumptions. To read the testimonial in this way is to read into it
not only the northern radical's own ideologically ambiguous relationship to imperialism, but what almost seems a nostalgia for
this ambiguity itself—as if, merely by conjuring away a *false* universal (modernism, or the "literary"), one would thereby be able
to produce a *true* particular. (18)

Perhaps Beverley, Sommer, and Yúdice would be willing to accept Larsen's diagnosis in these respects. First, modernism, as the
hegemonic literary-cultural paradigm, is indeed the framework of assumptions from which and out of which an alternative must be de-
vised. And modernism did indeed impose a particular brand of aesthetic utopianism on the Latin Americanist left, which, on having
been revealed to be insufficient or catastrophic, must now be shed.
Within that context, Beverley, Sommer, and Yúdice underwrite testimonio criticism's attempts at doing without the aesthetic fix, at
renouncing a cultural politics based on the hegemony of modernist
aesthetic claims, and at claiming the "true" particularity of the testimonial subject's recourse to the unguarded possibility of the extraliterary real. These attempts may undoubtedly be still swamped in
"epistemic murk," to use Michael Taussig's apt expression.[19] Nevertheless, insofar as they constitute rigorous if unfinished attempts at
breaking away from the auratic practice of the postauratic, which
has always organized and seemingly circumscribed the field of the
Latin Americanist literary representation of the hegemonically oppressed, they do not seem open to challenge, or at least to immediate
vanquishment, from a perspective intent on salvaging the representational possibilities of literary realism in postliterary times.

Larsen criticizes unwanted remnants of "a modernist discourse
of aesthetic utopianism" (*Reading* 17) in contemporary critical prac-

tice, but, insofar as his project contemplates the possibility of "a genuinely realistic portrayal of contemporary life in Latin America" (20),
the question to Larsen would be whether he can in fact argue for the
possibility of a present or future realism that would not be an auratic practice under the terms defined. If so, it would be the first such
realism indeed—since realism, by tendentially assuming the transparency of its own discourse as one free of ideological presuppositions (it is not ideology but truth that guides the realist hand, by definition), has always fully identified itself with the auratic extreme.[20]
The question may not bc just for Larsen, since the very possibility of
a renewal of the literary stands or falls with it; and with it also, the
possibility of an emancipatory cultural politics that could proceed
outside and beyond the mournful confines of identitarian lamenta-
tions, commemorations, and ultimately dubious secrets, guarded or
unguarded, in the real.

We seem to be caught in a predicament: either we renounce,
from the perspective of radical solidarity with the subaltern, the
representational pretensions of high literature, and thus the traditional presumption of the aesthetic to mediate the movement for
general social emancipation; or we renounce such a renunciation by
reaffirming the possibility of an aesthetic practice (and reflection)
with a legitimate claim to the expression of social truth. In the first
case, we run the risk of fetishizing subaltern production, of blindly
reaestheticizing it as the perceptual ground for a reconfiguration of
critical practice that will always be excessive with respect to its object; in the second case, we are seemingly forced to state an essentialist epistemology conversant with the truth of the world and in
full control of its own conditions of production.

My final reference is to Nelly Richard's notion of the "hyperliterary," developed in the context of an interpretation of Diamela
Eltit's *El padre mío*. In *El padre mío*, which transcribes the testimonial ramblings of a Chilean schizophrenic vagrant, the resources
of testimonio seem to be turned against themselves. The extraliterary dimension of testimonial production is here also constituted by
the indexical reference to the singularity of a pain beyond any possibility of representation, except that *El padre mío* refuses to be read,
as much as it refuses to read itself, as an identitarian construction.
The testimonial subject, as Richard says, here projects himself "as
an image lacking all interiority and profundity," to complicate "the

idea of testimonio as a vector of social consciousness and of an identitarian formation . . . rooted in ethos-sharing" ("Bordes" 4; my translation). For Richard, the erratic singularity of el padre's voice configures a hyperliterary space where testimonio exceeds its condition as a "document" of social reality and as a "monument" of Latin Americanist representation (9). If that is so, is *El padre mío* the site of a restitutional excess strong enough to undo Latin Americanism's aura and yet weak enough to allow for its conceptualization as a merely aberrant, all-too-abject exemplary instance? How do we read it, as literature, beyond literature?

EIGHT The Order of Order: On the Reluctant
Culturalism of Anti-subalternist Critiques

Populist Historicism

The order of order, the value of value, the measure of measure, the reason of reason: all these expressions, which are actually one and the same, refer to a classic aporia, solved by Leibniz by recourse to the principle of sufficient reason. The principle of sufficient reason, a founding principle of European philosophical modernity, reads: "Nihil est sine ratione," there is nothing without a reason. If there is nothing without a reason, reason must have a reason, and there must be a reason for the latter. The question about the value of value, or, perhaps more clearly, the value of values, is still a question within the purview of the principle of reason. But one of the paradoxes of an accomplished globalization is that it leaves us without a ground to question its very ground: it is in that sense the material confirmation of Pascal's God as ontotheological sphere or Borges's Aleph. In the history of European thought nature was always taken to be the ground of culture. If the reduction of nature through hypercommodification has been accomplished in late capitalism, then culture becomes groundless ground: meanings circulate within it but do not have recourse to a "natural" outside that can properly found them. This is a corollary of Fredric Jameson's theory of postmodernism, as well as of Willy Thayer's notion of indifferentiation in real subsumption and of Michael Hardt and Antonio Negri's empire of control, but one that hasn't been quite thought out yet. If values have in the past been taken to be not simply meaningful but in fact the principle of meaning, the question of the value of values must now be seen to constitute an ideologeme related to previous forms of historical existence within modernity. This loss of ground of values in contemporary times has, however, made Beatriz Sarlo say that "values are at stake. And we should not allow conservatives to have a monopoly on this claim. It was a mistake to adopt a defensive attitude, thereby implicitly accepting that only conservative critics or traditional intellectuals were capable of confronting an issue central to political and artistic theory. The values debate is the great theme of the end of the century" ("Cultural Studies" 120).

Sarlo's essay, "Cultural Studies and Literary Criticism at the Crossroads of Values," must be read in the context of the discussion mentioned in the introduction and then again in chapter 7 concerning what Mabel Moraña calls "teorización sobre Latinoamérica a nivel internacional" (international Latin Americanism ["Boom" 50; my trans., here and below]). A number of Latin American intellectuals have sharpened their critical knives on what they regard as a major Latin Americanist sellout of Latin America into the global market taking place primarily, if not exclusively, through the U.S. academy and, in particular, through Latin Americanist subaltern and postcolonial studies, sometimes—not always—simply identified with metropolitan-led "cultural studies" *tout court*.[1] Those critiques are not made solely against "international" Latin Americanists: Mario Vargas Llosa's analysis and ultimate condemnation of the work of José María Arguedas is a case in point. In Vargas Llosa's interpretation, Arguedas is made to stand in for a host of Peruvian and other Latin American contemporary intellectuals said to be unable, in their indigenist neurosis, to understand supracultural historical forces that have been changing the face of Andean societies and would continue to do so if subalternist intellectuals (along with other admittedly more pernicious elements) would just stop interfering. Vargas Llosa says: "Neither Indian nor white, neither indigenist nor hispanist, the Peru that is emerging to last is still a mystery of which we can only say for certain, but with absolute certainty, that it will have nothing to do with the images used by José María Arguedas in his works to describe it—to fabulate it" (*Utopía* 335; my trans.). Not bad for a professed antidogmatist: this and other similarly strong opinions seem to be ultimately based on nothing but a desire to delegitimize Arguedas's thinking on subalternity in Peru. But Vargas Llosa's book ought to serve to remind us that positions that are quite close to "international" subalternism (a minority affair in the best of cases) are relatively widespread in Latin America. Many Latin Americanist critics would share the objections against postcolonial and subaltern studies, and many Latin American intellectuals, local or not, organic or not, are also involved in what in the voice of some of the critics would seem a type of thinking exclusively promoted by the global metropoli.

A certain amount of babelic confusion is probably unavoidable. Néstor García Canclini, himself an obvious target of critique (although not a subalternist and not a U.S. Latin Americanist), makes the point in one of his contributions to these debates that "hybridity studies have discredited Manichean approaches that used to oppose frontally the dominant and the dominated, the periphery and the metropoli, senders and receptors. They in turn show the multipolarity of social initiatives, the oblique character of power, and the reciprocal borrowings taking effect in the midst of inequality and difference" ("Debate" 44; my trans.). García Canclini is, however, in the name of hybridity studies, not questioning the easy binarisms of the antisubalternist critics, who make the rather unhybrid claim that subalternism is a first world imposition on Latin America, but is rather supporting these critics, since it is precisely subaltern studies that is today presumed guilty of bringing back to life Canclini's Manichean games. In the background of these polemics there are a number of developments, each of them, of course, affecting the various participants differently, that may be summarized, in their effects, as follows: first, national or regional particularisms or both resent reductive representational practices coming from the metropolitan location standing in as a signifier of universality; second, local interests resent what they perceive as an overwhelming colonization of their discursive space by intellectual and political agendas emanating from other locations that cannot be made their own without a varying but always present degree of violence; and third, personal histories resent powerful interpretive frameworks, which are felt as a threat to the moral right of self-interpretation. These geopolitical, cultural, and theoretical objections concerning unequal exchange bear heavily on metropolitan-based institutional intellectuals, who may very well have tried to incorporate a certain amount of self-reflexivity into their work but who still see themselves constrained by their own institutional location into types of discursive behavior that they are unable to control.

But if power is, in relative terms, on the side of the metropolitan-based institutional intellectual, and if unequal exchange tends to favor capital accumulation on the investor's side, it is also true that power is always contested and that games of validation happen in many ways. It is not clear whether the metropolitan intellectual is in every case always a purely metropolitan intellectual, since what Vicente Rafael has called the "immigrant imaginary" seems to have developed a hegemony of sorts within the transnational academy ("Cultures" 102–07). It is equally dubious that the local intellectual can always assert his or her adscription to locality in unmediated ways. In terms of fact, the ongoing debate has been initiated by scholars whose association with the transnational academic sphere is long-standing, which automatically turns their interpellation into a matter of intellectual and not social position. Things become even more complicated when we remember that the fundamental target of their questioning tends to be the metropolitan-based intellectual's interest in Latin American subalternity, in its various relational forms. Although the international regime of unequal exchange in knowledge distribution is a contextual problem that should not be eliminated or moved out of sight, it would nevertheless be wrong to reduce this debate to an issue of relatively disempowered professionals from the Latin American semiperiphery confronting their comfortably settled brothers and sisters from the capitalist core.

Some of the participants in the debate suggest that the postcolonialist or subalternist work they would like to indict is but a neo-orientalism that will not speak its name. Moraña, echoing the comment by Nelly Richard that was cited in chapter 7, charges subalternism with a "critical neoexoticism that keeps Latin America in the place of the Other, a pretheoretical, marginal, calibanesque site in relation to metropolitan discourse," thus becoming a practice whose function is "a pseudo-integration of what is Latin American into an exotic theoretical apparatus, created for other historico-cultural realities, and providing the illusion of a rescue of a Latin American third-worldist specificity that cannot overcome, in many cases, the commomplaces of 1960's criticism" ("Boom" 50; my trans., here and below). Latin Americanist subalternism, for Moraña, would use Latin America as an empty site for cultural colonization. As in the classical neocolonial economy, U.S.-based subalternist intellectuals would regard Latin America as "an importer of manufactured products from centers which become wealthy through their sales to the very same markets that supply them with raw materials" (53). Subalternists would thus betray not simply their scholarly subject of inquiry but also the very presuppositions that frame their critical and political work.[2]

As we remember, Richard similarly remarks that "perhaps the political consciousness of Latin Americanism requires, in order to continue to be mobilized by utopias of change, a mechanism for the production of an Other that must take the form of a radical exteriority regarding . . . the all-too-familiar metropolitan bibliography" ("Intersectando" 351; my trans., here and below). She warns that "such an operation, when elevated to emblematic status, brings with it the problem of confining the force of 'the Latin American' into a mute or savage exteriority with regard to discursive norms and their cultural mediations: an exteriority that contains such Latin American force in an extra- or prediscursive domain, anterior to the codes of symbolic interaction, and thus condemns it to remain marginalized from the categories, interpretations and representational battles in which metropolitan critical knowledge about Latin America is involved" (352). But Richard's observations are formulated from a position of critical interiority vis-á-vis what is common to the cultural-postcolonial-subaltern studies paradigms. Although she refers to her "resentment against cultural studies as a globalizing metadiscourse" which "overdetermines local usages of the categories of subalternity and periphery" and "threatens the erasure . . . of cultural singularity" (346), she also states that it is possible to understand cultural studies analysis as "a multiple and relational process of conflictive and negotiated reinscriptions of the alterity-difference tension, able to intervene in every new discursive context about difference" (347). The relation between cosmopolitan Latin Americanism and Latin American reflection is thus "politically modifiable, from both sides, if a watchful self-critical consciousness . . . makes us revise, every time we speak, our own game of enunciation" (349). Richard's appeal to a radical situational consciousness leads her to assert the need for a self-probing search in critical writing and thinking (in other words, for the self-critical cultivation of style) as a means to escape the constantly dangerous reifications of discourse and knowledge that are part and parcel of participation in any institutional enterprise. Her work does not involve a recourse to value thinking as the ground of critical practice: it marks, rather, a sustained attempt to refuse value as ground for the sake of a constant interruption of sedimented meaning, which makes her position consistent with subalternism. Indeed, one of the fundamental positions of subalternism is its critical refusal of any kind of orientalist representation.

Hugo Achugar, like Moraña, is clear in his overall rejection and condemnation of Latin Americanist subalternist thinking, which in his opinion cannot—and should not—be distinguished from an American-led globalization that threatens to homogenize and reduce all regional and national specificities to a pervasive ahistorical sameness. Subalternism is for Achugar particularly pernicious as it indulges in a willful forgetting of the Latin American intellectual tradition—the "Latin American thinking," which is said rather uncannily to start with Andrés Bello's work—for the sake of "brokering" into the Latin American market an English-language thinking that, despite its protestations to the contrary, once exported, is objectively nothing more than the cultural arm of the global bourgeoisie (see "Leones" 383).

If postcolonial studies, as Arif Dirlik has put it, is in a significant sense a response to the crisis of reason originated in the collapse of actually existing socialism, it is not the only response.[3] An alternative way of dealing with contemporary problems is to opt for a retrenchment into past forms of critical reason, particularly because such a retrenchment seems to serve a tactical function in terms of determining the actual inadequacies of alternative paradigms. It is then easy to say that postcolonial studies are too close for their own good to the workings of transnational capital and can therefore serve more or less unwittingly an ideological function of legitimation regarding the evils of globalization. In other words, to use Enrique Dussel's terms, for at least some of their critics postcolonial studies would be functional, and not critical, vis-à-vis current hegemonic articulations; whereas for their antagonists the nonfunctionality of retrenchment equally preempts the latter's usefulness from the point of view of critical thinking (see "Globalization").

Both Achugar and Moraña tend to conflate postcolonialist and subalternist positions within a certain ideology of multiculturalism that Dirlik had already condemned as constitutively incapable of challenging the present order, because it is in fact consonant with it. What is perhaps erased or lost in these critical positions is the extent to which subalternist thinking situates itself in opposition to the soft multiculturalism that goes along with capital-led globalization. Although Latin American subalternism, different in this from South Asian subaltern studies, is far from taking the Latin American nation-states as primary discursive referents, except perhaps in a critical sense, that does not mean that subalternism swallows whole any kind of general antinationalist position and even less that it has embraced some kind of allegiance to the sort of identity politics promoted by the global "culture-ideology of consumerism."[4] The subalternist critique of the Latin American national spaces has effective antecedents in what Rodolfo Stavenhagen and others, working alongside indigenous groups in Latin America, started to develop already long ago as a critique of the nation as a space for exclusion based upon the spectralization of the old colonial situation into an "internal colonialism" which continues to the present day.[5] These critiques no doubt still undermine the prestige of many criollo-led anti-imperialist nationalist projects, which are suffering these days from an acute lack of credibility, given the simultaneous, and perhaps more formidable, attack of transnational corporations and their allies (the World Bank and the International Monetary Fund, for instance) on national sovereignty; in other words, given what we have already studied in previous chapters regarding the passage to the social regime of control in the real subsumption of society under capital.

But this contemporary crisis of the nation-state is for Achugar not a sufficient reason to liquidate local-national collective histories as the proper ground for Latin American thinking. Achugar emphasizes, quite reasonably, the need for local memory and a sense of history, and this need could and probably should be the basic source for what Jorge Castañeda, Néstor García Canclini, and George Yúdice called a "regional federalism" able to withstand the negative force of unequally homogenizing globalization (see chap. 1 on these issues). However, to the extent that Achugar makes the programmatic value of this regional federalism dependent on negating it to subalternist projects, which would then be involved not in a truly resistant regional federalism, but rather in some blind if unintentional obedience to the obscure dictates of global capital, something like an "our-Americanist" mentality would seem to develop potentially through his critique. I mean by that, through the reference to Martí's essay, a commitment to the notion that only a salvaging of national values such as those handed over by the hemispheric national histories in their integrationist (or centrifugal, as Cornejo Polar used to call them) efforts can help us sustain the possibility of a regional identity, which is then perceived to be the only effective bastion against total submission to cultural imperialism.[6] Obviously enough, the nationalist projects that started to emerge with Martí and others were powerful and historically influential constructs that should be credited with a fair amount of social and political accomplishments. However, attempting to resuscitate them from the ruins of state-centered *desarrollismo* must be admitted to be a fairly problematic enterprise. John Beverley uses the term *neo-Arielismo* to refer to precisely that position: "neo-Arielism . . . seeks to posit again literature and literary intellectuals—now, however, in the mode of Angel Rama's idea of a left modernist literary culture—as the bearers of Latin America's cultural originality and possibility. . . . Subaltern studies shares with cultural studies . . . a sense that democratization implies the displacement of hermeneutic authority to popular reception, whereas the neo-Arielist position seems to depend on a claim for the continued hermeneutic authority of the traditional or 'critical' intellectual" (Beverley and Sanders, "Negotiating" 255).[7] "Ariel" of course refers to José Enrique Rodó's 1900 essay of the same title, in which he expounds on the spirituality of a certain "Latinity," whose guardianship was entrusted to the Latin American intellectual "youth," as the only real defense against the encroachment of U.S. imperialism.

It would seem as if the main thrust of Sarlo's contribution to this complex debate is to disengage from any kind of social-political reductionism for the sake of a double vindication: a vindication of artistic value, on the one hand, and, on the other, a vindication of the need to retrieve value thinking at the service of a cosmopolitan project of nation building that would refuse all essentialisms of the identitarian variety. Sarlo's attack on what she calls cultural studies hinges on a recourse to a notion of critical thinking that makes aesthetic value its proper ground. I will attempt to show that there is a certain "essentialism of anti-essentialism" at work in her essay, which limits the cosmopolitan scope of her words and might even reintroduce, through the back door, and possibly counterintentionally (just as in the case of Moraña or Achugar), a sort of antipopulist populism as the ultimate horizon of critical thinking. Sarlo's position, which is more positive in its proposals than Moraña's or Achugar's and arises out of a different mood, will prove to be not as different from neo-Arielism as it might seem at first sight.

As I mentioned in the introduction, what is primarily at stake in this debate is an understanding of the current order of critical thinking, which is also a critical understanding of the very order of order. Whether the true order of things is spontaneous, as some of the liberal theoreticians have argued,[8] or, as was widely believed in the recent past by important sectors of the critical intelligentsia, can only result from constructivist ideologies such as socialism or national populism, a critical perspective on globalization that might at the same time manage to say something pertinent in connection with specific histories and localities must remain attentive to history without using history as a site for retrenchment and must avoid functionalization of history by the ruling regimes of capital. As Ernesto Laclau puts it, the first task for a critical project today is to understand the order of order as placed beyond, and dependent on, a necessary deconstruction of the very alternative between market and social regulation.

For Laclau, the crisis of reason associated with the fall of actually existing socialism and the subsequent weakening of all national-popular projects in the face of the global triumph of transnational capitalism is in fact dependent on "the very notion that 'social regulation of the production process' is dialectically linked to its opposition to market regulation conceived as wholly based on the individual pursuit of profit" (*New Reflections* xiii). In a strong sense, the identity-difference politics associated with what is known as "new social movements," which are clearly in the background of both postcolonial and subaltern studies, is a direct consequence of the destabilization of the market-social regulation polarity. Social regulation can no longer aspire to encompass the totality of the social, and market regulation these days bases some of its ideological strategies on the targeting of microgroup rather than individual consumption.

Under these circumstances it would seem as if any group claim concerning rights and privileges would feed directly into the antinationalist logic of the transnational market, whereas the point of view of social totality would depend on a notion of "the homogeneous and indivisible nature of [national] community" (xiii), which of course a new politics of difference inspired by social movements has denounced as wrong and ineffectual. But showing that this apparent differend is in fact the product of a previous ideological articulation (the self-feeding polarity of social in contrast to market regulation) that needs to be dismantled might go a long way toward reconstructing the possibility of a situated or markedly contingent critical reason, which would then place itself in an oblique position vis-à-vis libertarians (of the neoliberal and group-identity varieties) and communitarians (of both the socialist and the national-popular kind).

Both libertarian and communitarian perspectives (which I would have to call precritical perspectives in the sense outlined above) are linked not simply by their common assumption of the market-social regulation polarity but also by their common grounding in a notion of socially shared value, regardless of the fact that the values they respectively uphold are different. Nuances are many and turn any possible attempt at categorization into a rather complicated exercise in cognitive mapping. For instance, there are some libertarians and some communitarians who would insist on the privileging of universalist values, access to which, since Kant, has been a matter of aesthetic taste. But there are other libertarians and communitarians who would be radical in their critique of universalism, holding that no universalism, including the historical-materialist one, can transcend the epistemic limits of Eurocentric colonial history. Their values tend therefore to follow counterhegemonic histories and have a basis on notions of collective identity understood as counteridentities of resistance to dominant paradigms.

I have no desire to take sides with either the libertarians or the communitarians within or without subaltern studies. I want, rather, to help move the debate beyond merely situational parameters. My presupposition is that value thinking, which starts to be explicitly thought out as grounded thinking and a thinking of ground in Sarlo's essay, is the relatively unthought hermeneutical horizon of a sizable amount of Latin American(ist) anti–cultural studies positions and, a fortiori, of anti–postcolonial and anti–subalternist studies positions;

and, furthermore, that value thinking is only superficially understood as a commitment to aesthetic values. Aesthetic ideology—of a
Schillerian not a Kantian variety, to mention Paul de Man's important distinction—is ultimately founded on a (no matter how residual)
historicist populism—as indeed it always was in German idealism
and, generally, in Romantic thought. It is tempting to take up and
follow through de Man's distinction in the context of this debate,
which is certainly a distinction not just between Kant and Schiller,
but also between what we could call a Kantian and a Schillerian attitude in the critical tradition. In a nutshell: "There seems to be always
a regression from the incisiveness and from the impact, from the
critical impact of the original [the original is Kant]. . . . So there is . . .
an attempt to account for, to domesticate. . . . And that leads them
to texts like those of Schiller, which undertake to do just that. Out
of a text like Schiller's *Letters on Aesthetic Education,* or the other
texts of Schiller that relate directly to Kant, a whole tradition in Germany . . . and elsewhere has been born: a way of emphasizing, of
revalorizing the aesthetic, a way of setting up the aesthetic as exemplary, as an exemplary category, as a unifying category, as a model for
education, as a model even for the state" (de Man, *Aesthetic Ideology*
130). I am not suggesting that there necessarily is a conscious domestication of Kantian aesthetics at stake in the opposition to subalternism, but there certainly would seem to be a taking-for-granted of
Schillerian aesthetics as the only possible aesthetics (and definitely
as a model for the state, as we will see later). Critics who prejudge
the inability of subaltern studies to deal with literature in an aesthetic sense—to deal with the aesthetic tradition in rigorous terms
other than their own—are mistaken and are engaging in a Schillerian reading of subalternism, which would prefer to be Kantian (see
chap. 9 below). I contend that there is always a historicist element
in value thinking and that it tends to be expressed rather unavoidably along populist lines in the context of a political debate. To dig
up the residue of historicist populism in the influential critiques of
Latin Americanist postcolonial and subaltern studies is the purpose
of what follows.

In his defense of historicism, Fredric Jameson refers to the possibility of an absolute historicism that "grounds the possibility of
a comprehensive theory of past societies and cultures in the structure of the present, of capitalism" ("Marxism" 174). The experience

of historicism is thus for Jameson not a refusal of history; on the contrary, "whatever its theoretical contradictions, existential historicism must be honored as an experience, indeed, as the fundamental inaugural experience of history itself, without which all work in culture must remain a dead letter" (158). I would like to claim the status of absolute historicism for that which subaltern studies attempts to do, but I will retain the name of populist historicism to refer to an always insufficient kind of historicism, thwarted by its confusion of the part and the whole, and intent upon hegemonic seizure. *Absolute historicism*, if such can be a motto for subalternism, would meet the conditions Dipesh Chakrabarty requires of subalternist historiography: "I ask for a history that deliberately makes visible, within the very structure of its narrative forms, its own repressive strategies and practices, the part it plays in collusion with the narratives of citizenship in assimilating to the projects of the modern state all other possibilities of human solidarity" ("Postcoloniality" 290).

By historicist populism, then, I mean a mode of thinking horizontally based on the positing of community values, in the understanding that such community values can and should embody a communal universality that would then be the ground for a seizing and suturing of the social on the part of a given class or interclass formation whose strategy is to make itself stand for the social whole. It is a mode of thinking best suited to, and codeterminant of, a national-popular state form. To the extent that subaltern studies finds its point of departure in a critique of the national-popular state apparatus, and particularly in societies marked by a colonial past, historicist populism must be the target of subalternist critique. The second part of this chapter initiates such a critique by concentrating on Sarlo's proposal for a renewed value thinking. If for Sarlo a debate on values is the great debate of our time, then it seems to me that the question of subaltern studies is the question about what it is that values always necessarily obscure.

Absolute Historicism

There is nothing wrong with nostalgia, but it is significant that Sarlo's essay begins with a nostalgic comparison of the function of literary criticism in past epochs of Latin American history. In particular she points out that literary criticism in Argentina around the turn of the twentieth century was a highly influential practice with enormous implications regarding the construction of a "modern public sphere," "national culture," and "state policy" ("Cultural Studies" 115–16). She also identifies the 1960s and 1970s as the last great moment of the critical debate on aesthetic and literary values, still based on their relevance for national politics and state formation (116). Sarlo shows with these references the deep involvement of the ideological discourse on literary values with the construction of the national-populist state, incipient early in the century and poised for either collapse or revolutionary triumph in the Argentinian 1960s and 1970s. Her investment in that particular form of state discourse is consistent with Moraña's and Achugar's. At a certain level of her argumentation Sarlo advocates a residual national populism, even if only under the guise of a nostalgia for it, through her more straightforward attempts at salvaging the literary aesthetic, which she sees as jeopardized by the current cultural studies–dominated and market-driven transnational state paradigms.

Sarlo's recourse to "personal experience" toward the end of her essay retrospectively but decisively frames it to some extent as a vindication of national (or at any rate regional) rights over against a market-driven demand for Latin American third-worldism along the lines of Moraña's denunciations: "Whenever I have been on a panel with European and North American colleagues in order to judge videos and films, we have had trouble in establishing common ground on which to make decisions: they (the non-Latin Americans) look at Latin American videos with sociological eyes, emphasizing their social or political merits and overlooking their discursive problems. I tend to judge them from an aesthetic perspective, placing secondary importance on their social and political impact. They behave like cultural analysts (and, on occasion, like anthropologists), whilst I adopt the perspective of an art critic" (Sarlo, "Cultural Studies" 122–23).

The conclusion to be extracted from this recurring nightmare is the same one that was proposed by Moraña in her essay cited earlier: "Everything seems to indicate that as Latin Americans we should produce objects suited to cultural analysis, whilst others (basically Europeans) have the right to produce objects that are suited to art criticism. The same could be said of women or the working class: they are expected to produce cultural objects while white males produce art. This is a racist perspective even when it is adopted by those on the international Left" (Sarlo, "Cultural Studies" 123). And so it is. Sarlo and Moraña are dead right in their perception, shared by Richard, that the production of abjection is one of the fundamental strategies and easy resources of a lot of what goes under the name of transnational-left Latin Americanism in contemporary times. But Sarlo's diagnosis is largely or solely based on the vindication of value thinking as the right medicine for cultural studies–based racist orientalism. I will contend that values, the basic resource of disciplinary societies, are not the right medicine. A revamped value thinking can hardly approach the difficulties confronting the task of geocultural thinking in contemporary times.

The general recourse to tradition that is involved in the thinking of values might satisfy some historicist leanings, and yet it leaves us with no resource in terms of accounting for the tendential present. In globalization (provided it could ever be accomplished) the nation-state would no longer be and could not itself declare the standard of knowledge. If, in Paul Bové's words, "history has been the principle within and according to which modern state systems organize knowledge" ("Afterword" 381), we must also realize that value thinking has been the principle of that principle. The old historian Henry Charles Lea, in speaking of the Spanish Inquisition, said that it formed "a power within the state superior to the state itself" (*Inquisition* 357). The state found its legitimacy in the historical transcendence that grounded it: but the ground of transcendence could not be read without the state itself. We would adapt Lea's words to values. Values are consubstantial to state thinking, which leaves them without a ground when what is at stake is not the need to rebuild a previous state form as a defense against transnational capital but is rather the necessity to think through what Bové calls "the transitional space between state and superstate (or no state) and the national and transnational forms of capital" (385). I think the Latin American critics of cultural studies have made short shrift of this predicament, which is actually the predicament of our times (or at least a part of it). But the present has a long history.

Sarlo herself says that it would be useless to confront contemporary problems with old arguments. The value argument is, however, an old one, because its genealogy, from a philosophical perspective, can be traced back along a continuous line down to Platonism and the Platonic Idea—and thus to the very beginnings of European historicism, now in Karl Popper's sense.[9] Nietzsche attempted an over-coming of Platonism precisely through the notion of a transvalua-tion of values. But Heidegger showed with sufficient finality in his work on Nietzsche, which is not so secretly also a work against Nazi historicism, that the Nietzschean transvaluation, in its recourse to the notion of European nihilism, is still based on a metaphysics of presence transcendentally dependent on what it desires to over-come.[10] A debate on values, instead of reintroducing a critical dimen-sion in an all-too-market-driven world, is more likely to risk ending up in a surreptitious but no less anachronistic return to an epoch of European metaphysics that European thinking has already suffi-ciently examined and critically laid to rest. What is true for European thinking is in my opinion true a fortiori for what may be attempted in societies that have long been subject to European colonialism. A debate on values, whether those values are deemed to be universalis-tic or tradition bound, could accomplish various things, but it could never generate the possibility of a thinking attuned to the conditions of our present, provided that the present, as Bové claims, makes a difference, because it would always already be hopelessly entangled in the ontological historicity of the European past—and of its plane-tary epiphenomena. There is a complicity between European colo-nialism and the history of being, which we ignore at our own risk. The Latin American post-independence and national-popular states, through their essential reliance on tools of empire such as Chris-tianity and imperial languages, for instance, are consubstantial in their very constitution with an ontology of politics, or a politics of ontology, which has everything to do with their colonial history and its neo- or postcolonial continuations.[11] There is certainly no Latin American "fault" in this, which is simply a fact of history. But his-tory keeps changing: if there is any reality behind all the talk about the relative weakening of the nation-state and the disappearance of the national-popular state and its replacement by a transnational regime of capital, then the conditions for thinking have shifted. The world is now at the threshold of a change which, granted, will not necessarily erase values from the cultural-political repertoire—no more than the critique of ontotheology has erased the ontotheologi-cal ground of many thinking projects in the present. However, imag-ining their erasure might do more for the understanding of what is coming than proposing or furthering their reconstitution. Values are ideal repositories of sedimented ideology. Doing without them remains critical for the undoing of the European-historicist residue in the service of materialist thought.

It seems to me that the real differend between a radicalized, and therefore subalternist, Latin American cultural studies and what I, following Beverley, will call a tendential neo-Arielism has to do with the difference between state thinking and what Bové calls a thinking of the "interregnum." As we saw in chapter 3, speaking of a "criticism that intends to respond to the various crises and opportunities induced and afforded by globalization and the so-called end of the Cold War" ("Afterword" 373), Bové refers to the "fissure" between "the discoveries and disclosures" to be expected given "the insistence upon economic and civilizational rupture" and "the persistence of our intellectual resources which we constantly attempt to reconfigure in order to make them do the work needed to transform this putatively new world (order?) into something recognizable" (373–74). The notion of interregnum refers to the time-space marked by a certain kind of now, namely, "that place and time when there is as yet no rule, when there are ordering forces but they have not yet summoned their institutional rule into full view" (385). From the point of view of intellectual work, this generates a particular form of betweenness with important implications: "the fact of being within modernity and the state while trying to be in but not of postmodernity and globalization produces as yet unfulfilled demands for thinking, a process that can only be satisfied in a movement that does not work within the tread-marks of previous intellectual systems themselves principally attendant upon either modern state formations (and their epiphenomena) or romantic embrasures of local 'struggles' against 'global' forces" (377). I think tendential neo-Arielists are by and large engaged in a salvaging movement of what is past, while some of the people they critique are attempting to think in the interregnum. This "querelle" is therefore, in one perspective, simply a version of the patterned disputes between the emergent and the dying (which remains spectral, and continuously resurrects through the structure of the "neo" that was considered in chapter 3).

If values are the ground of thinking, or the reason for reason, as the metaphysical tradition teaches us, how could one then imagine a thinking without ground that would not quickly vanish into the utopia of a groundless thinking? In other words, how can it be possible to think without a ground? In political theory and the theory of art? In cultural studies? This is the question properly being asked every time one hears talk of essentialism or anti-essentialism, including strategic essentialism. I agree with Sarlo that the sort of academic thinking that has come to be internationally identified as cultural studies has perhaps not yet produced a satisfactory answer to this question, even though the necessity for it has been repeatedly announced. The issue is not whether cultural studies—particularly in its Latin Americanist and subalternist avatar—has come up with an appropriate answer, because answers at this level cannot really be improvised. It is not fair to judge an intellectual current by its worst possible work. The question is, rather, whether cultural studies can open itself, in some radical way, to that sort of questioning. If it can, then the indictment of cultural studies from the perspective of a necessary return to a thinking of values—be they local, national, continental, universal, or aesthetic (which might encompass them all)—that would alone hold the possibility of critical thinking is, it would seem, not simply reductive or superficial but misguided in its very presuppositions.

And yet something like an appropriate answer to the question regarding the possibility of anti-essentialist thinking is in my opinion present in the work of Laclau, and in his insistence on the "infinitude of the social": "any structural system is limited, . . . it is always surrounded by an 'excess of meaning' which it is unable to master and . . . consequently, 'society' as a unitary and intelligible object which grounds its own partial processes is an impossibility" (*New Reflections* 90). The discovery of the infinitude of the social is precisely the undoing of ground in the political sense. It is from this perspective that Laclau proposes his concept of ideology: "The ideological would not consist of the misrecognition of a positive essence, but exactly the opposite: it would consist of the non-recognition of the precarious character of any positivity, of the impossibility of any ultimate suture. The ideological would consist of those discursive forms through which a society tries to institute itself as such on the basis of closure, of the fixation of meaning, of the non-recognition of the infinite play of differences. The ideological would be the will to 'totality' of any totalizing discourse" (92).

Value thinking fulfills the ideological function thus defined in an eminent sense. It is also clear, however, that the ideological function needs to be fulfilled, since, as Laclau says, "the social only exists as the vain attempt to institute that impossible object: society" (92). Nevertheless, a distinction ought then to be made between a critical articulation of thinking, which thinks *about* the ideological function of social closure through the always essentialist appeals to value as ground or suture, and a populist articulation, which forfeits its critical dimension for the sake of the political expediency of reaching closure by recourse to value thinking, that is, to a thinking *from* values. A thinking of the interregnum or for the interregnum, insofar as it presents itself as a critical and not a populist project, cannot therefore exhaust itself in either a return to values or in any kind of radical local culturalism. Indeed, both options can be now revealed to be modifications of one and the same option: whether the proper place or abode of values is understood to be beyond the local or within the local, value thinking cannot overcome its populist-historicist horizon as a thinking of the conditions of possibility for largely vanquished and thus tendentially residual forms of historical understanding. This is not to say that these forms will not return: they will, necessarily, perhaps eternally, but always under the guise of unavoidable farce, in the well-known Marxian sense.

Value thinking is only possible today, in my opinion, on the basis of an ideological populism that can take only one of two forms: either it takes the form of a dogmatics of antidogmatism, as in the sort of neoliberal worldview that, in the Latin American context, we have come to identify with Vargas Llosa; or it takes the opposite form of an antidogmatics of dogmatism, as in any culturalist position that takes itself as resistance to some global dominant from a localist perspective or to some local particular deemed to be insufficient on universalist grounds. In the first case, the populist dogmatics of antidogmatism insists on the need to accept the spontaneity of things over against social engineering or any kind of rational constructivism; in the second case, the populist antidogmatics of dogmatism invokes rational constructivism at the service of singularized social projects undertaken under the banner of cultural identity. If neoliberalism can be taken to be the general name for the former, and culturalism for the latter, we must still distinguish between culturalist culturalism, that is, a culturalism bent on preserving the local particular, as in Achugar and perhaps Moraña, and anticulturalist culturalism, as in Sarlo, which is a universalist kind of culturalism that claims a European Enlightenment genealogy. I think most of the critics of transnational cultural studies (and no doubt also some of the very practitioners of transnational cultural studies in any of its modalities, including some subalternists) fall into the various possibilities afforded by these culturalisms. The possibility of a thinking beyond values must measure itself over against these varieties of populist historicism.[12]

The first and most obvious objection to the presumption that a thinking without values is possible is that formulating the project is already a value-laden move, since there is no such thing as a project without a reason for it, and values are nothing but reasons. Hence the very project of a thinking without values would be secretly undertaken in the name of a value that will not speak its name: an abject or obscene value, in other words, a value that cannot enter into consideration, that is barred from the scene of inquiry. The insight that is barred into blindness or the excess that will not enter the scene, since it stages it, does not, however, constitute an insurmountable objection to the question about the possibility of raising questions in the name of nothing, of no value. The question of thinking without a ground can be rephrased as a question about asking under no name, in the name of nothing: a nameless thinking, or a nameless asking. The objection that there is a value to valuelessness is thus answered in the reflection that it is not valuelessness that is attempted but rather the possibility of a thinking that refuses value as a standard for thinking, as the principle of thinking, or as the barring ground: an improper thinking, unprincipled, even unnameable—but from whose very unnameability something like a "great debate" may hang. Perhaps the great debate of the beginning of the century is a debate not on values but rather on that which values obscure, which would not be the ground of values. That values may be groundless, the question of an absolute historicism, is in fact a closer question to the spirit of our times. And then one has to wonder what exactly is at stake when one says that values are at stake.

Sarlo understands that we have come to "a crossroads" or "a new scene" and that it is organized as such by a change in the production of knowledge. The change originates in the devaluation of values as a result of a historically conditioned "split" in the practice of reading. If reading, Sarlo claims, has traditionally organized a "common ground" for both "intellectual" and "nonintellectual" reading practices (or, we could say, "expert" and "amateur" reading practices, in order to smooth out, if not quite eliminate, the exclusionary polarization of the former distinction), the common ground has vanished from under our feet as, first, the hegemonic ascent of audiovisual media in the global sphere imposes "a new alphabetization" based on "speed" and "the ability to surf" (or "slide," "*deslizarse*"), and, second, something like a "hypertechnification" in the intellectual field has led to a destructive impasse: "Even when we profess the negative metaphysics that teaches us that there are no longer any great truths to be reached by immersing ourselves in the written word, nor totalities that must be constructed from a mass of fragments, we are experts in profound reading who, paradoxically, recognize the futility of a metaphysical pretension of profundity" ("Cultural Studies" 117). Our technique, in other words, can no longer be reconciled with our values. That this has been so for a long time—hence the Heideggerian notion that "technology is nothing technological"—does not need to concern us now.[13]

For Sarlo something like a new awareness of the split between technique and value has led to, among other things, a change in the organization of knowledge affecting both the national and the international public spheres, which she sums up in the phrase "the social redemption of literary criticism by cultural analysis" ("Cultural Studies" 118). Cultural analysis amounts, in Sarlo's characterizations, to a "postmodern epistemology" based on relativism and culturalism. Sarlo defines it as an all-too-blind or overly quick acceptance of the Foucauldian-Bourdieuan-Certeauian notions that discourse is power, that discursive struggles aim for cultural legitimation, and that there is such a thing as the possibility of a good fight, committed to altering social power relations by engaging in discursive struggles on the part of the subaltern. This is Sarlo's version of what could be alternatively and perhaps more efficiently described using Stuart Hall's notion that cultural studies emerges when we realize that "culture will always work through its textualities—and at the same time . . . textuality is never enough" (Hall, "Cultural Studies" 271).

If these changes redefine the intellectual academic scene by promoting efforts such as the abandonment of previous disciplinary masteries (for instance, literary-critical mastery), the crossroads is constituted by the fact that culturalist ideology, in Sarlo's sense, loses some ground even if it also gains some. The new affirmation of something other than the very value of technique in cultural studies, which operates the social redemption of aesthetic thinking (or of literary thinking in the traditional sense), leads to an abyss: the loss of the principle of sufficient reason in the aesthetic realm is the loss of the value of value. For Sarlo—moving now in an anticulturalist sense, but without making the justification for her steps totally explicit—the values associated with symbolic production, that is, with world interpretation, can only be based on aesthetic value. Aesthetic value would be the overarching principle that could give value to value: the ground of value. It is this ground that seems to have been placed offstage by the new scene, the excess that could never be accounted for by cultural studies. In that sense, "the paradox we face could also be considered one in which cultural studies is perfectly equipped to handle almost everything in the symbolic dimension of the social world, *except art*" (Sarlo, "Cultural Studies" 122). For Sarlo, the "never-enough" of textuality has seemingly given way in cultural studies to an abandonment of textuality in an abject form of arbitrary foreclosure. Cultural studies becomes for her nothing but a culturalism that prematurely forecloses the question of textuality in its eminent aesthetic sense.

If cultural studies can only be said to constitute a legitimating ideology for discursive struggle aiming at the conquest of cultural capital in postliterary times, what it can only miss, for essential reasons, is a sort of spectral surplus that, in this case, is not simply generated by cultural capital, but itself generates any and all possible forms of cultural capital. In other words, cultural studies, in Sarlo's determination, misses out on the possibility of accounting for cultural capital's capital—it cannot itself ask the question of ground, of aesthetic value. "There is an extra in [Silvina] Ocampo that is totally absent in [Laura] Esquivel. Art is about this something extra. And the social importance of a work of art, in a historical perspective, depends on this something extra" (123).

Cultural studies does not necessarily have to negate that: it simply does not have to turn it into an absolute ground for reading or thinking. Sarlo's essay would only amount to a final indictment of cultural studies, Latin American or otherwise, if cultural studies could not respond to the objection that it exhausts itself in culturalism—that culturalism leaves no remainder, or surplus, for or from a cultural studies perspective. But that is not the case. Sarlo's argument is a version of the old metaphysical objection to postmetaphysics. If postmetaphysics wants to think the possibility of a thinking without ground, the residual metaphysician will say, "yes, but that desire amounts to a new foundation for thinking." If cultural studies dares think the possibility of a culturalism without ultimate ground (that is, if it thinks the nonculturalism of culture), then the defender of aesthetic values will say, "yes, but that can only be done by foreclosing the notion of ground." Sarlo's objection is that cultural studies forecloses the question of aesthetic value, which is in her account the only possible ground for determining the social significance of symbolic practices in a historical sense. By foreclosing aesthetic value, that is, by barring from the scene of writing that which makes writing possible, cultural studies "would be losing sight of the object cultural studies is trying to construct" (122). Sarlo's essay, which is built upon the positing of aesthetic ground as the ultimate horizon of cultural practice, works then as an indictment of what I have called culturalist culturalism, but by the same token it does not abandon the horizon of anticulturalist culturalism. Sarlo's culturalism amounts to a historicism of the enlightened variety, where aesthetics comes to occupy the ground a properly culturalist culturalism would have assigned to cultural identity in some collective sense. I think this point would also work to describe Moraña's and Achugar's thinking, even if in their case the appeal to aesthetic grounds is tempered through an alternative mask. For Moraña and Achugar what a radicalized cultural studies would tend to foreclose is the very possibility of an our-American historicism. Hence their objections to subalternism. They are closer to identitarian thinking than Sarlo is.

Sarlo's objection can be dealt with by arguing that cultural studies *does not have to* accept the presupposition that a thinking that is not based on aesthetic values is thereby barred from reflection on aesthetic values. The refusal to accept aesthetic value as a standard for thinking is not necessarily a regression into a sociologism that will not speak its name: it is—it could be—a wager for an unnamed project, an aporetic thinking of the valuelessness of value which, however, makes of its ungrounded moorings its very condition of possibility. Cultural studies is not in itself culturalist because its very logic makes it move against the ground of value, and thus also

260 // THE EXHAUSTION OF DIFFERENCE

against itself as ground.[14] Just as the essence of technology is not itself technological, cultural studies is not in itself cultural, but it could be, in its essential possibility, a thinking of the world as negative totality, as I argued in chapter 1. As a thinking of the interregnum that proceeds out of an abandonment of value thinking through a rigorous examination of the social articulations of culture, it ought to exert itself in a fundamental way through the reduction of all transcendence. Negation is the work of interruption. Interrupting narratives of totality is the groundless and reckless ungrounding of world globalization. For the sake of what?

The ruptural horizon for a thinking of the interregnum that can go under the name of subaltern cultural studies cannot itself be understood as a variety of populist historicism.[15] To borrow Stuart Hall's phrase, "the explosion of cultural studies along with other forms of critical theory in the academy represents a moment of extraordinarily profound danger" ("Cultural Studies" 273). But, again in Hall's phrase, "dangers are not places you run away from but places that you go towards" (273). The populist danger in cultural studies, in any of the varieties underlined above, lies in a premature (or belated) use of what Hall, following Homi Bhabha, calls "the arbitrary closure" (264), which I suppose is quite similar to what Jacques Derrida and Laclau have theorized as the moment of "decision."[16] "Decision" is the proper terrain of the political, in the sense that a decision imposes "an arbitrary closure" in knowledge for the sake of political action. The decisional moment in cultural studies "holds theoretical and political questions in an ever irresolvable but permanent tension" (Hall, "Cultural Studies" 272) precisely because there is never a proper time for it: if there were a proper time for a decision to be made or for a closure to be reached, then the decision, in a radical sense, would fail to be such, and the closure would forfeit its arbitrariness. Finding a proper time for political closure is however the mark of populist historicism—just as finding the proper time for theoretical closure would be the mark of some scientific project with which cultural studies has just as little to do.

Thinking the interregnum thus stands here for an interpretative enterprise, affirming an irresolvable tension between the theoretical and the political, which poses "no theoretical [or political] limits from which [to] turn back" (Hall, "Cultural Studies" 268). Its radical openness to the making of a decision marks it off from any kind of value thinking—indeed, it posits value thinking as the "extraordinarily profound danger" of cultural studies in Hall's sense (that is, its internal corruption). Nelly Richard, as we saw, uses the word *pronunciamiento* to refer to the need for the interruption of "the unlimited chain of indefinitions" for the sake of a conjunctural political practice ("Intersectando" 359). I do not think Larry Grossberg means anything different by what he calls the politically based "radical contextualism" of cultural studies: "This contextualism affects every dimension of cultural studies. It affects the most fundamental concepts that define the discourse of cultural studies, which now cannot be defined outside the particular context or field of study and struggle. . . . The very relationships between culture and society are themselves contextually specific, the product of power, and hence they cannot be assumed to transcend particular contexts" (*Bringing* 254). The model of critical reason defended here is a markedly contingent one, in the sense that reason is precisely what establishes itself in the difference between theory and discursive practice, including political practice, linking them both relationally through punctual acts of singular closure.

I want to underline this thorough elimination of nonabsolute or culturalist historicism, in the sense defined, from the theoretical understanding of subaltern cultural studies, up to and including the very notion of culture as ground, not just because, as Popper has shown, culturalist historicism is always value thinking in a strong sense but also because only its postulates can prescribe in advance what the proper moment for political closure is. A thinking of arbitrary closure has of course other dangers as well—making mistakes, making the wrong decision—but a populist closure of its field of engagement is the one against which it ought to constitute itself. In the refusal of hegemonic closure (that is, of a suture of the social inspired by any kind of hegemonic project) this thinking of the interregnum is attuned "to the agency of the subaltern in its struggle against domination" (Beverley and Sanders, "Negotiating" 242), not because of any ethical or culturalist voluntarism but because the subaltern is what is left out of any and all hegemonic closures.

To conclude: Sarlo's critique shares with Moraña, Achugar, and others the failure to account sufficiently for a particular historical predicament that I have called, using Bové's term, the "interregnum." Given the ungrounded, abyssal historical positioning of the interregnum itself, the interregnum cannot even claim the present as ground. Temporally, it occupies rather something like a time gap —the time gap of unaccomplished globalization or of the passage to empire, which will remain our host for a long time to come. The interregnum is in that sense the figure of an untimeliness that believes not in eternity but rather in its own radical historicity. I associate that untimeliness with Laclau's notion of the infinitude of the social. That the social only gives itself to us under the form of an unmasterable excess constitutes or determines my own investment in subalternism. For Laclau "the social is not only the infinite play of differences. It is also the attempt to limit that play, to domesticate infinitude, to embrace it with the finitude of an order. But this order— or structure—no longer takes the form of an underlying essence of the social; rather, it is an attempt—by definition unstable and precarious—to act over that 'social,' to *hegemonize* it" (*New Reflections* 91). The understanding of social order as the product of a more or less collective decision that sutures infinitude by way of a hegemonic closure is also the understanding that such an order opens itself necessarily to a second-degree order, an order of order, as it were, which is the relation of subalternity permanently implied by any and all hegemonies. A critical perspective on the infinitude of the social is therefore a kind of absolute historicism and also necessarily a radical opening to the subaltern position, calling as such for the permanent destabilization of hegemonic ideology and the passage to a thinking beyond hegemony.

"I get mad when I hear the word identical," *Calabazas had
continued. "There is no such thing. Nowhere. At no time.
All you have to do is stop and think. Stop and take a look."*
—Leslie Marmon Silko, *Almanac of the Dead*

NINE Hybridity and Double Consciousness

It is now a commonplace in cultural studies discourse to say that
reifications (or "essentializations") of ethnicity, whether literally
meant or practically used, like reifications involving gender or
national identity, are not good from a political perspective, particularly because they seem to depend on an inversion, rather than a
negation, of the hegemonic positions against which they struggle.
The common response invokes hybridity as a counterconcept strong
enough to dissolve the dangers of either hegemonic or counterhegemonic reification and by the same token able to ground a fluid-
enough politics of identity/difference that might warrant the cultural redemption of the subaltern. Nevertheless, the political force
of hybridity, such as it may be, remains to a large extent contained
within hegemonic politics.

As an analytical tool for Latin American studies, hybridity is
genealogically linked to the historically antecedent notions of transculturation and heterogeneity. "Transculturation" was born in the
1930s, and it appeared in the writings of Fernando Ortiz as the key
concept of an ideology of social integration whose main target was
to provide an imaginary basis for the construction of the post–1929
national-popular state. Its critical success, perhaps culminating in
Angel Rama's work, has everything to do with the fact that the
national-popular state formation was dominant in Latin America
from the 1930s until the 1980s. "Heterogeneity," which is a notion

developed by Antonio Cornejo Polar the late 1970s in a double relationship of antagonism and supplementarity with transculturation, insisted on a critique of the national-popular ideology as its main strategic function because that ideology was already coming undone through its very failure to accomplish national integration: heterogeneity as a critical concept simply signaled the fact that, from the point of view of what was heterogeneous to the dominant social articulation, for instance, indigenous ethnicities in Peru, transculturation was a powerfully threatening instrument of social subordination, not of redemption.[1]

The Latin American dominant state formation starts to change in a major way after the public debt crisis of 1982, which is not just concomitant with real changes in the structure of world capitalism but is also partially caused by them. The notion of hybridity as a master concept for Latin American social thought develops in the late 1980s, in the work of Néstor García Canclini, as the epistemological anchor for a cultural politics that could control or adjust to a number of epiphenomena derived from the then-emergent state formations, dubbed neoliberal by most, and coconstituted through a multiplicity of transstate processes that the new configuration of capital—that is, finance capitalism—made unavoidable. Just as for García Canclini "modernism is not the expression of socioeconomic modernization but the means by which the elites take charge of the intersection of different historical temporalities and try to elaborate a global project with them" (*Hybrid Cultures* 46), it could be said as well that for him hybridity, in its normative or theoretical aspect, also expresses a will to "take charge" of the present by the new intellectual elites. Hybridity thus abandons its heuristic specificity as a mere concept to become an entire political program: "perhaps the central theme of cultural politics today is how to construct societies with democratic projects shared by everyone without making everyone the same, where disintegration is elevated to diversity and inequalities (between classes, ethnic groups, or other groups) are reduced to differences" (106).

Arif Dirlik refers to "the [contemporary] need to overcome a crisis of understanding produced by the inability of old categories to account for the world" ("Postcolonial Aura" 352). Polarities such as traditional/modern, center/periphery, development/underdevelopment, and even identity/difference come under strong questioning from political and ideological positions grounded in emergent social realities. As Dirlik says (although he might have a hard time making his terminological case in Latin America), in the mid-1980s postcoloniality comes to occupy the terrain "that in an earlier day used to go by the name of Third World" (329). Postcoloniality will have come to name the very conditions of existence of the intellectual class in times of global capitalism. But for Dirlik the abolition of binarisms, and with them all foundationalism for the new planetary regime of capital, has gone too far: "While capital in its motion continues to structure the world, refusing it foundational status renders impossible the cognitive mapping that must be the point of departure for any practice of resistance and leaves such mapping as there is in the domain of those who manage the capitalist world economy" (356). Dirlik recommends a necessary adjustment: "The question . . . is . . . whether, in recognition of its own class-position in global capitalism, [the intelligentsia] can generate a thoroughgoing criticism of its own ideology and formulate practices of resistance against the system of which it is a product" (356). Only under that condition, in Dirlik's terms, could postcolonial thinking aspire to articulate itself as a counterhegemonic force in some real sense.

John Kraniauskas was perhaps the first to formulate an objection to García Canclini's position along the lines suggested by Dirlik's principle of ideology critique. Kraniauskas notes that the processes of territorialization—that is, both de- and reterritorialization—that in *Hybrid Cultures* set the parameters of cultural hybridization are always already subject to a reading whose effects are insufficiently thought out in García Canclini's text. For Kraniauskas, "reterritorialization may not only present itself as tradition, or as what Deleuze and Guattari call 'neoarchaisms,' but as the production of new subjects of a socio-cultural order which, like capital, is specifically transnational (postnational). In other words, reterritorialization may also be located—indeed, especially so—in openness and cosmopolitanism [and hybridity] too" ("Hybridity and Reterritorialization" 150). From that perspective, just as transculturation was not simply the name for a phenomenological process of cultural integration in national-popular societies but was also an ideological discourse determinant to the production of that very integration (that is, just as for the concept of transculturation a distinction could always be made between its constative and performative aspects),

hybridity might in the present come close to becoming, on its performative side, a sort of ideological cover for capitalist reterritorialization—and even a key conceptual instrument for the very process
of naturalization of subaltern exclusion. Hybridity needs, in that
sense, a corrective counterconcept that might do to it what heterogeneity, in the work of Cornejo Polar, did to transculturation ideology: reveal its limits, or indeed its ideological character. The point
is not to criticize García Canclini's work, since it has given us pre-
cious tools that remain necessary to reflect on the Latin American
present; it is rather to continue it by pushing one of its guiding concepts to the point of making it show some of its relatively unnoticed
conditions of possibility.

To argue for hybridity against the reification of cultural identities
as some kind of recipe for perpetual flexibility overdoes its usefulness once it is made clear that hybridity can also produce a form
of conceptual reification. It certainly becomes a reified notion as it
assumes the performative role of naming a space "where disintegration is elevated to diversity and inequalities . . . are reduced to differences." As hybridity moves through the power-knowledge machine
toward its particular form of conceptual closure, it keeps us from
understanding that the world is something more, and other than,
the sum of its subjects: in other words, that a politics of subjectivity
does not exhaust politics altogether. I want to propose a particular
understanding, or critique, of hybridity along the lines of a double
articulation that might enable us to retrieve it at the service of what
I have called perspectival or relational subalternism. By that I mean
an understanding of the subaltern position in merely formal terms,
as that which stands outside any given hegemonic articulation at any
given moment. Relational subalternism can perhaps, as I will try to
show, offer a sort of abyssal ground for a critique of the social able
to see beyond some crucial ideological narratives of the present, and
thus freer to confront the "central axis of conflict" in Paul Gilroy's
sense. For Gilroy, writing a few years ago about the near future, "the
central axis of conflict will no longer be the colour line but the challenge of just, sustainable development and the frontiers which will
separate the overdeveloped parts of the world (at home and abroad)
from the intractable poverty that already surrounds them" (*Black
Atlantic* 223).

Walter Mignolo has used the conceptual pair "allocation/relocation" to point out that "identities are dialogically constructed within a structure of power. Hegemony and subalternity are two major players in this scenario: hegemony with the power of allocating meaning, subalternity as a relentless place of contestation and reallocation of meaning" ("Allocation" 1). Subalternity is the site, not just *of* negated identity, but also *for* a constant negation of identity positions: identities are always the product of the hegemonic relation, always the result of an interpellation and, therefore, not an autonomous site for politics. With difference or hybridity, as with identity, the problem is elsewhere and cannot be circumscribed to the subjective terrain. A subalternist politics would entail for Mignolo the necessary theorization of that elsewhere, under "the double experience of simultaneously dwelling within the epistemology of Western modernity *and* in the difference created by modernity's subjugation of alternative epistemologies" ("Espacios" 8; my trans., here and below). Mignolo's "border epistemologies" are based on the force of a double consciousness that "incorporates civilization to barbarism at the same time that it negates the hegemonic concept of civilization" (8). For him, "borderless capitalism" paradoxically creates the conditions to "rearticulate modern epistemology in the encounter with local knowledges" (15). Against the danger that contemporary reflection can only rather feebly oppose capitalist flexible accumulation with a flexible identity under the name of hybridity, Mignolo's reflection alerts us to a possible alternative: a radicalization of the interplay between "local histories" and "global designs" on the grounds of their mutual incommensurability might lead into new determinations for thinking historically and geopolitically that would not appeal to identity/difference or to its domestication as hybridity as a primary referent. A certain concept of subalternity might do for hybridity what heterogeneity did for, and to, transculturation. The next section, which aims to show some structural limits of identity politics, is a prologue to my proposal concerning a subalternism in double articulation.

Economic Calculation and the Difficulties of the "New Order"

Pierre Bourdieu has recently described neoliberalism as the global "new belief" that comes to conform "a [political] program for the methodical destruction of collectives." For Bourdieu such a program is based on an ideological embrace of the notion that "the economic world" of late capitalism and its flexible accumulation is "a pure and perfect order" ("Essence" my trans. here and below 3). He is referring to, among other things, Friedrich A. Hayek's theorization of the market as the most likely mechanism to help bring about and then sustain "the spontaneous order" of things (Hayek, *Fatal Conceit* 83–84 and passim). Bourdieu presents this ideological new belief, which equates a natural or spontaneous order of the real to the logic of the market, as a particular kind of rational constructivism—that is, a rationalization of the world—that simply conceals itself as such. He calls it a "utopia," whose active *"mise en oeuvre"* depends on an "immense political labor" simultaneously denied as such because it apparently constitutes a merely negative form of politics. The political labors of neoliberalism drive us toward a sort of negative globality that hides pernicious effects under its virtues and merits. In Bourdieu's words:

> This movement, made possible by the politics of financial deregulation, towards the neoliberal utopia of a pure and perfect market is accomplished through the transforming and, it needs to be said, destructive action of all its political measures . . . , attempting to bring into question all the collective structures capable of setting obstacles to the logic of the pure market; the nation, whose margin for manoeuver ceaselessly decreases; labor groups, with, for instance, the individualization of salaries and careers as a function of individual competence and the resulting atomization of workers; collectives for the defense of workers' rights, unions, associations, cooperatives; the family itself, which, through the constitution of markets based upon age groups, loses a part of its control on consumption. (3)

Although Bourdieu strangely omits from his list of collective institutions all explicit reference to ethnicity, race, or indeed subaltern cultures and alternative historicities, as neoliberalism also does, his emphasis on the hidden (or negative) constructivism of the neoliberal project is already important enough: for one thing, it undermines neoliberalism's claim to an unmediated or unpolitical access to reality. But he also wonders whether one could expect that the "extraordinary mass of suffering" such a political-economic regime has produced and will continue to produce can one day start a countermovement "capable of arresting our march towards the abyss" (3). Only the collective subjectivities endangered by their suffering could initiate it. To the extent that Bourdieu is here proposing a counterprogram to the neoliberal utopia based on the political radicalization of collective subjectivities, he is proposing a form of identity politics.

Bourdieu refers to the "extraordinary paradox" according to which the *"mise en oeuvre"* of the neoliberal utopia is proceeding smoothly precisely because the residual resistance of what he calls the old order of things keeps it going through the very fact of resistance: "It is actually the permanence or survival of the institutions and agents of the old order undergoing dismantlement, and all the work of all the categories of social workers, and also all the social solidarities, familial or of other kinds, which make it possible that the social order does not sink into chaos in spite of the growing volume of the population which is made to live under precarious conditions." The dove of neoliberalism does not fly in the void: it needs the air of the old order. The effects of neoliberalism, in other words, are hidden by the resistances it encounters "from those who defend the old order pushing the resources it guarded, in the old solidarities, in the reserves of social capital which protect a large segment of the present social order from a fall into anomie." Bourdieu labels these forces of conservation (which certainly would not exclude in principle other manners of subaltern identification, such as those based on race, gender, language, or ethnicity) "forces of resistance," which could become "subversive forces" if they could just be channelled into serving "the rational pursuit of collectively elaborated and approved goals." To these forces of conservation/resistance/subversion befalls the task of holding open the hope of showing that public interest "will never be served . . . by the accountant's vision . . . that the new belief presents as the supreme form of human accomplishment" (3). The response to representational calculation, which is the hidden power of the neoliberal utopia, can only be, for Bourdieu, the rational appeal to a notion of social totality sought in and through the memory of what is vanishing.

Bourdieu's reasoning would seem persuasive: if those forces of conservation that strive to keep memory alive are themselves paving the way for the advance of neoliberalism as a political program for their destruction, then it is time for them to stop serving inimical interests. Once neoliberalism is revealed to be not simply a practical triumph of instrumental rationality but in fact an ideology feeding on the negation of alternative instrumentalizations, then alternative instrumentalizations can be rallied from their abjection into actively resisting that which destroys them. If so, however, the collective identities and solidarities of the old order would have nothing but a reactive function. This is what I would consider precarious in Bourdieu's attempt to counter the very precariousness of the present social order. Bourdieu's precariousness is symptomatic of the larger one of identity politics *tout court.* If collective identity, under one or another manifestation, attempts to present itself as a radical countermove to neoliberal globalization, it can only be because it would have the power to react to the neoliberal destruction of collective identity. Beyond its persuasiveness, one ought to note, a kind of tautology seems to mark this line of argumentation—as indeed tautology rather fittingly marks in every case the final limit of any kind of politics based on identity.

Although identity politics, increasingly under the guise of a politics of hybridity (that is, a politics based on flexible identification rather than on monistic claims to self-presence), has consistently been theorized over the last few years as an effective countermove to neoliberal globalization, its necessary appeal to the reconversion of forces of conservation into forces of subversion would seem overly optimistic. Support for a politics of collective identity can be a good tactical tool, but the minute we cease to understand identity politics tactically and move on toward assuming a strategic function for it we condemn ourselves to a likely irrelevance in the best of cases.[2] I agree with Bourdieu that public interest is not to be served by an accountant's perspective, which is perhaps only the extreme form of what Martin Heidegger calls the "representational-calculative world-view."[3] I find it much harder to believe that the traditional forces of conservation, including the nation-state in its present if tendentially residual configuration (but also in any and all ancestral identities and in any and all forms of collective solidarity), even if defined in a nonessentialist, flexible manner, can turn themselves into forces of subversion against the "*precarisation*" of life brought about by the advance of the neoliberal utopia. The rational pursuit of collectively elaborated ends and goals—which is another form of referring to a collectively assumed rather than substantially inherited social identity—if it is to be accomplished on the basis of the retrieval and conversion of residual solidarities fostered by the old order, cannot by itself counterbalance the epochal pull of flexible accumulation. Something else would be necessary.

Lisa Lowe, in a manner more typical of North American–style identity politics, attempts to offer that supplement through a sustained appeal to what we could call a form of critical identitarianism based on a tactical double game of identification and deidentification. Its possibility opens up once the opposite conceptual poles of any given identity claim, that is, either "assimilationist" or "nativist" inversion (*Immigrant Acts* 73), or, in an alternative vocabulary Lowe does not herself use, (partial) universalism or extreme particularism, are renounced in favor of what she calls "material hybridity" (75): "the materialist concept of hybridity conveys that the histories of forced labor migrations, racial segregation, economic displacement, and internment are left in the material traces of 'hybrid' cultural identities; these hybridities are always in the process of, on the one hand, being appropriated and commodified by commercial culture and, on the other, of being rearticulated for the creation of oppositional 'resistance cultures'" (82). We should note that Lowe's double possibility for the hybrid nevertheless retraces Bourdieu's notion that "the [residual] collective" can either sustain or subvert the social order. The difference between Bourdieu's and Lowe's theories is that, whereas Bourdieu's notion of rationality must sustain itself in a projected vision (or mnemonic trace) of social totality, for Lowe "the convergence of determinations [cannot] be conceived as contained within anything like . . . 'totality.'" Lowe does recognize that "if the society structured-in-dominance and its oppositional responses remain unavailable to the groups and individuals . . . , then domination functions and persists precisely through the [ideological] unavailability of this structure" (93). However, for Lowe that unavailability is only as ideological as its opposite would be. Totality is, for her, nothing but a name for a hegemonic closure of the social accomplished at the price of selective disfranchisement and subalternization. Thus, her proposal is not for the pursuit of rationally elaborated collective goals on the basis of residual identities, but is rather for "conceptions of collectivity that do not depend upon privileging a singular subject as the representative of the group [and] do not prescribe a singular narrative of emancipation. Engagement with these cultural forms is not regulated by notions of identity or by modes of identification; a dialectic that presupposes differentiation and that crosses differences is always present as part of the process of engagement" (170).

Lowe's vision seems more attuned than Bourdieu's to the fact that the "old order" depended on hegemonic closures whose retrieval from history's repository will do nothing for a number of social groups or singularities—the subaltern—that were disfranchised in and by them. To the extent, for instance, that "transnational capital is 'parasitic' upon institutions and social relations of the modern nation-state, deploying its repressive and ideological apparatuses, manipulating the narratives of the liberal citizen-subject, as well as rearticulating modern forms of gender, temporality, and spatialization" (Lowe 171), it should be said that Bourdieu's forces of conservation, which were construed during centuries of capitalist development and which are consubstantial with colonialism, slavery, patriarchy, racism, and class domination, have enabled the neoliberal utopia to take off and are themselves implicated in its violence. The neoliberal utopia has historical roots in the capitalist world-system going back to its very inception, and it cannot be properly considered a "new order" coming to us from nowhere. In Enrique Dussel's words:

> . . . modernity, to be able to manage the immense world-system . . . must accomplish or increase its efficacy through *simplification*. It is necessary to carry out an abstraction (favoring *quantum* to the detriment of *qualitas*) that leaves out many valid variables (cultural, anthropological, ethical, political, and religious variables; aspects that are valuable even for the European of the sixteenth century) that will not allow an adequate, "factual" or technologically possible management of the world-system. This *simplification* of complexity encompasses the totality of the life-world, of the relationship with nature (a new technological and ecological position that is no longer teleological), of subjectivity itself . . . , and of community (a new intersubjective and political relation). A new economic attitude—practico-productive— will now establish itself: capitalism. ("Beyond Eurocentrism" 13)

Neoliberalism, understood either as the moment of the real subsumption of society into capital or as the highest stage of capitalism under the form of finance capital, is an intensification of capitalism, not an alternative system. There is in that sense no absolute historical rupture or fissure between the new and the old, even if and when the new and the old can be shown to be indeed different. It is not just that Bourdieu's old order is supporting the advance of neoliberalism by resisting it and thus giving it a ground to grow on. Neoliberalism itself is also supporting the old order by, in a sense, resisting it and thus giving it a ground to grow on. Bourdieu understands in the (residual) "survival of the old order" the presence of a number of collective social identities that are said to be simultaneously undergoing and resisting dismantlement. Those identities must now, he says, become forces of subversion. But social identities cannot be kept in storage to be used for a resistant or a subversive end whenever the occasion arises; social identities are mere shifters, and they only mean what the present makes them mean. The old order, always already based on the terror of world simplification, should not be retrospectively understood as the salvational repository of collective identities, whether rationally constructed or ancestrally inherited, over against their dissolution in the neoliberal utopia. Collective identity is rather, and since the onset of modernity has never been anything but, the tactical invention of a countercalculation to the calculation of the market. As a countercalculation, it is still caught up within the basic parameters of the accountant's mentality. As a negative or resistant form of calculation, as a counterreification or counterfetish against the fetishism of commodities, and thus dependent, in spite of itself, on its very logic, collective identity is therefore still (or always already) appropriate pasture for neoliberalism and the triumph of negative globality.

The old order is to be understood, in at least one of Bourdieu's senses, not as a sort of populist possibility or reserve for the realization of either present or future collective social identity, but rather as the order out of which the neoliberal utopia grows over against its own apparent negations—as indeed Bourdieu himself also shows. The new order is simply the consummation (one of the many possible potential consummations but precisely the one we have) of the old one, and the presumed epic battle between neoliberal globalization and collective identities is really not a battle for the future but is rather the very face of the past as it evolves into the present.

Lowe's notion of "material hybridity" goes a long way toward admitting all that, up to the statement that her "dialectic of difference" belongs "to a new mode of cultural practice that corresponds to the new social formation of globalized capitalism" (170). Her risk is the inability to move beyond precisely an adjustment to transnational capital. Lowe's abandonment of the notion of social totality, which Bourdieu had refused to contemplate, leaves her open to the critique that her material hybridity cannot go beyond the horizon of identitarian representation and that the game of tactical identification and deidentification finds an absolute limit in a politics of the subject. But the world cannot be reduced to the subject. If Bourdieu's precariousness was the conception of resistance as reactive formation, Lowe's precariousness is that her active stance toward differentiation cannot position itself beyond the ideological interpellation of transnational capital. If to capitalism's flexible accumulation Lowe can only counterpose a flexible identity (or hybridity), then her brand of identity politics, even if understood or redesigned ambivalently as a dialectics of difference, has also ceased to be tactical and becomes strategic: identity politics, whether hybrid or not, becomes in effect all there is in the realm of the political—a simplifying counterpart to capitalism's world simplification, unable, in spite of itself, to move beyond tautology.

The becoming-strategic of identity politics is for Bourdieu the recourse to a massive appeal to collectively planned and approved political goals whose function is to preserve the collective, no matter how rationally, as a counterbalance or even a subversion of the neoliberal regime of social control. For Lowe, it is the translation of the "terrain of politics" "away from an exclusive focus on the abstract unified subject's relationship to the state or to capital, and toward those institutions, spaces, borders, and processes that are the interstitial sites of the social fomation in which the national intersects with the transnational" (172). In either of the two cases, selected here as representatives of vast fields of intellectual reflection, a strategically conceived identity politics is doomed to failure not simply because it can never be strong enough to counter neoliberalism, but also because it is not different from it: it belongs to its logic, and it is produced by it. If neoliberalism is the subjection of the social to an economic calculation understood or presented as spontaneous, and thus "pure and perfect" in its mathematical or extreme form, strategically understood identity politics is also the subjection of the social to an extreme form of economic calculation—although perhaps then the criterion of what is "economic" needs to be expanded to include its etymological sense, that is, the administration, the rule and regimentation, of what mediates between inside and outside in any human sense.

If neoliberalism is not the final discovery of the natural order of things but a form of historically based rational constructivism (a world rationalization, in other words), it is necessary to go one step beyond and think that its ostensible counterpart, the appeal to the perpetual reconstruction of collective identity either through identification or through deidentification, is also a form of rational constructivism. It is of course possible to opt between modalities of world rationalization, but that the option exists should not lead us to essentialize any one of its poles into a recipe for salvation. If essentialist thinking can be shown to be the paradoxical ground of neoliberal ideology, essentialist thinking is also in final terms the paradoxical ground of strategic collectivism. No appeal to the old order as the repository of collective values or to the new as the ground of a possible "dialectical unification across difference" (Lowe 173) can substitute for a critical understanding of what is behind both the old and the new, that is, human history in the terrible complexity of its workings.

Historical identity, any notion of a historical collective, is always a function of economy in its expanded sense: of the relations between and inside groups. There is no possible separation between the sum total of those economic relations such as they have been and the planetary triumph of finance capitalism, flexible accumulation, or the neoliberal utopia such as it is today. There is no real battle between the old order and the new order if the former is understood as the order of collective identity/difference and the latter as the order of neoliberal globalization. Rather, collective identities, which can only be developed as a reaction to a threat of whatever kind, have been elaborated historically in and through an essential relationship with an economic world-system that antedates and is the absolute precondition for the neoliberal order. But the neoliberal order, conversely, has only come into existence precisely because collective identities have furthered its growth, even in resisting it. The historical triumph of capitalism condemns collective identity (or difference) to an always already reactive function—therefore, collective identity and any ideology of collective identity can never constitute an alternative to neoliberal globalization: they are simply the calculating social response to economic calculation, and they will not supersede their essential frame. The strategic task is then not to reconstruct or salvage either identities or differences but to explore the possibility of moving beyond identity and its dissolution, into a different mode of thinking that will not need to believe in rational constructivisms, that is, that will not need to believe in ideology as the extreme remedy for a dignified form of social and historical existence, be it personal or collective.

Beyond the Local/Global Thing

The relationship between the local and the global is ubiquitous in critical discourse and has come to be accepted within cultural studies as a fundamental justification of its own enterprise. It is a complicated relationship that perhaps hides more than it reveals. Slavoj Zizek has recently offered an understanding of it in Hegelian terms:

> Today the basic political antagonism is that between the universalist "cosmopolitical" liberal democracy (standing for the force corroding the state from above) and the new "organic" populism-communitarianism (standing for the force corroding the state from below). . . . This antagonism is to be conceived neither as an external opposition nor as the complementary relationship of the two poles in which one pole balances the excess of its opposite . . . but in a genuinely Hegelian sense—each pole of the antagonism is inherent to its opposite, so that we stumble upon it at the very moment when we endeavour to grasp the opposite pole for itself, to posit it "as such." ("Spectre" 3)

If Zizek is correct, a thinking of the local is the mere dialectical inversion of the ideology of flexible accumulation understood as the present regime of capital. It cannot antagonize or "undo" the social regime of control: it can only sustain it. The conclusion is then that locality, as the dialectical correlative of global capitalism and of its dominant political manifestations, does not form the privileged site for an alternative to global dominance: it is in fact one of its faces. There is no choice between particularism and universalism, because you get them both at the same time. Zizek's definition of the local-global relationship is not contradictory with that given by Stuart Hall: "what we call 'the global' is always composed of varieties of articulated particularities. . . . The global is the self-presentation of the dominant particular. It is a way in which the dominant particular localizes and naturalizes itself and associates with it a variety of other minorities" ("Old and New Identities" 67). The global is for Hall simply a specific hegemonic articulation. His notion of the global as the local dominant is also consistent with Zizek's observation that "each pole of the antagonism is inherent to its opposite."

For Hall, "one of the things which happens when the nation-state begins to weaken, becoming less convincing and less powerful, is that the response seems to go in two ways simultaneously. It goes above the nation-state and it goes below it. It goes global and local in the same moment. Global and local are the two faces of the same movement from one epoch of globalization, the one which has been dominated by the nation-state, the national economies, the national cultural identities, to something new" ("Local" 27). What is that "something new"? Hall, writing in 1990, was optimistic and pessimistic regarding its configuration, and he was both in rather complicated ways, since in a sense his main reason for pessimism was overturned into its opposite. Recognizing that capitalism moves dialectically, "on contradictory terrain," he denounced the false claims prophesying a thorough homogenization and instrumental rationalization of the world in order to state that the new form of capital understands "that it can only, to use a metaphor, rule through other local capitals, rule alongside and in partnership with other economic and political elites. It does not attempt to obliterate them; it operates through them. It has to hold the whole framework of globalization in place and simultaneously police that system: it stage-manages independence within it, so to speak" (28–29).

In other words, for Hall "globalization cannot proceed without learning to live with and working through difference" ("Local" 31). One can have two alternative positions regarding these conclusions: on the one hand, one can say that, if such is indeed the case, then the reign of the local is phantasmatically shadowed and imperialized by the global itself, and it is only a false reign that must be understood as such; or, on the other hand, one can say, as Hall chooses to say, that difference, as the contradictory terrain for the advance of capital, is not only a site of integration but is also a site of resistance; not the terrain for history's final closure, but its site of opening. If local difference is primordially a site for the opening of history through its residual power of resistance, then everything depends on the empowerment of local difference. History can be reconstructed as what Hall calls "a minority event" (35) through the unearthing of the hidden histories of the unspoken in the very precariousness of their manifestation. This is then the moment of particularism, the moment of ethnicity, and the moment of the margin: a triumphant moment where we can rediscover the revolutionary potential of the local through what Hall calls "the aesthetics of the hybrid, the aesthetics of the crossover, the aesthetics of the diaspora, the aesthetics of creolization" (38–39). And a moment where, to our jaded surprise, we can discover "in entirely new forms which we are only just beginning to understand, the same old contradictions, the same old struggle. Not the same old contradictions but continuing contradictions of things which are trying to get hold of other things, and things which are trying to escape from their grasp" (39). In other words, we can discover what is simply the ground of politics, which we had thought was lost to globalization. Except that politics is now understood most directly and even exclusively as identity politics.

Hall's option in favor of hybrid "ethnicity," understood as a counterpolitics of the local in the new epoch of globalization, represents what has come to constitute a powerful mainstream in contemporary thinking. Hybrid ethnicity, as shorthand for a politics of the local, is not however an unproblematic concept. Nothing guarantees that hybrid ethnicity, even as a normative and not simply a descriptive concept, can successfully arrest the pull of capital toward a full colonization of the life world; perhaps the colonization of the life world is, in our times, accomplished through identity politics, as a pessimistic reading of Hall's very definition would allow one to conclude. A counterpolitics of the local, insofar as it is itself a result of the movement of global capital, is always essentially open to hijacking by the movement of global capital itself: it can be tamed and reduced to a mere mechanism for identity consumption, in much the same way as one is prompted to consume products of various kinds. Identity is always open to commodification by the cultural-ideological apparatus of global capitalism. Difference, either in its major sense as civilizational difference or in its minor sense as the sheer possibility of nondominant identifications, can lose its edge; it can be coopted and put at the service of capital as the transcendental subject of history. The optimistic wager in favor of a politics of difference as a liberationist counterpolitics of the local is nothing but an optimistic wager. Does it then remain a feasible tool with which to theorize the viability of a break that might offer once again the possibility of a counterhegemonic thinking as a basis for political practice?

Hall's "continuous dialectic between the local and the global" ("Old and New Identities" 62) in contemporary times makes the local pole of the binary relationship theoretically incapable of generating what Ranajit Guha, talking about the function of negation in subaltern consciousness, called "a semiotic break," which he understood as "[the violation of] that basic code by which the relations of dominance and subordination are historically governed in any particular society" (*Elementary Aspects* 36). To the extent that a thinking of locality, that is, any identity thinking and any thinking of difference, is systematically and dialectically linked to the *pensée unique* (if there is only one) of global capital, as Zizek and Hall argue, identity thinking feeds at the same time from and into the "basic code" (if there is only one) of global dominance. This does not mean that the struggle between the local and the global, or between the particular and the universal, is no longer, as Ernesto Laclau put it, "one of [the] basic dimensions" of emerging politics (*Emancipation[s]* 1). Rather, it means that the struggle between the particular and the universal has to be redefined precisely in order better to serve the goals of a democratic politics. It has to be understood as the ideological mask of an antagonism that can be alternatively represented.

A perspectival or relational notion of subalternity (as opposed to its essentialist counterpart, whereby the position of the subaltern could always be determined in advance out of some specific positivity) can help toward that goal. Subalternism finds its field of incidence in the study of the cultural or experiential formations that are excluded from any given hegemonic relation at any particular moment of its own history. There would seem to be a basic theoretical incompatibility between any cultural politics aiming at hegemonic articulations and a subalternist politics. Hybridity has today developed into a code word associated to a large extent with hegemonic politics. There are then strong reasons to seek a critical alternative to hybridity thinking from a subalternist perspective. It is possible to initiate a critique of the antisubaltern functions of hybridity thinking and at the same time retain a programmatic political position. A logic must be found for cultural studies work that does not confine itself to the dialectics of the global and the local.[4] The next section presents it under the notion of the double articulation.

A Double Register of Thinking.

Michael Walzer is right when he says that "the production of difference in self and society is the dominant feature of . . . modern history" (*Thick* 37), but perhaps not quite in the sense he means. Walzer seems to overlook that the production of difference in contemporary times is not just a consequence of simple particularisms, but is rather, necessarily, a hybrid event, since it can only happen within the dialectical horizon outlined above ("each one of the [local-global] poles is inherent to its opposite"). There is no particularism but in the context of a universalism that sets it as such. Walzer's failure to theorize that relationship as dialectical limits his otherwise useful distinction between "thick" and "thin" moralities.

Walzer starts his argument from the assertion that there is a kind of new world order characterized by an ostensible "commitment to democratic government and an equally pervasive, and more actual, commitment to cultural autonomy and national independence" (ix). The contemporary contrast between a universal ideology and "an extraordinarily intense pursuit of the 'politics of difference'" (ix) would seem difficult to handle for political theory, Walzer says, but only insofar as we do not come to the realization that "the crucial commonality of the human race is particularism: we participate, all of us, in thick cultures that are our own. With the end of imperial and totalitarian rule, we can at last recognize this commonality and begin the difficult negotiations it requires" (83). Thick morality is therefore a consequence of particularism: particularism's content in every case.

"Thinness" or "minimalism" is the extrapolation of that presumed commonality into a transcultural realm: I use my thin morality when I approve or disapprove of social and cultural practices going on elsewhere, basing my judgment on practical but not substantial reason. For Walzer "if there is . . . no single, correct, maximalist ideology, then most of the disputes . . . that arise within a particular society and culture have to be settled—there is no choice—

from within" (49). We are all caught within our own thick practices, which make "the leap from inside to outside, from the particular to the general, from immanence to transcendence" (48) a mere matter of thin interpretation but not the genuine object of philosophy: "To construct a theory out of an actual thick morality is mostly an interpretive (rather than a philosophically creative) task" (49). For Walzer we are all necessarily constrained by a particularism that allows for some interpretation of what remains outside it (that is, other particularisms), but that can never express the latter's truth (or indeed their falsity).

It is possible to reformulate Walzer's distinction between thick and thin morality by noting that there is no thick morality that is not always already crossed through with thin interferences; in other words, thick morality is always already hybrid, never properly exhausted by any given particularism. There is no escaping the need for minimalism, as Walzer proves when he discusses the "commonality of particularisms," which we could perhaps rephrase using Etienne Balibar's notion of the "unconditional." Minimal commonality, based as it is on a negative force or on the very force of negativity, can offer the possibility of going beyond both thick and thin ideologies: it leads us into a different realm of experience, away from the commonplace realization that we are destined to move forever between particularist and universalist ideologies.

For Balibar the introduction of "the unconditional into the realm of politics" ("Ambiguous Universality" 65) is a consequence of what he calls "ideal universality," meaning the perpetual presence, within any particularism, of "some open or latent insurrection" expressed in the form of an absolute or infinite claim "against the limits of any institution," that is, of any kind of particularism (64). Ideal universality, in Balibar's terms, "can be demonstrated to be true or absolutely justified only *negatively*, by refuting its own negations (or by displaying its internal negativity)." It is an absolute demand that defines its terms negatively, understanding freedom as noncoercion and equality as nondiscrimination (66).

Ideal universality is opposed by Balibar to what he terms "fictitious or total universality" (61), a concept that is similar in its ethical implications to Walzer's notion of "thick morality." "Fictitious or total universality is effective as a means of integration . . . because it leads dominated groups to struggle against discrimination or inequality in the very name of the superior values of the community: the legal and ethical values of the state itself. . . . To confront the hegemonic structure by denouncing the gap or contradiction between its official values and the actual practice—with greater or lesser success—is the most effective way to enforce its universality" (Balibar, "Ambiguous Universality" 61–62). Walzer refers to this kind of internal critique as "the subversiveness of immanence," saying that "social criticism in maximalist terms can call into question, can even overturn, the moral maximum itself, by exposing its internal tensions and contradictions" (*Thick* 47). But this insistence on internal contradictions and gaps cannot transcend the parameters given by the hegemonic structure itself. The internal critique of fictitious universality has as its counterpart an acceptance of normalization, that is, an always already internalized agreement to the rules of the hegemonic game: "Hegemony liberates the individual from immediate membership, but which individual? It requires and develops subjectivity, but which subjectivity? One which is compatible with normality" (Balibar, "Ambiguous Universality" 62).

In those terms, only a "subversiveness of immanence" would seem possible for any kind of differential politics based on Hall's ethnic hybridity in its dialectical confrontation with the global as local dominant. The politics of ethnic hybridity seems to reach exhaustion in the potential universalizing of a resistance which the system itself produces and can therefore always potentially reinstrumentalize. At the same time, however, it is possible to say that the positing of an aporetic or heterogeneous dimension, that of a radicalized minimalism or an ideal universality based on negative insurrection, might open the way for a different kind of political and theoretical possibility. I think it is best developed through what I have called a double articulation.

Lawrence Grossberg and Jennifer Daryl Slack have pointed out the centrality of a theory of articulation in the work of Stuart Hall and generally in cultural studies (see Grossberg, "History" and Slack, "Theory"). For Hall "an articulation is . . . the form of the connection that *can* make a unity of two different elements, under certain conditions," where "the 'unity' which matters is a linkage between that articulated discourse and the social forces with which it can, under certain historical conditions, but need not necessarily, be connected" (Grossberg, "On Postmodernism" 141). I want to retain that definition and then double it in the following sense: the "unity" I will try to establish, at a theoretical level, is not simply a unity between an ideology and its subject, but is rather a linkage between a project for cultural-political practice and a theoretical endeavor within which the conditions of possibility of that same political practice can also be defined as conditions of impossibility. I am calling it "perspectival subalternism," using an expression suggested by Veena Das ("Subaltern" 310). With it we can break out of the trap of hybridity thinking as the ultimate horizon of (counter)hegemonic cultural work.

The notion of a double articulation is not new. Its more famous formulation perhaps continues to be Gayatri Spivak's notion of "strategic essentialism," as presented in "Subaltern Studies: Deconstructing Historiography," her introduction to Selected Subaltern Studies.[5] For the sake of consistency with my own terminology I will translate strategic essentialism as tactical essentialism. Spivak's stated intention was to align work done within subaltern studies with her own practice of deconstruction. That meant, first of all, showing that subaltern studies does not move through any serial positing of subaltern subjectivity in any way other than as what she calls "theoretical fictions" ("Subaltern Studies" 7, 12). This is because subaltern consciousness can only be determined as "the absolute limit of the place where history is narrativized into logic" that is, as a negative form of consciousness, always already cathected by the elite, that will not result in any triumph of self-awareness or self-determination but that produces itself through cognitive displacement and failure: "if . . . the restoration of the subaltern's subject position in history is seen by the historian as the establishment of an inalienable and final truth of things, then any emphasis on sovereignty, consistency and logic will . . . inevitably objectify the subaltern and be caught in the game of knowledge as power" (16).

However, for Spivak "a restorative genealogy cannot be undertaken without [a] strategic [that is, tactical] blindness" that allows the genealogist to claim "a positive subject-position for the subaltern" (16). The tactical use of positivist essentialism is then to proceed as if it were possible to suspend the heterogeneity of subaltern consciousness in order to postulate a unified field of subaltern consciousness "in a scrupulously visible political interest" (13). The utopian or idealist or humanist notions of self-determination and an unalienated consciousness can then, contradictorily enough, be broached "within the framework of a strategic [i.e., tactical] interest in the self-alienating displacing move of and by a consciousness of [subaltern] collectivity" (14).

The relation between the tactical essentialism contained in subalternist theoretical fictions and the radicality of subalternism as a thinking of negativity (insofar as subalternism is the thinking of whatever is left outside of, that is, negated [and therefore also "cathected"] by, a hegemonic relation at any given moment) is to be thought not dialectically but through the notion of a double articulation or double register whereby the subalternist will be able to engage both radical negativity and tactical positivity simultaneously and distinctly. This is not too far from Balibar's differentiation between a fictitious universality and an ideal universality. I will call the first register *fictitious register* and the second *negative register.*

The fictitious register is invoked in every case on the basis of political necessity. The hegemonic relation is precisely what excludes the subaltern as such. However, no political work can be done outside the labor of hegemony. Political action either tendentially changes or consolidates the hegemonic relation as presently constituted. But any hegemonic change will proceed to a seizing of the social in whose closure the subaltern—in the sense of the internally excluded or subordinated within that particular kind of hegemonic rearticulation—will reemerge as such, if in different ways from the previously constituted. In other words, hegemonic politics can always abolish some subalternities but can never abolish them all—it needs them as that on which it constitutes itself. There is then a necessary and irreducible difference between hegemonic politics and subalternism, and it is that difference that calls for subalternism's double articulation. The subalternist insistence on hegemony's outside, that is, on the constitutive negativity of hegemony, should then be seen as an affirmative insistence—I hope that much is clear. There is a difference between positivity and affirmation. If hegemonic politics in general can be considered to be a politics of the positive, they are never yet affirmative to the extent that they are made possible by what they foreclose as a result of their very constitution—which is precisely the object of subalternist affirmation.

In "Marx after Marxism: Subaltern Histories and the Question of Difference" Dipesh Chakrabarty tackles what he thinks is "an

almost insoluble problem in writing subaltern history" and asks
whether there are "ways of engaging with the problem of the 'universality' of capital that do not commit us to a bloodless liberal pluralism that only subsumes all difference(s) within the Same" (13). For
Chakrabarty the question has to do with the necessary thinking
of commodity fetishism in contemporary times. If the form of the
commodity has to do with the conflict between "real labour" and
"abstract labour," then Chakrabarty will insist that "real labour" is
not the same thing as "natural labour." "Real labor" is already socially mediated, that is, it is always already culturally mediated. It
therefore bespeaks of an irreducible heterogeneity at its core: "It can
find a place in a historical narrative of capitalist transition (or commodity production) only as a Derridean trace of something that cannot be enclosed, an element that constantly challenges from within
capital's and commodity's—and by implication, History's—claims
to unity and universality" (14). That trace is precisely and constitutively the trace (but there is always more than one, and not all of
them depend on commodity production) of the subaltern, the cin-
der that remains after the conflict between real and abstract labor
has taken place in every case. The subaltern therefore appears within
historical narrative as "what fractures from within the signs that tell
of the insertion of the historian (as a speaking subject) into the global
narratives of capital. It is what gathers itself under 'real labour' . . . ,
the figure of difference that governmentality . . . all over the world
has to subjugate and civilize" (15) by either including it within the
hegemonic articulation through a successful ideological interpellation (as in all populisms) or by proceeding to its nonhegemonic incorporation through naked capture. Hegemony also effectively seizes
what it does not include by producing it as excluded, as left over, as
remainder.

If that is so, then "subaltern histories written with an eye to difference cannot constitute yet another attempt . . . to help erect the
subaltern as the subject of modern democracies, that is, to expand
the history of the modern in such a way as to make it more representative of society as a whole" (15). In other words, subaltern histories
are not populist histories. In Chakrabarty's formulation, the point of
subaltern history as such is to unconceal the incommensurabilities
and heterogeneities "inscribed in the core" of capital/commodity.
"Or, to put it differently, the practice of subaltern history would aim

to take history to its limits in order to make its unworking visible" (16). It is thus a counterrepresentational practice. The visibility it aims for is the visibility of what has been rendered invisible through, for instance, the conflict between real and abstract labor. But the visibility pertaining to any kind of hegemonic politics is precisely the opposite: it aims to dwell within the working of history, as its goal is either to sustain the given hegemonic relation or to establish a new one.

It is said that the focus on unworking, on counterrepresentation, on deconstruction, that is, the exclusive insistence on the negative register as a register which withholds positivity even if based upon affirmation, is not sufficiently political. As John Beverley puts it, "the truth *of* the subject, of its location in the Real, is not the same as truth *for* the subject. . . . Social struggles are not between science and ideology but rather between contesting classes and group ideologies, which may or may not invoke science or an idea of science in their self-legitimization . . . but do always involve what Spivak calls the 'metalepsis' of positing the (subaltern) subject as sovereign cause" ("Does the Project" 244–45). Kraniauskas makes the same point when he states that Chakrabarty's notion of "real" labor implies "a temporality which may remind us of other 'forms of worlding' but which does not itself 'world' " ("Hybridity in a Transnational Frame" 122). For Kraniauskas it is necessary to move from the theorization of the radical negativity of subaltern temporality to the uncovering of "the historicity of cultural forms where heterogeneous histories flow into and nourish vibrant alternative and/or insubordinate worlds" (122). Hence the need for a hegemonic project that can sustain such critical enterprise, for entering the political field at the level of interpellation and representation. Without it, a subalternist politics will be deprived of a way to ever lay a claim to practical success within any hegemonic articulation.

The notion of the double articulation of subalternist thinking seems apposite to a resolution of the seemingly aporetic relationship between the negative presentation of the subaltern as such and the political need for hegemonic action. A more recent model was given by Jacques Derrida's call for a New International in *Specters of Marx*. For Derrida, the first articulation—what I am calling the fictitious register—would still work within an idealist logic—as all populist, that is, hegemonic logics necessarily do: "Let us accept provisionally the hypothesis that all that is going badly in the world today is but a measure of the gap between an empirical reality and a regulating ideal" (*Specters* 86). Within this first articulation the imperative to intervene critically and politically in order to attempt to close the gap between the regulating ideal of democracy and the empirical facts that keep the democratic ideal outside the everyday experience of many is an important and necessary one. It calls for hegemonic politics of the kind theorized by Laclau and Chantal Mouffe as both democratic and popular struggles: that is, positional struggles and systemic struggles, struggles for recognition and struggles for redistribution, identity politics and class politics, solidarity politics and representational politics. Derrida's second articulation describes the negative register in the subalternist position. "Beyond the 'facts,' beyond the supposed 'empirical evidence,' beyond all that is inadequate to the ideal, it would be a question of putting into question again, in certain of its essential predicates, the very concept of the said ideal [of democracy in our historical terms]" (86–87).

The first articulation by itself would lead to a conceit with what Walzer calls thick descriptions, according to which we cannot step outside of our own skin, or barely can; we are always already determined by our world, we cannot get rid of our own experiential prejudices; and all we can do is make sure that our prejudices are consistently maintained. Derrida calls this "a fatalist idealism" (*Specters* 87), which is as such always caught up in a sort of unavoidable essentializing of the life-world. But the second articulation, by itself, would lead to a permanent critique without remainder, to an absolutist position of negation, and to a kind of European nihilism in the Nietzschean-Heideggerian formulation (Heidegger, *Nietzsche* 4s: 1–187). Derrida calls it "an abstract and dogmatic eschatology in the face of the world's evil" (*Specters* 87). There is a sense in which subalternist negativity falls victim to the limitations of both registers, taken individually. Thus, a radicalized embrace of subaltern negativity may at the same time fall prey to fatalist idealism (for instance, when historians understand that they are themselves always already constrained by disciplinarity and the historicity of capital and can only point to the "real" labor of the other as an unworkable limit, an unreachable "beyond") and to dogmatic eschatology (since that unworkable limit would then be used as a marker of the permanent destabilization of knowledge, without reprieve). Only a simultaneous dwelling within both registers, where one would work as an automatic corrective of the other, might allow for the formulation of a critical enterprise that would avoid the pitfalls of fatalist idealism and dogmatic eschatology. Such simultaneous dwelling is what is understood by subalternist affirmation.

A subalternist politics that explicitly adopts the need for its double articulation can be tactically hegemonic, or populist, without sacrificing its historical commitment to subaltern consciousness and the unworking of privilege. But it can also be tactically negativist without indulging in Jacobin dreams of revolutionary terror. Its strategic position—its "proper" in de Certeau's sense—is then of course the double articulation itself.[6] We are perhaps now ready to return to the notion of hybridity and explore how it may itself be made newly productive when understood under the double register. But we cannot do so without further exploring the conditions under which a thinking of the double register makes itself possible as a thinking of unrestricted affirmation.

Savage Hybridity

The concept of hybridity is complex and particularly suggestive because it can be used to subsume phenomena that derive both from territorialization and from deterritorialization. In the latter case, hybridity refers to processes of loss in previously determined positions (that is, hybridity would increase in today's world because there is deculturation, and deculturation is a net loss, beyond reprieve). In the former case, hybridity refers to the positivity such loss structurally or constitutively entails (there is no deculturation without reculturation, and reculturation could even produce—under certain circumstances—a threat to the very economy of the system). Hybrid reterritorialization and hybrid deterritorialization are then two—different—sides of the same coin.

The positive (or transgressive) side would imply that it is possible to place hybridity at the service of a critique of hegemonic identities that might tendentially serve the cause of decolonization or of resistance against the Eurocentric colonization of the imaginary. The negative or reticent side would suspend such redemptive teleology by claiming that it remains excessively entangled in a modernizing or progressive idealism that, as such, is not only insufficiently materialist but is also always already Eurocentric in its historical conditions of possibility. Both sides dwell as virtualities in the concise definition of hybridity provided by Gyan Prakash:

> Postcolonial criticism . . . seeks to undo the Eurocentrism produced by the institution of the West's trajectory, its appropriation of the other as History. It does so, however, with an acute realization that postcoloniality is not born and nurtured in a panoptic distance from history. The postcolonial exists as an aftermath, as an after—after being worked over by colonialism. Criticism formed in this process of the enunciation of the discourses of domination occupies a space that is neither inside nor outside the history of Western domination but in a tangential relation to it. This is what Homi Bhabha calls an in-between, hybrid position of practice and negotiation, or what Gayatri Chakravorty Spivak terms catachresis: "reversing, displacing, and seizing the apparatus of value-coding." ("Postcolonial Criticism" 8)

This very transversality or tangentiality vis-à-vis any of the two poles of the relationship of hegemonic domination gives hybridity the conceptual possibility of dwelling in ambivalence, of being able to opt for either transgression or reticence. But such structural undecidability of the hybrid position would seem to impose a political price, to the extent that, by giving a choice in practical terms, it voids the *necessity* for a specific practice against Eurocentric subjectivation. This is perhaps what Dirlik has in mind when he remarks that "since postcolonial criticism has focused on the postcolonial subject to the exclusion of an account of the world outside of the subject, the global condition implied by postcoloniality appears at best as a projection onto the world of postcolonial subjectivity and epistemology" ("Postcolonial Aura" 336).

The necessary circumscription of hybridity thinking to the terrain of a politics of the subject limits its theoretical and practical effectiveness. However, the potential radicalization of hybridity as a thinking of subjectivization allows space for a new understanding, itself transversal vis-à-vis both the transgressive and the reticent options. I will use Bhabha's option of "savage hybridity" to move toward the possibility of a concept of hybridity beyond the transgressive-reticent game. The radicalization of hybridity as savage hybridity could lead into an experience of thought based on the double articulation. If savage hybridity correspond to the negative register, what I will call cultural hybridity belongs in its fictititious side.

Hybrid subjectivity, through its very undecidability qua hybrid, preempts the closure of any discursive position around either identity or difference. Hybrid subjectivity, at its limit, does not some times allow for identity and some times for difference, but rather simultaneously undermines both identitarian and differential positions, which are driven into aporia. More than the site for ambivalence, hybridity, as diasporic ground or abyssal foundation for subjective constitution, is a nonsite or it is ambivalence itself. It is therefore not a place for subjective conciliation. On the contrary, it points to the conditions of possibility for the constitution of the sociopolitical subject as at the same time conditions of impossibility because the subject, through its constitutive, hybrid undecidability, is always already split. This is savage or nomadic hybridity: not what grounds a subject in an antagonistic relation to the state or capitalist domination, but precisely what ungrounds it, or the very principle of its ungrounding vis-à-vis any conceivable operation of state or social regime constitution. Against savage hybridity, since the split subject is nevertheless constituted as such, even through deconstitution, since there is state, and there are social regimes, hybridity finds a second life as cultural hybridity, which is an ideological response to the sociostatal interpellation that produces it. Hence its new hegemony in late-capitalist cultural discourse. Hybridity has come to be the "empty signifier" of contemporary cultural politics in precisely that second sense, that is, as cultural hybridity.

In Laclau's terms, an empty signifier is the placeholder for a founding universality, to be occupied by any element in a chain of equivalences that, through always contingent historical circumstances, develops a hegemonic function. A hegemonic relationship is for Laclau the specific relationship between the particular and the universal that obtains in any given historical moment. His postulate that hybridity is today a privileged instrument handed over by history that could facilitate a more active process of planetary democratization contributes to the enthronement of the hybrid as the empty signifier for a new hegemonic articulation. Laclau is then not too far from the kind of cultural politics underwritten by García Canclini on the basis of a similar assignment of democratic value to the concept.

Laclau affirms "the centrality of the concept of hybridization in contemporary debates": "hybridization is not a marginal phenomenon but the very terrain in which contemporary political identities are constructed" (*Emancipation[s]* 50). For Laclau, "modernity started with the aspiration to a limitless historical actor, who would be able to ensure the fullness of a perfectly instituted social order. . . . The starting point of contemporary social and political struggles is, on the contrary, the strong assertion of their particularity, the conviction that no one is capable, on its own, of bringing about the fullness of the community" (51). Thus the linkage between particularism and hybridity becomes crucial for him, since it is precisely the passage from the particular to the hybrid, or the conversion of the particular into a specific kind of hybridity, that can today, in his opinion, found a new hegemony. Picking up on the transgressive-reticent option of cultural hybridity (itself a version of the dual possibilities earlier found in Bourdieu, Lowe, and Hall), Laclau says: "Difference and particularisms are the necessary starting point, but out of it, it is possible to open the way to a relative universalization of values which can be the basis for a popular hegemony. This universalization and its open character certainly condemns [*sic*] all identity to an unavoidable hybridization, but hybridization does not necessarily mean decline through the loss of identity: it can also mean empowering existing identities through the opening of new possibilities" (*Emancipation[s]* 65).

Hybridization defines for Laclau the contemporary realization that no particularism can overcome its own finitude. As he explains it, from a formal point of view, the finitude of any particularism places it in the position of an element in a chain of equivalences that can only define itself as such through its antagonistic relationship with that which denies it. The systematicity of the chain of particularisms, or of differences, that is, its moment of totalization, of conversion into a system, is only possible on the basis of a constituting negativity. This constituting negativity of particularism or difference introduces within it a moment of universalist identity that "destabilizes or subverts those differences" (53). It is a negative universality: "that 'something identical' can only be the pure, abstract, absent fullness of community, which lacks . . . any direct form of representation and expresses itself through the equivalence of the universal terms" (57).

Such negative universality paradoxically constitutes the very possibility of linkage for a hegemonic articulation on the basis of the hybridization of particularisms. Laclau's cultural politics, like García Canclini's, "wholly accepts the plural and fragmented nature of contemporary societies but, instead of remaining in this particularistic moment, it tries to inscribe this plurality in equivalential logics which make possible the construction of new public spheres" (*Emancipation[s]* 65). Laclau seems then to accept what I referred to as cultural hybridity. But I would claim that his logic also offers the means to theorize savage hybridity as the aporetic radicalization of its cultural concept: "if all identities depend on the differential system, unless the latter defines its own limits [that is, unless the system becomes a *system*], no identity would be finally constituted. . . . If we had a foundational perspective we could appeal to an ultimate ground that would be the source of all differences; but if we are dealing with a true pluralism of differences, if the differences are *constitutive*, we cannot go, in the search for the systematic limits that define a context, beyond the differences themselves" (52).

Laclau is pointing at the aporetics of differential thinking. No differential thinking can establish closure in its self-determination without a systemic or foundational ground that gives it a principle of constitution. In the absence of such a foundation, the impossibility of closure of the system of differences is its aporetic relation. It cannot be solved logically, and it is thus a limit for thought. Politically, as we have seen, it results in the possibility of creation of a historically contingent hegemonic relationship: in it, one of the elements in the differential chain will occupy the place of the impossible object or empty signifier, becoming thus a ground that does not ground, a principle of reason on the abyss. The transgressive version of cultural hybridity insists on this political resolution of the aporetic conflict and dwells on it, embracing it as the possibility of a hegemonic change. The reticent version dwells in skepticism or in the memory of a loss. And savage hybridity is the very terrain of the aporetic relationship.

As such the latter calls for the theorization of a remainder within and beyond all hegemonic closures. This remainder or reserve, which by definition would be excluded from the cultural politics of hybridity, or from the politics of cultural hybridity, is beyond all difference and all identity, and it is at the same time the condition of (im)possibility of both. It marks the site of an abyssal exclusion, beyond any principle of reason, and it marks the (im)possible locus of enunciation of the subaltern perspective, beyond the subject. In Laclau's terms, "the only way out of [the theoretical] difficulty [the impossibility of systematicity creates] is to postulate a beyond which is not one more difference but something which poses a threat to (that is, negates) all the differences within that context— or, better, that the context constitutes itself as such through the act of exclusion of something alien, of a radical otherness" (*Emancipation[s]* 52). What constitutes the system of differences is what negates the system of differences. And what negates the system of differences is undecidably other. Savage hybridity, as expression of the radical finitude of all particularism, is that beyond. Savage hybridity is *not*, to be sure, the subaltern. But, as the "other side" of the hegemonic relationship, savage hybridity preserves, or holds in reserve, the site of the subaltern, just as it preserves the site of a subalternist politics. It is not so much a locus of enunciation as it is an atopic site, not a place for ontopologies but a place for the destabilization of all ontopologies, for a critique of totality—*and* a place for the possibility of an *other* history.[7] In Chakrabarty's terms, it is the limit where history looks at its own undoing, or the constitutive trace of the real within the real. But it is also the place where articulation becomes possible with, in Kraniauskas's terms, "alternative social forms of *conscious* memorisation. Those forms which carry ongoing and renewed responses—narratives, images and histories—figure (temporalize) experiences of subalternization to the abstract 'time of capital'" ("Hybridity in a Transnational Frame" 123). Grossberg's definition of Hall's concept of articulation must be quoted again: articulation is the establishment of a linkage between an "articulated discourse and the social forces with which it can, under certain historical conditions, but need not necessarily, be connected" (Grossberg, "On Postmodernism" 141). Savage hybridity is the (abyssal) ground for linkage, as well as the opening of that first hegemonic articulation between a discourse and a given social force (the fictitious register) to a second articulation: the political and theoretical articulation between the fictitious register itself and the radical contingency of an affirmed subalternity, which is the negation of what hegemony negates and thus the possibility of an other history.

Hybridity is then, as Bhabha says, "at once very cultural and very savage" (*Location* 158). In its cultural sense, hybridity, which inscribes itself within the fictitious register of the double articulation, is but the consequence of its own primary repression: it allows us to find a position within any of the hegemonic relations that constitute us. It is then synonymous with any position in the (dialectical) game of identity and difference that marks locality in the contemporary world: all localities are hybrid, since all localities are the intersection of given particularisms and what negates them. In its savage and delocalized sense, however, hybridity, which in its cultural version seeks the crossing-over of borders and the (relative) erasure of limits, finds a fold or a second kind of crossing. There is no beyond the hybrid, since the hybrid is the beyond. As a counter-limit savage hybridity is the ne-plus-ultra of any limit, and thus the limit of limit, and an impossible possibility. As impossible possibility, it marks the constitutive split of any (hybrid) subject position. It could then be understood as a critico-transcendental concept in the Kantian sense, simultaneously a producer and a destroyer of all foundations and of all teleologies, and similar to what Kant terms "the sublime." According to Kant, given the "perception that every standard of sensibility is inadequate for an estimation by reason of" what remains under the categorization of the sublime, the experienced displeasure turns into pleasure in the simultaneous perception of our "supersensible vocation, according to which finding that every standard of sensibility is inadequate to the ideas of reason is purposive and hence pleasurable" (*Critique of Judgment* 115). That is, the trembling in front of the thing, the fear suffered by the imagination before the excess of the supersensible as supersensible ("the thing is, as it were, an abyss in which the imagination is afraid to lose itself" [115]), becomes a source of satisfaction once the supersensible is recaptured by reason as a faculty higher than the imagination. In Kant's words, "what makes this possible is that the subject's own inability uncovers in him the consciousness of an unlimited ability which is also his, and that the mind can judge this ability aesthetically only by that inability" (116). It is known that Kant relates that "unlimited ability" with the ability of reason to relate to "the idea of the absolute whole" (117). That way, the end of reason, or its teleological aim, comes to be recaptured through the very failure of teleology: the conditions of impossibility of the understanding of the thing now appear as its very conditions of possibility. And a thinking of totality is once again possible.

In the terms of our discussion, the inability of the cultural notion of hybridity to reach logical closure, that is, the inability of the hybrid to offer itself as a stable order of subjectivization, frees up the possibility of a critical concept of the hybrid as a teleological aim of thought in its move toward the capture of social totality. If the hybrid is an abyss in which the imagination is afraid to lose itself, that abyss can be turned into the "proper" site of a subalternist politics. Savage hybridity is the region of Balibar's ideal universality and of Walzer's transcendent minimalism. It is the (im)possible place or the articulatory nonplace of the subalternist double articulation.

The hypostasis of the hybrid in mainstream postcolonial and cultural studies, although more or less secretly dependent on its savage possibility, generally follows its tamed or cultural possibility over against the former: in terms of our discussion in the previous chapter, it is Schillerian rather than Kantian. Cultural hybridity generally disavows savage hybridity. Savage hybridity can be understood as the radicalization of the reticent version of cultural hybridity on the basis of its constitutive negativity: it turns a reticent understanding of cultural change into a principle of counterhegemonic praxis, and it places it at the service of the subaltern position in the constitution of the hegemonic system. The hegemonic relation—any hegemonic relation—must then be understood, not as a full hybrid body, but as a (quasi-)socioideological totality that is only made possible through the negation or exclusion of the subaltern other. The subaltern position structurally marks the failure of hybrid totalization: the remainder of the hegemonic relation, that is, its negative register.[8]

Dirlik remarks that "the hybridity to which postcolonial criticism refers is uniformly between the postcolonial and the First World" ("Postcolonial Aura" 342). Cultural hybridity always appears in its mainstream formulation as critical of Eurocentrism, since it aspires to a displacement of Eurocentrism as the hegemonic ideological formation in the history of modernity. But Dirlik, repeating Kraniauskas's argument in reference to García Canclini, understands that the apparent ideological fragmentation that accompanies global capitalism at the superstructural level "may represent not the dissolution of [Eurocentric] power but its further concentration" (347). That is what Kraniauskas understands as capitalist reterritorialization. From it, in Dirlik's words, "the managers of this world situation themselves concede that they . . . now have the power to appropriate the local for the global, to admit different cultures into the realm of capital (only to break them down and remake them in accordance with the requirements of production and consumption), and even to reconstitute subjectivities across national boundaries to create producers and consumers more responsive to the operations of capital. Those who do not respond . . . need not be colonized, they are simply marginalized" (351)

From that marginalization one cannot expect the effective constitution of cultural hybridities in the sense ostensibly promoted by García Canclini or Laclau, by Bourdieu, Lowe or Hall: the democratization of the public spheres within transnational capitalism does not reach so far. But from that marginalization the memory of an alternative hybridity depends absolutely. If it could ever break through, it would determine a semiotic break, to use Guha's expression, with unpredictable consequences for the present hegemonic articulation and its limited set of particularisms and universalities.

The Exteriority of Ambivalence

I began this chapter with a reflection concerning the need to open up contemporary notions of hybridity into wider modalities of world interpretation. Hybridity categories, once they solidify into a strategic political project, circumscribe political life to subjective agency. But subjective agency does not exhaust the political. Ultimately, the postulation of subjective agency as the limit of the political remains caught up within a Cartesian game of calculation and countercalculation that is by its very nature unable to break through and beyond the internalization of hegemony. Some appeal to a position of exteriority remains necessary in order to restitute the possibility of what, following Balibar, we could call "unconditional insurrection." Unconditional insurrection does not name a voluntaristic project of world revolution. It names, rather, the possibility of an other history, of an alternative historical memory: a memory made possible by the simple fact that things could be, and could have been, other than what they are. Historical reason is always contingent. Its contingency preserves within itself the very order of critical reason. And no critical reason is possible that cannot imagine itself confronting always alternative historical contingencies.

The notion of the double register presented here preserves just such possibility. Gilroy prefers the term "double consciousness," which he adapts from W. E. B. Du Bois, to refer to a specific structure of subaltern consciousness within modernity. Black diaspora subaltern consciousness would incorporate the double possibility of a "politics of fulfilment" and a "politics of transfiguration." A politics of fulfilment is based on "the notion that a future society will be able to realise the social and political promise that present society has left unaccomplished. . . . [it] demands that bourgeois civil society live up to the promises of its own rhetoric. It creates a medium in which demands for goals like non-racialised justice and rational organization of the productive processes can be expressed. It is immanent within modernity and is no less a valuable element of modernity's counter-discourse for being constitutively ignored" (Gilroy, *Black Atlantic* 37). A politics of fulfilment is thus a politics of the fictitious register, dwelling on Walzer's subversiveness of immanence. It is a hegemonic politics, in the sense that it plays itself out within the limits of the given hegemonic articulation.

A politics of transfiguration, hoaver, "strives in pursuit of the sublime, struggling to repeat the unrepeatable, to present the unpresentable" (Gilroy, *Black Atlantic* 37). Its "basic desire is to conjure up and enact the new modes of friendship, happiness and solidarity that are consequent on the overcoming of the racial oppression on which modernity and its antinomy of rational, Western progress as excessive barbarity relied" (38). For Gilroy, this "resolutely utopian politics of transfiguration . . . partially transcend modernity, constructing both an imaginary anti-modern past and a postmodern yet to come" (37). Notwithstanding its positive or utopian content, Gilroy's politics of transfiguration incorporate a negative register, which I have defined as the formal condition for unconditional insurrection. The absolute condition for a politics of transfiguration, rather than the presentation of a utopian content, is the preservation of a mnemonic trace pointing to the possibility of a savage outside: an exteriority without positivity, a transhistorical remainder whose force is the appeal to an "otherwise" understood as the negation of what hegemony negates. This is the *affirmative* site of subalternist politics, which thus appears as a site beyond hegemony: the nonsite that, by making possible historical subjectivation, affirms the radical ambivalence of historical subjectivation and drives any politics of fulfilment against their own limit.

The subalternist position undoes hybridity thinking, that is, the hegemonic thinking of the passage to empire, by sharing in a savage hybridity which is, in Spivak's words, "the absolute limit of the place where history is narrativized into logic" ("Subaltern Studies" 16)— and therefore also an absolute refusal to narrativization itself. But from this refusal, from the nakedness that results, something like a force able to confront "the central axis of conflict" begins to emerge. I think Latin American cultural studies is in at least as good a position as any other discursive field to open itself to it—provided that we do not tell ourselves stories.

///

I have attempted throughout this book to move toward the aporetic moments of Latin Americanist knowledge and to push Latin Americanist fulfilment against its limit. My intent is not merely critical; it is also preparatory. If there is to be a politics of Latin American cultural studies that may have a chance at grasping what the political is, in other words, a politics that would not be merely administration, but one that could conceivably have some effect in preparing a transformation, I believe that it must be articulated through as relentless and savage a practice of clearing as possible. Call it a labor of the negative, without which any positivity is only, at best, a pile of good intentions. Or call it critique. A Latin Americanism of fulfilment, which always already accepts and has accepted its historical submission to translational imperatives and the burdens (and, I suppose, the glories) of location, cannot stake a claim to go, beyond itself, toward the atopian or excessive region that perhaps no academic Latin Americanism has ever reached, but on which, nevertheless, something like a transfiguration depends. This is not abstract thought or mysticism of any kind. Latin Americanism, whether historically constituted or rebellious, has a subordinate place in university discourse: there are also hegemonic politics to be played in that terrain. How can we play them from a position of force if all we ever do is submit to the directives of university discourse, always linked to the discourse of the master (who wants us located and placed where it can see us), in the alarming delusion that accommodation will give us power and will stand us in good stead? But political force within the university is hardly it. "It" has more to do with pushing the institutional limits of disciplinary thinking, as much as we are able to, in order to see what happens then. Is that not our final responsibility, as Latin Americanists, toward Latin America? And, beyond responsibility, is that not also our enjoyment?

NOTES

Introduction: Conditions of Latin Americanist Critique

1   It would be difficult to mention all the participants in these debates, many of whom have not yet published their work. But see recent issues of *Revista de crítica cultural, Revista iberoamericana, Journal of Latin American Cultural Studies,* and *Cuadernos americanos.* See also chapter 8 of this book. The debates, in plural, may however be one and the same debate, since they share so many intersecting characteristics. The most recent contribution at the time of this writing is Abril Trigo's "Why Do I Do Cultural Studies?," a level-headed and useful attempt to navigate conflictive options that will nevertheless not go beyond staking out one possible position among others. Latin Americanists know that the discussions I refer to go well beyond published work and manifest themselves almost obsessively at professional conferences and in e-mail discussions. Four books that were published after I finished writing this book will have influence in fueling the debate, although I myself have not been able to include them in my musings here: Román de la Campa, *Latin Americanism,* Doris Sommer, *Proceed with Caution When Engaged with Minority Writing in the Americas,* John Beverley, *Subalternity and Representation,* and Walter Mignolo, *Local Histories/Global Designs.*

2   *Our-Americanist* refers to the well-known essay, written in 1891, by José Martí, "Nuestra América" ("Our America").

3   Of course cultural studies developed in Britain during the 1960s and 1970s and was reinstitutionalized in the United States in the late 1980s. See Dennis Dworkin, *Cultural Marxism in Post-War Britain,* for a history of its early development. See Lawrence Grossberg, Cary Nelson, and Paula Treichler, *Cultural Studies,* for its first major manifestation in the United States. The history of Latin American cultural studies is yet unwritten. My point is that what is now emerging as a full-blown field of inquiry in Latin American studies has its own regional history, which is only partially indebted to the British and North American and Australian precursors. That history also has a totally different genealogy as well as different conditions of social and intellectual inscription.

4   We should credit Immanuel Wallerstein with the development of these concepts. See in particular *The Modern World System 1.*

5   I am bracketing the otherwise obvious fact that cultural studies not only interacts with and develops from the literary field but also from history, sociology, anthropology, and communication studies in particular. But I must leave it to scholars from those disciplines to elucidate the influence cultural studies has on them (and vice versa).

6   See, however, Wander Melo Miranda, "Projeçoes de um debate," and Eneida Maria de Souza, "A teoria em crise."

7   This is not to say that some Spanish-language literary Latin Americanists, whether U.S.-based or not, are not putting up a fierce opposition.

They are, but their contributions tend to be more subdued and behind the scenes. I venture to say that it was easier for the Brazilians to thematize the literary-cultural studies debate because of the vast network of scholars associated with ABRALIC. In the United States, unfortunately, and in spite of the existence here of similar networks, the division of the previously unified field continues with little mediation but with at times considerable effects at various levels of professional life—including institutionally corrupting effects such as the politicization of tenure decisions.

8   On contemporary financial capitalism see Giovanni Arrighi, *The Long Twentieth Century*, and Fredric Jameson, "Culture and Finance Capital."

9   I do not mean to condemn all historicisms, as there is one I like: absolute historicism, in Jameson's sense. See Chapter 8. By the same token I am not opposed to aesthetics. It is rather the combination of aesthetics and historicism as the theoretical-political horizon that I find lacking today. See Jameson, "Marxism and Historicism" for an interesting structural-historical differentiation of historicisms in European thinking.

Chapter One: Global Fragments

1   See also Manegold, "A Woman's Obsession Pays Off," for more of the same if from a different angle. For rich treatments of recent U.S. representations of Latin Americans along similar lines, see George Yúdice's comments on Joan Didion's *Salvador* in "Testimonio and Postmodernism," and Fredric Jameson's analysis of Robert Stone's *A Flag for Sunrise* in "Americans Abroad."

2   Jameson asks "Is global Difference the same today as global Identity?" at the end of his analysis of Frampton's proposal for a critical regionalism in architecture. Jameson wonders whether "pluralism and difference are not somehow related to [late capitalism's] own deeper internal dynamics" (*Seeds* 205, 204).

3   The essay by Deleuze that Hardt refers to is "Postscript on the Societies of Control."

4   My use of the notion of "time-lag" is indebted to Homi Bhabha's invention of the term as a powerful tool of postcolonial studies: "in each achieved symbol of cultural/political identity or synchronicity there is always the repetition of the sign that represents the place of psychic ambivalence and social contingency . . . [the] time-lag [is] an iterative, interrogative space produced in the interruptive overlap between symbol and sign, between synchronicity and caesura or seizure . . ." ("Postcolonial Authority" 59). See also Walter Mignolo, "Postcolonial Reason," for further references and articulations.

5   See also Yúdice's essay "Globalización y nuevas formas de intermediación cultural" for these and related issues.

6   One does not quite know whether Petras and Morley are engaging in wishful thinking or something else when they say that "the incapacity of the institutional intellectual to provide adequate responses to the pressing

problems confronting liberal-democratic regimes has already set in motion the formation of nuclei of young intellectuals with ties to the political and social movements. . . . The current crisis in Latin America may force members of the new generation of intellectuals who cannot be or choose not to be absorbed by the system to fight against it and to reconstitute themselves through organic ties to popular movements" (*US Hegemony* 156).

7 It is fair to say that Hardt and Negri's notion of the "multitude," in which they cipher the possibility of an outside to empire, does not in itself constitute a thinking of the outside: it is a thinking of immanence. This is perhaps the most markedly original aspect of their book. See *Empire* (60–66) and chapter 3 of this book for further discussion. In terms of deconstruction and messianic justice, "the necessary disjointure, the de-totalizing condition of justice, is indeed here that of the present—and by the same token the very condition of the present and of the presence of the present. This is where deconstruction would always begin to take shape as the thinking of the gift and of undeconstructible justice, the undeconstructible condition of any deconstruction, to be sure, but a condition that is itself *in deconstruction* and remains, and must remain (that is the injunction) in the disjointure of the *Unfug* . . . in the waiting and calling for what we have nicknamed here without knowing the messianic" (Derrida, *Specters* 28). See Jameson's comments on the Derridean messianic toward the end of "Marx's Purloined Letter."

8 But see, for instance, Bhabha, *The Location of Culture*, or Rey Chow, *Writing Diaspora*, for different accounts of intellectual work in the context of postcolonial reason. See also Bruce Robbins, *Secular Vocations*, in reference to the contemporary "professional" intellectual.

Chapter Two: Negative Globality and Critical Regionalism

1 I am referring to the influential account by Jean-François Lyotard in *The Postmodern Condition*. For instance, "the grand narrative has lost its credibility, regardless of what mode of unification it uses, regardless of whether it is a speculative narrative or a narrative of emancipation" (37).

2 I follow Ernesto Laclau's application of the linguistic notion of empty signifier to the sphere of political theory in *Emancipation(s)* 36–46 and passim.

3 I first found the notion of *critical regionalism* in Fredric Jameson's *Seeds of Time*. Jameson takes it from Kenneth Frampton. The notion of "region" designates "not a rural place that resists the nation and its power structures but rather a whole culturally coherent zone (which may also correspond to political autonomy) in tension with the standardizing world system as a whole" (*Seeds* 191–92). What Frampton says about modern architecture can sometimes be rather uncannily applied to geopolitical epistemics: "Critical Regionalism tends to flourish in those cultural interstices which in one way or another are able to escape the optimizing

thrust of universal civilization. Its appearance suggests that the received notion of the dominant cultural centre surrounded by dependent, dominated satellites is ultimately an inadequate model by which to assess the present state of modern architecture" (*Modern Architecture* 327). See also my book *Tercer espacio,* especially chapters 1 and 4.

4 John Kraniauskas offered the definition of subaltern studies as "the critique of the total apparatuses of development" at the meeting "Cross-Genealogies and Subaltern Knowledges," at Duke University, October 1998.

5 On the relationship between contemporary epistemologies and the market, see Brett Levinson's typescript "The State/Market Duopoly," which I read after I had written this chapter. But my argument is indebted to numerous conversations with Levinson—beyond what would be quotable in any case.

6 The Gulbenkian Commission makes the case that cultural studies challenges the division between the humanities and the social sciences. But John Guillory presents an interesting argument that cultural studies should pay particular attention to systems theory, one of whose merits is to have a claim to dissolving the difference between natural science and social science: "Systems Theory has a beachhead in the university now in the new discipline of Cognitive Science, which may be the first discipline to overcome the distinction between social science and natural science" ("System" 18). See also Wallerstein, "Open the Social Sciences" 6.

7 On "area-based knowledge" see the Social Science Research Council's "Proposal to the Ford Foundation for Core Support of a New Joint International Program": "Traditional area studies is primarily knowledge *about an area.* Area-based knowledge starts with knowledge about an area, but then applies that knowledge to processes, trends, phenomena that transcend any given area" (2).

8 For a more detailed presentation of the New York–based Social Science Research Council's new position on area studies see Prewitt's "Presidential Items."

9 Sklair, *Sociology of the Global System* 75; see also 75–77, 129–69.

10 Others have already initiated the critical examination of the ideology of identity and difference within cultural studies. See in particular Lawrence Grossberg, "Identity and Cultural Studies: Is That All There Is?" (revised and expanded as "Cultural Studies in/and New Worlds") for an analysis that departs from the position that identity/difference have become more central to cultural studies than they originally were, given the influence of "so-called postcolonial theory and critical race theory" ("Identity" 87). At the moment of sending this text to press, Gareth Williams's *The Other Side of the Popular,* which engages with these issues in many fascinating ways, is about to be published.

11 Something similar could be said about Cornejo's concept of "literature," despite his effort and marked interest to include within it oral symbolic

productions. See Walter Mignolo, "La lengua, la letra, el territorio" and *The Darker Side of the Renaissance*, for a questioning of the concept of "literature" as an inadequate category to account for the complexity of Latin American symbolic-verbal production.

12 See, for instance, Cornejo Polar, *Sobre literatura y crítica latinoamericanas*, and also *Escribir en el aire*. The first pages of *Escribir* repeat the "anxious" formulation about postmodernity I have been discussing. "Heterogeneity" in Cornejo Polar's sense has recently generated some important essays: see Friedhelm Schmidt, "¿Literaturas heterogéneas o literatura de la transculturacion?"; Mabel Moraña, *"Escribir en el aire"*; and Hugo Achugar, "Repensando la heterogeneidad latinoamericana."

13 "Modernization theory is almost inextricable from the idea of the three worlds" and "modernization theory is not merely some adventitious appendage of the idea of three worlds, it is constituent to the structural relationship among the underlying semantic terms" (Pletsch, "Three Worlds" 571, 576).

14 In my opinion, a strong case could be made that the notion of "narrative fissure" is more productive than the well-known and overabused Lyotardian notion of "the end of metanarratives" to discuss postmodern phenomena.

15 In "Civil Society, Consumption, and Governmentality in an Age of Global Restructuring" George Yúdice refers to both Jorge Castañeda and Néstor García Canclini in connection with the concept of "regional federalism," explicitly formulated by Castañeda (17). The pertinent texts are Castañeda's *Utopia Unarmed* and García Canclini's *Consumidores y ciudadanos*.

16 Yúdice has pioneered work in this decisive conceptual area in Latin American cultural studies. See his "Consumption and Citizenship" (8) and also "Globalización y nuevas formas de intermediación cultural."

17 A good discussion of the dangers of a compulsive politics of identity in the context of the cultural survival of minorities can be found in several of the essays included in Amy Gutmann, *Multiculturalism*. See especially the essays by Kwame Anthony Appiah, "Identity, Authenticity, Survival"; Charles Taylor, "The Politics of Recognition," and Jürgen Habermas, "Struggles for Recognition in the Democratic Constitutional State."

18 See Richard Barnet and John Cavanagh's *Global Dreams*.

Chapter Three: Theoretical Fictions and Fatal Conceits
The translation of the epigraph is my own.

1 For Wallerstein "the world-system is in mutation now. This is no longer a moment of the minor, constant cumulation of cycles and trends. 1989 is probably a door closed on the past. We have perhaps arrived now in the true realm of uncertainty. The world-system will continue, of course, to function, even function 'well.' It is precisely because it will continue to

function as it has been functioning for 500 years, in search of the cease-less accumulation of capital, that it will soon no longer be able to function in this manner" (*Geopolitics* 15). *Geopolitics and Geoculture* is entirely devoted to explaining some of the conditions of our "uncertainty."

2 On the "four discourses" the basic source is Lacan's *L'envers de la psych-analyse*. See also Bruce Fink, *The Lacanian Subject* 129–37.

3 Berger's book, *Under Northern Eyes*, "about the ways in which profes-sional discourses on Latin America have contributed throughout the twentieth century to U.S. efforts to control and manage events in the Americas" (1), is an impressive reconstruction of U.S. Latin American studies and their political context (as well as their function in context-production) since 1898. Pike's *The United States and Latin America* studies "how it is that ambivalent myths and stereotypes of civilization and nature seem to lie at the heart of American attitudes toward Latin Americans" (xiii) and how "domination" (xv) has a lot to do with it. Both books tell a splendid story.

4 See Berger, *Under Northern Eyes* (xi–xii) on new trends in Latin American studies in the 1990s: all of them are substantially implicated in the study of culture.

5 For Jameson all literatures have produced "national allegories," in the sense that texts, "even those which are seemingly private and invested with a properly libidinal dynamic—necessarily project a political dimen-sion in the form of . . . an allegory of the embattled situation of the pub-lic . . . culture and society" ("Third-World Literature" 69; see also 79–80). It would be interesting to know if his analysis, dating back to 1986, would today be modified for the literature of the present in light of the increasing reduction of the national as primary cultural referent.

6 I borrow the term *fatal conceit* from Friedrich Hayek's influential book with the same title. I suppose that by *theoretical fiction* I mean nothing more than a fatal conceit at the point of its historical emergence, that is, when it can still be productive. Hayek's selective application of his term to what he calls constructive rationalizations of the world, meaning the various forms of historicisms, is too restrictive in my opinion: antihistori-cisms of various kinds, including Hayek's own, can also work as forms of fatal conceit, and they invariably do when their time comes.

7 The notion of the "empty signifier" as the representation of a communi-tarian absent fullness is explicitly developed by Laclau in "Why Do Empty Signifiers Matter to Politics?" He says: "Politics is possible because the constitutive impossibility of society can only represent itself through the production of empty signifiers" (44). I suggest that national literature can be thought to have constituted an empty signifier under a previous ar-ticulation of the state form, but it can no longer occupy such a position; however, under certain conditions, the neoliterary possibly could.

8 These are familiar themes in Hardt and Negri's *Empire*, which is discussed in chapter 2. I use the term *neoimperial* with a view to my own textual

consistency, but there is a family resemblance between "empire" and the "neoimperial" in several important features.

9   For "the unmasterable excess of the social" see Laclau, *New Reflections on the Revolution of Our Times* 90, and chapter 8 below.

10 See Antonio Negri and Michael Hardt, *Labor of Dionysus* 14 and passim, for a parallel reflection.

11 For Marx, "the development of fixed capital indicates to what degree general social knowledge has become a direct force of production, and to what degree, hence, the conditions of the process of social life itself have come under the control of the general intellect and been transformed in accordance with it. To what degree the powers of social production have been produced, not only in the form of knowledge, but also as immediate organs of social practice, of the real life process" (*Grundrisse* 706). I owe my attention to this concept to Virno, who quotes the *Grundrisse* passage in "Virtuosity and Revolution," on 209. See Jon Beasley-Murray, "We the People."

12 Hardt and Negri make of the multitude the only conceivable agent for the creation of a counter-empire. See especially 60–64, 194–95, 209–18, and passim. Although I have some doubts about the philosophical underpinnings of the notion, which seem to me overly engaged with a metaphysics of productionism that in essence (i.e., from the perspective of what Heidegger would call "the history of Being") would not be different from the very history of the capitalist formation, it is nevertheless intriguing to think of the multitude, in Virno's terms, as a moniker for a virtuoso practice of knowledge: could we then talk of a "multitudinous practice of Latin Americanism"? I dedicate this note to Jon Beasley-Murray. See the final pages of his "Towards an Unpopular Cultural Studies," a paper presented at the Cross-Genealogies and Subaltern Studies Conference at Duke University, in October 1998, which marks the first attempt I know of to use the concept of the multitude in Latin American subaltern studies.

13 I have already referred to Derrida's notion of the absolute justice of the messianic claim in chapter 2. See Derrida, *Specters of Marx* 28. On Balibar's "ideal universality" see "Ambiguous Universality" 64, and chapter 9 below. I pursue the notion of a double register of intellectual practice rather centrally in chapter 9.

14 Guha's refers to "the corpus of historical writings on peasant insurgency" as "prose of counterinsurgency." He describes three types of discourse, "primary, secondary, and tertiary, according to the order of their appearance in time and their filiation" ("Prose" 47). Because the subaltern as such rarely produce their own texts, the subalternist must read against the grain and interpret insurgency and subaltern negation through the prose of counterinsurgency. Guzmán's text is a classic example of tertiary prose of counterinsurgency for the Mexican Revolution.

15 On subaltern negation see Guha, *Elementary Aspects of Peasant Insurgency in Colonial India*, chapter 1. But for recent (and forceful) engagements with the notion that there is no politics (or political subjectivity)

without subaltern negation see Slavoj Zizek, *The Ticklish Subject* 188 and passim, and Jacques Ranciére, *Disagreements* 1–19.

Chapter Four: Restitution and Appropriation

1   This would be one effect of the expansion of funding for Latin American-ist scholarly projects by Western foundations. See James Petras and Morris Morley, *US Hegemony under Siege,* for an extreme assessment of the price to be paid. For Latin American integration into transnational circuits of cultural consumption, see Néstor García Canclini, *Hybrid Cultures* and *Consumidores y ciudadanas,* and Oscar Landi, *Devórame otra vez.* See Beatriz Sarlo, *Escenas de la vida posmoderna,* for a rather contrary appre-ciation.

2   For Samuel Huntington the political struggles of the next decades "will not be primarily ideological or primarily economic. The great divisions among humankind and the dominating source of conflict will be cul-tural. . . . The clash of civilizations will dominate global politics" ("Clash" 22). This is where area studies may become strategically important again: "The West will increasingly have to accommodate these non-Western modern civilizations whose power approaches that of the West but whose values and interests differ significantly from those of the West. This will require the West to maintain the economic and military power necessary to protect its interests in relation to these civilizations. It will also, how-ever, require the West to develop a more profound understanding of the basic religious and philosophical assumptions underlying other civiliza-tions and the ways in which peoples in those civilizations see their inter-ests" (49). See Huntington, *The Clash of Civilizations and the Remaking of the World Order,* for a more detailed explanation of these views. For the opposite source of interest in area studies see Leslie Sklair, *Sociology of the Global System* 129–69.

3   On Abraham's sacrifice, its connection with the Western sense of respon-sibility, the sense of a double responsibility to Other and other, and related themes see Jacques Derrida, *The Gift of Death,* and in particular 82–115.

4   See Bartra's 1981 collection of essays entitled *Las redes imaginarias del poder político,* where many of the themes explored in *Jaula* are already announced.

5   On the connections among state formation, popular culture, and the Mexican Revolution see the important collection edited by Gail Joseph and Daniel Nugent, *Everyday Forms of State Formation.*

6   For West (and correctly in my opinion), the cultural politics of differ-ence constitutes a worldwide phenomenon of aesthetic-political practice whose inception must be marked in the 1980s. Let me quote West to counterbalance Hartman's interpretation: "The new cultural politics of difference are neither simply oppositional in contesting the mainstream . . . for inclusion, nor transgressive in the avant-gardist sense of shock-ing conventional bourgeois audiences. Rather, they are distinct articu-

lations of talented (and usually privileged) contributors to culture who desire to align themselves with demoralized, demobilized, depoliticized and disorganized people in order to empower and enable social action and, if possible, to enlist collective insurgency for the expansion of freedom, democracy and individuality" ("New Cultural Politics" 19–20). Obviously, excesses are possible, but to focus exclusively on them means to engage in reactive politics.

7   See Derrida, "Some Statements and Truisms," 84, 88–90, for stabilizing and destabilizing jetties and a critique of deconstruction*ism* as theory.

8   Quoted in Bennington, *Legislations* 83; see 83–84 for a further twist on ressentiment and its abyssal and abysmal dimensions.

9   The "incipient saying of being" is part of the title of the second part of the 1941 lecture series published in English as *Basic Concepts* (*Grundbegriffe*), entirely devoted to the Anaximander fragment (see 49). It was tempting to engage in a sustained analysis of this text and "The Anaximander Fragment" to show restitutional thinking as essential to the Heideggerian enterprise, even since *Being and Time*. But finally I chose to limit myself to a few comments and this note.

10 The sources of *Being and Time* are superbly studied by Theodor Kisiel in what has become the standard book on the subject, *Genesis of Heidegger's Being and Time*.

11 Gareth Williams's essay on the aftermath of the Salvadoran war ("Subalternity and the Neoliberal *Habitus*") has a great deal to say about these issues. For instance, "the notion of a possible site of resolution within the thought of subalternity merely transforms the subaltern subject position into a nodal point of social intelligibility around which hegemonic programs or populist political solutions can be articulated. Such practices, however, tend to reflect little more than a thought invested in the neohegemonic stabilization of the subaltern's destabilizing force. As such, it is a thought grounded in the constitution and maintenance of social intelligibility and of translatability over and above the destabilizing promise of subaltern heterogeneity and difference. The question, of course, is how to think subaltern heterogeneity and difference from within institutional thought" (140).

12 One could refer to books such as *Drawing the Line*, by Oriana Baddeley and Valerie Fraser, to understand Santí's and Hartman's irritation in the face of deeply reductive aesthetic interpretations based on identity restitution of a particularly blind sort. One example of bad art history: "Because our interests are concentrated around the *Latin American* features of Latin American art, or the essentially Latin American issues which it raises, we have tended to exclude works which, for example, take the processes of composition and construction as their only subject matter. Since such purely reflexive abstract art deliberately avoids specificity it cannot be illuminated by being considered within a Latin American context" (3). A close equivalent would be to exclude from Latin American literature

everything that is not to some explicit degree connected to political abjection or magical realism. Another close equivalent is the refusal of so many to accept that, say, a thinking that refers to Heidegger could have any possible relevance, other than an imperialist relevance, for Latin American reflection. A further close equivalent is the abandonment of theoretical reflection on the basis that theoretical reflection does not belong to the Latin American tradition except in its derivative form as "ensayismo." Latin Americanism has had to put up with a great deal of that kind of attitude throughout its history; it is still a fairly prevalent attitude. When, on top of simply existing, it hides its deep demagogy and anti-intellectualism under the guise of political progressivism, as it often does, then it comes very close to sheer hypocrisy.

Chapter Five: The National-Popular in Candido and Borges

1   "To know Brazil was to know these displacements, experienced and practised by everyone as a sort of fate, for which, however, there was no proper name, since the improper use of names was part of its nature. Widely felt to be a defect, well-known but little reflected upon, this system of displacement certainly did debase ideological life and diminished the chances for genuine thought" (Schwarz, *Misplaced Ideas* 28.) "Genuine thought" translates the Brazilian word "reflexão" (see "Idéias" 22).

2   As "idéias fora do lugar" is the first chapter of *Ao vencedor as batatas,* one of the two volumes Schwarz devoted to the nineteenth-century novelist (*Ao vencedor as batatas* and *Un mestre na periferia do capitalismo: Machado de Assis*).

3   There is a necessarily orientalist bias in subalternism as there is a necessarily orientalist bias in any enterprise that claims to obtain its legitimacy by studying human alterity. A critique of subalternist orientalism in Latin American subaltern studies has been done by Gareth Williams, from an on-the-other-hand sympathetic or internal self-positioning, in two sister essays, "Fantasies" and "After Testimonio." I subscribe to them and state my agreement.

4   See on these issues, beyond the already cited "On Some Aspects of the Historiography of Colonial India" (ch. 3), two other programmatic essays by Ranajit Guha: "Dominance without Hegemony and Its Historiography" and "The Small Voice of History."

5   I consider John Beverley's *Against Literature,* in all the richness of its self-conscious ambiguity, the inaugural text preparing and announcing the possibility of a new paradigm for Latin Americanist reflection in the humanities.

6   See Veena Das's "Subaltern as Perspective" where it is stated that "subalterns are not . . . morphological categories, but represent a perspective in the sense in which Nietzsche used the word" (324). The subaltern perspective is actively erased in superregionalism precisely because super-

regionalism, in its transculturating zeal, seeks an integration with the hegemonic perspective.

7 I take the expression *situational consciousness* from Jameson ("Third-World Literature" 85). In "Postmodernism and the Market" Jameson refers explicitly to the Sartrean underpinnings of the term: "The Sartrean concept of the situation is a new way of thinking history as such" (288). In another passage he refers to situational consciousness as "a demystifying eyeball-to-eyeball encounter with daily life, with no distance and no embellishments" (286).

8 See Carlos Vilas, "Neoliberal Social Policy," for a concise account of the specific costs of neoliberalism on the Latin American subaltern classes and also of the differences between the national-popular or Keynesian-Fordist and the neoliberal Latin American states. A more extensive treatment of the impact of neoliberalism on Latin America can be found in Victor Bulmer-Thomas, *The New Economic Model in Latin America and Its Impact on Income Distribution and Poverty.*

9 But see Brett Levinson, "The State/Market Duopoly," for a non-neoliberal account of the market in its contemporary duopolic relationship with the state, which is no longer a nation-state.

10 Althusser's final insistence on denarrativization is interesting in this context: "my objective: never to tell myself stories, which is the only definition of materialism I have ever subscribed to" (*Future* 169); "'Not to indulge in story-telling' still remains for me the one and only definition of materialism" (221). Beverley ends the introduction to his *Subalternity*, after referring to his own Althusserianism, saying: "Would it be possible to have a work of 'theory' that would be composed entirely of stories? Perhaps that is what is still worth thinking about in Borges, despite his overtly reactionary politics (or are those politics related to his function as a storyteller as well)?" (24). Well, I think the objective of Borges's stories is in almost every case to open into a space of de-narrativization. If pushed, I might (with the later Althusser) say the same regarding all theoretical work. I dedicate this note to John Beverley.

11 Gyan Prakash, "Writing Post-Orientalist Histories of the Third World" 394–403 passim. See also Rosalind O'Hanlon and David Washbrook's contestation in "After Orientalism" 141–67, and Prakash's response: "Can the 'Subaltern' Ride?" 168–84.

Chapter Six: The End of Magical Realism

1 See Antonio Cornejo Polar, *La formación de la tradición literaria en el Perú* 137–55, for an illuminating commentary on those cultural struggles in Peruvian history. See also Rama, *Transculturación narrativa en América Latina* 11–116, where the conflict is studied as a conflict between "regionalism" and "modernization," and "Los Procesos de transculturación en la narrativa latinoamericana" 203–33.

2   See Clifford, "On Ethnographic Surrealism" 117–51. See also Denis Hollier, *College of Sociology*. Enrico Mario Santí has mentioned the influence
of the College de Sociologie in Octavio Paz's *El laberinto de la soledad*
("Introducción" *[Laberinto]* 98–106), but much remains to be done in the
wider context of Latin American contemporary literature.

3   As we saw in chapter 4, Taussig's *Shamanism, Colonialism, and the Wild
Man* adds other insights into Latin American magical realism. See also
Taussig's *The Devil and Commodity Fetishism in South America* and
Fredric Jameson's "On Magic Realism in Film," for work on magical real-
ism that departs from Bloch's notion of noncontemporaneity (Bloch 97–
116). The recent compilation of articles by Lois Parkinson Zamora and
Wendy B. Faris, *Magical Realism*, is very useful, although I find the edi-
torial position highly controversial. See also Amaryll Chanady, *Magical
Realism and the Fantastic*, and, of course, Irlemar Chiampi, *O realismo
maravilhoso*.

4   For Fernando Ortiz' development of the notion, see *Contrapunteo cubano
del tabaco y el azúcar* 129–35. See also Gustavo Pérez Firmat's essay on
Ortiz in *The Cuban Condition* 16–33.

5   The concept of transculturation has been thematized, from different critical positions, in books and texts that were published (or in manuscripts I
have had access to) after this chapter was finished. Let me mention Gareth
Williams's (in *The Other Side of the Popular*) and John Beverley's (in *Subalternity and Representation*) critiques as for the most part, if not totally,
consistent with my own. Let me also refer to John Kraniauskas's "Hybridity in a Transnational Frame" as what I would consider a useful res-
suscitation, since Kraniauskas's purpose is to understand (critically) transculturated phenomena for the sake of a historical phenomenology of Latin
American cultural practices. See also Román De la Campa, *Latin Americanism*, Doris Sommer, *Proceed with Caution*, and Walter Mignolo, *Local
Histories/Global Designs*, for other interesting uses.

6   They have not remained unread by, among others, Forgues, William Rowe,
Cornejo Polar, or Martin Lienhard, but they have remained mostly unread
in the sense that they have not been thought to bear on the Latin American literary and cultural tradition, where they enforce a deep destabilization. Although this is not the place to elaborate on it, I tend to understand
Arguedas's critical self-positioning vis-à-vis Latin American writing in *El
zorro*'s primer diario (7–23) from that particular problem. Arguedas had to
feel that his boom contemporaries remained willfully blind to what was
for him a literally blinding light. See Rama's comments in "Procesos" 225–
26.

7   For Jameson, in words that will resonate for any reader of Arguedas's last
novel, "Third-world texts, even those which are seemingly private and invested with a properly libidinal dynamic, necessarily project a political
dimension in the form of national allegory: the story of the private individual destiny is always an allegory of the embattled situation of the public

third-world culture and society" ("Third-World Literature" 69). Jameson has received a lot of criticism for that sentence, but I haven't found a text where those words do not ultimately prove true: perhaps the controversy surrounding them, and certainly in the case of Franco, arises from a misunderstanding concerning the term *allegory*. In any case, for Arguedas's last novel, those words should constitute something like an epigraph.

8   In particular, Lienhard, *Cultura popular andina y forma novelesca,* and Cornejo Polar, *Las universos narrativos de José María Arguedas.* But see also their shorter essays cited in the bibliography.

9   Sara Castro-Klarén may be quoted to give an example of a critical state of affairs that has possibly started to change in recent years: "*El sexto* as well as *El zorro de arriba y el zorro de abajo* are minor narrative works . . . [where] a desire to denounce reality dominates. As a consequence, those works are weak in structure and in narrative development" (*Mundo* 200; my trans.). (I agree with Castro-Klarén about *El sexto.*)

10   See Cornejo, Polar, *Sobre literatura y crítica latinoamericans,* "Nuevas reflexiones sobre la crítica latinoamericana," and *Escribir en el aire.* See also Mabel Moraña's study of the notion of "heterogeneidad" in Cornejo, "*Escribir en al aire:* Heterogeneidad y estudios culturales."

11   In "Ideología de la transculturación" Moraña uses Patricia D'Allemand's phrase to refer to Rama as an " 'interlocutor silenciado' pero de innegable fecundidad (en las teorizaciones actuales)" the "silent interlocutor" but of an undeniable fecundity (in contemporary theorizations)] (7).

12   "Yo no soy un aculturado" (*Zorro* 257). Apparently Arguedas had wanted that text to appear as a foreword to the novel, but it has always been published at its end. See *Zorro* xxviii.

13   On Chimbote, see César Caviedes, "The Latin American Boom-Town in the Literary View of José María Arguedas."

14   See Julia Kristeva's analysis of depression and melancholia, *Black Sun.* The black sun is a well-known symbol in Latin American literature: it can be found in Ernesto Sábato's *Sobre héroes y tumbas* as well as in Julio Cortázar's *Rayuela,* for instance. Arguedas improves on that image by denying its expressive sufficiency.

15   On the general topic of literary autobiography in Arguedas, see Ignacio Díaz Ruiz's interesting monograph, *Literatura y biografia en José María Arguedas.* See also Mario Vargas Llosa, "Literatura y suicidio," on literature and suicide in Arguedas. Vargas Llosa's *La utopía arcaica,* book is an ideological attempt to minimize Arguedas's historical importance while recognizing his talent as a storyteller, see chapter 8.

16   With his customary precision Cornejo Polar remarks: "the death of the narrator . . . leads to the interpretation of that atrocious fact as a silent sign which permeates . . . the discourse that precedes it and announces it" ("Ensayo" 304; my trans., here and below).

17   Gustavo Gutiérrez remarks that when Arguedas says that the second cycle is about to begin or has already begun, he does not mean that the first one

is over: "His ver life fell prey to the clash between the cycles" (Gutiérrez, Romualdo, and Escobar, *Arguedas* 37). For an extended interpretation of the two cycles' imagery as a reference to an "anthropocentric turn [which] does not imply the disappearance of the mythical or the religious," see Pedro Trigo, *Arguedas*, (236; my trans.), which includes Gutiérrez' commentary on Trigo's essay "Entre las calandrias." José Miguel Oviedo suggests that the notion of the beginning of the fire lark cycle might also have to do with the political events developing in Peru at the time of writing: the "military revolution" and its indigenist rhetoric. Arguedas would have had, according to Oviedo, tremendous difficulty dealing with the political implementation of changes affecting indigenous societies, which he could not simply oppose. For Oviedo that was the "detonante" of Arguedas's suicide ("El ultimo Arguedas" 145). See Sybila Arredondo's presentation of Arguedas's correspondence between 1966 and 1969 to understand further Arguedas's psychological and intellectual crisis, *"El zorro de arriba y el zorro de abajo* en la correspondencia de Arguedas."

18 See, for instance, among other possible texts, José Matos Mar's *Desborde popular y crisis del estado;* the classic *Buscando un inca,* by Alberto Flores Galindo; and the pertinent sections of Orin Starn, Carlos Iván DeGregori, and Robin Kirk's *The Peru Reader.* Of course Arguedas's suicide is *also* an expression of radical skepticism about the formation of a Peruvian state of justice. Arguedas's novel turns the national allegory on its head, or breaks it, while at the same time being entirely contained within it. It was that sense that I had in mind when I said earlier that Arguedas takes the Jamesonian model as far as it can go in order to turn it against itself, the affirmation of a new "cycle" of historical time notwithstanding.

19 The "unwriting" of Latin American history signals for González Echevarría the beginning of the writing of the "archive," a "mode beyond anthropology" (*Myth* 15). Archival writing is for him the "razing" of the "various mediations through which Latin America was narrated, the systems from which fiction borrowed the truth-bearing forms, erased to assume the new mediation that requires this level-ground of self and history" (17). But for González Echevarría "what is left for the novel after *Los pasos perdidos* and *Cien años de soledad"* is simply "fiction itself" (18). The "voiding of the anthropological mediation" results in "a relentless memory that disassembles the fictions of myth, literature and even history" (20, 23), but such memory is itself the literary system as a fictional system. Although González Echevarría's model is powerful, it doesn't yet provide for the possibility of developing strong internal distinctions regarding archival writing. There is a sense in which Arguedas, by ultimately "voiding the anthropological mediation," also at the same time destabilizes the archive as literary system. If *Los zorros* is indeed archival writing, it is so only to the extent that it is also antiarchival, for it shows the very pretense of archival constitution as always already insufficient, always already invested in a project of "overcoming modernization" through an intensifi-

cation of modernism. There is an interesting hesitation in *Myth and Archive:* toward the end of the first chapter, after explaining the notion of the archive as that which puts an end to the anthropological paradigm, González Echevarría doubts his own words by saying: "the current mode, *perhaps* beyond the anthropological mediation, the locus on which my own text is situated" (40; my emphasis). Perhaps the limits of the archive are also the limits of transculturation, which *Los zorros,* much more so than *Los pasos perdidos* or *Cien años de soledad,* and even in essentially different and opposite ways, thematizes. Arguedas, with his last novel, announces the voiding of the archive itself, or its loss: not archival gaps, but the archive as gap.

20   See Jean-Luc Nancy, *L'oubli de la philosophie* 70–71. Nancy's entire book is concerned with the thinking of the connections between meaning and signification in senses that have influenced the writing of this chapter.

Chapter Seven: The Aura of Testimonio

1   On "national security" see Noam Chomsky, "The Fifth Freedom"; Juan Rial, *Las Fuerzas Armadas;* Brian Loveman and Thomas Davies, *The Politics of Antipolitics* 163 and passim; Alain Rouquié, *The Military and the State in Latin America;* and Lawrence Weschler, *A Miracle, a Universe* 111–23, among other possible sources.

2   See Daniel Mato, "Construcción de identidades pannacionales y transnacionales en tiempos de globalización." Mato understands the "irruption and growing political and cultural importance of new base organizations and political and social movements organized around local, ethnic, class, gender, and generational identities among others" (218; my translation) as a direct response to globalization in contemporary times. See also Yúdice, "Postmodernity and Transnational Capitalism in Latin America" 7 and passim.

3   The notion of literature as colonial discourse in the case of Latin America has been presented by John Beverley: "Latin American literature [is endowed] with an ambiguous cultural role and legacy: literature (or, less anachronistically, *letras*) is a colonial institution, one of the basic institutions of Spanish colonial rule in the Americas; yet it is also one of the institutions crucial to the development of an autonomous creole and then 'national' (although perhaps not popular-democratic) culture. [Contemporary literature] still bears the traces of this paradox" (*Against Literature* 2). See also Angel Rama, *La ciudad letrada.*

4   See for instance Hugo Achugar, "Notas sobre el discurso testimonial latinoamericano" 279–81. Elzbieta Sklodowska quotes Angel Rama declaring that he was the one to recommend that *Casa de las Américas* establish testimonio as a new category for their literary contest in January 1969 (Sklodowska, *Testimonio* 56). In *Literature and Politics in the Central American Revolutions* Beverley and Marc Zimmerman argue that in the mid-1960s the popularity of ethnographic life stories such as those by

Oscar Lewis and Ricardo Pozas and of more directly political testimonial accounts, such as, in Cuba, the ones inspired by Ernesto Che Guevara's *Episodios de la guerra revolucionaria cubana,* was in fact responsible for the canonization of the genre only a few years later *(Literature* 173–74). Yúdice emphasizes the sense of cultural-literary belligerence against the mostly liberal supporters of boom-like literature attached to these institutional beginnings of testimonio ("Testimonio and Postmodernism" 26). In fact, however, boom literature was destined to occupy hegemonic ground for the next fifteen years. In the early to mid-1980s a certain exhaustion with boom and postboom fiction came together with the solidarity movement and the general horror in the face of repression in Argentina and civil wars and government atrocities in Central America to assure a widespread popularity for testimonio.

5   The extraliterary aspect of testimonio has been expressly emphasized by Beverley and Zimmerman: "In principle, testimonio appears . . . as an extraliterary or even antiliterary form of discourse" *(Literature* 178); "[testimonio] functions in a zone of indeterminacy between" antiliterature and "a new, postfictional form of literature, with significant cultural and ideological repercussions" (179). In contrast, Sklodowska concludes that the unmediated testimonio has such a strong relationship with the word that it can be considered an actualization (or historical genre) of the novel understood as "theoretical genre" (97; my trans.)

6   The connection of testimonio criticism and 1980s solidarity movements was suggested by Yúdice and discussed during the panel "Testimonio y abyección" (Latin American Studies Association Meeting, Atlanta, March 1994). This is a story that has not been told yet and is awaiting its teller.

7   See Achugar, "Historias paralelas/Historias ejemplares," for a sharp discussion of the elemental importance of those three features in the academic institutionalization of testimonio.

8   Beverley and Zimmerman state: "literature has been a means of national and popular mobilization in the Central American revolutionary process, but that process also elaborates or points to forms of cultural democratization that will necessarily question or displace the role of literature as a hegemonic cultural institution" (207). I do not think that the Central American revolutionary process causes a hegemonic shift concerning literature's cultural capital; rather, a shift in literature's cultural capital creates the ideological framework for that argument.

9   Testimonio is generally thought to have reached full maturity as a genre in connection with revolutionary struggle in Central America in particular. For Antonio Vera León Latin American testimonio models itself "on the revolutionary project of putting the workers in control of the means of production as the way to eliminate the domination and repression produced by capitalist modernity" ("Hacer hablar" 184; my trans.) See, however, Gareth Williams, "Translation and Mourning," for a response to Vera León and a highly persuasive conceptualization of testimonio as an

identity-producing discourse on the basis of radical loss: "[In testimonio] the discursive reconfiguration of personal and collective experience . . . is ultimately facilitated by a movement of mourning in which loss of original selfhood is fought against and reconciled to itself by its absorption and translation into the very basis of cultural resistance and survival" (97). I am indebted to Williams for the notion that testimonio is a primary cultural manifestation of identity politics—indeed, for an understanding of the production of identity on the basis of an introjecting resistance to as well as assimilation of original loss. For Williams, discourses of identity in contemporary Latin American testimonio must be understood as phenomena of mourning and of its peculiar dialectics of lamentation and commemoration. In reference to Rigoberta Menchú, for instance, Williams says: "The reconfiguration of one's life through discourses becomes equatable with a process of mourning in which the incorporation and assimilation into the self of painful severance—from one's cultural laws, one's past, one's language, from the body of a tortured and murdered mother and brother, from a father killed in the act of resisting—is a remembrance of loss which, nevertheless, is also seen to permit a new process of becoming" (94). I am arguing that the identity-politics dimension of testimonio grows immensely during the 1980s and 1990s, and that such an identitarian dimension is dominant today in testimonio's cultural capital. In fact, leaving aside considerations of literary quality or formal interest, the overwhelming presence of *Me llamo Rigoberta Menchú* in discussions of testimonio seems directly related to the identitarian, rather than to the social-revolutionary, dimension in testimonio's cultural capital. See also, in reference to the connection between testimonio and identity politics, Yúdice, "Testimonio y concientización" 208 ("those texts focus on the ways that difference oppressed groups . . . practice their identity not just as a resistance to oppressors but also as affirmative culture, as practical aesthetics" [213]); Marín, "Speaking Out Together" 53, 55, 59, 65. For a different and intriguing take on the issue (insofar as testimonio's general capability to induce solidarity at the service of the social emancipation of the subaltern is quite radically called into question), see Zimmerman's "El *otro* de Rigoberta." But Zimmerman is, in my interpretation, still supporting the general notion that testimonio articulates, or even primarily articulates, identity dimensions in people's lives.

10   This correctly should be spelled "Machu Picchu." See Enrico Mario Santí, "Introducción" [Neruda], for a sharp interpretation of Neruda's orthographic addition. According to Santí, "the supplemental letter [is] not a mere typo: it is the mark of a gazing point that is at once exterior and inferior to the American being, and from which the mediated gaze of the chronicler stands revealed—as well as his deliberate and scandalously occidental interpretation" (90).

11   See Vincent Gugino, "Ethos" 195–209, for an interpretation of Neruda's dwelling ("morada") as "the turning in need to a without, a *chora* that is

at the same time a site of potential participation" anticipating or seeking "a possible encounter" (195). Although my reading of Neruda's gesture
toward that encounter does not follow Gugino's reading, I don't regard
mine as incompatible with his: Neruda's "morada" is overdetermined. Let
me also suggest the possibility of reading Neruda's famous verse through
G. W. F. Hegel's appropriation of the Greek proverb *Idou Rodos, idou kai
to pedema* ("Here is the rose, dance here") in his *Hegel's Philosophy of
Right* (26).

12 This notion of "total representativity" is equated by Fredric Jameson to
testimonio's drive toward "a multiplication of proper names" ("De la sustitución" 128), and the implied notion that testimonial anonimity "is not
something one dives into, but rather something one must conquer" (130;
my trans. here and below). Jameson goes on to talk about testimonio as
expressive of "zero degrees of desire," since for him, in testimonio's subjective positioning, "experience moves backward and forward between two
polarities or dialectical limits regarding the individual subject: one is the
collective or peasant ritual, always present . . . the other one is history in
the sense of brutal irruption, of catastrophe, the history of others, which
bursts into the peasant community from the outside, and moves specifically in the peasant *space* as such from outside" (130–31).

13 However, it needs to be constantly kept in mind that by testimonio, no
matter how much we choose to emphasize in our reading the voice of
the testimonal subject, we also generally mean a text in which an act of
transcription has taken place. Vera León's splendid essay on the testimonial transcription, "Hacer hablar," settles the fact that the testimonial text
is, always already, "the space where the transcriptor builds his or his authority" (191). Vera León's conclusion points to the unsettling fact that testimonio itself, in its canonical examples, is never free of contamination
from the sort of critical practice, based on the production of abjection,
which I am here calling "auratic practice of the postauratic": "In the testimonial process the life of the 'other' is not just the real referent the text
alludes to . . . . Hence, the text can be read as a place of unresolved tensions . . . where a narration is negotiated that documents the other's life
as well as the ways of telling it, which are also ways of imagining it and
of appropriating it for writing" (195; my trans.). "Hacer hablar is in several
important senses at the genealogical foundation of my own text."

14 I am appropriating, as well as referring to, Jacques Derrida's notion of the
"dangerous" supplement, developed in the analysis of Rousseau's references to masturbation. See Derrida's *Of Grammatology* 141–64.

15 For a similar notion of the operativity of the secret in Menchú's text, but a
different interpretation of how the secret was textually intended, see Williams, "Translation" 95–97.

16 "Announcing limited access is the point, not whether or not some information is really withheld. Resistance does not necessarily signal a genuine epistemological impasse; it is enough that the impasse is claimed in

this ethico-aesthetic strategy to position the reader within limits" (Sommer, "Resisting" 409). Even though resistance does not *necessarily* signal an epistemological impasse, the implication of Sommer's analysis throughout her essay is that resistance in the subaltern text in fact creates that impasse for the reader: whether impasse exists becomes undecidable, and the undecidability is itself a part of the impasse.

17 "Resistant Texts and Incompetent Readers" is the title of the essay Sommer published in *Latin American Literary Review*, which is a partial version of the longer article I am referring to.

18 A metacritical analysis on some aspects of testimonio production and interpretation is also offered by Robert Carr, although from a different perspective and one lacking in the Latin Americanist specificity that Larsen develops. Carr's project is "to map the contexts and implications of First World intellectuals occupied with Third World texts" ("Re-presentando el testimonio 91).

19 *Epistemic murk* in the sense in which Taussig uses the expression can be briefly described as the engagement of fictitious realities whose allegorical as well as literal effect is "a betrayal of Indian realities for the confirmation of colonial fantasies" (*Shamanism* 123). It is not an accusation against Latin Americanists but simply a call for the recognition of a fact that marks, structurally and inevitably, our discourse.

20 Although it probably has nothing to do with what Larsen has in mind when he talks about realism, I cannot let the opportunity pass to cite a Latin Americanist disciplinary text that paradoxically seems to go a long way toward ridding itself of auratic practices by almost paroxystically intensifying them to their extreme: Ruth Behar's *Translated Woman*. It is a strange sort of text, in that it is an ethnobiography-cum-testimonio where the traditional mediator figure at times becomes the testimonial subject herself. It is a maddening text: it problematizes the authorial position because it takes to an extreme the irreducible conflict between political desire and epistemic constraints; it pretends to translate without ignoring that translation shows the original to be dead, that it in fact kills the original; it allegorizes the relationship between anthropologist and subject as that between a wetback and her coyote, maybe even the worst kind of coyote; it calls itself redemptive ethnography knowing full well that there is no redemption actually happening anywhere; it denounces its own malinchismo; it purports to go beyond the self-other division without actually bothering the self-other division. *Translated Woman*, as a Latin Americanist text, has some claim to go beyond Latin Americanism, to come close to a region of writing without disciplinary entitlement, without permission. It problematizes the notion that the Latin American testimonial-ethnographical subject is the ground of disciplinary thought, at the same time that it challenges the reader to move beyond disciplinary thought toward a raw encounter with its imaginary basis, or its basis in the imaginary.

Chapter Eight: The Order of Order

1   There are of course serious intellectual differences among cultural studies, postcolonial studies, and subaltern studies, but they are not always marked by this critique. The reader ought to keep in mind that what is targeted in subaltern studies as wrong is not always judged in the same way by cultural or postcolonial studies scholars. However, what is targeted as wrong in cultural studies or postcolonial studies is always also an *a fortiori* feature of subalternism.

2   Some of the first objections raised against the contemporary avatar of cosmopolitan Latin Americanism are to be found in Gareth Williams, "Fantasies of Cultural Exchange in Latin American Subaltern Studies," and George Yúdice, "Estudios culturales y sociedad civil." See also Mario Cesareo, "Hermenéuticas del naufragio y naufragios de la hermenéutica"; John Beverley's response, "Respuesta a Mario Cesareo"; and Federico Galende, "Un desmemoriado espíritu de época." For a spirited defense of literary values against cultural studies encroachment, see Leyla Perrone-Moisés, "Que fim levou a crítica literária?" All this is not to take originality away from Moraña's position. Perhaps Moraña, with Achugar and, to a certain extent, Sarlo, is the first to establish a critique not as internal to the paradigms being discussed, but rather as intellectual break from them (Perrone-Moisés does not break away because she was never "inside"). Another critique, at times coincidental with some of the ones under consideration but not as drastic as them, is Santiago Castro-Gómez's "Modernidad, latinoamericanismo y globalización," which was published after this chapter was written. See also his edited book, with Eduardo Mendieta, *Teorías sin disciplina,* which puts together many of the essays I am concerned with and adds some new ones. Again, this important book reached me when this chapter was already written, but I am glad to have the opportunity of at least mentioning it. Finally, see Abril Trigo, "Why Do I Do Cultural Studies?"

3   Dirlik is critical of postcolonial studies. Addressing the antifoundationalism in postcolonial studies, Dirlik says: "While capital in its motion continues to structure the world, refusing it foundational status renders impossible the cognitive mapping that must be the point of departure for any practice of resistance and leaves such mapping as there is in the domain of those who manage the capitalist world economy" ("Postcolonial Aura" 356). His admittedly foundationalist proposal to confront the crisis of reason is however different from what I am about to call "historical retrenchment" in the text.

4   See Beverley's "Does the Project of the Left Have a Future?" for his call for a return to a strategic, nation-based populism as a means to reconstitute the possibility of a popular front alliance. A populist political strategy is not the same thing as populist historicism: a strategy can be conceived along antifoundationalist lines. See also the last chapter of *Subalternity and Representation.*

5   See Stavenhagen, *Las clases sociales en las sociedades agrarias,* and also his recent *Ethnic Conflict and the Nation-State.* There is a long genealogy of Latin American scholars and intellectuals whose positions mark a Latin American tradition of subalternist thinking; there is certainly no need to go back to Bartolomé de Las Casas. However, a history of Latin American subaltern(ist) thinking still needs to be written. For a consideration of these issues, see Walter Mignolo, "Are Subaltern Studies Postmodern or Postcolonial?"

6   A distinction between centripetal and centrifugal forces in the construction of a national culture is the structuring concept in Antonio Cornejo Polar's *La formación de la tradición literaria en el Peru.*

7   In "From Populism to Neoliberalism" Gareth Williams says: "The history of the [LASA conferences] is, at least in part, the history of Latin American Latinamericanists often rightfully protesting that US Latinamericanism's interests and concerns were very often far removed from the local engagements and reflections of intellectuals and critics in, say, Caracas, Lima, or Buenos Aires. . . . However, the underlying cultural nationalism which maintained, legitimized, and bolstered the critique of US Latinamericanism and its practices as inherently and often unreflexively imperialistic . . . is increasingly destitute as a valid position from which to critique the hegemonization of contemporary knowledge production" (6). Other aspects of Williams's argumentation are fully consistent with mine. Achugar explicitly rejects the term *neocriollismo* (which he identifies with a "fundamentalism" it is not meant to refer to ["Leones," 381 n1]), but he comes repeatedly to *"nuestro americanismo"* as a possibly fair formulation of where he wants to stand (383, 386). Cornejo Polar makes an ominous and wistful reference to the "not very honorable end of Hispanic Americanism" (poco honroso final del hispanoamericanismo) ("Mestizaje" 344) in a contribution on the use of Spanish (and Portuguese) over against English as the "genuine" Latin American languages for intellectual production. Although those words are targeted at the reliance on English as the main language of cosmopolitan Latinamericanism, they are made ambiguous given the Latin American linguistic and cultural heterogeneity that Cornejo himself so masterfully theorized. In spite of that ambiguity, however, a heartfelt and poignant defense of the "Nuestra América" tradition is at stake in Cornejo's remarks—and this affective investment equally marks Moraña's, Achugar's, and Sarlo's texts (although not Richard's). It is certainly not to be dismissed on supposedly unemotional intellectual grounds given that emotion may be the very heart of the matter under discussion.

8   I am referring to Friedrich A. Hayek's influential theory of "the spontaneous order of the market." See *The Fatal Conceit* 83–84 and passim. See also Carl Susstein, "The Road from Serfdom" 38–40.

9   Popper pays central attention to Plato in *The Open Society and Its Enemies.* However, he traces the beginnings of European historicism to Hera-

clitus and his aristocratic notion of a "law of destiny": "No conceivable experience can refute it. But to those who believe in it, it gives *certainty* regarding the ultimate outcome of human history" (1: 9). Just as "Heraclitus' philosophy is an expression of a feeling of drift; a feeling which seems to be a typical reaction to the dissolution of the ancient tribal forms of social life" (1: 17), in the background of my argument in this chapter is my belief that contemporary forms of historicist populism are a reaction to the dissolution of the national-popular state form. It is interesting to note that Popper detects in Heraclitus a certain "relativism of values" that will be thoroughly canceled out by Plato in his recourse to Eternal Ideas as the only possible ground for a well-run republic.

10 Heidegger's Nietzsche interpretation places Nietzsche as the great philosopher of the inversion of Platonism. Nietzsche's "transvaluation" is his historical resetting of values in the perspective of so-called European nihilism from their old idealist or foundationalist Platonic base. See the beginning of a very long explanation comprising several volumes that starts in section 20 of the second volume: "Truth in Platonism and Positivism. Nietzsche's Attempt to Overturn Platonism on the Basis of the Fundamental Experience of Nihilism" (*Nietzshe* 2: 151–61). It is precisely because Nietzsche "inverts" Platonism, and remains therefore caught up in it, that he would be the last thinker of metaphysics, its "consummator," in the double sense of one who brings metaphysics to full fruition and at the same time liquidates it into the beginning of a new age. In the Heideggerian interpretation, which I accept, "values" are totally involved in the first sense but not in the second sense.

11 Although I lack space to go into it, I would like to refer here to Heidegger's *Parmenides*, in which he traces the European notion of empire to the transformation of the notion of truth by the Romans. The inheritance in Latinate Europe of the Roman-imperial language solidified the language of ontology into a particular experience of the political. See Heidegger, *Parmenides* 17–70 and passim. See also my "Ten Notes on Primitive Imperial Accumulation."

12 Two remarks are perhaps in order here: the first is that even neoliberalism can be understood as a radical form of culturalism. Value thinking is certainly firmly entrenched among some of its illustrious theoreticians—Hayek, Samuel Huntington, and Francis Fukuyama, to name the first three that come to mind. See also the numerous appeals to cultural values in Barry Levine, *El desafío neoliberal*. The second remark is to repeat that an avowed adscription to postcolonial or subaltern studies does not necessarily mean the practitioner is mechanically free of culturalist thinking (but that is a different problem).

13 See Heidegger, "Question" 317: "Because the essence of technology is nothing technological, essential reflection upon technology and decisive confrontation with it must happen in a realm that is, on the one hand, akin to the essence of technology and, on the other, fundamentally different

from it." To the extent that the contemporary notion of culture is an "enframing" of the world that shares essential characteristics with the notion of technology (i.e., culture is a technology for life in identitarian thinking and its variations, including hybridity thinking), a radicalized cultural studies that would attempt to understand culture would also have to go to a realm of thinking that must be "fundamentally different from it."

14 In *Bringing It All Back Home*, Lawrence Grossberg writes, "cultural studies does not believe that culture can be explained in purely cultural terms, nor does it believe that everything is culture; rather it believes that culture can only be understood in terms of its relations to everything that is not culture. In this sense, cultural studies is always materialist" (255).

15 See, however, Jon Beasley-Murray, "Peronism and the Secret History of Cultural Studies," on the properly populist origins of the international expansion of cultural studies through the work of Laclau—and then Laclau and Chantal Mouffe. Although I don't think Laclau's recent work has a populist ground, it has to a certain extent developed out of a rigorous thinking of populism. This might even be true for the work of the Birmingham Centre of Cultural Studies in general. Beasley-Murray's essay has influenced my own perspective. While the article claims that cultural studies "forgets" the state, it stops short of investigating how a thinking of the state in Bové's interregnum might differ from state thinking in Deleuzian-Guattarian ways.

16 Decision is of course inseparable from undecidability and regulated by it. It does not therefore ground an irrationalist "decisionism" in the political or indeed the theoretical terrain—the thinking of decision as the proper terrain of the political marks and remarks the radically contingent nature of political action "in the last instance," but it doesn't therefore authorize just any old action, any old decision. See in particular Laclau, "Deconstruction, Pragmatism, Hegemony" 48–60 and Derrida, "Remarks on Deconstruction and Pragmatism." Richard Beardsworth's excellent *Derrida and the Political* is an analysis of the political implications of Derrida's thought from the central concept of aporia, which calls for a constant decision in the face of final undecidability. See also Derrida's *Specters of Marx* on justice. Derrida's considerations of "the messianic" arbitrate a radical, undeconstructible difference between historicist and contingent decisions. This is not to say that all contingent decisions are good ones— or even that all decisions taken out of historicist grounds are ethically or politically faulty.

Chapter Nine: Hybridity and Double Consciousness

1 See Fernando Ortiz, *Contrapunteo cubano del tabaco y el azúcar*; Angel Rama, *Transculturación narrativa en América Latina*; and Antonio Cornejo Polar, *Sobre literatura y crítica latinoamericanas*.

2 I am using the terms *strategic* and *tactic* in Michel de Certeau's sense: "I call a 'strategy' the calculus of force-relationships which becomes possible

when a subject of will and power . . . can be isolated from an 'environment.' A strategy assumes a place that can be circumscribed as 'proper' and thus serve as the basis for generating relations with an exterior distinct from it . . . Political, economic, and scientific rationality has been constructed on this strategic model.

I call a 'tactic,' on the other hand, a calculus which cannot count on a 'proper' (a spatial or institutional location), nor thus on a borderline distinguishing the other as a visible totality. . . . A tactic insinuates itself into the other's place, fragmentarily, without taking it over in its entirety, without being able to keep it at a distance" (*Practice* xix).

3   "[The] objectifying of whatever is, is accomplished in a setting-before, a representing, that aims at bringing each particular being before it in such a way that man who calculates can be sure, and that means be certain, of that being. . . . The whole of Western metaphysics taken together . . . maintains itself within [that] interpretation of what it is to be and of truth that was prepared by Descartes" (Heidegger, "Age" 127).

4   Gayatri Spivak's warning against a sacralization of an alternative version of the local and the global, that is, the diasporic or migrant and the ontopological, also recommends the development of alternative categories: "to see absolute migrancy as the mark of an impossible deconstruction, and to see all activity attaching to the South as ontopologocentric, denies access to the news of subaltern struggles against the financialization of the globe. . . . Subalternity remains silenced here" ("Ghostwriting" 71.) See also her "Diasporas Old and New," which argues against the complacency of dialectical, or not dialectical enough, categories: "Feminists with a transnational consciousness will also be aware that the very civil structure here that they need to shore up for gender justice can continue to participate in providing alibis for the operation of the major and definitive transnational activity, the financialization of the globe, and thus the suppression of the possibility of decolonization" (251). On "ontopology" see note 7 below.

5   I do not think that Spivak uses the expression *double articulation*. Her recent work, however, rehearses that structure in various ways. See, for instance, her comment that "our relationship to capitalism, Derrida's and my relationship to imperialism, indeed feminism's relationship to both . . . shares the structure [found in Derrida's work] of the relationship between possibility and the principle of reason," which would be a version of it ("Responsibility" 39). In "Diasporas" she will call that structure "aporetic," claiming that it is the very "basis of a decolonization of the mind" (251).

6   See note 2.

7   Ontopology is "an axiomatics linking indissociably ontological value to being-present to one's situation, to the stable and presentable determination of a locality, the *topos* of territory, native soil, city, body in general" (Derrida, *Specters* 137). See also Spivak, "Ghostwriting" 71.

8   This is perhaps an appropriate place to refer to Grossberg's essay "Cultural Studies in/and New Worlds," where a similar impatience with the

limits of a politics of the subject is vented through a different but perhaps not all that incompatible logic. Grossberg proposes to replace "theories of difference" with "theories of otherness" on the basis that difference cannot be understood apart from a Cartesian-Kantian temporalizing representation. Difference is in that sense, for him, "a fundamental logic of the formations of modern power" (354). For Grossberg, most "work around identity in cultural studies" is predicated on a principle of differential negativity grounded on language and signification, one of whose effects is the displacement and abjection of subaltern agency vis-à-vis dominant positions. He thus proposes to move "from a temporal to a spatial logic of power" and "from a structural to a machinic theory of power" (354). I cannot summarize in this space his very complex and elaborate argumentation, but I would say that my own view, by claiming that the subaltern position is spatially, not temporally, articulated as the constitutive outside of hegemony and that savage hybridity is the destructuring constitution of all identity structures, can be read "machinically" as providing, first, a phenomenological-material field that is not prediscursive or preterritorial (364); second, a field of differentiation for subject positions along myriad determinations (364); and third, a field for (de/re)territorialization on a distributive basis (366). This is so because my notion of subalternity is relational, not differential. Subalternity is not primarily a difference from the dominant but is rather a correlate to it. Accordingly, those three machinic productions would be radically crisscrossed by power relations whose right understanding would not depend on a privileging of consciousness or on the attribution of either a lesser or a greater subjectivity to the subaltern. Both the privileging of consciousness and the relative distribution of subjectivity would be rather understood as always already produced by hegemonic assemblages, as spatial effects of power, in other words, which operate multiply and heterogeneously throughout the socius and produce all positivities as well as all investments in lack or negation. I would also claim, however, that Balibar's notion of "unconditional insurrection," which I have presented as the very condition of the negative register of the double articulation, seems to provide a better vector for political praxis than Grossberg's admittedly provisional notion of "agency," which he develops on the basis of a "belonging without identity" whose ability to mobilize seems unclear (371).

WORKS CITED

Achugar, Hugo. "Historias paralelas/Historias ejemplares: La historia y la voz del otro." *Revista de crítica literaria latinoamericana* 36 (1992): 49–71.

———. "Leones, cazadores e historiadores: A propósito de las políticas de la memoria y del conocimiento." *Revista iberoamericana* 180 (1997): 379–87.

———. "Notas sobre el discurso testimonial latinoamericano." Chang-Rodríguez and De Beer 279–94.

———. "Repensando la heterogeneidad latinoamericana (a propósito de lugares, paisajes y territorios)." *Revista iberoamericana* 176–77 (1996): 845–61.

Achugar, Hugo, and Gerardo Caetano, eds. *Mundo, región, aldea: Identidades, políticas culturales e integración regional.* Montevideo: FESUR-Goethe Institut, 1994.

Adelman, Jeremy. "Latin America and Globalization." *LASA Forum* 29.1 (1998): 10–12.

Adorno, Theodor. *Minima Moralia: Reflections on Damaged Life.* Trans. E. F. N. Jephcott. London: New Left, 1974.

Althusser, Louis. *For Marx* Trans. Ben Brewster. London: Verso, 1990.

———. "Freud and Lacan." Althusser, *Lenin and Philosophy* 189–219.

———. *The Future Lasts Forever: A Memoir.* Trans. Richard Veasey. New York: New Press, 1993.

———. "Ideology and the Ideological State Apparatus. (Notes toward an Investigation)." Althusser, *Lenin and Philosophy* 127–86.

———. *Lenin and Philosophy and Other Essays.* Trans. Ben Brewster. New York: Monthly Review. 1971.

———. *Sur la philosophie.* Paris: Gallimard, 1994.

———. "La transformation de la philosophie. Conference de Grenade (1976)." In *Sur la philosophie,* 139–78.

Amin, Shahid, and Dipesh Chakrabarty, eds. *Subaltern Studies 9: Writings on South Asian History and Society.* Delhi: Oxford University Press, 1996.

Anderson, Perry. *The Origins of Postmodernity.* New York: Verso, 1998.

Appadurai, Arjun. "Disjuncture and Difference in the Global Cultural Economy." Robbins, *Phantom Public Sphere* 269–95.

Appiah, Kwame Anthony. "Identity, Authenticity, Survival: Multicultural Societies and Social Reproduction." Gutmann 149–63.

Arguedas, José María. *Señores e indios.* Montevideo: Arca, 1976.

———. *El zorro de arriba y el zorro de abajo.* Ed. Eva Marie Fell. Madrid: Archivos, 1990.

Arias, Arturo, Albert Fishlow, and Charles R. Hale. "Latin America and Globalization: Responses to Jeremy Adelman's Paper." *LASA Forum* 29.1 (1998): 12–15.

Arredondo de Arguedas, Sybila. "*El zorro de arriba y el zorro de abajo* en la correspondencia de Arguedas." Arguedas, *Zorro* 275–95.

Arrighi, Giovanni. *The Long Twentieth Century: Money, Power, and the Origins of Our Times.* New York: Verso, 1994.

Baddeley, Oriana, and Valerie Fraser. *Drawing the Line: Art and Cultural Identity in Contemporary Latin America.* London: Verso, 1989.

Balibar, Etienne. "Ambiguous Universality." *Differences* 7.1 (1995): 48–74.

———. "Is There a 'Neo-Racism'?" Balibar and Wallerstein 17–28.

Balibar, Etienne, and Immanuel Wallerstein. *Race, Nation, Class: Ambiguous Identities.* New York: Verso, 1991.

Barnet, Richard, and John Cavanagh. *Global Dreams: Imperial Corporations and the New World Order.* New York: Simon, 1994.

Bartra, Roger. *La jaula de la melancolía: Identidad y metamorfosis del mexicano.* Mexico: Grijalbo, 1987.

———. *Las redes imaginarias del poder político.* Mexico: Era, 1981.

Beardsworth, Richard. *Derrida and the Political.* London: Routledge, 1996.

Beasley-Murray, Jon. "Peronism and the Secret History of Cultural Studies: Populism and the Substitution of Culture for State." *Cultural Critique* 39 (1998): 189–217.

———. "Towards an Unpopular Cultural Studies: The Perspective of the Multitude." Paper presented at the Cross-Genealogies and Subaltern Studies Conference, Duke University, October 1998.

———. "'We the People:' Intimations of General Intellect in Latin America." *Cultural Studies,* forthcoming.

Behar, Ruth. *Translated Woman: Crossing the Border with Esperanza's Story.* Boston: Beacon, 1993.

Bell, Steven, Albert H. Le May, and Leonard Orr, eds. *Critical Theory, Cultural Politics, and Latin American Narrative.* Notre Dame: U of Notre Dame P, 1993.

Bennington, Geoffrey. *Legislations: The Politics of Deconstruction.* London: Verso, 1994.

Berger, Mark T. *Under Northern Eyes: Latin American Studies and U.S. Hegemony in the Americas, 1898–1990.* Bloomington: Indiana University Press, 1995.

Beverley, John. *Against Literature.* Minneapolis: University of Minnesota Press, 1993.

———. "Does the Project of the Left Have a Future?" *boundary 2* 24, no. 1 (1997): 35–57.

———. "¿Posliteratura? Sujeto subalterno e impasse de las humanidades." *Revista de la Casa de las Américas* 190 (1993): 13–24.

———. "Respuesta a Mario Cesareo." *Revista iberoamericana* 174 (1996): 225–33.

———. "Sobre la situación actual de estudios culturales." Typescript, 1996.

———. *Subalternity and Representation: Arguments in Cultural Theory.* Durham, N.C.: Duke University Press, 1999.

Beverley, John, José Oviedo, and Michael Aronna, eds. *The Postmodernism Debate in Latin America.* Durham, N.C.: Duke University Press, 1995.

Beverley, John, and James Sanders. "Negotiating with the Disciplines: A Conversation on Latin American Subaltern Studies." *Journal of Latin American Cultural Studies* 6 (1999): 233–57.

Beverley, John, and Marc Zimmerman. *Literature and Politics in the Central American Revolutions*. Austin: University of Texas Press, 1990.

Bhabha, Homi. *The Location of Culture*. London: Routledge, 1994.

———. "Postcolonial Authority and Postmodern Guilt." Grossberg, Nelson, and Treichler 56–68.

Bloch, Ernst. *Heritage of Our Times*. Trans. Neville Plaice and Stephen Plaice. Berkeley: University of California Press, 1991.

Borges, Jorge Luis. "Avatares de la tortuga." Borges, *Prosa* 1: 199–204.

———. "El etnógrafo." Borges, *Prosa* 2: 355–57.

———. "The Lottery in Babylon." *Collected Fictions*. Trans. Andrew Hurley. New York: Penguin, 1999. 101–06.

———. "La perpetua carrera de Aquiles y la tortuga." Borges, *Prosa* 1: 187–92.

———. *Prosa completa*. 2 vols. Barcelona: Bruguera, 1980.

———. "Tlön, Uqbar, Orbis Tertius." Borges, *Prosa* 1: 409–24.

Bourdieu, Pierre. "L'essence du néolibéralisme." *Le Monde Diplomatique* (March 1998): 3.

Bourdieu, Pierre, and Loïs Wacquant. "On the Cunning of Imperialist Reason." *Theory, Culture, and Society* 16.1 (1999): 41–58.

Bové, Paul. "Afterword: 'Global/Local' Memory and Thought." Wilson and Dissanayake 372–85.

Brotherston, Gordon. "Regarding the Evidence in *Me llamo Rigoberta Menchú*." *Journal of Latin American Cultural Studies* 6 (1997): 93–103.

Bulmer-Thomas, Victor, ed. *The New Economic Model in Latin America and Its Impact on Income Distribution and Poverty*. New York: St. Martin's 1996.

Burgos-Debray, Elizabeth, and Rigoberta Menchú. *Me llamo Rigoberta Menchú y así me nació la conciencia*. México: Siglo XXI, 1981.

Butler, Judith. *Bodies That Matter: On the Discursive Limits of "Sex"*. New York: Routledge, 1993.

———. "Imitation and Gender Insubordination." Fuss 13–31.

Candido, Antonio. "Literature and Underdevelopment." *On Literature and Society*. Ed. and trans. Howard Becker. Princeton: Princeton UP, 1995. 119–41.

Carr, Robert. "Re-presentando el testimonio: Notas sobre el cruce divisorio Primer mundo/Tercer mundo." *Revista de crítica literaria latinoamericana* 36 (1992): 73–94.

Carroll, David, ed. *The States of "Theory": History, Art, and Critical Discourse*. New York: Columbia University Press, 1990.

Castañeda, Jorge. *Utopia Unarmed: The Latin American Left after the Cold War*. New York: Knopf, 1993.

Castro-Gómez, Santiago. "Modernidad, latinoamericanismo y globalización." *Cuadernos americanos* 67 (Jan.–Feb. 1998): 187–213.

Castro-Gómez, Santiago, and Eduardo Mendieta, eds. *Teorías sin disciplina:*

Latinoamericanismo, poscolonialidad y globalización en debate. Mexico: Porrúa, 1998.

Castro-Klarén, Sara. *El mundo mágico de José María Arguedas.* Lima: Instituto de Estudios Peruanos, 1973.

Caviedes, César. "The Latin American Boom-Town in the Literary View of José María Arguedas." Mallory and Simpson-Housley 57–77.

Cesareo, Mario. "Hermenéuticas del naufragio y naufragios de la hermenéutica: Comentarios en torno a *Against Literature.*" *Revista iberoamericana* 174 (1996): 211–23.

Chakrabarty, Dipesh. "Marx after Marxism: Subaltern Histories and the Question of Difference." *Polygraph* 6-7 (1993): 10–16.

———. "Minority Histories, Subaltern Pasts." *Postcolonial Studies* 1.1 (1998): 15–29.

———. "Postcoloniality and the Artifice of History. Who Speaks for 'Indian' Pasts?" Guha, *A Subaltern Studies Reader.* 263–93.

———. "The Time of History and the Times of Gods." Lowe and Lloyd 35–60.

Chanady, Amaryll. *Magical Realism and the Fantastic: Resolved versus Unresolved Antinomy.* New York: Garland, 1985.

Chang-Rodríguez, Raquel, and Gabriella de Beer, eds. *La historia en la literatura iberoamericana.* Hanover: Ediciones del Norte, 1989.

Chiampi, Irlemar. *O realismo maravilhoso: Forma e ideologia no romance hispano-americano.* São Paulo: Perspectiva, 1980.

Chomsky, Noam. "The Fifth Freedom." *Turning the Tide: U.S. Intervention in Central America and the Struggle for Peace.* Boston: South End, 1985.

Chow, Rey. *Writing Diaspora: Tactics of Intervention in Contemporary Cultural Studies,* Bloomington: Indiana UP, 1993

Clifford, James. "On Ethnographic Surrealism." *The Predicament of Culture: Twentieth-Century Ethnography, Literature, and Art.* Cambridge: Harvard University Press, 1988. 117–51.

Cornejo Polar, Antonio. "Un ensayo sobre *Los zorros* de Arguedas." Arguedas, *Zorro* 297–306.

———. *Escribir en el aire: Ensayo sobre la heterogeneidad socio-cultural en las literaturas andinas.* Lima: Horizonte, 1994.

———. *La formación de la tradición literaria en el Perú.* Lima: Centro de Estudios y Publicaciones, 1989.

———. "Mestizaje e hibridez: Los riesgos de las metáforas. Apuntes." *Revista iberoamericana* 180 (1997): 341–44.

———. "Nuevas reflexiones sobre la crítica latinoamericana." *De Cerventes a Orovilca: Homenaje a Jean Paul Borel.* Madrid: Visor, 1990. 225–35.

———. *Sobre literatura crítica latinoamericanas.* Caracas: Facultad de Humanidades y Educación, Universidad Central de Venezuela, 1982.

———. *Los universos narrativos de José María Arguedas.* Buenos Aires: Losada, 1973.

Das, Veena. "Subaltern as Perspective." Guha, *Subaltern 6* 310–24.

de Certeau, Michel. *The Practice of Everyday Life*. Trans. Steven Rendall. Berkeley: University of California Press, 1984.

De la Campa, Román. *Latin Americanism*. Minneapolis: U of Minnesota Press, 1999.

Deleuze, Gilles. "Postscript on the Societies of Control." *October* 59 (winter 1992): 3–7.

de Man, Paul. *Aesthetic Ideology*. Ed. Andrzej Warminski. Minneapolis: University of Minnesota Press, 1996.

Derrida, Jacques. *The Gift of Death*. Trans. David Wills. Chicago: University of Chicago Press, 1995.

———. *Of Grammatology*. Trans. Gayatri Chakravorty Spivak. Baltimore, Md.: Johns Hopkins University Press, 1976.

———. *Politics of Friendship*. Trans. George Collins. New York: Verso, 1997.

———. *The Post Card: From Socrates to Freud and Beyond*. Trans. Alan Bass. Chicago: University of Chicago Press, 1987.

———. "Psyche: Inventions of the Other." *Reading de Man Reading*. Minneapolis: University of Minnesota Press, 1989. 25–65.

———. "Remarks on Deconstruction and Pragmatism." Mouffe 77–88.

———. *Specters of Marx: The State of the Debt, the Work of Mourning and the New International*. Trans. Peggy Kamuf. New York: Routledge, 1994.

———. "Some Statements and Truisms about Neologisms, Newisms, Postisms, Parasitisms, and Other Small Seismisms." Carroll 63–94.

Díaz Ruiz, Ignacio. *Literatura y biografía en José María Arguedas*. Mexico: UNAM, 1991.

Dirlik, Arif. "The Postcolonial Aura: Third World Criticism in the Age of Global Capitalism." *Critical Inquiry* 20 (1994): 328–56.

Dussel, Enrique. "Beyond Eurocentrism: The World-System and the Limits of Modernity." Jameson and Miyoshi 3–31.

———. "Globalization and the Limits of Modernity." Lecture given at Duke University, January 1998.

Dworkin, Dennis. *Cultural Marxism in Post-War Britain: History, the New Left, and the Origins of Cultural Studies*. Durham, N.C.: Duke University Press, 1997.

Eltit, Diamela. *El padre mío*. Santiago: Zegers, 1989.

Eltit, Diamela, and Paz Errázuriz. *El infarto del alma*. Santiago: Zegers, 1994.

Ferguson, Russell, Martha Gever, Thinh T. Minh-ha, and Cornel West. *Out There: Marginalization and Contemporary Cultures*. New York: New Museum of Contemporary Art, 1990.

Fink, Bruce. *The Lacanian Subject: Between Language and Jouissance*. Princeton, N.J.: Princeton University Press, 1995.

Flores Galindo, Alberto. *Buscando un inca: Identidad y utopía en los Andes*. Havana: Casa de las Américas, 1986.

Forgues, Roland. *José María Arguedas, de la pensée dialectique a la pensée tragique: Histoire d'une utopie*. Toulouse: Ed. France-Ibérie Recherche, 1986.

———. "Por qué bailan los zorros." Arguedas, *Zorro* 307–15.

Fox, Jonathan, ed. *The Challenge of Rural Democratization: Perspectives from Latin America and the Philippines.* London: Cass, 1990.

Frampton, Kenneth. *Modern Architecture: A Critical History.* London: Thames and Hudson, 1985.

Franco, Jean. "The Nation as Imagined Community." Veeser 204–12.

———. "What's Left of the Intelligentsia? The Uncertain Future of the Printed Word." *NACLA Report on the Americas* 28, no. 2 (1994): 16–21.

Fraser, Nancy. "Rethinking the Public Sphere: A Contribution to the Critique of Actually Existing Democracy." Robbins, *Phantom Public Sphere* 1–32.

Fukuyama, Francis. *The End of History and the Last Man.* New York: Free Press, 1992.

Fuss, Diana, ed. *Inside/Out: Lesbian Theories, Gay Theories.* New York: Routledge, 1991.

Galende, Federico. "Un desmemoriado espíritu de época: Tribulaciones y desdichas en torno a los Estudios Culturales (una réplica a John Beverley)." *Revista de crítica cultural* 13 (1996): 52–55.

García Canclini, Néstor. *Consumidores y ciudadanos: Conflictos multiculturales de la globalización.* Mexico: Grijalbo, 1995.

———. *Culturas híbridas: Estrategias para entrar y salir de la modernidad.* Mexico: Grijalbo, 1990.

———. "El debate sobre la hibridación." *Revista de crítica cultural* 15 (1997): 42–47.

———. *Hybrid Cultures: Strategies for Entering and Leaving Modernity.* Trans. Christopher Chiappari and Silvia L. López. Minneapolis: University of Minnesota Press, 1995.

Gereffi, Gary, and Lynn Hempel. "Latin America in the Global Economy: Running Faster to Stay in Place." *NACLA Report on the Americas* 29, no. 4 (1996): 18–27.

Geyer, Michael, and Charles Bright. "World History in a Global Age." *American Historical Review* 100 (1995): 1034–60.

Gilroy, Paul. *The Black Atlantic: Modernity and Double Consciousness.* Cambridge: Harvard UP, 1993.

Gómez Mango, Edmundo. "Todas las lenguas: Vida y muerte de la escritura en *Los zorros* de Arguedas." Arguedas, *Zorro* 360–68.

González Echevarría, Roberto. *Myth and Archive: A Theory of Spanish American Narrative.* Cambridge: Cambridge University Press, 1990.

Greenblatt, Stephen. *Marvelous Possessions: The Wonder of the New World.* Chicago: University of Chicago Press, 1991.

Grossberg, Lawrence. *Bringing It All Back Home: Essays on Cultural Studies.* Durham, N.C.: Duke University Press, 1997.

———. "Cultural Studies in/and New Worlds." Grossberg, *Bringing* 343–73.

———. "History, Politics and Postmodernism: Stuart Hall and Cultural Studies." Morley and Chen 151–73.

————. "Identity and Cultural Studies: Is That All There Is?" Hall and Du Gay 87–107.

————, ed. "On Postmodernism and Articulation: An Interview with Stuart Hall." Morley and Chen 131–50.

Grossberg, Lawrence, Cary Nelson, and Paula Treichler, eds. *Cultural Studies.* London: Routledge, 1992.

Gugelberger, Georg, ed. *The "Real" Thing: Testimonial Discourse in Latin America.* Durham, N.C.: Duke University Press, 1996.

Gugelberger, Georg, and Michael Kearney. "Voices for the Voiceless: Testimonial Literature in Latin America." *Latin American Perspectives* 18.3 (1991): 3–14.

Gugino, Vincent F. "On Ethos." Diss. SUNY-Buffalo 1991.

Guha, Ranajit. "Dominance without Hegemony and Its Historiography." Guha, *Subaltern 6.* 210–309.

————. *Elementary Aspects of Peasant Insurgency in Colonial India.* Delhi: Oxford University Press, 1983.

————. "On Some Aspects of the Historiography of Colonial India." Guha, *Subaltern Studies 1* 1–8. Rpt. in Guha and Spivak 37–44.

————. "The Prose of Counterinsurgency." Guha and Spivak 45–86.

————. "The Small Voice of History." Amin and Chakrabarty 1–12.

————, ed. *Subaltern Studies 1: Writings on South Asian History and Society.* Delhi: Oxford University Press, 1982.

————, ed. *Subaltern Studies 6: Writings on South Asian History and Society.* Delhi: Oxford University Press, 1989.

————, ed. *A Subaltern Studies Reader, 1986–1995.* Minneapolis: University of Minnesota Press, 1997.

Guha, Ranajit, and Gayatri Chakravorty Spivak, eds. *Selected Subaltern Studies.* New York: Oxford University Press, 1988.

Guillory, John. *Cultural Capital: The Problem of Literary Canon Formation.* Chicago: University of Chicago Press, 1993.

————. "System without Structure: Cultural Studies as Low Theory." Typescript, n.d.

Gulbenkian Commission. *Open the Social Sciences: Report of the Gulbenkian Commission on the Restructuring of the Social Sciences.* Stanford, Calif.: Stanford University Press, 1996.

Gutiérrez, Gustavo. "Entre las calandrias." Trigo, *Arguedas* 240–77.

Gutiérrez, Gustavo, Alejandro Romualdo, and Alberto Escobar. *Arguedas: Cultura e Identidad Nacional.* Lima: EDAPROSPO, 1989.

Gutmann, Amy, ed. *Multiculturalism: Examining the Politics of Recognition.* Princeton, N.J.: Princeton University Press, 1994.

Guzmán, Martín Luis. *El águila y la serpiente.* Mexico: Porrúa, 1987.

Habermas, Jürgen. "Struggles for Recognition in the Democratic Constitutional State." Gutmann 107–48.

Hall, Robert B. *Area Studies: With Special Reference to Their Implications for*

Research in the Social Sciences. Social Science Research Council Pamphlet 3 [New York], May 1947.

Hall, Stuart. "Cultural Studies and Its Theoretical Legacies." Morley and Chen 262–75.

———. "The Local and the Global: Globalization and Ethnicity." King 19–39.

———. "Old and New Identities, Old and New Ethnicities." King 41–68.

Hall, Stuart, and Paul Du Gay, eds. *Questions of Cultural Identity.* London: Sage, 1996.

Halperín Donghi, Tulio. *The Contemporary History of Latin America.* Trans. John Chasteen. Durham, N.C.: Duke University Press, 1993.

Hardt, Michael. "The Withering of Civil Society." *Social Text* 45 (winter 1995): 27–44.

Hardt, Michael, and Antonio Negri. *Empire.* Cambridge: Harvard University Press, 2000.

Hartman, Geoffrey. "The Philomela Project." *Minor Prophecies: The Literary Essay in the Culture Wars.* Cambridge: Harvard University Press, 1991. 164–75.

Hayek, Friedrich A. *The Fatal Conceit: The Errors of Socialism.* Chicago: University of Chicago Press, 1988. Vol. 1 of *The Collected Works of F. A. Hayek.* Ed. W. W. Bartley III.

Hegel, Georg W. F. *Hegel's Philosophy of Right.* Trans. T. M. Knox. London: Oxford University Press, 1967.

Heidegger, Martin. "The Age of the World Picture." *The Question Concerning Technology and Other Essays.* Trans. William Lovitt. New York: Harper, 1977. 115–54.

———. "The Anaximander Fragment." *Early Greek Thinking.* Trans. David Farrell Krell and Frank A. Capuzzi. San Francisco: Harper, 1984. 13–58.

———. *Basic Concepts.* Trans. Gary E. Aylesworth. Bloomington: Indiana University Press, 1993.

———. *Basic Writings.* Ed. David Farrell Krell. New York: Harper: 1977.

———. *Being and Time.* Trans. John Macquarrie and Edward Robinson. New York: Haper and Row, 1962.

———. *Nietzsche.* Trans. David Farrell Krell. 4 vols. San Francisco: HarperCollins, 1991.

———. *Parmenides.* Trans. André Schuwer and Richard Rojcewicz. Bloomington: Indiana University Press, 1992.

———. "The Question concerning Technology." Heidegger, *Basic Writings* 287–317.

Heilbrunn, Jacob. "The News from Everywhere: Does Global Thinking Threaten the Social Science? The Social Science Research Council Debates the Future of Area Studies." *Lingua Franca* May-June 1996: 49–56.

Herlinghaus, Hermann, and Monika Walter, eds. *Posmodernidad en la periferia: Enfoques latinoamericanos de la nueva teoría cultural.* Berlin: Langer, 1994.

Hollier, Denis, ed. *College of Sociology (1937-39)*. Trans. Betsy Wing. Minneapolis: University of Minnesota Press, 1988.

Hopenhayn, Martín. *Ni apocalípticos ni integrados: Aventuras de la posmodernidad en América Latina*. Santiago: Fondo de Cultura Económica, 1994.

Huntington, Samuel. "The Clash of Civilizations?" *Foreign Affairs* 72, no. 3 (1993): 22-49.

———. *The Clash of Civilizations and the Remaking of the World Order*. New York: Simon and Schuster, 1996.

Jameson, Fredric. "Americans Abroad: Exogamy and Letters in Late Capitalism." Bell, Le May, and Orr 35-60.

———. *The Cultural Turn: Selected Writings on the Postmodern, 1983-98*. New York: Verso, 1998.

———. "De la sustitución de importaciones literarias y culturales en el Tercer Mundo: el caso del testimonio." *Revista de crítica literaria latinoamericana* 36 (1992): 117-33.

———. "Marx's Purloined Letter." *New Left Review* 209 (1995): 75-109.

———. "Marxism and Historicism." 2 Jameson, *Syntax of History*. Minneapolis: University of Minnesota Press, 1988. 148-77. Vol. 2 of *The Ideologies of Theory, 1971-1986*.

———. "Culture and Finance Capital." Jameson, *The Cultural Turn* 136-61.

———. *The Political Unconscious: Narrative as a Socially Symbolic Act*. London: Methuen, 1981.

———. "Postmodernism and the Market." Zizek, *Mapping Ideology*. 278-95.

———. *Postmodernism, or, The Cultural Logic of Late Capitalism*. Durham, N.C.: Duke University Press, 1997.

———. *The Seeds of Time*. New York: Columbia University Press, 1995.

———. "Third-World Literature in the Era of Multinational Capitalism." *Social Text* 15 (fall 1986): 65-88.

Jameson, Fredric, and Masao Miyoshi, eds. *The Cultures of Globalization*. Durham, N.C.: Duke University Press, 1998.

Joseph, Gail, and Daniel Nugent. *Everyday Forms of State Formation: Revolution and the Negotiation of Rule in Modern Mexico*. Durham, N.C.: Duke University Press, 1994.

Kamuf, Peggy. *The Division of Literature, or, The University in Deconstruction*. Chicago: U of Chicago P, 1997.

Kant, Emmanuel. *Critique of Judgment*. Trns. Werner Pluhar. Indianapolis: Hackett, 1987.

———. *Critique of Pure Reason*. Trans. Norman Kemp Smith. New York: St. Martin's, 1965.

Kaplan, Amy, and Donald E. Pease, eds. *The Cultures of U.S. Imperialism*. Durham, N.C.: Duke University Press, 1993.

Keenan, Thomas. *Fables of Responsibility: Aberrations and Predicaments in Ethics and Politics*. Stanford, Calif.: Stanford University Press, 1997.

King, Anthony, ed. *Culture, Globalization and the World-System: Contempo-*

rary Conditions for the Representations of Identity. Binghamton: Dept. of Art and Art History, SUNY-Binghamton, 1991.

Kisiel, Theodor. *The Genesis of Heidegger's* Being and Time. Berkeley: University of California Press, 1995.

Kraniauskas, John. "Hybridity and Reterritorialization." *Travesía* 1, no. 2 (1992): 143–51.

———. "Hybridity in a Transnational Frame: Latin-Americanist and Postcolonial Perspectives on Cultural Studies." *Nepantla-Views from South* 1, no. 1 (2000): 111–37.

Kristeva, Julia. *Black Sun: Depression and Melancholia.* Trans. Leon S. Roudiez. New York: Columbia University Press, 1989.

Lacan, Jacques. "L'envers de la psychanalyse: Les quatre discours." Séminaire 1969/70. (unpublished Seminar).

Laclau, Ernesto. "Deconstruction, Pragmatism, Hegemony." Mouffe 47–67.

———. *Emancipation(s).* London: Verso, 1996.

———. *New Reflections on the Revolution of Our Time.* London: Verso, 1990.

———. "Why Do Empty Signifiers Matter to Politics? Laclau, *Emancipation(s)* 36–46.

Landi, Oscar. *Devórame otra vez: Qué hizo la televisión con la gente, qué hace la gente con la televisión.* Buenos Aires: Planeta, 1992.

Larsen, Neil. "Latin America and 'Cultural Studies.'" *Latin American Literary Review* 40 (1992): 58–62.

———. *Reading North by South: On Latin American Literature, Culture, and Politics.* Minneapolis: University of Minnesota Press, 1995.

Latin American Subaltern Studies Group. "Founding Statement." Beverley, Oviedo, Aronna 135–46.

Lea, Henry Charles. *The Inquisition in the Spanish Dependencies.* 1908. New York: Macmillan, 1922.

Levine, Barry, comp. *El desafío neoliberal: El fin del tercermundismo en América Latina.* Bogatá: Norma, 1992.

Levinson, Brett. "Neopatriarchy and After: *I, Rigoberta Menchú* as Allegory of Death." *Journal of Latin American Cultural Studies* 5 (1996): 33–50.

———. "The State/Market Duopoly." Typescript, 1999.

Lienhard, Martin. "La 'andinización' del vanguardismo urbano." Arguedas, *Zorro* 321–32.

———. *Cultura popular andina y forma novelesca: Zorros y danzantes en la última novela de Arguedas.* Lima: Tarea Latinoamericana Eds., 1981.

———. *La voz y su huella: Escritura y conflicto étnico-cultural en América Latina 1492–1988.* Lima: Horizonte, 1992.

Lomnitz-Adler, Claudio. *Exits from the Labyrinth: Culture and Ideology in the Mexican National Space.* Berkeley: University of California Press, 1992.

Loveman, Brian, and Thomas M. Davies Jr., eds. *The Politics of Antipolitics: The Military in Latin America.* 2nd ed., rev. and ex. Lincoln: University of Nebraska Press, 1989.

Lowe, Lisa. *Immigrant Acts: On Asian American Cultural Politics.* Durham, N.C.: Duke University Press, 1996.

Lowe, Lisa, and David Lloyd, eds. *The Politics of Culture in the Shadow of Capital.* Durham, N.C.: Duke University Press, 1997.

Lyotard, Jean-François. *The Postmodern Condition: A Report on Knowledge.* Trans. Geoff Bennington and Brian Massumi. Minneapolis: University of Minnesota Press, 1984.

Macherey, Pierre. *In a Materialist Way: Selected Essays.* Ed. Warren Montag. Trans. Ted Stolze. London: Verso, 1988.

Mallory, William, and Paul Simpson-Housley, eds. *Geography and Literature: A Meeting of the Disciplines.* Syracuse, N.Y.: Syracuse University Press, 1987.

Manegold, Catherine S. "The Rebel and the Lawyer: Unlikely Love in Guatemala." *New York Times* 27 Mar. 1995: A1.

———. "A Woman's Obsession Pays Off—At a Cost." *New York Times* 26 Mar. 1995, sec. 4: 1.

Marín, Lynda. "Speaking Out Together: Testimonials of Latin American Women." *Latin American Perspectives* 18.3 (1991): 51–68.

Martí, José. "Our America." *José Martí Reader: Writings on the Americas.* Ed. Deborah Shnookal and Mirta Muñiz. New York: Ocean Press, 1999. 111–20.

Marx, Karl. *Grundrisse: Foundations of the Critique of Political Economy. (Rough Draft).* Trans. Martin Nicolaus. London: Penguin, 1993.

Mato, Daniel. "Construcción de identidades pannacionales y transnacionales en tiempos de globalización: consideraciones teóricas y sobre el caso de América Latina." *Diversidad cultural y construcción de identidades.* Caracas: Tropykos, 1993. 211–31.

———. "On the Complexities of Transnational Processes: The Making of Transnational Identities and Related Political Agendas in 'Latin' America." Typescript, n.d.

Matos Mar, José. *Desborde popular y crisis del estado: El nuevo rostro del Perú en la década de 1980.* Lima: CONCYTEC, 1988.

Menchú, Rigoberta. *Me llamo Rigoberta Menchú y así me nació la conciencia.* Ed. Elizabeth Burgos-Debray. Mexico: Siglo XXI, 1981.

Mignolo, Walter. "The Allocation and Relocation of Identities." Typescript, n.d.

———. "Are Subaltern Studies Postmodern or Postcolonial? The Politics and Sensibilities of Geocultural Location." *Dispositio/n* 46 (1994): 45–73.

———. "Colonial and Postcolonial Discourse: Cultural Critique or Academic Colonialism?" *Latin American Research Review* 28, no. 3 (1993): 120–34.

———. *The Darker Side of the Renaissance: Literacy, Territoriality, and Colonization.* Ann Arbor: Michigan University Press, 1995.

———. "Espacios geográficos y localizaciones epistemológicas. La ratio entre la localización geográfica y la subalternización de conocimientos." *Dissens: Revista internacional de pensamiento latinoamericano* 3 (1997): 1–18.

———. "La lengua, la letra, el territorio (o la crisis de los estudios literarios coloniales.)" *Dispositio* 28–29 (1987): 137–60.

———. *Local Histories/Global Designs: Coloniality, Subaltern Knowledges, and Border Thinking.* New York: Princeton University Press, 2000.

———. "Postcolonial Reason: Colonial Legacies and Postcolonial Theories." Typescript, n.d.

Miranda, Wander Melo. "Projeçoes de um debate." *Revista brasileira de literatura comparada* 4 (1998): 11–17.

Mohanty, S. P. "Us and Them: On the Philosophical Bases of Political Criticism." *Yale Journal of Criticism* 2, no. 2 (1989): 1–31.

Moraña, Mabel. "El boom del subalterno." *Revista de crítica cultural* 15 (1997): 48–53.

———. "*Escribir en el aire:* Heterogeneidad y estudios culturales." *Revista iberoamericana* 170–71 (1995): 279–86.

———. "Ideología de la transculturación." Typescript, n.d.

Moreiras, Alberto. "Ten Notes on Primitive Imperial Accumulation: Ginés de Sepúlveda, Las Casas, Fernández de Oviedo." *Interventions* 2 (2000): 343–63.

———. *Tercer espacio: Duelo y literatura en América Latina.* Santiago: ARCIS/ Lom, 1999.

Moretti, Franco. *Modern Epic: The World System from Goethe to García Márquez.* Trans. Quintin Hoare. London: Verso, 1996.

Morley, David, and Kuan-Hsin Chen, eds. *Stuart Hall: Critical Dialogues in Cultural Studies.* London: Routledge, 1996.

Mouffe, Chantal, ed. *Deconstruction and Pragmatism.* London: Routledge, 1996.

Nancy, Jean-Luc. *L'oubli de la philosophie.* Paris: Galilée, 1986.

Negri, Antonio, and Michael Hardt. *Labor of Dionysus: A Critique of the State-Form.* Minneapolis: University of Minnesota Press, 1994.

Neruda, Pablo. *Canto general.* Ed. Enrico Mario Santí. Madrid: Cátedra, 1991.

O'Hanlon, Rosalind, and David Washbrook. "After Orientalism: Culture, Criticism, and Politics in the Third World." *Comparative Studies in Society and History* 34 (1992): 141–67.

Ortiz, Fernando. *Contrapunteo cubano del tabaco y el azúcar.* Barcelona: Ariel, 1973.

Oviedo, José Miguel. "El último Arguedas: Testimonio y comentario." *Cuadernos hispanoamericanos* 492 (1991): 143–47.

Pérez, Hildebrando, and Carlos Garayar, eds. *José María Arguedas: Vida y obra.* Hildebrando, Lima: Amaru, 1991.

Pérez Firmat, Gustavo. *The Cuban Condition: Translation and Identity in Modern Cuban Literature.* Cambridge: Cambridge University Press, 1989.

Perrone-Moisés, Leyla. "Que fim levou a crítica literária?" *Folha de São Paulo* 25 Aug. 1996: 5–9.

Petras, James, and Morris Morley. *U.S. Hegemony under Siege: Class, Politics, and Development in Latin America.* New York: Verso, 1990.

Pike, Fredrick B. *The United States and Latin America: Myths and Stereotypes of Civilization and Nature.* Austin: University of Texas Press, 1992.

Pletsch, Carl E. "The Three Worlds, or the Division of Social Scientific Labor, circa, 1950–1975." *Comparative Studies in Society and History* 23 (1981): 565–87.

Podestá, Guido. "*El zorro de arriba y el zorro de abajo:* Las paradojas de una literatura menor." Pérez and Garayar 97–105.

Popper, Karl. *The Open Society and Its Enemies.* 2 vols. Princeton, N.J.: Princeton University Press, 1966.

Prakash, Gyan. "Can the 'Subaltern' Ride? A Reply to O'Hanlon and Washbrook." *Comparative Studies in Society and History* 34 (1992): 168–84.

———. "Postcolonial Criticism and Indian Historiography." *Social Text* 31–32 (1992): 8–19.

———. "Writing Post-Orientalist Histories of the Third World: Perspectives from Indian Historiography." *Comparative Studies in Society and History* 32 (1990): 383–408.

Prewitt, Kenneth. "Presidential Items." *Items: Social Science Research Council* 50. 2–3 (1996): 31–40.

———. "SSRC, ACLS, and the Reexamination of Area Studies." *LASA Forum* 27. 1 (1996): 10–12.

Rafael, Vicente. "The Cultures of Area Studies in the United States." *Social Text* 41 (1994): 91–111.

Rama, Angel. *La ciudad letrada.* Hanover: Ediciones del Norte, 1987.

———. "José María Arguedas transculturador." *Arguedas, Señores* 7–40.

———. "Los procesos de transculturación en la narrativa latinoamericana." *La novela en América Latina: Panoramas 1920–1980.* Veracruz: Universidad Veracruzana, 1982. 203–33

———. *Transculturación narrativa en América Latina.* Mexico: Siglo XXI, 1981.

Ranciére, Jacques. *Disagreements: Politics and Philosophy.* Trans. Julie Rose. Minneapolis: University of Minnesota Press, 1999.

Readings, Bill. *The University in Ruins.* Cambridge: Harvard University Press, 1996.

Rial, Juan. *Las Fuerzas Armadas: ¿Soldados-políticos garantes de la democracia?.* Montevideo: CIESU, 1986

Richard, Nelly. "Bordes, diseminación, postmodernismo: Una metáfora latinoamericana de fin de siglo." Paper presented at the International Colloquium, "Las culturas de fin de siglo en América Latina." Yale University, April 8–9, 1994.

———. "Intersectando Latinoamérica con el latinoamericanismo: Discurso académico y crítica cultural." *Revista iberoamericana* 180 (1997): 345–61.

Rivera Cusicanqui, Silvia. "Liberal Democracy and *Ayllu* Democracy in Bolivia: The Case of Northern Potosí, Bolivia." Fox 97–121.

Robbins, Bruce, ed. *The Phantom Public Sphere.* Minneapolis: University of Minnesota Press, 1993.

———. *Secular Vocations: Intellectuals, Professionalism, Culture.* London: Verso, 1993.

Rosaldo, Renato. Foreword. García Canclini, *Hybrid Cultures* xi–xvii.

Rouquié, Alain. *The Military and the State in Latin America.* Trans. Paul E. Sigmund. Berkeley: University of California Press, 1987.

Rowe, William. *Mito e ideología en la obra de José María Arguedas.* Lima: Instituto Nacional de Cultura, 1979.

Said, Edward. *Culture and Imperialism.* New York: Knopf, 1993.

———. *Orientalism.* New York: Vintage, 1979.

Sandoval, Chela. "U.S. Third World Feminism: The Theory and Method of Oppositional Consciousness in the Postmodern World." *Genders* 10 (spring 1991): 1–24.

Santí, Enrico Mario. "Introducción." Neruda. *Canto general.* 13–99.

———. "Introducción." Santí, *Laberinto* 11–136.

———, ed. *El laberinto de la soledad,* by Octavio Paz. Madrid: Cátedra, 1993.

———. "Latinamericanism and Restitution." *Latin American Literary Review* 40 (1992): 88–96.

———. "Sor Juana, Octavio Paz, and the Poetics of Restitution." *Indiana Journal of Hispanic Literatures* 1, no. 2 (1993): 101–39.

Santiago, Silviano. "Reading and Discursive Intensities: On the Situation of Postmodern Reception in Brazil." Beverley, Oviedo, and Aronna 241–49.

Sarduy, Severo. "Imágenes del tiempo inmóvil." Typescript, n.d.

Sarlo, Beatriz. "Cultural Studies and Literary Criticism at the Crossroads of Values." *Journal of Latin American Cultural Studies* 8 (1999): 115–24. Rpt. of "Los estudios culturales y la crítica literaria en la encrucijada valorativa." *Revista de crítica cultural* 15 (1997): 32–38.

———. *Escenas de la vida posmoderna: Intelectuales, arte y videocultura en la Argentina.* Buenos Aires: Ariel, 1994

Schmidt, Friedhelm. "¿Literaturas heterogéneas o literatura de la transculturación?" *Nuevo Texto Crítico* 14–15 (1994–95): 193–99.

Schwarz, Roberto. "As idéias fora do lugar." *Ao vencedor as batatas.* 4th ed. São Paulo: Duas Cidades, 1992. 13–28.

———. *Un mestre na periferia do capitalismo: Machado de Assis.* 2nd ed. São Paulo: Duas Cidades, 1991.

———. "Misplaced Ideas: Literature and Society in Late-Nineteenth-Century Brazil." *Misplaced Ideas: Essays on Brazilian Culture.* Trans. John Gledson. London: Verso, 1992. 19–32.

Silko, Leslie Marmon. *Almanac of the Dead.* New York: Penguin, 1992.

Sklair, Leslie. *Sociology of the Global System.* Baltimore, Md.: Johns Hopkins University Press, 1991.

Sklodowska, Elzbieta. *Testimonio hispanoamericano: Historia, teoría, poética.* New York: Lang, 1992.

Slack, Jennifer Daryl. "The Theory and Method of Articulation in Cultural Studies." Morley and Chen, 112–27.

Smith, Paul. *Discerning the Subject.* Minneapolis: University of Minnesota Press, 1988.

Social Science Research Council. "Proposal to the Ford Foundation for Core

Support of a New Joint International Program." Typescript. New York: SSRC, 1996.

Sommer, Doris. *Proceed with Caution When Engaged with Minority Writing in the Americas.* Cambridge: Harvard University Press, 1999.

———. "Resistant Texts and Incompetent Readers." *Latin American Literary Review* 40 (1992): 104–08.

———. "Resisting the Heat: Menchú, Morrison, and Incompetent Readers." Kaplan and Pease 407–32.

Souza, Eneida Maria de. "A teoria em crise." *Revista brasileira de literatura comparada* 4 (1998): 19–29.

Spitta, Silvia. *Between Two Waters: Narratives of Transculturation in Latin America.* Houston, Tex.: Rice University Press, 1995.

Spivak, Gayatri Chakravorty. "Diasporas Old and New: Women in the Transnational World." *Textual Practice* 10 (1996): 245–69.

———. "Ghostwriting." *Diacritics* 25 (summer 1995): 65–83.

———. "Responsibility." *boundary 2* 21, no. 3 (1994): 19–64.

———. "Subaltern Studies: Deconstructing Historiography." Guha and Spivak 3–32.

Starn, Orin, Carlos Ivan de Gregori, and Robin Kirk, eds. *The Peru Reader: History, Culture, Politics.* Durham, N.C.: Duke University Press, 1995,

Stavenhagen, Rodolfo. *Las clases sociales en las sociedades agrarias.* Mexico: Siglo XXI, 1969.

———. *Ethnic Conflicts and the Nation-State.* New York: St. Martin's, 1996.

Stoll, David. *Rigoberta Menchú and the Story of All Poor Guatemalans.* Boulder: Westview, 1999.

Stowe, Harriet Beecher. *Uncle Tom's Cabin: or, Life Among the Lowly.* London: Penguin, 1981.

Susstein, Carl R. "The Road from Serfdom." *New Republic* 29 Oct. 1997: 36–43.

Taussig, Michael. *The Devil and Commodity Fetishism in South America.* Chapel Hill: University of North Carolina Press, 1980.

———. *The Nervous System.* New York: Routledge, 1992.

———. *Shamanism, Colonialism, and the Wild Man: A Study in Terror and Healing.* Chicago: University of Chicago Press, 1987.

Taylor, Charles. "The Politics of Recognition." Gutmann 25–73.

———. "Two Theories of Modernity." *Public Culture* 11, no. 1 (1999): 153–74.

Thayer, Willy. *La crisis no-moderna de la universidad moderna. (Epílogo del conflicto de las facultades).* Santiago: Cuarto Propio, 1996.

———. "Fin del 'trabajo intelectual' y fin idealista/capitalista de la historia en la 'era de la subsunción real del capital.'" *Espectros y pensamiento utópico. La invención y la herencia: Cuadernos ARCIS-LOM* 2 (n.d): 172–93.

Trigo, Abril. "Why Do I Do Cultural Studies?" *Journal of Latin American Cultural Studies* 9 (2000): 73–93.

Trigo, Pedro. *Arguedas: Mito, historia y religión.* Lima: Centro de Estudios y Publicaciones, 1982.

Vargas Llosa, Mario. "Literatura y suicidio: El caso Arguedas (*El zorro de arriba y el zorro de abajo*)." *Revista iberoamericana* 110–111 (1980): 3–28.

——. *La utopía arcaica. José María Arguedas y las ficciones del indigenismo.* Mexico: Fondo de Cultura Económica, 1996.

Veeser, H. Aram, ed. *The New Historicism.* New York: Routledge, 1989.

Vera León, Antonio. "Hacer hablar: La transcripción testimonial." *Revista de crítica literaria latinoamericana* 36 (1992): 181–99.

Vilas, Carlos M. "Neoliberal Social Policy: Managing Poverty (Somehow)." *NACLA Report on the Americas* 29, no. 6 (1996): 16–25.

Virno, Paolo. "Virtuosity and Revolution: The Political Theory of Exodus." Virno and Hardt 189–210.

Virno, Paolo, and Michael Hardt, eds. *Radical Thought in Italy: A Potential Politics.* Minneapolis: University of Minnesota Press, 1996.

Wallerstein, Immanuel. *Geopolitics and Geoculture: Essays on the Changing World-System.* Cambridge: Cambridge University Press, 1991.

——. *The Modern World-System 1: Capitalist Agriculture and the Origins of the European World Economy in the Sixteenth Century.* San Diego: Academic Press, 1974.

——. "Open the Social Sciences." *Items: Social Science Research Council* 50.1 (1996): 1–7.

Walzer, Michael. *Thick and Thin: Moral Argument at Home and Abroad.* Notre Dame: University of Notre Dame Press, 1994.

Weschler, Lawrence. *A Miracle, a Universe: Settling Accounts with Torturers.* Hardmonsworth: Penguin, 1990.

West, Cornel. "The New Cultural Politics of Difference." Ferguson, Gever, Minh-ha, and West 19–36.

Williams, Gareth. "After Testimonio: Latinamericanism, Orientalism, and the Elusive Loss of the Upper Hand." Typescript, n.d.

——. "Fantasies of Cultural Exchange in Latin American Subaltern Studies." Gugelberger 225–53.

——. "From Populism to Neoliberalism: Formalities of Identity, Citizenship, and Consumption in Contemporary Latinamericanism." *Dispositio/n* 49 (1997 [2000]): 13–42

——. *The Other Side of the Popular: Neoliberalism and Subalternity in Latin America.* Durham N.C.: Duke University Press, forthcoming.

——. "Subalternity and the Neoliberal *Habitus:* Thinking Insurrection on the El Salvador/South Central Interface." *Nepantla-Views from South* 1, no. 1 (2000): 139–70.

——. "Translation and Mourning: The Cultural Challenge of Latin American Testimonial Autobiography." *Latin American Literary Review* 41 (1993): 79–99.

Wilson, Rob, and Wimal Dissanayake, eds. *Global/Local: Cultural Production and the Transnational Imaginary.* Durham, N.C.: Duke University Press, 1996.

Yúdice, George. "Civil Society, Consumption, and Governmentality in an Age of Global Restructuring." *Social Text* 45 (1995): 1–25.

———. "Consumption and Citizenship." Paper presented at the Conference on Globalization and Culture, Duke University, November 1994.

———. "Estudios culturales y sociedad civil." *Revista de crítica cultural* 8 (1994): 44–53.

———. "Globalización y nuevas formas de intermediación cultural." Achugar and Gaetano 134–57.

———. "Postmodernism in the Periphery." *SAQ* 92 (1993): 543–56.

———. "Postmodernity and Transnational Capitalism in Latin America." Yúdice, Franco, Flores 1–28.

———. "Testimonio and Postmodernism." *Latin American Perspectives* 18, no. 3 (1991): 15–31.

———. "Testimonio y concientización." *Revista de crítica literaria latinoamericana* 36 (1992): 207–27.

Yúdice, George, Jean Franco, and Juan Flores, eds. *On Edge: The Crisis of Contemporary Latin American Culture.* Minneapolis: University of Minnesota Press, 1992

Zamora, Lois Parkinson, and Wendy B. Faris, eds. *Magical Realism: Theory, History, Community.* Durham, N.C.: Duke University Press, 1995.

Zimmerman, Marc. "El *otro* de Rigoberta: Los testimonios de Ignacio Bizarro Ujpán y la resistencia indígena en Guatemala." *Revista de crítica literaria latinoamericana* 36 (1992): 229–43.

Zizek, Slavoj, ed. *Mapping Ideology.* London: Verso, 1994.

———. "The Spectre of Ideology." Zizek, *Mapping* 1–33.

———. *The Ticklish Subject: The Absent Centre of Political Ontology.* London: Verso, 1999.

INDEX

Alberto Moreiras is Associate Professor of Romance
Studies and Literature at Duke University. He is
the author of *Tercer Espacio: Literatura y Duelo en
América* and *Interpretación y Diferencia.*

Library of Congress Cataloging-in-Publication Data
Moreiras, Alberto.
The exhaustion of difference : the politics of Latin
American cultural studies / Alberto Moreiras.
p. cm.
Includes bibliographical references and index.
ISBN 0-8223-2726-0 (cloth : alk. paper)
ISBN 0-8223-2724-4 (pbk. : alk. paper)
1. Latin America—Civilization—Study and teaching
'(Higher)   2. Latin American literature—Study and
teaching (Higher)   3. Latin Americanists—United
States.   4. Criticism (Philosophy)   I. Title.
F1409.9 .M67   2001   980'..71'1—dc21   2001023945